THE RIVALS

THE RIVALS

America and Russia

Since World War II

ADAM B. ULAM

NEW YORK / THE VIKING PRESS

Preface

There are several ways of approaching the problem of the present and the future relations of the United States and the Soviet Union. One can see them as reflecting the arithmetic of the nuclear weapons in the possession of two Great Powers, of the two nations' means of inflicting or avoiding total destruction in the case of an all-out war. Or one can discuss them in terms of a moral calculus: What is their respective share of responsibility for the present unhappy state of international affairs? Which of the two ideologies and political systems is superior and promises more for the world? Or, without neglecting either the weapon or the moral question, one can view the present situation and prospects for the future as arising mainly from certain historical developments, certain social and cultural changes, which have taken place within both countries since the time, twenty-five years ago, when they emerged as rivals and as the only remaining Great Powers. The present book, then, attempts to relate these issues to the history of Soviet-American relations during the past twenty-five years. The future of international affairs, of peace, will for a long time depend mostly on America and Russia. Their outright confrontation could lead to disaster. The continuation of their present and mostly antagonistic coexistence would, while avoiding a major war, perpetuate a high degree of international tension and local though not necessarily localized conflicts. It is only a firm determination on the part of both countries to go beyond the antagonisms which could lay the foundations of real peace.

A study of the history of the past twenty-five years cannot give a clear view of the future. Yet it can suggest which of our hopes and fears are realistic and which are not, which changes in Russia favor a *rapprochement* with the United States, which developments in America threaten her influence in the world and hence the future of democratic institutions.

I have not atttempted here to give a history of the Cold War or of international relations in general since 1945. Rather, this is a study of the main causes and manifestations of Russia's and America's policies toward each other, and of their implications and effects on the international scene as a whole.

I must once again express my debt and gratitude to my secretary, Mary Towle, and my editor, Mrs. Elisabeth Sifton. The Russian Research Center at Harvard was the pleasant setting in which the book was written. I cannot mention all my colleagues and students who have been of help, but I must cite in this connection my research assistants, Messrs. Sanford Lieberman and Alfred DiMaio.

ADAM B. ULAM

Cambridge, Massachusetts
March 1971

Contents

Preface   *v*

Part I. The Era of American Omnipotence

  1. Stalin   *3*
  2. Roosevelt   *28*
  3. Truman   *63*
  4. Neither Alliance nor Cold War   *102*
  5. Great Decisions—Great Misunderstandings   *124*

Part II. New Worlds Emerging

  6. A Neglected Lesson   *155*
  7. Almost Peaceful Coexistence   *194*
  8. The Point of No Return   *239*
  9. The Third World   *270*

Part III. Lost Opportunities

  10. Khrushchev's Gamble:
      What the Russians Sought in Cuba   *299*
  11. American Overcommitment and Its Consequences   *341*
  Conclusion: The Immorality of Unrealism   *383*

Index   *397*

I

The Era of American Omnipotence

1

Stalin

O n June 11, 1944, millions of Soviet citizens could read in *Pravda* an official government release specifying the extent of American aid received between October 1, 1941, and April 30, 1944. Thus they learned about the following items of Lend-Lease delivered to the U.S.S.R.: "6,430 aircraft and in addition 2,442 aircraft received from the U.S. on account of British obligations; 3,734 tanks . . . 206,771 trucks . . . 3,168 anti-aircraft guns . . . 5,500,000 pairs of army boots . . . food deliveries [of] 2,199,000 tons." [1] The total amount of material received from the United States during the specified period amounted to 7.4 million tons.

The date of the release was not accidental: it followed by five days the landing of the Allied armies on the Continent. By the same token, few in the West were likely to take notice of the Soviet communiqué; everybody's attention was riveted on the beaches in Normandy from which British, American, and Canadian soldiers were striking out all over northern France. In the Soviet Union the average citizen was also not likely to realize the full import of the news: Even with the tide of the war having shifted in favor of Russia and her allies, *his* life was too grim and the sufferings inflicted on his country too vast for him to be impressed by material help rendered by the West.

Yet the mere existence of the published communiqué had a po-

[1] *Soviet Foreign Policy During the Patriotic War: Documents and Materials* (London, 1945), II, 87.

tential significance hardly inferior to the events taking place in Normandy. The Soviet Government was never wildly enthusiastic about letting its people know about how much aid it was receiving from the West. That it authorized a release spelling out in detail and accurately the vast help it was getting from the capitalists [2] was undoubtedly an expression of relief and gratitude that the invasion of France, promised for so long, was finally taking place. This was in line with Stalin's own handsome acknowledgment published in the Soviet press on June 13: The Western Allies, he said, in mounting a huge amphibious operation, succeeded where Napoleon and Hitler had failed. "One must admit that military history does not know a similar enterprise so broadly conceived on so huge a scale so masterfully executed." Suspicious Soviet officials had doubted until the last day that the invasion would take place, but now they hastened to make amends for their criticisms and barely veiled slights of the past two years.

But simple gratitude could not entirely explain the Soviet motives in publicizing the extent of Allied help. Nor is the importance of this help truly assessed by comparing the Soviets' own production in the critical categories with the figures for American and British supplies. *Postwar* Soviet accounts tried to minimize the extent of American aid, and in contrast some American officials took pains to point out that in view of the Russians' precarious military situation until the summer of 1943, massive American help, especially in such categories as trucks and food, might well have spelled the difference. But interesting and inconclusive as such a debate may be, the importance of the Soviet publication of the data on Western aid at that particular moment lay elsewhere. To those Russians in the know (as distinguished from rank-and-file citizens), the figures spelled out the enormous power the United States could exert in the postwar world as well as in the settlement of the war. Here was America conducting war in several theaters, the two main ones separated by vast distances, furnishing food and supplies to Britain and other partners in the Grand Alliance. Yet with all those commitments and responsibilities, she was still capable of furnishing help to the U.S.S.R. on this vast scale. The performance of American industry was even more fantastic if one bore in mind that the American consumer, much as he grumbled about shortages and rationing, enjoyed a standard of living which would

[2] Figures about the supplies from Britain and Canada were also included, and in proportion to the population and resources of those countries, they were at least as impressive as those of American help.

be considered luxurious in many countries even in peacetime. And for all the efforts to push civilians into essential occupations, America still did not resort to those comprehensive measures of mobilization of man- and womanpower which were the rule in practically all belligerent states. It was an awesome and unprecedented spectacle: a democracy which developed compulsory military service only in 1940, whose army but four years before had had to simulate guns with wooden models during war games, performing such miracles of production. History offered nothing comparable to this preponderance in one country of everything that constituted the sinews of power under twentieth-century conditions. To a man with a sense of history, the accounts of Allied successes or setbacks in Europe or in the Pacific would have been secondary to the news from Detroit and a hundred other industrial centers and to the statistics on American farm production.

Such a man was in fact directing Russia's destinies. Being Marxists, Stalin and his closest associates were not likely to duplicate the folly of the Japanese, who had believed that a surprise attack and the samurai spirit would enable a country producing 7 million tons of steel to overcome one with an annual *peacetime* production of 75 million. He was not a man like Hitler, who could in incredibly lighthearted manner declare a war on the United States just to oblige an ally. Stalin's whole career as dictator had been a testimony to his belief that production figures were a direct indicator of a given country's power. Even in the 1920s, Stalin used to talk with the highest respect of America's industrial potential and extol American industrial techniques as an example to Soviet managers and planners. Now the United States wartime performance must have convinced him that America was not merely the most advanced capitalist country but an economic colossus in a class of its own. With the landing of General Eisenhower's armies on the Continent,[3] this enormous American potential was now being supplemented by the presence of Anglo-American armies aiming at the heart of Germany and Europe. If the battle of Stalingrad marked the end of the period where any doubt could still be entertained that Germany and her allies would lose the war, then the Anglo-American invasion of France marked the opening of a new decisive phase: the next few months would decide the fate of Europe and the world for at least a generation.

[3] The Russians had always considered the Italian campaign as a rather secondary theater of operations.

Nowhere was this fact realized so clearly as in the Kremlin. To foreigners, the Soviet Union seemed at the apogee of her power: Russian armies were scoring one success after another, and their summer offensive, undertaken in conjunction with the Western invasion, would free the last areas of Soviet soil from the Germans. During that summer of 1944, prosaic production figures could not compete in the public mind with the almost uninterrupted flow of Soviet victories. Superficially, it appeared that no matter what the concluding months of the war would bring, its end would find the Soviet Union the greatest military power in the world. But such comforting conclusions could not be endorsed by Stalin and his fellow members of the Politburo of the Communist Party of the U.S.S.R. They knew that the end of the war would find Russia in a fearfully weakened state. We must now move a bit ahead and consider some of the grim statistics which would await the Soviet leaders in May and September 1945, at the moment of apparent triumph: the capitulations of Germany and Japan.

The grimmest figure relates to the Soviet Union's losses in human lives. One estimate has the country's population decline by 24 million between 1941 and 1945.[4] The lowest consensus for deaths directly and indirectly attributable to the war is 20 million—that is, upward of 10 per cent of the prewar total. (What would have been the state of American society in 1945 had it lost 16 million lives in the war?) Less shattering from the human point of view but still significant for a statesman was the extent of material devastation. The frantic campaign to industrialize and modernize Russia which had claimed so many sacrifices between 1929 and 1941 was now very largely undone. The state plan for 1941 had provided for production of 22.4 million tons of steel; in 1945, the U.S.S.R. could produce only 10.6 million tons. Russia's agriculture, hard hit by collectivization, was just beginning to recover at the onset of the war and the German occupation of the main farm areas.

Everything considered, the recovery of the Russian economy would be amazingly fast. But in 1944 and 1945, all one could say was that the end of the war would find the Soviet economy largely in ruins and that it would take a tremendous effort to restore it—quite apart from the traditional Soviet ambition of catching up with the most advanced economies of the West.

It is an intriguing commentary on the psychology both of the leaders

---

[4] Warren Eason, "Population Changes," in Allen Kassof, ed., *Prospects for Soviet Society* (New York, 1968), p. 220.

and the general public in the West that these enormous problems faced by Russia were but dimly perceived. Of course, the devastation wrought upon the country could not be concealed from Western journalists—in fact, official Soviet accounts stressed it in describing German barbarism and the heroic resistance and endurance of the Soviet people—and the inevitably formidable job of reconstruction was palpably obvious to friend and foe. Yet somehow this was almost never related to the problem of Russia's *strength* or to her ability to dictate much of the shape of the postwar world. Winston Churchill, hugely apprehensive as he was about Russia's postwar role, seemed wholly lacking in any realization that the Soviet Union's bargaining position could be affected by her wartime losses and problems of recovery. On the contrary, both in his diplomatic activity at the time and in his writings later on, Churchill gave testimony to his conviction that, with the war over, Russia would be an invincible colossus bound to have her way on every point of the European settlement unless checked by the most determined and concerted action.

The explanation for this blind spot is not difficult to find. Western statesmen, like the public in general, were overcompensating for a previous low opinion of Russia's fighting potential and of the cohesion of her political system. It was now secretly and shamefully recalled that when the Germans struck in June, 1941, the British and American general staffs had given the Red Army no chance of withstanding the German onslaught for more than a few months. As late as the fall of 1942 and the crucial phase of the battle of Stalingrad, best "informed circles" had been skeptical of the Soviet ability to hold out. Even stronger was an outright feeling of guilt. Soviet armies had borne the brunt of land fighting. They had contained and then defeated the Germans—as against the disastrous record of the French-British forces in 1940. Any one of the major battles on the Eastern Front dwarfed the campaigns in North Africa and Italy, in terms both of total numbers involved and of casualties. But even for as hardboiled a politician as Churchill, awareness of Soviet losses and sacrifices at times crowded out the remembrance of Soviet perfidy in signing a treaty with Hitler and the revulsion at the design to dominate the reborn Polish state.

Thus both remorse and an overreaction to an earlier slighting estimate of the Red Army's strength and fighting ability impelled Western statesmen to conjure up the Soviet armed forces as not only invincible but able to draw upon seemingly unlimited manpower. Even more important was their conviction that the Soviets would be able to keep huge armies even after peace had been concluded, while in the West public opinion would force a very rapid pace of demobilization.

Much of this remorse on the part of the British and American statesmen would have been assuaged by the knowledge that their original doubts about the Soviet Union's ability to survive were more than shared by Joseph Stalin. We *now* know (Khrushchev and some other Soviet officials have chosen to divulge this) that on receiving the news of the German attack in 1941, Stalin had what amounted to a nervous breakdown which compelled him to leave the conduct of state affairs to others, and it took him almost two weeks to compose himself sufficiently to address the people. As for the size of the Soviet armed forces, common sense should have told Western leaders that in view of Russia's terrible losses and the needs of her industry and agriculture, those forces could not be appreciably greater than those of the West. (We now know that at the moment of German capitulation, the United States had more men under arms than the U.S.S.R.[5]) Common sense should also have argued that the needs of the Soviet economy would compel a fairly rapid pace of demobilization. Yet for many years after the war, the vision of multimillion-man Soviet armies ready to sweep to the English Channel at a moment's notice beguiled political and military leaders in Britain and the United States. Here again a corrective is supplied by a subsequent revelation of Khrushchev: by 1948 Soviet armed strength was reduced to 2.8 million. In view of the great Soviet commitments in Eastern Europe and its garrisons in Germany, this was hardly an abnormally high figure.

But the element of Russia's weakness most unsuspected in the West concerned neither her material resources nor the strength of her armies but the solidity of her political system. Stalin was not far wrong when he described the foreigners' prewar view as follows: "As is well known, the foreign press often expressed views that the Soviet social system is 'a risky experiment' destined to collapse, having no real roots in life, and imposed upon the nation by the organs of the secret police, that you need but a small push from the outside to destroy this house of cards.' " [6] After the battle of Stalingrad such voices were completely stilled. More than that, even the most inveterate critics of the Soviet

[5] Khrushchev gave the Soviet figure for May, 1945, as 11 million (*Pravda*, January 15, 1960). The corresponding figure for the United States was 12 million (U.S. Department of State, *Documents on Disarmament 1945–1959* (Washington, 1960), I, 682.
[6] Speech of February 9, 1946, quoted in J. V. Stalin, *Works* (in Russian; Stanford, Calif.), II, 6.

regime were willing to grant that the war had forged a sacred union between government and people. Yet as the previous prophecies of the doom of Communism had been vastly exaggerated, so now the appraisals of monolithic unity of the peoples of the U.S.S.R. and their devotion to Stalin were excessive. It was ignored or overlooked that the war had shown not only the strength and endurance of the people but, especially in its earlier phases, panic and defections at the approach of the enemy, indifference, if not indeed a positive welcome, to the first phase of the German occupation. (It was, in fact, only the incredible cruelties and exactions of the invader which turned most Ukrainians and Belorussians against the Germans.) There was really no excuse for this ignorance: decrees of the Supreme Soviet in 1944 and 1945 had ordered the dissolution of several national districts and regions. When Stalin was pronouncing his boastful panegyric on national unity, his secret police had just concluded the forcible resettlement of hundreds of thousands of their inhabitants—such as the Crimean Tatars, the Chechen-Inguish, etc.—throughout the Soviet Union. Anti-Soviet partisan activity by Ukrainian nationalists was to continue into 1947.

The most important and piquant detail here is the fact that the belief that the Soviet system rested largely upon the organs of the secret police was shared by none other than Stalin himself. Certainly nothing but this belief of Stalin's could explain the fact that upon their return from captivity, Russian prisoners of war were treated with suspicion —and many of them were to exchange German prison camps for forced-labor camps in their own country. Here literature contributes horrifying details beyond any of the revelations offered subsequently by the Soviet regime. Solzhenitsyn's *One Day in the Life of Ivan Denisovich* contains the story of a brave and loyal Soviet naval officer sentenced to forced labor for no other dereliction than that of accepting a present from a British comrade-at-arms in wartime. And the author of the novel was himself a victim of the morbid suspicion with which Stalin and his regime viewed their own people, a nation that had endured hardships and sacrifices on so vast a scale. An artillery officer with a spotless record, Solzhenitsyn was arrested and sentenced for the sole crime of making, in a private letter, a mildly derogatory remark about Stalin. This was the beginning of many years of imprisonment and detention which was to give the writer that insight into the horrors of Stalin's camps and prisons, horrors which he was to describe so shatteringly many years afterward.

But our concern here must be with the role that Stalin's assessment of his people's loyalty played in Russia's postwar strength and policy. The test of the war did not dissipate Stalin's conviction that his regime had to rely on repression. I have used the word "morbid" in describing suspicions about the loyalty of ex-prisoners of war and attitudes toward the slightest criticism of the leader. But granted the premises of Stalin's regime, and his mentality, is this term justified? The war was bound to create in the people who had fought so bravely and suffered so cruelly the feeling that they had earned the right to a better and freer life than the one they had known before the Germans struck. Patriotic exaltation and excitement would not last long after the enemy's capitulation: what would be increasingly recalled and resented would be the mistakes and exactions of one's own government. Those who had gone into battle for "country and Stalin" would now expect Stalin to do something for *them*. The very extent of the people's expectations urged those with the mentality of Stalin and his associates to be especially vigilant in isolating and extirpating any trouble spots.

The war had bereaved virtually every Russian family, not excluding that of the despot himself.[7] If life was not going to be freer after the nightmarish experiences of the war, the Russians could at least hope that it would become easier from the material point of view, that they would not be mercilessly hustled to produce more and more as they had been for over a decade before the war, that the average citizen would not be viewed by the regime mainly as a producer. Even in peacetime the Russian worker had lived in considerable anxiety: unexcused absence or tardiness in work was punished by a prison term; factory accident might be classified as sabotage with even more fearful penalties; a nonfulfillment of the assigned quota could have drastic consequences for the engineer, manager, or even minister. The collectivized peasant, though by the late 1930s he had begun to breathe more freely than during the horrors of forced collectivization in 1928–33, was in fact a serf of the state: his work load and manner of living were much more minutely prescribed than for his ancestor in Czarist Russia before the emancipation of the peasants. And as in the old days, he was tied down to the soil: any absence from his community had to be approved by the authorities. Granted that the task of rebuilding Russia's shattered economy was to be formidable, it still could be

[7] Yakov Dzhugashvili, Stalin's son by his first marriage, died in a German camp under circumstances which still have not been fully explained. According to Svetlana Aliluyeva, Yakov's wife was imprisoned by the Soviet secret police shortly after his capture.

expected that the end of the war would see the end of those degrading restrictions which put the Russian industrial worker on virtually the same level with a convict laborer and the peasant in the category of a serf. Finally, while abundance could not be expected in a half-ruined country, it was reasonable to expect a better life for the consumer.

On all those counts, popular hopes and aspirations were to be cruelly disappointed. Soviet historians had often denounced the Czarist governments for their ingratitude to their people. They would quote the famous manifesto of Alexander I to his people thanking them for their heroic stance during Napoleon's invasion, graciously conferring various privileges on the upper classes, but telling the vast bulk of Russia's population, the peasants, with unconscious humor that their services to the Fatherland had been of such magnitude that their reward had to come from God. But, as things were to turn out, the imperial autocrat had been more generous than Stalin was now. At the beginning of the great industrialization drive of the 1920s, which had cost Russia so dearly, Stalin had exclaimed: "We are fifty or a hundred years behind the advanced countries. We must make good this distance in ten years. Either we do it or they crush us." Now, especially in view of the miraculous performance of American industry during the war, this urgency was even more strongly felt. Though the war was over, the consumer was still to be given a very low priority; there was no relaxation in industrial discipline; the peasants still lived in virtual bondage; and forced labor camps, far from being disbanded, were filled with new inmates, many of them former defenders of their country.

Such, in brief, was the balance of Russian weaknesses and of her rulers' fears when the war with the Axis was entering its last phase in the summer of 1944. The moment of victory was to find the Soviet Union enfeebled and devastated on a scale unprecedented in the past by countries *defeated* in a major war, and her rulers would feel compelled to rule in the future as they had in the past.

Stalin's fears and assumptions concerning his own people have already been mentioned. When it came to foreign powers and statesmen, Stalin, as in certain other respects, was a fast learner. Right after the German invasion, in those cruel months in the summer and fall of 1941, he had been peremptory and brutal in his requirements for help from the West, especially from the English, whom he still regarded as a rapacious, imperialist race. Among the extensive set of proposals for an Anglo-Soviet alliance handed to Foreign Secretary Anthony Eden on December 15 when he arrived in Moscow, which had just been saved from German occupation, was one for a *secret* protocol: a demand that Britain accept the gains the Soviets had chalked up under their bargain with Hitler up to 1941—i.e., agree to the Soviet annexations of the Baltic states, eastern Poland, and parts of Rumania. In return, the U.S.S.R. was willing to allow the British to have postwar military bases in France, the Low Countries, Norway, and Denmark, while Bavaria and the Rhineland were to be detached from Germany. In plain English, this was a scheme for the division of the Continent between the two Great Powers. Yet not since the Hundred Years' War had England entertained such ambitions on the Continent.

Even more interesting was Stalin's implied attitude toward the United States, which had just entered, or more properly been pushed into, the war. Clearly he anticipated more trouble from the Americans than from the British. In fact—and it is amazing that a man as astute as Churchill failed to see this—the proposed treaty was an attempt to combine with the British against the United States and to exclude the latter from any major influence on the postwar European settlement. How paradoxical all this must have seemed only a year or so later,[8] for the Soviets soon convinced themselves that the Americans were more pliable concerning Soviet wishes and suggestions than the British.

This amenability was principally demonstrated with the issue of the second front in France. On this, both President Roosevelt and his Chiefs of Staff were much more willing to meet Soviet wishes for a speedy invasion of Europe than were the British, with their memories of the huge losses of World War I and the debacle of 1940. (If a large-scale invasion of France had taken place in 1942 or even 1943, most of the ground troops would obviously have come from Britain.) But perhaps even more eye-opening to Stalin was the report on American official mentality which Molotov brought from his Washington visit in 1942. Roosevelt had spoken to him quite freely (and unnecessarily, one may add) about the evils and dangers of Western imperialism. Following the war, said the American leader, many of those colonies—and he obviously included Britain's Asiatic possessions among them—would have to be put under international trusteeship until they could achieve independence. It was a valuable hint of the deep chasm

---

[8] The British, influenced also by Secretary Hull's warning that the United States did not acknowledge the Soviet annexations of 1939 and 1940, refused to sign any treaty including frontier provisions.

which separated the thinking of the American administration from that of Churchill—and a testimony to the magic properties the Americans attached to the words "international" and "internationalized."

Throughout 1942 and 1943, Stalin's fears of British-American solidarity vis-à-vis the U.S.S.R. were thus gradually dispelled, as well as his notions of the cunning of British imperialists and the implacable hostility of American capitalists toward Communists. In fact, public opinion in both countries appeared more enthusiastically pro-Soviet than the respective governments'. Stalin's alliance with Hitler of 1939–41 was being forgotten or rationalized as a natural and desperate step in view of the British and French intention in 1939 to "push Hitler eastward." [9] The delay in opening a second front and the inadequacy of such substitutes for it as the invasion in North Africa in 1942 and Italy in 1943 was criticized not only by fellow travelers and radicals but by people like Wendell Willkie with his impeccable Wall Street credentials.

Being a cautious and suspicious man, Stalin continued to hedge his bets. Was it *completely* inconceivable that the Western capitalists would fail to invade Europe *en masse* or even make a separate treaty with Germany? Not even Stalin could believe that such a deal could be made with *Hitler*. But suppose German generals and conservatives overthrew Hitler and made approaches for peace? Throughout 1942, Stalin in his public announcements continued to draw the distinction between the genuine interests of the German nation and nationalism and Hitler. "As long as the Hitlerites were occupied in reuniting German lands, the Rhineland, Austria, etc., they could with justification be considered nationalists. But after they occupied foreign territories and enslaved European nations . . . [they] became imperialists." And perhaps the most famous statement in the same vein: "The experience of history shows that Hitlers come and go but the German nation, the German *state, remains*." [10] This was perhaps intended as a hint to the "good Germans" that the Russians more than the Western Allies understood the difference between Germany's legitimate claims and Hitlerism, but just as likely it was a hint to those officials in the

[9] If such, in fact, had been the intention of Chamberlain's and Daladier's governments, why did they then go to war after Hitler's attack on Poland and continue in it after the destruction of the Polish state? This question was not being asked then any more than it is now by the still considerable number of historians and polemicists who cling to this absurd view.

[10] J. V. Stalin, *The Great Patriotic War of the Soviet Union* (5th ed.; Moscow, 1950), pp. 49 and 59. My italics.

West who might think of a separate peace: we can beat you at that game, so hurry up and open a real second front.

In fact, of the Big Three, Russia had the greatest need for a complete defeat and occupation of Germany, not just the destruction of Hitler. Any resolution that left Germany a power would mean renewed and terrible dangers to the U.S.S.R. and would be seen as such by every Russian. There are things which are beyond the power of the most absolute despot. A separate peace with Germany could have meant curtains for Stalin and he knew it. If there were rumors current in 1943 that contacts were being made between the Soviets and the Germans with a view to a separate peace, they were most likely spread by the Russians themselves to impress their allies with the urgency of establishing a second front.

At the Casablanca conference in January, 1943, Roosevelt and Churchill pronounced the famous formula of "unconditional surrender," and this should have stilled Stalin's suspicions. But within a few weeks the Western Allies felt compelled because of heavy losses to suspend temporarily their convoys to northern Russian parts. The Russians could well have argued that after Stalingrad their allies knew a Russian collapse was unlikely and there was pressing need to help the Soviets *advance,* but by November, at the Teheran conference, Stalin appeared convinced that there was no likelihood of Britain and America ganging up on the Russians.

Stalin had approached the conference rather warily. While Churchill and Roosevelt had brought with them their Chiefs of Staff, Stalin's delegation contained no high-ranking military leaders except for his old friend Marshal Voroshilov, who in view of his age (he was sixty-two) and lack of competence in modern warfare no longer held an active command.[11] Stalin's decision here showed his apprehension about exposing his generals to contacts with the West. But the decisions, and even more the atmosphere surrounding the conference, must have convinced Stalin that such precautions were unnecessary. The British were not able and the Americans were not willing to frustrate major Soviet aspirations, and both were in fact deeply divided both on the merits and on the way of dealing with Soviet demands.

---

[11] Stalin's suspicion of his generals was such that no high-ranking officer was allowed any prolonged contact with his Western colleagues. In 1939, following the Soviet-Nazi Pact, discussions between the Germans and Russians on the technicalities of the division of Poland and contacts between the two armies bogged down because for long the Soviets would not send an officer of sufficiently high rank as military attaché to Berlin.

In their separate ways Roosevelt and Churchill went far in appeasing their awesome partner. In the vain hope of obtaining Russian concurrence to a modification or postponement of the massive invasion of northern France, Churchill initiated a discussion of the Polish problem in terms which probably surpassed Soviet expectations.[12] Roosevelt ostentatiously took Stalin's side in some disputes with Churchill and tried to jolly him up. Thus, between his two partners with their different anxieties and approaches, Stalin was able to dominate the conference. In reading its proceedings one is struck by how much of it consisted of *his* demands and *his* requests for explanation, while the leader of the most powerful country in the world and the prime minister of the country which had held out alone for more than a year were usually on the defensive.

After Teheran, therefore, Stalin could not possibly imagine that covertly the United States and Britain were preparing some horrendous intrigue against him. By the same token, lingering doubts must have remained as to whether Churchill's wiles would not prevail and the French invasion scheduled for May would not be postponed or its dimensions changed [13]—hence the relief and unfeigned gratitude on that day in June, 1944. But it was also in the nature of the Soviet system and the man who both ran and epitomized it that the relief and gratitude could not persist for long. Soon they were joined, if not replaced, by apprehension about the future.

The great success of the Normandy landing should have removed the last vestiges of Western guilt feelings vis-à-vis Russia. Insofar as the Soviet *regime* was concerned, such a feeling was altogether illogical: it was after all the result of Stalin's own policy that the Germans struck and brought his government to the brink of disaster. But insofar as the sufferings of the peoples of the Soviet Union were concerned, the mixture of admiration and concern felt throughout the West was both natural and proper. But now that a great Anglo-American army was fighting on the Continent it might have been expected that the Allied statesmen would assess the Russian problem, the key one in any forthcoming peace settlement, realistically without undue sentimentality or feeling of guilt.

[12] See my *Expansion and Coexistence: The History of Soviet Foreign Policy 1917–1967* (New York, 1968), pp. 352–57.
[13] General Deane, then head of the American mission in Moscow, puts it perhaps too strongly. "The [Russian] General Staff had never been convinced that the May date agreed upon in Teheran was not a part of a deception plan that the western powers were using against their Russian ally." John R. Deane, *The Strange Alliance* (New York, 1947), p. 150.

If generals are proverbially ready to fight the last war, then the American experience with planning for peace in the waning moments of World War II is a melancholy demonstration that statesmen may err by thinking excessively about the last peace settlement. The United States had not joined the League of Nations, and it was now recognized that the sequence of events leading to World War II was rendered possible largely through her absence in the international organization and hence its ineffectuality. It followed, then, in the opinion of leading senators and State Department officials that the first priority in establishing peace was to create a comprehensive world organization in which the Big Three (or Four, since many American officials believed that China was potentially if not actually a major power) would faithfully collaborate in the interests of peace. Thus a feeling of guilt over the original American abstention now dictated what was to become a frantic preoccupation with the establishment and structure of the United Nations.

This whole sequence of reasoning was questionable on both historical and logical grounds. Even without the United States, the League of Nations would have been able to preserve peace had its main sponsors—i.e., Britain and France—been able and willing to respond decisively to such violations of international peace as the Japanese move into Manchuria in 1931 and Hitler's remilitarization of the Rhineland in 1936. But they were not willing—that is, the electorates of these democracies simply could not get excited over developments in foreign lands until the balance of power shifted in favor of the Axis. In fact, the existence of the League hampered rather than strengthened the ability of the democratic nations to face down the challenge of the totalitarian states: liberals and socialists, especially in Britain, insistently claimed that it was not only sinful but unnecessary for the democracies to rearm, for "threats to peace should be handled by the League of Nations." The true lesson of the interwar years should have been that an international organization can function well only if its major members share certain basic premises about world order, and that it can preserve peace only if they are able and willing to meet any threat to it with a preponderance of force.

On the first count, it should have been obvious that the United Nations would from the outset have less chance to succeed than its prewar predecessor. Most of the original members of the League had been united by a certain similarity of political institutions and social premises; the two principal members, Great Britain and France, were status-quo powers, and even Italy and Japan did not exhibit during the first decade of the League's existence any ambition to upset the world order. Of the four proposed principal members of the United Nations, one, the U.S.S.R., was clearly a state based upon political and social principles vastly different from those underlying the governments of the United States and Britain. The future of another one, China, was still uncertain, but whatever would happen to Chiang Kai-shek's regime, it was unlikely, to put it mildly, that China would become a democracy within the foreseeable future. To assume that these states could hold together in the absence of a common enemy was to assume a great deal.

Yet this very assumption was the cornerstone of the American planning for the postwar world. The United Nations was projected not only as a useful institution (which in fact it has occasionally been) where the Great Powers, if their interests so dictated, could reach agreement on this or that issue when direct diplomacy would be inconvenient, but as an institution *necessary* for preserving peace in the postwar world and as an instrument for the creation of a new world where imperialism, aggressive nationalism, and restrictive tariff walls would gradually recede and where the frontiers of freedom and commercial and cultural intercourse among nations would be constantly expanded.

Russia's cooperation in setting up the United Nations was viewed by the Americans as a key to the success of the whole scheme. As Secretary Hull put it to members of the Senate in briefing them on the general proposals for the United Nations, among the pivotal questions "The first was to keep Russia solidly in the international movement." [14] This rather awkward phrase was meant to convey that: (1) no international organization could hope to preserve peace without Russia, and (2) it was the Western powers that had to plead with Russia to enter the proposed organization (and, presumably, offer her concessions) rather than vice versa. It is no exaggeration to say that the Americans viewed this as the key issue of postwar politics, surpassing in importance the resolution of the thorny Polish problem and even the eventual resolution of the problem of Germany. Membership in the U.N., they believed, was somehow bound to "domesticate" the U.S.S.R., assimilate her goals and aspirations if not her institutions to those of democratic nations. That the U.S.S.R. could enter the United Nations and yet pursue the same policies she would

[14] *The Memoirs of Cordell Hull* (New York, 1948), II, 1659.

pursue were she not a member did not seem to have occurred to many of the American planners. At Dumbarton Oaks, Secretary Hull expressed the prevailing hopes: "The Soviet Union has made up its·mind to follow the course of international cooperation. . . . It is only through international cooperation that she can advance her general economic interests, her industrial development, her social welfare. . . . Like some other nations at various times and under various circumstances, the Soviet Union might get off the line but . . . she would have to come back into line in time because she would discover that any course other than cooperation was against her own interests." [15]

One cannot accuse the Russians of undue hypocrisy on this issue. On the contrary, throughout all the discussions leading to the formation of the United Nations Organizations, Stalin maintained a perfectly sensible and aboveboard position: if the Big Three maintained a general agreement, then peace would be secured; if they disagreed, then no structural contraptions, voting procedures, etc., would be capable of maintaining a secure and peaceful world. Yet the Russians —as they observed, undoubtedly with a mixture of puzzlement and secret amusement, the Americans' preoccupation with "declarations of principles," procedural minutiae, etc.—would not have been human not to take advantage of their allies' strange infatuation.

Roosevelt and his advisers were convinced that the American people would not sanction U.S. involvement in the United Nations unless the structure and spirit of the organization reflected that relentless idealism which they currently attributed to their own actions and goals. If they and their representatives in the Congress were not satisfied on this point they might well relapse into isolationism. America's two main partners were thought, despite widespread admiration for their war effort, incapable of matching America's disinterested virtue in international affairs; Britain being imperialist and Russia Communist. Senator Vandenberg, the Republican Party's most influential spokesman on foreign policy, noted in his diary for May 26, 1944, that there was widespread suspicion that "Russia and Britain virtually agreed what they are to get out of the postwar world and that Roosevelt acquiesced." [16] The only way to secure public approval for America's continuing association with those two rather sinful states was to project it under the auspices of a wider international organization the democratic per-

[15] *Ibid.*, p. 703.
[16] Arthur H. Vandenberg, Jr. (ed.), *The Private Papers of Senator Vandenberg* (Boston, 1952), p. 103.

fection of whose procedures would filter out, so to speak, the selfish interests of the Great Powers.

The tragic predicament of American policy-makers is portrayed in this exchange between Secretary of State Hull and Vandenberg: "If we postpone planning our League until we get a Peace everything will blow up," said the Secretary of State, to which Vandenberg retorted: "I want you to go ahead with your League Conversations . . . but . . . I do not think you have any right to expect this Senate Committee [on Foreign Relations] either to endorse your plans in advance or to agree that your League shall bind us regardless whether the Peace satisfies the American conscience or not." [17] This was the strange and unreal way in which the Secretary of State and an influential legislator of the world's most powerful state tended to think of international affairs: no discussion of concrete issues, of the real sinews of international affairs such as military and economic power, of what could be obtained through well-informed and tenacious diplomacy. It would not have occurred to these two veteran politicians to discuss politics in Tennessee or Michigan in terms of such vague generalities. The road to a disillusioning and precarious peace was thus being paved with eloquent but ineffectual declarations and with nobly conceived but unrealistic schemes of international collaboration.

There were, to be sure, American officials who realized the complexity of dealing with the Russians and erecting a stable structure of peace—such as George Kennan, General Deane, head of the military mission in Moscow, and, to some extent, Ambassador Harriman. Nor must we overdo the motif of American naïveté about Russia; while it was real and extensive enough, Roosevelt for one, as we shall see, was shedding this naïveté rather rapidly when death cut short both his education and leadership. But accommodation to Russia was the prevalent mode—the war against Germany was not yet quite won and there was a fairly longish contest with Japan still in the future, in which it was believed by people as unsentimental about the U.S.S.R. as the Joint Chiefs of Staff that Soviet help would be of the essence. The basic miscalculation, the father of most of the mistakes made by the United States vis-à-vis Russia to the early 1950s, was the strange unawareness of America's enormous strength and Russia's relative weakness.

The most important and fateful miscalculation, however, touched not on Russia but on the Americans' real incomprehension as to what the international order is or could be in this sinful and complex world.

[17] *Ibid.*, p. 105.

And it was epitomized by the attitude both of public opinion and the government toward Great Britain.

Attitudes and policies toward Britain had undergone a subtle but extremely important change during the war. On the surface, Anglo-American military and political collaboration was intimate, relations between the two leaders extremely cordial. Churchill was accorded tumultuous welcomes on his frequent visits to the United States and remained the embodiment of the Western resolve to stand up to the dictators and to defend freedom. But, increasingly, Churchill the leader of an embattled democracy was distinguished from Churchill the imperialist, Britain from the British Empire. As one reads various memoirs and accounts of the period (such as Sherwood's book on Hopkins) one gets a strong impression that to many Americans in responsible positions British imperialism loomed as much of a potential threat to peace as unreconstructed Russian communism. Vandenberg worried about possible British plans for *further* aggrandizement. Secretary Hull was bent upon destroying the British imperial tariff preference as a price for postwar American economic aid. This was an attitude natural in a life-long free trader, but hardly an indication of a sensible set of priorities. Though it is unlikely that Roosevelt's attitude was as violently anti-imperialist as presented in his son's book,[18] it is clear that he saw the whole colonial system both as an evil and as a danger to peace, and that he would have liked a system of international trusteeships to replace it and eventually to guide all the dependent territories to independence.

In principle this position was both reasonable and just. The colonial system could not in the nature of things—especially in Asia—long survive the end of the war. But ill-informed American pressure was not going to contribute to its *orderly* liquidation or to the evolution of new political devices that might save the new states from anarchy, civil wars, militarism, and all the evils which have in fact beset so many of them. (Even under the most optimistic prognosis for the United Nations, it was fantastically unrealistic to expect that it would or could exercise tutelage over the vast areas being emancipated from colonialism.) More important, the American attitude on this thorny problem revealed a fallacy about the nature of international affairs which was to have long-lasting and tragic results. The war had *not* come because of the real or alleged evils of imperialist British rule in India or French rule in Indochina, or because Hitler and Mussolini were evil men. It came

[18] Elliott Roosevelt, *As He Saw It* (New York, 1945).

principally because France and Britain had been weak and confused in their counsels and because their resolution to resist came too late, and the strength and intelligence to do so effectively, never. If feasible international order was to be built, United Nations or no United Nations, Britain and France would have to continue to have important overseas commitments. Weakening and humiliating them, even if only psychologically, would make it less likely that they would have the resources and especially the will to play such a role. The proper American policy at the end of the war should not have been to award points, so to speak, to various countries depending on their virtues or derelictions— to reprimand the British for their imperialism, to punish the French for their ignoble performance in 1940 and for de Gaulle's obduracy— but to ensure that the maximum resources were being mobilized for a stable peace. Without American understanding, the dilemma of Great Britain, where the electorate anyway was sure to demand a curtailment of imperial responsibility, would only be accentuated, and the relinquishment of empire, instead of being done in a reasonable fashion, would turn into headlong flight, which would then compel America to assume a quasi-imperial role. The history of the last twenty-five years is a melancholy commentary on this sequence of events. They were not unforeseeable in those days of 1944, when Hull worried about the imperial tariff preference and various senators suspected Churchill of being out to grab more real estate.

Some of these implications of American foreign policy were very much on Churchill's mind, however. He contemplated with a sinking heart the postwar perspectives: a ruined British economy; an empire with massive troubles—India, Palestine, the whole problem of the British presence in the Near East. These burdens, which even before the war were overtaxing the resources of a small island, would be magnified by the wartime losses of foreign investment and shipping, and by the task of policing Germany. In view of these perspectives, the Prime Minister felt the only hopeful course was to stick resolutely by America and try to educate the Americans in the complexities of world politics. Some time before, he had in fact abdicated any independent policy for Britain for a share, which was to diminish as time went on, in the formulation of joint American-British policy. This was a realistic recognition of America's preponderant role in the war effort, but it also reflected a hope that recognition of America's leadership would enable him to steer U.S. policy in what he considered desirable directions. A sane foreign policy, for Churchill, was based on three important assumptions. First, a stable peace required agreement, whether tacit or explicit, on spheres of influence among the Great Powers—hence, his attempts, a bit on the sly, to draw out Stalin on the extent of Russia's territorial ambitions in Europe and a possible agreement on spheres of influence. Second, Britain would require a considerable dose of economic aid even after the end of the war if she was to be able to maintain part of her commitments abroad. Third, future East-West relations depended on a firm attitude vis-à-vis Stalin and a demonstration of Anglo-American unity when dealing with the Russians. (This was somewhat inconsistent with his private approaches to the Soviet dictator.) Were America, he believed, to become discouraged with world politics, she would lapse back into isolation and leave Britain alone to face the enormous postwar might of the Soviet Union. Like practically everybody in the West, Churchill overestimated Russia's strength as well as her capabilities for aggression.

In the pursuance of these goals, the Prime Minister courted vigorously American public opinion and deferred more and more to the wishes of the President and other American leaders. But the very intensity of this courtship was to prove, to use an economist's term, counterproductive. For the Americans, Russians were difficult to get along with, hence they had to be and most often were appeased, while British agreement on most issues of wartime strategy and postwar planning was taken for granted. Thus Secretary Hull unbosomed himself to some senators: "Malcontents in this country . . . were doing their best to drive Russia out of the international movement by constant attacks and criticisms. . . . Unless it was possible to prevail upon newspapers, commentators and columnists to refrain from this line of activity . . . it would be difficult for any international undertaking, such as that offered by us, to succeed." [19] The British were not assumed to be as sensitive, or rather their sensitivity was not deemed of equal importance.

Churchill's task was hugely complicated by the fact that a large portion of the British public and most politicians connected with the Labour Party shared the American conviction of the sinfulness of imperialism. In fact, it has traditionally been the British left which instructed American liberals as to the evils of the British establishment, as this term would be used now, and the hopeful aspects of the Soviet experiment. Whenever in the course of the war the Allies dealt with

[19] Hull, op. cit., II, 1659.

people whose history was not of unsullied liberal virtue—Darlan in North Africa, Badoglio in Italy—there was usually vigorous outcry on both sides of the Atlantic. These protests reached a crescendo in December, 1944, when British troops engaged in fighting the Greek Communist guerrillas who, Churchill believed, were bent upon seizing the country after its liberation from the Germans. The picture of the heroic Churchill of 1940 was becoming dimmer. To many in England and the United States he was becoming Churchill the reactionary, not a man to lead his country into a postwar era of democracy, social progress, and peace through the United Nations.

Moreover, Churchill's influence on Roosevelt and his advisers, the very cornerstone of his tactics, was visibly declining. On the surface it was an almost perfect partnership of two great leaders, but one could detect Churchill's occasional exasperation with the President's simplistic anti-imperialism and naïveté concerning the Russians, and the President's irritation at his friend's flamboyance and constant stratagems. Was the relationship influenced by a partially crippled man's unconscious resentment of his partner, who though older exuded energy and was a hedonist? Was it traditional American diffidence vis-à-vis British wiles? In any case, on the all-important issue of how to deal with the Russians, the President had no confidence in Churchill's advice until it was too late.

One may question the soundness of Churchill's tactics—his excessive penchant for playing the wartime leader, at a time when militarily the issue had already been decided, led to his neglect of domestic politics and thus contributed to his party's catastrophic defeat in the 1945 elections. Indeed, was not his whole strategy misdirected in terms of his own objectives? Had the British acted more "difficult," it is possible that their point of view would have received more recognition in Washington. And his deference to the American position prevented Churchill from exhibiting greater cordiality toward de Gaulle, thus planting the seeds of a bitter resentment which was to cost Britain and Europe dearly. At least the British should have understood the importance of assuaging French pride and of restoring France to a position of power and self-confidence. Yet in dealing with the French, they often matched American tactlessness vis-à-vis themselves. Most of all, Churchill neglected to do any homework on Russia, which remained for him a puzzling, if not frightening, phenomenon. For all his tempestuous sessions with Stalin, he had a sneaking admiration for the despot (who in turn, according to his daughter, liked Churchill personally). The complex personality of a dictator fearful of his own people, apprehensive of possible schemes among his associates (who lived in deadly fear of him),[20] and conscious of the great weakness of his country—all this escaped Churchill. And if he viewed Stalin as a sort of national chieftain with little of the Communist in his makeup, then it is not surprising that to the Americans he appeared as a sort of a Russian Boss Crump.[21]

But, as the records of the Big Three abundantly prove, it was Stalin who took the measure of the Englishman as well as the American. Their anxieties and hopes were fully perceived by him and masterfully played upon, while his own remained completely concealed from the Westerners.

One gets the impression of prudent weighing of several alternatives. For one, the Americans might awaken to the realization of their enormous power, become less accommodating; the Russians made certain cautious attempts to assuage some of the most obvious prejudices of those strange people. In May, 1943, the official dissolution of the Comintern undoubtedly had a positive effect on those elements in the United States which were apprehensive about the link between the U.S.S.R. and the world Communist movement. And the American Communists' dedication to the war effort, their repeated declarations that no social or economic problem should interfere with it, would have done credit to the American Legion. (Indeed, the American Communist Party came close to committing harakiri by transforming itself into a mere association; its head, Earl Browder, with a fervor which a few months later was judged by Moscow to have been excessive, eulogized the progressive character of Wall Street.) And it was little realized in America how great a concession and sacrifice the Russians felt they were making when they finally sanctioned the establishment of American bases on Soviet soil for shuttle-bombing of Germany.[22] To have on Soviet soil upward of one thousand military personnel belonging to a foreign (even if allied) country ran against the grain of the whole Soviet system, and Stalin must

[20] The Polish ambassador to the U.S.S.R. during the war recounted to the writer how during one of his audiences with Stalin the deputy chief of staff of the Red Army was summoned and Stalin, obviously in a bad humor, sharply admonished the general. The unfortunate officer, who undoubtedly had unflinchingly faced death on the battlefield, began to shake like a leaf and could barely stammer an excuse.

[21] Secretary Hull formed an even higher opinion of the dictator. While in Moscow he was treated handsomely by Stalin, and the old statesman, touched by this deference and perhaps also mindful of how Roosevelt kept him out of his inner councils, had this to say: "I thought to myself that any American having Stalin's personality and approach might well reach high public office in my own country." Hull, *op. cit.*, p. 1311.

[22] They became operative about the time of the Normandy landing.

have desired to please the Americans very much to make him authorize this abrupt departure from the Soviet tradition in such matters. (The only foreign military installations on Soviet soil had been those pursuant to the clandestine collaboration between the German army and the Russians from the mid-twenties until a few months after Hitler's coming to power.)

But pleasing Americans was sharply differentiated from appeasing them. The latter, Stalin must have felt, would inevitably make them escalate their demands, or rather turn their pleas for Soviet collaboration to demands. The very air of mystery which surrounded Soviet intentions and capabilities, the unfathomable behavior of Soviet officials from Stalin downward—now brusque and demanding, now dissolving in effusive sociability over gargantuan meals and vodka—all that was (rightly) held to be of great psychological importance in dealing with the Americans, although it is not suggested that such behavior was *entirely* contrived.[23]

On the eve of victory, the outlines of future Soviet foreign policy were concealed or had not yet been determined by Russia's master. One must not fall into the fallacy of ascribing to Stalin superhuman political acumen and assert that he alone of the three great leaders knew what he wanted and how to obtain it. On such crucial issues as the status of postwar Germany, Stalin's mind was obviously not quite made up. The Soviet position depended to some extent on what the Americans wanted and how strenuously they would stick to their demands. Might the Western Allies suddenly reverse their slogan of unconditional surrender and be inclined to negotiate with an anti-Hitler German group? To cope with this admittedly slight possibility, Stalin had a ready instrument in the Free German Committee set up in Russia in 1943, composed of some German Communists but mainly of captured German officers and soldiers. Its program was strictly nonideological, its proclamations called for the overthrow of Hitler and national unity afterward, and the national colors displayed in its journal were those of *imperial* Germany. It would have been impossible for a similar body to have functioned in the West without drawing fervent Soviet accusations that the Allies were scheming to perpetuate German militarism in order to turn it against the U.S.S.R. For the Soviets, the committee was a reinsurance that Britain and America would not monopolize the nationalist and conservative elements of any German movement that might oust Hitler.

[23] Many a Soviet official must have felt that for all of the Americans' indispensable help, they suffered very little compared with Russia's huge losses.

Few things were so devoutly desired by the Russians as Communist control of Eastern and Southeastern Europe. Apart from having regimes that were in ideological sympathy with the U.S.S.R., there were important strategic reasons. But here again several options were being kept open. The Soviets had withdrawn recognition of the Polish government in London in the spring of 1943, but they had not, as of the time of the Normandy landings, recognized a rival pro-Communist group, even though they were edging toward doing so. The Americans might prove unexpectedly obstreperous, and a compromise arrangement might be necessary. We know that as late as 1944, the Russians frowned upon the Partisan movement in Yugoslavia demonstrating too openly its Communist character and bombarded Tito and his followers, to their bafflement, with requests for moderation, even querying why Tito could not collaborate with Mikhailovich! The future and rapid satellization of Eastern Europe was far from being taken for granted. One might have to have recourse to spheres of influence, as insistently insinuated by the British, or the Americans might insist that free elections and multiparty governments decide the fate of Hungary or Bulgaria. It was, after all, the memory of the vivid indignation aroused in the United States when Russia fell upon Finland in the Winter War of 1939–40 which kept that unfortunate country from being absorbed into the Soviet bloc and subjected to one-party rule—even though Finland might have been expected to be treated more severely, having been an ally of Hitler, and having once been united to the Russian empire for more than a century.

Even the most improbable contingencies had to be kept in mind. The Americans might *really* put their enormous power behind the proposed United Nations, in which case problems of procedures and votes in that body would become of importance. It was undoubtedly with this possibility in mind that on February 1, 1944, it was suddenly decided that each of the sixteen constituent republics of the U.S.S.R. was to have its own foreign and defense ministries. This would give the Soviet Union a prima-facie case for arguing that in any future world organization it should be represented by sixteen or seventeen votes. None of the Supreme Soviet's deputies who wildly cheered Molotov's spech to this effect could have believed that the Ukraine or Azerbaijan would be allowed to have an independent foreign policy or army, but a few might have realized how it reflected Stalin's thoroughness in preparing for the battle for peace.

And this battle the despot waged as craftily and suspiciously as his over-all war direction.[24] All the threads of foreign policy were in his hand. In 1943, the two ambassadors Maxim Litvinov, from Washington, and Ivan Maisky, from London, were recalled and replaced by two younger diplomats, products of the Stalin era: the (then) very young Andrei Gromyko and Fyodor Gusev. Litvinov and Maisky were men of great knowledge of and popularity in the West—a fact which had probably saved them during the Great Purge, when the Soviet diplomatic corps had been decimated—and by the same token, and in view of the fact that they had come from the older revolutionary generation, were not entirely trusted by Stalin. His foreign minister, Vyacheslav Molotov, had for long subordinated himself slavishly to his master, but even so the Foreign Ministry was studded with secret-service men, and on exceptionally important issues Molotov was not allowed to make decisions.[25] None of the subordinates was allowed to know the entirety of the politico-military situation; that Stalin reserved for himself. He probably learned about American progress toward the atomic bomb sometime in 1944, but the chief of operations of the Red Army Staff, General Sergei Shtemenko, was told about it only after the Potsdam conference.

[24] The memoirs of Soviet generals have now bared details of Stalin's direction of the war effort. The over-all war situation had to be reported to him three times a day, once in person by the Chief of Staff. No prominent field commander was allowed to stay with his army group or in an over-all command position in Moscow for too long; they were all constantly shifted around. At every important operation the commanding general had at his elbow not only a representative of the Party, but at least one and usually two representatives of the High Command. This could not have contributed to the efficiency of operations but certainly assured that no general could monopolize the credit for a major victory, or more important, the undivided attention and affection of *his* staff and troops.

[25] Molotov was the only one of the entourage whom Stalin addressed by the familiar "thou" rather than by "you" or first name and patronymic. This did not keep Molotov's wife from being disciplined by the Party in 1940 or from being exiled after the war.

2

Roosevelt

Franklin D. Roosevelt died within less than a year of the landing in Normandy. In those ten months or so he was, by virtue of his office, the most powerful man in the world and the central figure of the Grand Alliance.

One generation separates us from the crowded events of 1944–45. It is certainly fair to say that there have been startling fluctuations in Roosevelt's historical reputation. The image of a colossus dominating the Grand Alliance, just as for a decade he had dominated American politics, has been eroded. For the most extreme among his detractors he had always been a dupe of the Russians. Even his most fervent partisans had to admit with the onset of the Cold War that the President and his entourage had been overoptimistic about Stalin's intentions and designs, and that he had been naïve in his appraisal of the Russians and their willingness or ability to cooperate within the United Nations in the spirit of its Charter. Then there was, to be sure, an insistent body of left-wing opinion that the trouble with American policies after the war lay precisely in their increasing departure from Roosevelt's precepts, that Russia's growing alienation from the West was largely a response to America's abandoning the path he had indicated and adopting a militantly anti-Soviet position on practically every outstanding issue of world politics. This view corresponds to, but needless to say is not connected with, the official Soviet position that Roosevelt's wise policies were first modified

28

and then abandoned by his successor under the pressure of conservative and militantly anti-Soviet circles in Britain and the United States.

Historical fashions follow politics, and after the resounding defeat of Wallace's Progressive Party candidacy in 1948, the thesis of the alleged betrayal of Roosevelt's policies by Truman was no longer maintained by serious historians and analysts of international affairs. With the 1960s, Vietnam, and what might be called an agonizing reappraisal of American foreign policy, the theme that "it is we who are guilty" became fashionable again, and in the works of the so-called historical revisionists responsibility for the Cold War was laid to a lesser or greater extent on American policies and their abandonment of Roosevelt's strictures about the necessity of getting along with and soothing the suspicions of the Russians. But since historical revisionism, like much of the "new politics" of the late sixties, has strong dogmatic underpinnings, it cannot credit American policies even under Roosevelt with transcending the social and economic background of their makers. One specimen of the revisionist approach to the history of our period, in fact, denies to the President any major role in the formulation of American policies during the war: "Although genial, Roosevelt was not a man of vision, not a Woodrow Wilson with a unique personal mission. Indeed he was in no sense either by training or instinct an intellectual or a technician, but rather a well-born patrician in politics. He preferred to procrastinate on critical decisions rather than to make them, but despite this quality of mind in the last analysis he always came down on the side of the considered opinion of his advisers." [1] Even historians and analysts with no ax to grind have of late emphasized the extent to which Roosevelt adhered to the judgment of his professional military advisers and how the purely military side of the war tended to crowd out political considerations.

All such judgments are of course profoundly influenced by what has happened since 1945. And since what has happened has in many ways been unfortunate, there is a very strong tendency for both conservative and leftist critics of American foreign policy of the last twenty-five years to lay the blame on the sins of omission and commission during the war years.

To be sure, the President's position *during the war* endowed him with powers virtually unparalleled for a democratic statesman. He was not surrounded by a War Cabinet, which restricted Churchill's freedom

[1] Gabriel Kolko, *The Politics of War: The World and United States Foreign Policy 1943–45* (New York, 1968), p. 349.

of action and, on occasion, as in the case of policy on India in 1942, actually overruled him. Churchill was not immune from constant parliamentary criticism, and at least on one occasion after the fall of Singapore, to the threat of a vote of no confidence by the Commons. But apart from the rigors and hazards of the Presidential election of 1944, Roosevelt could not be dislodged as President and Commander in Chief. It is still amazing to recall that there was no body of people, no council to coordinate the over-all war effort with foreign policy and postwar planning, to debate and decide on alternatives and priorities confronting the United States. Various structures of decision-making and policy and military planning crisscrossed and ultimately rested in only one person —the President of the United States.

Considerations of domestic politics had to be weighed in connection with various aspects of wartime strategy and diplomacy—certainly such issues as Poland and the allocation of resources between the Pacific and European theaters could not be considered apart from their political repercussions—but whatever the political risks involved in any issue concerning the conduct of the war, the ultimate decision was the President's and his alone. Roosevelt's critics in and out of the Congress were reduced to mere carping at his policies, and, except at the time of the Presidential election, these could not have very far-reaching consequences. It was unimaginable that the Congress would refuse funds for the pursuit of the war, and unlikely that it would try to arrogate to itself any of the powers of the Commander in Chief.

The immense extent of the President's wartime powers made even more vivid the contrast in the Executive position once peace was established. It is testimony to the American genius for organization and improvisation that the vast and intricate machinery of the war effort ran as efficiently as it did and that the transition following Roosevelt's death was so smooth. But the very efficiency with which the war effort was run concealed and accentuated the lack of any long-range policy behind it. In place of such a policy, the American leaders had only *hope*.

Yet all the goals and engagements contracted during the war were bound to be reviewed and criticized in political debate. That the United States would have the means to dominate or strongly influence international relations could not be taken for granted: it depended on Congressional willingness to authorize and finance considerable standing armed forces, and to continue economic aid to the erstwhile allies beyond the time when it could be related to or justified by the war effort. The postwar American involvement in world affairs would require much more than what would have been needed in the 1920s—not only willingness to shoulder obligations under an international organization, but the continuation of some form of compulsory military services, economic sacrifices, American soldiers serving and dying in distant lands. Though nobody in 1944 or 1945 could imagine how long-lasting or vast such commitments would in fact become, it still loomed as an almost impossible task to "sell" this many-sided involvement to the American people and their representatives.

The American people's willingness to shoulder such burdens was thought to depend heavily on their being convinced that at least some of the democratic idealism with which the country credited itself was shared by its partners. They would not readily join an international organization if it was going to be merely a new form of the concert of Great Powers, a place where deals, compromises, and spheres of interest were going to be arranged. The United Nations had to signal a new era in international relations where power politics was superseded by principles of justice, equality of nations, and democracy. This vision, however, could not be sustained if the growing dissonances between the Western Allies and the U.S.S.R. were stressed, and especially if the latter's character as a ruthless dictatorship bound upon both territorial and ideological expansion were to blot out the image of Russia sedulously cultivated in wartime: a brave nation with a regime which had abandoned its earlier dogmatism and proselytizing zeal and was certainly undergoing liberalization. At the time of the Russo-Finnish war, only a few years before but from the perspective of 1944 a century away, President Roosevelt had characterized Russia as a dictatorship as absolute as any in the world. To keep repeating or implying this truth in the midst of wartime partnership meant not only risking a widespread disillusionment which could spill into defeatism (wasn't this, after all, precisely what Dr. Goebbels and German propaganda were insistently proclaiming?) but also undermining the willingness of the American people to sanction any scheme of collective security after the war. "Darling, you are so American. You get what is and what you want all mixed up in your head," says an English girl to her boy friend in a novel dealing with World War II.[2] American public opinion, then as now, rebelled at the thought of an alliance based merely on identity of interests rather than on mutually shared democratic values and practice.

The Roosevelt approach to foreign relations and especially to the Russian problem emphasized, therefore, smoothing over or ignoring

[2] John Hersey, *The War Lover* (New York, 1959), p. 388.

points of conflict. If in the process the United States had to make seemingly unpalatable concessions to Stalin, this could be rationalized by the imperative necessities first of keeping Russia in the war, something that until 1947 Americans erroneously believed could not be taken for granted, and then of securing her assistance against Japan. Most of all, it was believed that the United Nations would prove to be a corrective to any unjust settlements dictated by wartime expediency. Roosevelt's technique of negotiations at Teheran and Yalta was designed not so much to appease Stalin as to convert and "domesticate" him. The past sins of the Soviet regime, and its morbid suspiciousness, were attributed not to any inherent ideological or structural reasons but to a history of isolation and of distrust of the capitalist world. It was, after all, part of the American creed, now reinforced by the assimilation of Freudian psychology, that personal wickedness could in most cases be attributed to an unhappy and insecure childhood. Future historians would find embarrassing and pathetic Roosevelt's efforts at allaying Stalin's alleged insecurity and distrust of the outside world, at making him take a positive attitude toward Zionism, toward the Pope, etc. But all this corresponded to a very significant trait in the American mentality and world outlook. And when one reads today various prescriptions coming from both politicians and "experts" as to how to get along with Russia, Communist China, and the Third World, can one really claim that we have gained a great deal in sophistication and realism?

But beyond Stalin and the Russians, the real target of Roosevelt's diplomacy was the American people. Russia had to be presented in a hopeful or, if one prefers, unrealistic light because *Americans,* it was thought, had to be convinced and converted to participation in international affairs. It is impossible to say to what extent the President allowed for a failure in his approach, what alternatives he considered if Russia was not going to "play ball" or if the United Nations were to turn out impotent. His personal style was to exude optimism, to disregard and rebuke those advisers who raised the darker possibilities. His most famous utterance had been that the greatest thing we had to fear was fear itself. Yet there were obviously some serious apprehensions behind the veneer of confidence and optimism. To Robert Sherwood, who in 1944 conveyed to him Churchill's statement that the "United States was now at the highest pinnacle of power and fame," Roosevelt observed, "I'd hate to say it. Because we may be heading before very long for the pinnacle of our weakness." [3] For all his real or alleged naïveté, Roose-

[3] Robert E. Sherwood, *Roosevelt and Hopkins* (New York, 1950), p. 827.

velt had a unique grasp of the nation's psychology and a sober appreciation of how the people's mood could change, almost overnight, from
exultation to depression, from active and enthusiastic participation in
world affairs to a peevish withdrawal from "foreign entanglements." He
could not have foreseen the full turning of the wheel—how the faith in
America's inherent virtue and her freedom from the imperialist taint
would in the mind of not an inconsiderable part of public opinion be
replaced by a masochistic and self-lacerating image of the United States
as *the* imperialist power. But it was not difficult to see that the end of
the war would bring a drastic reduction of the vast powers held by the
federal administration, would sharply limit the people's willingness to
suffer heavy taxation, rationing, and compulsory military service. Also,
the Congress would tend to look more closely into what in fact had been
secret diplomacy among the Big Three (shades of Wilson and his "open
covenants openly arrived at"). The main outlines of the future world
organization and collaboration had to be hammered and nailed in while
the wartime spirit of elation and willingness to sacrifice was still strong.
And that in turn dictated avoidance of jarring and public dissonances
with the principal allies.

Such were then the reasons why the United States' enormous power
could not be translated into a proportionate influence in shaping the
peace.

Roosevelt felt that whatever the risks of his wooing and appeasing
Stalin, his hunches had to be played until and unless they were shown
to be definitely wrong. But if so, then what? The President might well
have believed that he could then make all the more impressive a case to
the American people for a new approach to international politics by
pointing out how far he had gone in trying to dissipate Stalin's suspicions
and to meet legitimate postulates of the Soviet Union.

In the spring of 1945, Roosevelt was very close to revising his estimate
of Stalin and turning in the direction recommended by Churchill, who
believed that Stalin's *faits accomplis* in Eastern Europe should be met
by appropriate countermeasures of the Western Allies. But he was too
weary to adopt a new line; and then, on the eve of what might have been
a decisive turn in Soviet-American relations, President Roosevelt died.
Truman inherited his powers and his advisers but not, certainly not in
the beginning, his self-confidence; and above all Truman never possessed
his predecessor's almost magical powers in swaying and educating public
opinion. The task of reorienting American foreign policy had to wait
until 1946–47, by which time the "provisional" arrangements concerning

Germany and Japan had hardened and the lines were drawn for the Cold War. In domestic and international politics alike, so much depends on timing. Had a decisive change in the official American attitude taken place between June, 1944, and the capitulation of Japan, when the situation was still fluid and the prestige of the Soviet and the Anglo-American sides still not committed to set positions, the fate of Europe and the world might well have been different.

Isolationism, we can now appreciate better than in 1944, was much more than a passing mood or a nostalgia for the time when two oceans really did protect the United States and allow it the happy luxury of not caring about the rest of the world. It was in large measure a society's realistic self-appraisal, an instinctive feeling that the country could not play a much more active role in world politics without at the same time damaging the desirable features of its domestic system. An activist foreign policy does not come easily or painlessly to a democracy. The very mechanics of the American system, such as separation of powers and the unique role of the Senate, had in the past handicapped the ability of the executive branch to pursue an activist foreign policy in *peacetime*. But a much more serious difficulty lay in the psychology of the American people. Weakened through the passage of time and the falling off of immigration after World War I, the links connecting millions of Americans to the countries of their origin still contributed to drastically different evaluations of the outside world and of America's stake in it by large groups of citizens. An even more basic difficulty lay in that mixture of superiority and diffidence with which Americans viewed themselves in relation to other nations. American institutions are held both superior to foreign ones and yet extremely fragile when exposed to the stresses of war and even of peacetime alliances with other countries.[4] For all its amusing and pathetic undertones, this attitude contained a sound psychological insight: a country shouldering world-wide responsibilities cannot expect its internal institutions to remain unaffected. Quite apart from the obvious requirements of a sizable

---

[4] This characteristic comes out most strikingly in the common reference to subversive doctrines and activities as being "un-American." The implication used to be that no undesirable acts or ideas could be home-grown, that contrariwise democracy originated and was developed on the soil of the United States. This assumption of national superiority has in recent years given ground to the argument that there is an inherent wickedness in the American style of life. We have heard civil strife being excused on the grounds that "violence is as American as cherry pie," and the nation's record of industrial and economic progress being condemned as leading to "alienation," which is supposedly more widespread and intense in the United States than anywhere else.

military establishment, a world role requires psychological warfare and intelligence establishments. And in American parlance propaganda and espionage have always been dirty words, their practice excusable only in wartime and certainly not on a large scale in peacetime. How sound this insight was we can appreciate only now. Under the impact of the Vietnam war, many of the mythical components of America's self-image have been stripped off, but the result has been not a greater maturity and realism in national self-appraisal but, alas, especially among the young, a confused and masochistic revulsion against their own society.

Thus both Stalin and Roosevelt in vastly different ways had to think of foreign policies primarily in terms of their impact on domestic politics. The despot had to gauge the psychological impact of any possible peace arrangement and the possibility, assuredly a distant one, of whether and how continued amity and collaboration with the West would erode the foundations of that absolute mastery which he and the Party held over Soviet society. Roosevelt had to question whether disenchantment over the terms of the peace would make the American people turn their back on the world and render fruitless all the sacrifices of the war.

This common concern for the domestic repercussions of the peace settlement led the dictator and the President to quite different conclusions as to what were the most important priorities for their countries. Stalin was after real estate: vassal states and spheres of influence to surround the U.S.S.R. These would strengthen Russia and permit her, behind this new socialist version of the *cordon sanitaire,* to pursue a policy of relative isolation from the West. The extent of that isolation would depend on the specific situation at the end of the war, but it was clear that Russia could not allow her political and ideological system to be corroded by too intimate an association with her allies. Churchill spotted this aspect of Soviet policy very perceptively when he said after the war that the Soviet regime was afraid of Western friendship no less than of open hostility. Even today, Soviet Russia—so much stronger and more prosperous than the ravaged, incredibly poor though proud country she was in 1945—while eager for a *détente* with the United States is still fearful of "ideological coexistence" with the non-Communist world or, in plain English, of having Soviet people exposed to ideas and contacts with the West.

Yet it was precisely this ideological coexistence which was the main objective of American policies. The principal means to that end would be the United Nations. The name was significant since it beckoned to a more comprehensive vision of international cooperation than any envisaged before. The old League of Nations postulated a fairly narrow concept of international cooperation, albeit one beyond its powers. The name "United Nations" implied a pattern of collaboration reminiscent of the wartime alliance. It was only the *first* objective of the United Nations to provide collective security and to banish war; eventually it was to be much more universal in scope and goals, and would propagate the spirit of internationalism. This spirit, it was hoped, would eventually take the edge off ideological differences and lead to friendlier and more open relations between nations, whatever their political and economic systems—i.e., to precisely what would later be described and rejected by *Pravda* as the "empty dream" of alleged "convergence" between the Soviet and Western systems, etc.

Thus in the late summer and early fall of 1944, the attention of American policy-makers was riveted as much on the Washington mansion of Dumbarton Oaks as to the battlefields of Europe, where Anglo-American and Russian armies were rapidly liquidating Hitler's European empire. For it was at Dumbarton Oaks that the structure and statutes of the United Nations were being discussed by the principal allies.[5]

President Roosevelt himself was a rather late adherent to the idea of an elaborate structure for the future world organization. At first he tended toward an organization on the model of the wartime United Nations. Just as of the many wartime allies only the Big Three (and to a lesser extent China) made decisions on policies and strategy, so in the peacetime United Nations Organization the four Big Powers would constitute a directorate charged with enforcing collective security, while on less important issues the smaller nations would share in decision-making. The four big powers would act as "policemen" in their particular geographic spheres while joining forces on really major threats to peace. To the President this scheme was quite different from the old and sinful system of spheres of influence coveted by Stalin and Churchill: a policeman is expected to act selflessly and on behalf of law and not to collect rewards from people on his beat. (This somewhat idealized version of the policeman's job was not challenged in the simple America of the 1940s; today it undoubtedly would be.) But to many both within and without the administration, the whole idea was reminiscent of spheres of influence, and besides it was not "international" enough:

[5] In effect between the Big Three, whose negotiations occupied by much the longer session, followed from September 28 by the conference between Britain, the United States, and China.

it lodged excessive powers in the big powers and tended to make the future United Nations merely a window dressing for the continuing domination by the major powers. By the time of the Dumbarton Oaks conversations, the President had been converted wholeheartedly to the new American plan which envisaged the United Nations pretty much as it was to shape up (with an exception to be noted below).

The new plan abandoned the idea of a superstructure built upon the foundation of big-power domination. The United Nations was to be a "thing in itself," certainly not a superstate but on the other hand not just a tool of one or even several major powers. It would be larger than the sum of its parts and also different in its spirit and approach to international problems. This concept was bound to please both conservative and liberal critics of the "policeman" concept of the organization. Conservatives (except the extreme ones, who would have no truck with the United States being part of any international organization) had been suspicious that the United States would be tricked and exploited by the wily British or unscrupulous Russians. The liberals would have liked an even more powerful body where some of the national sovereignty of the members would be sacrificed at the alter of true internationalism, but they were certainly pleased that the new scheme increased the role and importance of small states, as it had been a cardinal point with them that small units, whether in business or in world politics, are more virtuous than large-scale organizations.

The English, while acquiescing for obvious reasons in most of the features of the American plan, would have preferred a simple concert of the big powers. The traditionalist as well as the realist in Churchill wanted to include France and exclude China from the proposed list of permanent members of the Security Council. Insofar as the wider schemes of international organization were concerned, the Prime Minister looked forward to regional arrangements. What he was especially eager to see was a combination of the smaller European powers to balance, at least in part, the enormous weight Soviet Russia was to exert on the Continent after the defeat of Germany. Barring such an arrangement, he was quite skeptical that the U.N could do much good. And insofar as some proposals such as the trusteeship plan for dependent territories seemed to portend a threat to the British control of their colonies, the excessive internationalism of the American plan aroused his forebodings. In any case, here were the Americans spending a vast amount of time and energy on membership and voting arrangements, on sonorous declarations and preambles, instead of concentrating

on the real issue: the current and already too obvious Soviet designs
in Eastern and Central Europe and the postwar threat of Russia and
Communism.

The Soviet attitude was basically not much different. Privately, Stalin
had told the Americans more than once that safeguarding peace in the
postwar world would depend entirely on the Big Three, and he viewed
with amusement mixed with irritation the various peculiarities of the
American plan. America's solicitude on China's behalf at first aroused
his opposition. This in itself was due not to any ulterior motivation or
revulsion against Chiang, but simply to a belief that China did not
belong in the same club as the Big Three. And it was in honest exasperation that he argued with American spokesmen about their strange
conviction that small states were a repository of international virtues
of which the Great Powers (with the exception of the United States)
were, alas, incapable. Small powers, he told Harry Hopkins, very often
exploited and exacerbated differences between Great Powers. And today,
as one looks at the Middle East or Southeast Asia, one cannot deny
that at times Stalin offered sound and disinterested advice.

The Russians were quick to perceive, however, how seriously the
Americans viewed the U.N. Stalin could not fail to see how eager
Roosevelt was to obtain his cooperation, and how vital Russia's membership in the organization appeared to Washington. Stalin was too
shrewd a politician to bargain *directly* for territorial or other concessions in return for his adherence to the American plan. But the Soviets
exploited the Americans' preoccupation with the United Nations in an
indirect and clever manner. Serious objections would be raised to this
or that aspect of the American proposals, the Soviet position being
apparently inflexible; fearing the whole future of the United Nations
was endangered the American negotiators would be close to despair.
And then from the highest Soviet source an indication would be forthcoming that perhaps things were not so hopeless as all that, that an
accommodation might yet be reached. The Americans would hail the
subsequent compromise as a considerable Soviet concession and in their
relief would be much more willing to meet Russian demands on Germany and Poland.

Except on one occasion, and there Stalin retrieved his mistake very
quickly, the Russians never threatened or implied that they might stay
out of the United Nations altogether. Blackmail was not a technique
to be used with the American colossus. What is even more important,
the Soviets realized only too well how grave a threat to their interest

a United Nations in which they were not a member would be. Hence they were diligent to declare their enthusiasm for the principle of international cooperation, and at times they advanced proposals so far-reaching in their internationalism and in apparent willingness to abandon some attributes of national sovereignty as to be clearly impractical. Such was the proposal at Dumbarton Oaks that the Security Council have an international air force ready to spring into action at its command. It is clear that this could not have been meant seriously, but it obviously so embarrassed the American negotiators that it was *they* who had to object that this went too far and could not be accepted by the Senate.

Another astute Soviet bargaining device was the famous demand that each of the sixteen Soviet republics be given a seat in the Assembly; though the Assembly, it was believed at this stage, was not going to be of great importance (the nerve center of the projected U.N. being the Security Council), still the proposal was unpalatable. Not even the most pro-Russian official of the State Department could readily believe that the Karelo-Finnish or Uzbek republics were in any sense an autonomous let alone independent unit. When it came to foreign policy, choleric senators were likely to point out that an American state was much more independent vis-à-vis Washington and demand an additional 47 votes for the United States. At the same time, the Russian proposal was intended to appeal to the Anglo-Saxon feeling of fair play. Here was the U.S.S.R., as against Britain surrounded by its dominions and the United States by its South American clients (then, with the exception of Argentina, quite docile), all alone with no fellow Communist states. Should not this be recognized and compensated? There were, in addition, those bland and rhetorical Soviet arguments which could not be combated short of questioning Russian good faith. Each Soviet Union republic now had a foreign ministry, something which could not be claimed for New York or Nevada. Take the Ukraine, a country of 40 million which had suffered cruelly in the war: should it be excluded from the body in which Egypt and Ecuador were to be represented?

But an issue which caused even more apprehension and unhappiness on the American side was the one of voting procedures on the Security Council. That the permanent members of this body (who were, it was now agreed, to include China and France) would have the right to veto any decision of the Council was assented to by the Big Three. This already saddened the more extreme internationalists on the American and British side, who believed that the Council should reach decisions by a simple majority and the Great Powers should have no special privileges as against nonpermanent members of this body. But the Russians demanded that the veto should apply even to a vote on whether to have a discussion of an international dispute in the Council, even in the case when the Great Power which exercised it was itself a party to the dispute.

To the American government, let alone the public, it seemed to strike at the heart of the U.N. to deprive the Council of the right even to discuss and recommend a solution of an international crisis if a Great Power did not wish to be so inconvenienced. Was international law and morality to be applicable only to little fellows, while the big ones remained above them? The President felt the issue so important that the chief Soviet delegate was summoned at 7:30 in the morning to be lectured in some homely similes: "He pointed out that when husband and wife fell out with each other they stated their case to a judge and abided by his ruling: they did not vote in the case. The principle that any party in the dispute could be heard but could not vote, he said, had been imbedded by our forefathers in American law." [6] There must have been quite some head-shaking when the text of this interview reached Moscow. The noble principle enunciated by Roosevelt was not currently—and that with American acquiescence—being applied to the dispute between Poland and the U.S.S.R. Nor was it clear why the Soviet government should regulate its policies according to notions of the Americans' forefathers.

For the time the thorny problems of multiple representation in the Assembly and the Council veto were shelved, to be resolved at the next summit meeting, presumably. But Stalin was ready to pour oil on the troubled waters. On November 6 in a public speech he hailed Allied unity in the war: "An equally vivid demonstration of the stability (and unity) of the United Nations one sees in the decisions of the Dumbarton Oaks Conference about setting up a security organization following the war. . . . There are to be sure differences. . . . But different points of view exist at times among people in the same party. . . . The surprising thing is not that there are differences, but that there are so few of them and that they are really resolved almost always in the spirit of unity and accommodation between our three great countries." [7] The speech was delivered at the meeting of the Moscow Party organization celebrating

[6] Cordell Hull, *The Memoirs of Cordell Hull* (New York, 1948), II, 1700.
[7] J. V. Stalin, *Works* (in Russian; Stanford, Calif.), II (15), 164.

the anniversary of the Revolution, but the above passage was meant primarily to be read in Washington, where its content and tone must have cheered those who were beginning to despair of future Soviet collaboration.

People more perspicacious and cynical must have suspected that Stalin's hopeful and soothing words glossed over dissonances more ominous in their implications than those relating to the future international organization. For while diplomats discussed voting procedures, examined membership lists, etc., at Dumbarton Oaks, a much more important omen of things to come was taking place in Eastern Europe. Victorious Soviet armies were hammering out a Soviet sphere of influence. The strategy of the Soviet armies, now that the enemy was almost completely pushed out of the territory of the U.S.S.R., was clearly influenced by political considerations. Memoirs of Russian military commanders offer testimony. On October 28, Marshal Malinovski was called to the telephone and informed by Stalin that Budapest had to be taken forthwith. The commander of the Soviet armies in Hungary explained that other operations appeared for the moment advisable and less likely to incur prohibitive casualties. No, insisted Stalin, *political considerations* made capture of Budapest imperative, no matter what the cost in lives.[8]

And in the very month when the Dumbarton Oaks Conference began, the Warsaw uprising took place. With Soviet armies across the Vistula from the city, the underground Polish organization rose against the Germans at the order of the Polish exile government in London. Behind the subsequent drama lay a tangled and tragic history of Polish-Soviet relations.

The question of Poland epitomized the difficulties and differences separating the three great Allied powers. For the West it embodied a great moral problem. The war started after all over if not because of Poland's invasion by Hitler. The ringing tones of the Atlantic Charter and of other Allied declarations about securing freedom and democracy for nations enslaved by Hitler ought to have applied with special force to this most brutally treated victim of Nazi aggression and occupation. If Poland were to emerge from the war as a *de facto* Soviet satellite, what hope could be held for other East European countries where native Communist movements were stronger than in Poland and some of which had been German allies and harbored fascist governments?

By the same token, a successful resolution of the Polish problem was

[8] Severyn Bialer, *Stalin and His Generals* (New York, 1969), p. 614.

of supreme importance to the U.S.S.R. If Russia could have its way over Poland, she was likely to overcome Anglo-American scruples in regard to Rumania, Bulgaria, etc. Indeed, a dominant position in Poland was one of the principal objectives in the war. It would put the U.S.S.R. in a much stronger position against any resurgent and anti-Soviet Germany; a solution of the Polish problem would already contain a large part of the German one. In Teheran, Stalin had won Churchill's and Roosevelt's agreement to "move Poland westward," in Churchill's words —i.e., to let the U.S.S.R. retain those lands peopled largely by Ukrainians and Belorussians to compensate Poland for her loss of the eastern provinces seized with German Silesia and Pomerania and part of East Prussia. Not yet a hard and fast agreement, it was kept in the strictest secrecy; details were to be worked out later. But it is easy to see how much more of a prize Poland would become to Russia, which would stand to gain first by acquiring the eastern part of pre-1939 Poland and second by having her satellite in control of the industrial riches of Silesia.

The U.S.S.R. had broken off relations with the Polish government in the spring of 1943. While the direct cause of the breach was the notorious Katyn Forest massacre of Polish officers and men by Soviet forces, the original cause was the Poles' unwillingness to acquiesce in the loss of their eastern lands. Soon it became clear that the real Soviet aim in regard to that unhappy country was not only territorial concessions but a Polish government of its own choosing. With the Soviet armies entering ethnic Poland on July 27, a Polish Committee of Liberation, composed of Poles who endorsed the Soviet demands and headed by a Communist, was set up in the city of Lublin. To this body the Soviets turned over the civil administration of Polish territories freed from the Germans; they obviously envisaged it as the nucleus of the future government of Poland.

Certainly on the Western side there had been hope that the Teheran agreements could be modified in Poland's favor, but Stalin proceeded to treat the rather casual discussions as a pledged word of the West. He conducted diplomacy in a manner reminiscent of military campaigns: each verbal concession or even a hint of one became a veritable beachhead from which a new Soviet diplomatic offensive would be launched. "But you promised us at Teheran," "you assured us in your communication of last June," etc., was the constant theme of Soviet remonstrations. Soviet offensives were usually preceded and accompanied by saturation artillery fire. And so their diplomatic moves were assisted by a heavy barrage of propaganda. Had it not been an Englishman, Lord Curzon, who after World War I had prescribed the frontier between Poland and Russia which the latter now claimed? Was he, Stalin, to be less fair to his people than an English lord? By the time Roosevelt and Churchill, not famous for knowledge of East European history, could check with their experts, the Soviets had their beachhead firmly established and were pursuing an offensive on another sector. From territorial claims against Poland they gradually escalated their demands to having a Polish government they could approve of. And by establishing the Lublin Committee, they gave notice that they would demand a government of their own making.

The Polish government in London, while kept in the dark concerning the tentative decisions at Teheran, could be in little doubt as to the direction in which things were moving. It kept expostulating with Washington and London, pointing out the undoubted legal rights it had to the territories claimed by Russia and protesting the Soviets' mounting campaign of vilification, which was echoed by much of the left-wing press in Britain and the United States. Its pleas and protests were usually addressed to the legal and moral sides of the issue, and precisely because they were irrefutable in those terms they were bound to irritate Western politicians.

The Warsaw uprising was a desperate gamble by the legitimate Polish regime (1) to demonstrate to the world that it enjoyed the support of a large majority of people in occupied Poland (as against the Soviet line that it was nothing but a bunch of discredited politicians with no roots at home), and (2) to shame the British and Americans into supporting its claims. On the first count the uprising was convincing; the entire population of the city joined in the unequal struggle against the Germans. But on the second it was to prove unavailing.

The initiators of the uprising obviously counted on the Soviet armies, then just across the river, to take this opportunity to capture the capital of Poland. But the Red Army did not move. Conceivably crossing the Vistula was not at the time within its plans, but even if it had been, it is unlikely that Stalin would have chosen to crown with success an enterprise designed to raise the credit of the London government. The official Russian position on the uprising was, in Stalin's words, that it was unleashed by "a group of criminals . . . in order to seize power." British and American planes flying supplies to the insurgents were at first refused landing rights on Soviet territory.

The agony of Warsaw continued for eight weeks. The effect on public opinion in the West of the Russian armies standing by without helping was most powerful. Churchill, though displeased with the Polish exile government, was still moved to plead with Roosevelt for stronger pressure on Stalin. The latter was unwilling. In September, the Russians dropped supplies to the beleaguered Poles. In October, with the city utterly ruined, the remnants of the Polish underground forces capitulated to the Germans. The struggle had broken the spine of the Polish underground loyal to London, and thus made easier the task of transforming Poland into a Soviet satellite. For many Poles, Warsaw was to be a frightful lesson in political realism: in view of Stalin's ruthlessness and the indifference or inability of the Western allies to help, Poland, having been pushed by the horrors of German occupation to the limits of endurance, could not now be expected to resist another totalitarian power.

The shock of Warsaw did not swerve American policy from its aim of integrating Russia into an international organization. Roosevelt's messages to Stalin were at first pleading: "We must think of the reaction of world public opinion, if the anti-fascists in Warsaw are left to their own devices." [9] But the President shifted in his subsequent messages to Stalin to subjects he considered of more lasting importance: the voting procedure in the Security Council and working out of plans for joint operations against Japan. Churchill's anguish over the Russians' ruthlessness was joined with his bitterness at the Americans' unwillingness to pressure the Soviets more energetically to provide some help to the unhappy city. He tells us in his memoirs that he was tempted to threaten the Soviets with stopping all Western supplies unless they facilitated the task of supplying Warsaw by British and American planes. But without American concurrence he was helpless.

Churchill's unhappiness was increased by his irritation at the Polish government in London, which, by refusing to make timely territorial concessions to Russia, he felt helped bring about the tragic impasse. The loss of prewar eastern Poland was in a fair way a *fait accompli,* but by their bullheaded attitude the London Poles were endangering the independence of the rest of their country. By a tacit agreement with the President, Churchill was left the management of the Polish issue: it would not do for Roosevelt, with the election approaching—there was, after all, a large Polish-American constituency—to take too active a role in the quarrel. Polish visitors to the White House were given soothing but general statements, while Churchill had the humiliating task of

[9] *Correspondence of the Chairman of the Council of Ministers of the U.S.S.R. with Presidents of the U.S.A. and Prime Ministers of Britain 1941–5* (hereafter referred to as *Correspondence*) (Moscow, 1957), II, 154.

"working" on the London regime and trying to persuade it of something he himself did not quite believe—that Stalin did not want a Communist Poland. The central figure in this hopeless game was the Prime Minister, Stanislaw Mikolajczyk, whom Stalin finally deigned to receive in Moscow, *not* as head of an allied government but simply as a private individual.[10] The unhappy Polish politician was advised to seek his luck with the Lublin Committee, which expressed its willingness to accept him as the leader of the Provisional Government if he repudiated his London colleagues—a willingness that reflected the Russians' awareness that they needed a Polish politician of some popularity and standing among the people, and that the Lublin Poles were greatly deficient in this respect.

The tangled story of Poland and of the American attitude toward it epitomized the whole trouble with peacemaking as viewed from Washington. To obtain a Soviet signature on this or that declaration, to get Soviet agreement to a procedural question, Washington was willing to overlook or minimize concrete examples of Stalin's duplicity. It was equally unwilling to engage in hard-boiled bargaining with the Soviet Union. Yet in the absence of such bargaining, the shape of postwar Europe was being hammered out by the victorious Red Army. The American distaste for talking about spheres of influence did not prevent the Russians from *acquiring* one. Rumania capitulated in August. Finland signed an armistice in September. Bulgaria tried to get out of the war at the same time, but the Bulgarians' attempts to have conversations to this effect with the Allied Command in Italy had a paradoxical effect: the Soviet Union (upon whom Bulgaria had not declared war and with whom she consequently could have no peace negotiations) now declared war upon the small Balkan country and occupied it forthwith. Militarily, this expenditure of Soviet resources and subsequent casualties away from the main theater of war made as little sense as an Anglo-American landing in Norway would have. But politically the Red Army's presence in these countries made it probable that no matter what the future protocols, interallied control commissions, etc., the real power would be exerted by Moscow.

Churchill's anxiety on all these points must have been increased by the Anglo-American conference which took place in Quebec in Septem-

---

10 Mikolajczyk succeeded General Sikorski, who had died in an airplane crash in July, 1943. Many years later a German dramatist was to present his death as contrived by the British to appease Stalin. This absurd charge fits in with a popular posture of the 1960s: denigration of the Allies' wartime achievement, a fad which made commercial success out of many a mediocre book or play. Needless to say, there is no shred of evidence to support the charge.

ber, 1944. By now it was too late for Churchill to argue for decisive changes in strategy which would allow the Allied armies to get to Central Europe and parts of the Balkans before the Russians. This had previously been vetoed by the American government, which opted for a strategy determined by purely military considerations. It appeared now that the European war might soon be over, but this happy prospect brought some very unhappy possibilities. Would American economic help cease abruptly on V-E Day, before British industry could be reconverted to peacetime use? Would Britain's imperial interests—i.e., the recovery of those areas of the empire still held by the Japanese—be taken into account in American plans to deal the final blow to the Japanese? On both counts the proud Englishman had to appear as a supplicant.

This background helps to explain Churchill's acquiescence in the notorious plan for the pastoralization of Germany, which, having been worked out in the U.S. Treasury Department, passed into history as the Morgenthau Plan. It envisaged the destruction of Germany's heavy and medium industry; the main industrial areas of the Ruhr and the Saar and Silesia would be detached from Germany, to be partitioned into two separate states, their inhabitants relegated to mainly agricultural pursuits and their standard of living kept below that of any of the states Hitler had invaded. The plan reflected the vindictiveness then widely felt against the nation which had allowed itself to be used in Hitler's war against humanity. Roosevelt himself shared the mood, and the plan elaborated what he had said on the subject at Teheran. But Churchill, whose feelings toward the "Huns" were not any kindlier than those of the President, realized the plan's impracticality verging on sheer madness. For one thing, it had been hastily slapped together and was inconsistent: if the Saar was to go to France and the Ruhr "internationalized" (whatever that was supposed to mean), why destroy their industries? But most of all, how could one visit a Carthaginian peace on Germany and expect Europe as a whole to recover? The palpable incoherence of the Morgenthau Plan guaranteed that it could never be put into effect. But mere intimations as to its contents would go far to throw the Germans into the arms of Communism. For all the fears and hatred they felt toward the Russians, and for all the depredations the Red Army might visit on Germany, official Soviet propaganda was reverting more and more to Stalin's words that Hitlers come and go but Germany remains.

Churchill's acquiescence might well have been facilitated by the American promise to continue Lend Lease to Britain after the victory in Europe. The sheer impracticality of the Plan must also have convinced him that it would be dropped after a more rational scrutiny in Washington, as indeed was to be the case. But Churchill's account of the second Quebec conference is understandably brief and perfunctory. Decisions which could affect the course of history for generations were being made hurriedly and on largely emotional grounds. The President had a rather casual and impulsive way of reaching decisions, very often on the advice of people with no experience in international affairs, and little systematic thought was expended on topics of supreme importance, such as the postwar economic reconstruction of Europe, the future of France, or of the British Commonwealth in Asia.

Almost immediately after his return to Britain from Quebec, Churchill set out for Moscow. There can be little doubt that this was a rather desperate gambit to reach an understanding with Stalin on some of these most pressing issues. This was not *quite* going behind the back of the Americans, since no agreements could be kept secret from Roosevelt, but Churchill might have hoped that he could impress Stalin with the need for making some businesslike arrangements about spheres of influence. It is possible that he considered the fact that one could not be *absolutely* sure that Roosevelt would be re-elected, and that Stalin might jump at a chance to foreclose a deal before some strange faces appeared at the next Big Three meeting. If these naughty ideas were not in Churchill's head, it is hard to see why he went to Moscow at all, since he was bound to see Stalin at the summit meeting scheduled to take place after the elections, i.e., in two or three months.

As usual, the Americans were more alert to trickery on the part of close allies than by actual or potential antagonists. In a message to Stalin, Roosevelt was explicit: "in the current world war there is literally not a single problem, military or political, in which the U.S. is not interested. . . . Only we three, and only together, can decide the hitherto unresolved problems." [11] In answer, Stalin was all innocence: he had been given to understand that Churchill was coming to Moscow on behalf of the United States as well as Britain; now that Roosevelt denies it, he was puzzled as to what had brought the Prime Minister to Moscow, since Churchill had not informed him in advance.[12] To both

[11] *Correspondence*, II, 160.
[12] *Ibid.*, p. 162.

Churchill and Stalin the President insisted that Ambassador Averell Harriman attend the meetings of his two partners—a fairly unprecedented demand.

What would have been his reaction had Stalin made a similar request concerning Anglo-American meetings? Or Churchill vis-à-vis American-Soviet talks? Roosevelt's language to Churchill (as the message was actually drafted by Hopkins) is also of interest. "I have . . . instructed Harriman to . . . participate as my observer. . . . While naturally Averell will not be in a position to commit the U.S.—I could not permit anyone to commit me in advance—he will be able to keep me fully informed, and I have told him to return and to report to me as soon as the conference is over." [13] This does not imply an excessive faith that Churchill would make a full report, and the message has an imperious ring. Even Stalin usually eschewed personal pronouns, writing modestly "on behalf of the Soviet government" or "the Soviet people."

The irrepressible Prime Minister still tried. Managing on one occasion to shake off the friendly but inhibiting presence of Harriman, he propounded to Stalin his famous percentage plan.[14] Influence in various Balkan countries was to be apportioned between the two powers. Thus in Rumania, for example, Britain was to have 10 per cent influence and Russia 90; vice versa in Greece. Hungary (hardly a Balkan country!) was to be 50-50, etc. Stalin must have been strongly tempted to laugh or to ask "What will Roosevelt say?" but he merely put a tick on the paper with his pencil and politely told Churchill, who guiltily wondered whether they should not destroy the compromising document, that he might keep it.

That the Prime Minister indulged in such fatuous calculations was proof of the strain under which he had been laboring. There was not a chance of Washington acceding to such agreements. But quite apart from this point, what did the percentages mean? Why did Britain aspire to a 20 per cent influence in Bulgaria? In the absence of American agreement and in view of the fact that all those countries would be soon occupied by the Red Army and, in the case of Yugoslavia, by local Communist-led forces, there was no reason for the Russians to allow Britain as much as 1 per cent, and such in fact was to be the case. The one exception was to be Greece, but Stalin's abstaining from helping the

---

[13] Winston Churchill, *Triumph and Tragedy* (Boston, 1953), p. 219.
[14] In his *Memoirs,* Churchill includes Harriman as present at the talk, but he was not. See Herbert Feis, *Churchill-Roosevelt-Stalin* (Princeton, N. J., 1967), p. 488.

Greek Communists during their December, 1944, uprising was due not so much to any deference for Churchill's percentage plan but simply to the fact that the Red Army was not there and he could hardly have a reason for a head-on collision with the British.

Poland was not on the percentage list, and the implication was clear: the British were resigned that Poland would be *wholly* within the Soviet sphere while still hoping to save it from a purely Communist regime. Mikolajczyk was summoned to Moscow and there mercilessly bullied by Churchill to agree to Soviet territorial demands and to reach a compromise with the Lublin Poles. Though the Prime Minister loathed the latter and had no illusions as to their being Soviet puppets, he felt that with a quick solution of the Polish question, Stalin might be more accommodating in other areas and might leave Poland some shreds of independence. The Americans would appreciate this thorny problem being solved without their own involvement in its seamier details. The Polish Prime Minister, however, while leaning toward some accommodation with the Russians, was repudiated by his cabinet and resigned in November, 1944. The subsequent Polish government in London was virtually ignored by the British and the Americans.

While the atmosphere of the Moscow talks was quite cordial and a friendlier tone was to pervade Soviet-British relations for some time afterward, Churchill's mission was essentially barren of results. In the spring of 1942, the Russians had been willing to talk of dividing postwar Europe into spheres of interest with the British. But in two and a half years enormous changes had taken place in the power configuration, and from the British alone Stalin had little to fear and not much to expect. If anything, Churchill's abortive attempt must have increased the Russians' confidence that with skill and persistence they could arrange things in Eastern Europe pretty much to their liking.

The Soviets kept a hands-off attitude toward the Greek troubles which erupted in November-December, 1944. It appears certain that the Greek Communists' attempt to seize Athens was undertaken without Soviet inspiration or approval. To Churchill this suggested that the Russians were observing his percentage plan, which only shows how the most perspicacious statesmen can at times be subject to self-delusion.[15] But there was no reason for the Russians to clash with Western interests in areas where Soviet interests were not vitally engaged. The diplomatic

---

[15] From his letter to Foreign Secretary Eden on November 7: "Having paid the price we have to Russia for the freedom of action in Greece. . . ." Churchill, *op. cit.,* p. 286.

issue of greatest urgency for Stalin was still the Polish one, and he was not letting the Greek partisans deflect him from it.

While impatient, he was biding his time. The secret correspondence with Roosevelt and Churchill prior to the Yalta conference bore on three main topics: the location of the conference, the veto problem in the Security Council, and the procedure for voting. One was of little importance in itself but still symbolic: would the Big Three meet on Soviet soil or as preferred by Roosevelt in some Mediterranean location? Courtesy dictated that Stalin should yield: certainly Teheran had been his choice and was controlled by Soviet troops; Roosevelt was crippled and Stalin must have heard reports of his failing health. But he insisted on the Black Sea. On the veto he would not yield either, even with and perhaps because of Roosevelt's willingness to compromise and have the permanent members exercise the veto on all issues except that of procedure. On the most important Polish question he waited for an opening, and this came in Roosevelt's message of December 20.

He had heard, wrote Roosevelt, that the Lublin Committee was thinking of transforming itself into the Provisional Government of Poland. If so, he hoped that the Soviets "would be able to withhold the recognition of the Lublin Committee as Government of Poland until our meeting. . . . Couldn't you until that date continue to deal with the Committee on the present basis?" [16] This was all that Stalin needed—Soviet diplomacy had a new bridgehead. On December 27, he answered Roosevelt that the Soviet government had new evidence concerning the heinous activity of the London regime and its agents in Poland. The latter were killing Red Army soldiers. "If the [Lublin] Polish Committee proclaims itself a Provisional Polish Government . . . the Soviet Government would have no reason not to recognize it as such." [17] Would not Britain and the United States follow suit? The President was now thrown on the defensive. The United States could not as yet accept the Lublin Committee. "This by no means is caused by any special ties with the regime in London nor by any feelings toward the emigré Polish Government. But the United States has no proof that the majority of Poles support Lublin. Won't Stalin wait?" [18] Stalin on January 1, in his New Year's greetings, explained that he could not. The matter was out of his hands, much as he would like to oblige the President. The supreme authority in the U.S.S.R., namely the Presidium of the Supreme Soviet, had decided

[16] *Correspondence*, II, 173.
[17] *Ibid.*, p. 179.
[18] *Ibid.*, p. 180.

to recognize the Lublin group as the provisional government of Poland.

This is Stalin's diplomacy in quintessence. One wretchedly drafted sentence in Roosevelt's message provides an opening into which he rushes with alacrity and breathtaking brazenness. Prior to the American message of December 20, there was probably no intention on his part to press the issue so soon, but Roosevelt's feeble and pleading tone was an open invitation. What could Washington then say to retrieve the situation? That the Lublin Committee was a mere creature of the Russians, and that the august Presidium of the Supreme Soviet was also merely a puppet? (In fact, there is no record of a Presidium meeting on December 27!) But many in the West still thought that when it came to foreign policy, Stalin did not have a plenitude of powers, and that while he himself was personally friendly to the West there were some sinister forces in the Politburo who were less trusting. Needless to say, the Russians did nothing to dispel such rumors.

On both the U.N. and the Polish issues the Americans were then to be at a tactical disadvantage when they met the Russians at Yalta. Add to this the anxiety felt by the Chiefs of Staff that Russia definitely pledge her help against Japan once Germany collapsed or surrendered. By coincidence there was another psychological disadvantage under which the West's representatives labored as they gathered in the Czars' former resort in February. The recent setback by the Allied armies in the Ardennes had occasioned some alarm and pleas to Stalin to speed up his winter offensive. The latter was now rolling along.

But the United States' real bargaining power was, of course, enormous. Compared with the other belligerents in terms of resources, manpower, and casualties, the Americans had barely begun to fight. The President had just been elected to a fourth term, his prestige and power were enormous. That he would undertake the risks and discomforts of long sea and air travel was a touching testimony of how much he was willing to sacrifice for the goal of Allied unity. He looked forward not only to the settlement of the issues separating the West and Russia, but once more to gaining Stalin's confidence and dispelling the Russians' brooding distrust of the capitalist world.

After the war Yalta was to acquire a sinister reputation among some Americans. Allegedly it was there that China was sold down the river, there that the West first agreed to the disastrous German solution, etc. But in fact Yalta was not a sharp turn in the road to a frustrating peace. It was simply another stage.

It was the *mood* of Yalta rather than any concrete decisions reached there which did such great damage to Soviet-American relations. With the war in Europe practically won, with the Japanese being pushed inexorably back to their islands, there was no need for the Americans to be solicitous or to plead with the Russians rather than bargain. In view of their assumptions that the Pacific war might require invasion of Japan proper, and that what those professors from the Manhattan Project were saying about the new weapons could not be trusted, the hard-boiled Chiefs of Staff were not unreasonable in arguing that Soviet assistance in the war against Japan was of great importance. But common sense should have persuaded the American negotiators that the destruction of Japan as a military power was *at least* as important to the U.S.S.R. as to the United States. Russia was still carrying the main burden in the European war, the resistance of the Germans in the east being much stronger and their armies more numerous than on the western front. This also should have suggested how important the rapid defeat of Germany was to the interests of the U.S.S.R. In 1942 and 1943, Stalin, by way of pressuring for a second front, had at times insinuated that Russia might not be able to go on—i.e., might seek a separate peace with Germany. The West needed no such stratagems in 1945: the Russians were deathly afraid that the Germans, while fighting desperately in the East, would in effect open their front to the Allies in the West. They had every reason not to try the patience of the United States. At Yalta the Americans had the upper hand not only in material resources but also in the over-all tactical situation.

But they did not realize it, and they were thinking in different terms. The conference had to succeed in demonstrating the optimistic unity of the three participants, and its announced results could not clash with the moral principles according to which the American public believed international relations had to be regulated. Hence Roosevelt had to get some agreement on voting in the Security Council and some high-sounding declaration as to how nations liberated from German rule would be governed. Yet Stalin could not disparage Roosevelt or think he could pull the wool over his eyes. He must have been impressed by the President's enormous political skill. Who else could have brought America, engrossed in her own problems and determined to stay out of the war, from complete isolationism to virtual belligerency even *before* Pearl Harbor? The President had to be handled carefully. Constant maneuvering to get the better of his two partners was combined in Stalin with a sense of history and an awareness of the uniqueness of the Grand Alliance. He was probably sincere when he said that peace would remain secure as long as the three of them remained at the helms of their nations.

The details of the Yalta agreements are well known. The U.S.S.R. pledged to enter the war against Japan, but claimed tangible rewards. Otherwise, said the incorrigible Stalin, the Soviet people would not understand why they had to fight a nation with whom they had no particular quarrel. Southern Sakhalin and the Kuril Islands were to return to the U.S.S.R. Then came concessions at the expense of a third and friendly party—China. The Soviet Union was to recover the Manchurian Railway—i.e., the industrial complex she had sold in 1935 to Japan's puppet Manchukuo. She was to receive the base of Port Arthur and get special rights in Dairen. Mongolia was to be confirmed in her "independence"—i.e., her status as a Russian satellite. The United States was to second these demands on Chiang Kai-shek. While this part of the bargain was indelicate, it is quite likely that Chiang would have granted the demands even without American pressure, so eager was he to please Moscow and to obtain its pledge not to support the Chinese Communists.

The central problem of Germany received superficial treatment, final decisions being deferred until after victory. Provisionally, the country was to be divided into spheres of occupation by the Big Three and France.

On February 5, at a plenary session of the conference, Roosevelt made a fateful statement: while the United States would continue her efforts on behalf of peace, the Congress and the public were not likely to tolerate keeping American troops in Europe beyond two years after the war's end.[19] Stalin did not show any reaction to this statement. Yet it must have weakened America's hand in negotiations. Why should the Russians make undue concessions to the American viewpoint on Germany, etc., if within two or three years American troops were bound to leave Europe? Churchill's apprehension increased. What force was to balance the huge Red Army? Britain, with her small standing army and her inevitable postwar economic troubles? France, herself not immune from the Communist danger? The Prime Minister's interest in partitioning Germany into several states had now definitely vanished. He was also most voluble in protesting any excessive scheme of reparations. Britain did not wish to be tied to "Germany's corpse."

That the Americans agreed to the Russians' figure for German

[19] *Foreign Relations of the United States—Conferences at Malta and Yalta* (to be referred to as *Yalta Papers*) (Washington, 1955), p. 617.

reparations was largely because of what they felt was an important and far-reaching concession by Stalin. The Russians had agreed to the American proposal that procedural questions in the Security Council would be decided by a majority vote and that a permanent member would not be able to veto discussions of a dispute to which it was a member. The President "felt this was a great step forward which would be welcomed by all peoples in the world." [20] To the American participants this was probably the most valuable achievement of the Yalta Conference, one that would enhance if not indeed make possible America's wholehearted participation in the United Nations.

It is not surprising that on another question concerning the United Nations the Russians also showed themselves conciliatory. Having dragged out their demand to the point where its withdrawal or modification would be most effective, they announced that they no longer desired sixteen seats in the Assembly. Three would do. There is little doubt that this demand would have been dropped too, at an appropriate moment, but in their relief the Americans hastily agreed, and as a consequence the Ukraine and Belorussia are today members of the United Nations.[21] Only later did Roosevelt have second thoughts. Stalin had argued eloquently how he might have political difficulties (!) in the Ukraine and Belorussia if they were not represented in the U.N. In a communication to his Soviet friend, the President shared his anxiety lest *he* experience some difficulties in the United States. "Therefore it may be necessary for me to ask, so that the Congress and nation of the U.S. fully accept our membership in the U.N. for additional votes in the Assembly." [22] Stalin was understanding: the U.S. should have three votes just as the U.S.S.R. with its "two main republics." [23] But somehow the expected trouble in the Senate never did materialize, and we shall forever be tantalized by the question as to which two American states were slated for inclusion in the U.N. and what it would have meant to American politics.[24]

The amiable mood of Yalta dissipated whenever the Polish issue was discussed, which was often (at seven out of eight plenary sessions).

[20] *Ibid.*, p. 713.
[21] How often are the most obvious things overlooked by statesmen and analysts. If there was any validity to the Russian demand, the most obvious claimant for membership in the U.N. should have been by far the biggest and most populous of the Soviet Union Republics, the Russian S.S.R.
[22] *Correspondence*, II, 189.
[23] Again an unwarranted slight on the Russian Union Republic!
[24] Texas and Mississippi? The future Secretary of State, James Byrnes, present at Yalta, jokingly suggested Hawaii and Alaska.

In view of his "concessions," Stalin might well have thought that the bothersome issue would be finally disposed to his liking. But the question of the frontiers still gave trouble. Both Western Allies were resigned to the Soviet territorial vindications, though Roosevelt pleaded that "it would make it easier for me at home if the Soviet government could give something to Poland," [25] a rather odd way of asking the Soviets to take *less* from Poland than they intended. But Churchill was developing growing doubts as to the extent of Poland's compensation in German territory. It would be unwise, he argued, to "stuff the Polish goose so full of German food" that it might die of indigestion. A felicitous if ominous figure of speech, for don't most people look at the goose from one very special point of view? And to be sure, Stalin's view was that of consumer. In issuing orders to his commanders for the January offensive, he had asked them to spare the rich industrial basin of Silesia, which he now claimed for Poland. "Sheer gold," he said, placing his hand on the map of Silesia, which according to Marshal Konev indicated his solicitude for "fraternal Poland."

The exact western border of Poland was to be decided later. Roosevelt's attempt to make the Soviets modify their demands in the east was so feeble that it was bound to be ineffective.[26] But Stalin did not want to give the city of Lvov to Poland. He could not, he explained, be less pro-Russian and pro-Ukrainian than Lord Curzon!

The final communiqué of the conference put the British and American imprimatur on the Soviets' obtaining the desired frontier in the west. "The three Heads of Government consider that the eastern frontier of Poland should follow the Curzon line." [27] Pedants could object not only to the decision but to the language. The line suggested by Lord Curzon in 1920 did not run in the southern part of the disputed territory, and it was not supposed to be a definite border but merely a true line between Poland and Russia. Yet it had been a virtual certainty ever since Teheran that, barring a miraculous change in the Western powers' position, Russia would retain the gains she made under the Nazi-Soviet agreement of 1939.

The relative ease with which the Soviets obtained the approval

---

[25] *Yalta Papers*, p. 677.

[26] The President's statement deserves to be recorded: "I come from a distance and therefore have the advantage of a more distant point of view. There are six or seven million Poles in the United States. As I said in Teheran, in general I am in favor of the Curzon line. Most Poles are like the Chinese and want to save face." (This does not purport to be a literal rendition of the President's remarks.) *Ibid.*, p. 677.

[27] *Ibid.*, p. 974.

of their territorial claims on Poland put in sharper focus the disagreement as to the future Polish regime. Here there had been some stiffening in the Anglo-American position and a refusal simply to acknowledge the Lublin government. For all his irritations at this rather unexpected obstinacy, Stalin displayed patience. Seldom had his personal diplomacy been more masterful than on this issue at Yalta. He had an admirable knowledge of details which shamed his protagonists and put them on the defensive. He never resorted to crude threats but merely kept asking his interlocutors to imagine the ominous results which would follow from their stubbornness. True, the Lublin government was not a product of elections, but was de Gaulle's, which Britain and the United States now recognized? And while the French government had done nothing in the social sphere, his Polish government had already enacted far-reaching economic reforms. The London government? Say what you will, politicians who have been out of their country for five years inevitably lose touch with their people. (In fact, the London Polish regime was headed by a recent arrival from the Polish underground resistance, but neither Roosevelt nor Churchill remembered it.) To query whether British and American observers should not first report as to what was going on inside Poland, Stalin replied that the Poles were a proud nation that might resent foreign interference. And then his mood would change to one of sympathy for the troubles Churchill and Roosevelt had with *their* Poles: good people, excellent fighters, a nation that had produced great scientists and musicians, but alas, when it comes to politics quarrelsome and never satisfied. One may disagree with Hull's opinion that Stalin could have made a career in American politics, but one must grant that he would have been a dazzling success on Madison Avenue.

For the moment he obtained most but not all that he wanted. The Soviet protégé, the Provisional Government of Poland, was to be the nucleus of the future Government of National Unity. Democratic leaders from Poland and abroad would be invited to join; the process would be supervised by a commission in Moscow composed of Molotov and the British and American ambassadors. This meant a virtual though as yet not formal repudiation by the West of the legitimate government in London.

The decision on Poland set in melancholy perspective the Declaration on Liberated Europe issued by the conference and authored by the U.S. delegation. It pledged the Big Three to abide by the free verdict of the nations liberated from the Nazi yoke and to abide by the

verdict of free elections. Here was a classic example of the peculiarities
of the American approach to international politics. In terms of power
politics there could be some justification for yielding to Stalin. But then
why pretend to the point of self-deception that what is happening and
about to happen in Poland is in response to the free wishes of the
majority of its people? The declaration was not so much an exercise
in propaganda as an attempt at self-deception, and as the next few
months were to show the attempt was quite successful. How can you
turn a country over to a foreign power and yet demand that it be
done through free elections and in accordance with high principles of
morality and democracy?

The pace and contentiousness of the negotiations obviously tired
President Roosevelt. One assumes he shared the relief of his subordinate
who recorded in the conference log how upon boarding an American
ship "the crew served a delicious steak dinner to us, which was
a real treat after eight days of Russian fare." [28] All that sturgeon, caviar,
and vodka! The Russians had put themselves out for their visitors.
The Crimea had been utterly devastated in the war and the Russians
had improvised all the comforts and contrived to get lavish supplies
of food all the way from Moscow. And millions of Russians were still
starving. A small yet characteristic example of the insensitivity which
American officials often display toward foreigners and their problems.

However, the President grasped every opportunity to be pleasant
and obliging. Beyond the agreements and the declarations, his main
objective was to win Stalin's confidence. The Soviet ambassador in
Mexico, Umansky, had just died in a plane crash. The President offered to have an American plane transport his remains to Moscow or
(mindful of how Russians were wary of flights over their territory)
to a rendezvous with a Soviet plane in Alaska. The American people,
he added, had fond memories of Umansky. This was hardly true.
Umansky, whose service in Washington coincided with the Nazi-Soviet
Pact, had been shunned by the American government. Undoubtedly
surprised (there were nasty rumors that the crash had been arranged
by the Soviet secret service), Stalin gratefully accepted Roosevelt's
offer and even let an American plane bring the remains all the way
to Moscow.

The impression received by the Russians from the tone of the proceedings at Yalta was almost immediately translated into increased
pressure on East European countries occupied by the Red Army. In

[28] *Ibid.,* p. 560.

Rumania, King Michael was brutally coerced into appointing a Communist-dominated government. In Yugoslavia, Tito speeded the task of removing non-Communist elements of his regime and of scuttling the compromise with the royalists on which Churchill had placed so much hope. Some non-Communist leaders hastened to bow to the inevitable before they would find themselves in the predicament of the London Polish regime. President Beneš of Czechoslovakia, after a trip to Moscow in March, reorganized his government to include several Communists and entrusted the premiership to Zdenek Fierlinger, who while not yet a party member had, while ambassador in Moscow, become a thoroughgoing fellow traveler.

The Declaration on Liberated Europe was thus proving not so much ineffective as irrelevant. Such incantations could hardly work against the Red Army's actual or imminent presence, against the exhaustion of the people, and against the destruction of countries which urged politicians to seek accommodation with or to submit to the Russians and their local friends.

Troublesome Poland then bobbed up to the surface. The three-power commission situated in Moscow was to settle the details of the future Polish regime. To Molotov, this meant essentially taking the Provisional Government and decorating it with a few obliging figures. But the British and American ambassadors took their task seriously and began a real search for "democratic Poles." Most of their nominees were rejected by Molotov as either tainted with fascism and/or unacceptable to the Provisional Government, which now moved amidst the ruins of Warsaw, where it was dourly though mostly passively combated by a majority of the population. This in turn increased the severity of the Soviet secret-police detachments which moved in with the Red Army. Though weakened by the Warsaw catastrophe, the underground regime connected with London was still influential. In March, sixteen of its leaders were contacted and assured of immunity if they agreed to a conference with the Soviet military authorities. On their arrival in Marshal Zhukov's headquarters, they were arrested, and it was more than two months before any news of their fate was to reach the West.

Another consequence of the Polish situation, in itself minor, was to have a far-reaching psychological effect on the Americans in these last weeks of Roosevelt's life. As the Red Army pushed the Germans westward, it liberated American prisoners of war held in camps in

Poland. Their return home was now delayed unduly, and no American officers were allowed to inspect the facilities where their countrymen were being retained while awaiting passage home. Much of this could be explained by the inevitable red tape and chaotic wartime conditions.

But it was clear that the Russians did not want foreign observers on Polish soil and were not eager for the returning Americans to carry tales about the behavior of the Red Army and the Soviet secret police. Roosevelt's messages on the subject grew astringent in tone, and so did Stalin's replies. The President's irritation spread to the whole Polish issue. From Moscow, Ambassador Harriman, who could not be accused of being anti-Soviet, reported that the Russians were taking an increasingly brusque and peremptory tone. The President was not well, and he was not going to recast his whole foreign policy, but it must have become clear to him that all the amiability at Yalta was threatening to end in results exactly opposite from the ones he had expected. The usual American desire to be liked is accompanied by fear of being taken in, of being a sucker. And the Soviets' attitude now left little doubt that they thought they had taken the measure of their American friends and could disregard their objections. Stalin persisted to make moves and threats which even before had not been taken seriously but were now sorely trying the patience of the man who had put so much stock in his good will. For example, he canceled Molotov's forthcoming trip to the founding meeting of the U.N. in San Francisco on grounds that the Supreme Soviet required his presence. Roosevelt was by now heartily sick of the Supreme Soviet and the insulting implication that such excuses would be swallowed indefinitely. Though his messages were often drafted by someone else, the thrust of his warning to Stalin is unmistakable. On April 1, a long, rather imperious message reached the Kremlin. Stalin, it stated, should compare the Declaration on Liberated Europe with what his subordinates were doing in Rumania. "It was clear" that the Polish Provisional Government had no right to veto the people to be included in the future democratic regime, nor should it persecute political opponents in Poland. "It is essential" that the American and British ambassadors have the right to visit that country and see things for themselves. Were the Polish problem not solved promptly and justly, the unity of the Grand Alliance would be threatened. "You realize, I hope, that in the United States any policy of the government whether at home or abroad must have genuine support of the people. The American people make up their own mind and no exertions by the government can change their judgment. . . . I have been forced to wonder whether you fully realize this fact." [29]

Stalin's behavior throughout those last days of Roosevelt's life is a fascinating study of how an unusually clever man can make a grave psychological error and then compound it to the point of falling into a veritable panic. What could be behind this sudden American intransigence? Had Churchill finally persuaded the President to get tough? Then there must have been in the background the long-lasting and deeper anxiety that the Western Allies might pull some trick at the last moment. The Germans had obviously been eager for some sort of an agreement which would spare most of Germany from Russian occupation.

In March a German plenipotentiary had arrived in Switzerland with the view of ascertaining possible British-American conditions for a surrender of the German armies in northern Italy. The British loyally informed Moscow about General Wolff's move. Immediately the Russians demanded that their representative be present at *every stage* of negotiations. The Americans thought this demand unreasonable, but Churchill was willing for a Soviet representative to be present when and if the Germans actually offered to surrender, whereupon Molotov demanded an immediate end to all negotiations.

In a recent "revisionist" treatment the whole episode is given the hue of a deep Anglo-American intrigue to prevent northern Italy from falling into the hands of the Left. Warming to his subject, the author writes of "Roosevelt's coyness and feigned innocence." [30] This is clearly absurd: accepting military surrender by the enemy was always the business of the military commander in the given theater. The Anglo-American offer to have a Russian officer present in Field Marshal Alexander's quarters when and if the Germans would actually surrender already went beyond the usual practice in such matters. There was no Western representative when Field Marshal Paulus surrendered in Stalingrad in 1943, nor when the Finns surrendered to the Soviet Army in 1944. As to saving northern Italy from left-wing partisans, the problem could not arise, since upon liberation from the Germans the region would presumably pass under the authority of the Italian government, which was then supported by all the major political parties, including the Communists. Until the area could be turned over to civil

[29] *Correspondence,* II, p. 202.
[30] Kolko, *op. cit.,* p. 379.

authorities it was the duty of Field Marshal Alexander not to allow any derogation of the rights of the Rome government recognized by the Allies, including the U.S.S.R.[31]

But the problem of northern Italy was farthest from Stalin's mind when he exploded at the news of the negotiations. For all his confidence that he could handle his Western partners, he must have always feared a secret bargain between them and the Germans. And now this presumably was it! "If the Germans in northern Italy . . . want negotiations to surrender and open the front to the Western allies, it must mean that they have other, more serious aims concerning the fate of Germany." [32] The President's message, received in Moscow on April 1, tried patiently to explain the whole story: the negotiations were of the most preliminary type, a capitulation would not be signed unless the Russians were present. This in turn led to the truly paranoid outburst of Stalin's note of April 3. His sources, he wrote, informed him that the Germans in Italy had already agreed to surrender, and in return the Anglo-Americans would go easy on Germany after her defeat. More than Italy was involved, he wrote; the Germans would let the Anglo-American armies deep into their country while continuing to fight the Russians. But maybe Roosevelt was not fully informed? The whole matter had clearly been devised by the British. And now the Germans had stopped fighting in the West while continuing to fight the Russians!

It would have been most unpolitic for Stalin to send such messages even if the facts had been as he alleged. They were deeply insulting to the President, implying as they did that he was either a trickster or a figurehead ignorant of what was being done in his name, or a fool led by the nose by his British ally. As well as being insulting, Stalin's language bared what he had always been careful to conceal: Russia's real fears and sense of relative weakness. After imputing to the Anglo-Americans rather heinous behavior toward their allies,[33] he ended on a pleading rather than threatening note: "I and my colleagues would never take such a risky step since we realize that the momentary ad-

---

[31] What is one to think of Kolko's conclusion: "Any separate surrenders by the Germans in a major theatre of war would have enabled Anglo-American troops to fill in the vacuum, political as well as military." *Ibid.*, p. 379. What vacuum?

[32] *Correspondence,* II, 199.

[33] Including the charge that they *intentionally* misinformed the Russians about the coming German counteroffensive. General Marshall had told the Soviet staff that a German counterattack would be launched in Pomerania. Actually it came in Hungary. Had the Russians acted on the American advice they would have suffered a disaster.

vantage thus gained is nothing compared with the vast advantage which accrues from preserving and strengthening the trust among the Allies." [34]

A different man in the White House might well have answered in effect, "Assuming that things are as you allege, shall we now talk about Poland and Rumania?" But Roosevelt could not do this. His answer, though drafted by another's hand, still reflected his indignation: "It is with amazement that I read your message of April 3rd. . . . I cannot but feel extreme indignation about those who feed you such information, whoever they are, because of their disgraceful misinterpretation of my actions or those of my trusted subordinates." [35]

Stalin's reply of April 7 testified that he had cooled off. He did not mean to impute bad faith to anybody. Roosevelt should not be angry with those who provide Stalin with information; they are "honest and humble people." A message sent on the same day reverted to the Polish questions. The Russians were obviously eager to shift discussions away from the unfortunate Swiss negotiations. The message sent back in Roosevelt's name acknowledged drily that the matter could be relegated to the past. But even before it reached Moscow, on April 12, Franklin Roosevelt died.

[34] *Correspondence*, II, 205.
[35] *Ibid.*, p. 206.

3

Truman

The sudden death of President Roosevelt was felt by Churchill, he tells us in his memoirs, to be a veritable catastrophe. Apart from his genuine personal grief, the Prime Minister thought that Roosevelt was just coming around to his viewpoint concerning the Russians. His successor, he writes, for all his intelligence and vigor, lacked experience and knowledge in foreign affairs. It took time to become oriented in the complexities of his awesome office, and by then it was too late to retrieve what had been lost. The new leader, Churchill implied, lacked the self-confidence and prestige with which his predecessor had been so abundantly endowed.

Such judgments may well have been shared in Moscow. The Soviet dossier on Truman contained the frank but undiplomatic outburst by the then senator from Missouri, who in June, 1941, had said it was an excellent thing for Germany and the U.S.S.R. to be fighting each other and he hoped that they finished each other off. In 1945 this was not mentioned, but during the long years of the Cold War the Soviet reader of books and articles on American foreign policy would often be reminded of this cynical remark, which supposedly explained so much about American policy after 1945.

Stalin felt the need of a first-hand report. The Supreme Soviet somehow relented and allowed Molotov to go to San Francisco. On his way, the Soviet minister stopped off in Washington, where Truman read him a lesson on Poland—couched in a style which soon became familiar to various American politicians and to an unfortunate music critic who was to comment unfavorably on the singing of Miss Margaret Truman. He had never been spoken to like that before, exclaimed Molotóv. But knowing who his boss was, one must assume that the Soviet statesman was exaggerating.

Truman had a genuine admiration for Churchill, and indeed his first steps suggested that he would follow the Prime Minister's advice less reluctantly than Roosevelt: a joint message to Stalin of April 18 spoke sharply of Russian chicaneries concerning the formation of the new Polish regime. But the new President could not sharply reverse American policy, and the Russians may have sensed that it would be a grave psychological error at this point to show either compliance or hesitation.

Thus in San Francisco Molotov once again raised objections about the voting procedures and the membership composition of the United Nations. Virtuous, democratic Russia balked at the inclusion of Argentina, which was now entering upon her Peronist period. And Stalin's reply to the Truman-Churchill message was harsh and unyielding: It was not the Soviets who were sabotaging formation of the Polish Government of National Unity but the British and American ambassadors. Did he, Stalin, interfere with what the British were doing in Belgium or Greece? He now pushed his demands beyond what was agreed upon at Yalta. The Polish Provisional Government was to be merely enlarged, not broadly reorganized. As to the character of the new regime, Stalin proposed to adopt the Yugoslav example. This had an eloquence of its own, for, as Churchill was to object plaintively: "The trend of developments in Yugoslavia is such that I do not think that the ratio 50:50 as between our interests is being observed. Marshal Tito is a complete dictator. He himself admits that he is warmly devoted to the Soviet Union." [1]

The Prime Minister tried to impress his correspondent with the gravity of the problem: "I ask of you, my friend Stalin, do not underestimate the difference on issues which you may find unimportant, but which symbolize the deepest convictions [literally, the world outlook] of the English speaking democracies." [2] Stalin affected to scorn both pleading and covert threats. On May 4, with Germany's capitulation but days away, he replied with increased harshness, completely rejecting

[1] *Correspondence of the Chairman of the Council of Ministers of the U.S.S.R. with Presidents of the U.S.A. and Prime Ministers of Britain 1941–5* (hereafter referred to as *Correspondence*) (Moscow, 1957), I, 345.
[2] *Ibid.*, p. 349.

Churchill's argument. The people to be consulted on the new Polish regime must be "only those who have demonstrated concretely their friendship towards the Soviet Union, who honestly and frankly are ready to collaborate with the U.S.S.R." [3] Churchill's position made impossible any joint solution of the Polish problem, concluded the infuriated dictator. A copy of the message was sent to the President with what can only be considered a slighting addendum that Stalin was sending it to Truman because he understood the President to be "interested in the Polish problem."

Stalin's tone in these communications with the Western leaders following Roosevelt's death, especially on the Polish issue, suggests strongly that he felt that Truman's tough talk would not be followed by commensurate action, and that it would be wrong to give the impression that the Soviet Union could be swerved from its purpose by a few harsh words.

This was a correct appraisal of the situation. The dictator was not going to repeat the error of the month before, when on the news of the negotiations between the Germans and the Western military authorities he exhibited panic. Late in April, the British and Americans rejected Himmler's suggestion that the Germans might capitulate in the West while continuing to fight the Russians, and insisted on simultaneous capitulation to the Big Three. Stalin's reaction to this news was dignified and magnanimous: knowing Churchill, he said, he was sure that such would be the reply.

The compliment notwithstanding, Churchill continued to search for some lever for restraining Stalin over Poland and to save something of the independence of other East European countries. One gambit he had favored was "getting there first," and throughout the days preceding V-E Day he prodded the Anglo-American commanders to beat the Russians to such important cities as Berlin, Vienna, and Prague. But Churchill's scheme inevitably ran into American objections. Military objectives should not be sacrificed for political aims, it was held in Washington. Also, despite growing doubts it was thought unwise to alienate the Russians and further increase their suspicions. Frustrated in this line of argument, the Prime Minister switched to another gambit. The Anglo-American armies should not retreat upon the capitulation of Germany to their occupation zones as agreed previously with the Russians until and unless the latter became more amenable about

[3] *Ibid.*, p. 353.

Eastern Europe. This would have meant, to employ a metaphor invented much later, standing eyeball to eyeball with the Russians considerably to the east of the occupation zone assigned to the Western powers. In the same vein Churchill implored Truman to delay deploying major American military units from Europe to the United States and the Pacific.

Contrary to what is sometimes suggested in postwar Soviet literature, Churchill did not expect or wish for an armed clash with the Soviets. He hoped to forestall Soviet *faits accomplis* by threats of similar action on the part of the West in Germany and Austria. If he counted on any actual fighting it was at most against the Yugoslavs, who occupied the Italian province of Venezia Giulia and Trieste and refused to yield it to Field Marshal Alexander, the Allied commander in Italy. Churchill felt a personal grievance against the mercurial Yugoslav leader to whose charm he, like many others, had succumbed.

The American Joint Chiefs of Staff whose advice was now decisive with Truman would have no part of such games. With Germany defeated, their mind was now on the Pacific theater, and they still felt the imperative need of Soviet assistance against Japan. But it is doubtful that Churchill's formula could have worked, even if the Americans had been agreeable. The Western leaders had neither the political nor the psychological support in their own countries for a confrontation, to use another fashionable term, with the Russians. The European war was over, and in the United States there was relief mixed with an urgent desire to get on with the other part of the business—Japan. How would the Americans and British take a sudden avowal of a sharp crisis among the Big Three? Many in the West had their attention focused on San Francisco, where the foundations of a brave, new, and peaceful world were being laid. For them it would have been inconceivable that there should be raised even the merest possibility of a world-wide clash.

There was at this stage, then, no possibility of retrieving by one bold stroke all the mistakes the Western Allies had made in their policy vis-à-vis the Soviet Union since at least Teheran. Perhaps there would have been a chance were Roosevelt still at the helm. But without him, there was little probability that the Soviet Union would heed Western protests, even less of public opinion understanding or approving a tough course against her.

By the same token, there was no need to compound the previous errors, to depart from a friendly but somewhat distant and businesslike relationship with Russia in favor of a will-o'-the-wisp effort to recapture a cordial understanding. Soviet policy in Eastern Europe was by now probably unchangeable, but it could have been modified if the United States had endured a bit longer the strained tone of communications with Moscow. A good proof was the provisional solution of the Trieste problem. Following strong representation from Russia, Tito retreated from Trieste and agreed with the Allied command on a line of demarcation between their forces and his. The whole business was to bring some long-run dividends for the West. Stalin grew angry with Tito for tangling the lines of his over-all diplomacy for the sake of a miserable Adriatic port. The Yugoslavs were pained and surprised that the all-powerful Soviet Union would not stand loyally by and incur risks on behalf of her fellow Communists. This mutual irritation was to bring forth further complications culminating in the breach of 1948.

Had the impasse over Poland been allowed to deepen, Stalin would have modified his position. But on the Western side there was little taste and patience for such a test of nerves. Such was Churchill's innocent conceit and confidence in his persuasiveness that he was eager for a meeting of the Big Three, while the Americans wanted the thorniest issues cleared away *before* the meeting took place. Hence Truman dispatched Harry Hopkins to Moscow and Joseph E. Davies to London to prepare the ground for the conference.

The personalities of the two emissaries and the nature of their mission throw a glaring light on the deficiencies of American wartime diplomacy. Hopkins was thought best suited to restore a friendly dialogue between Moscow and Washington. He had been a confidential adviser of Roosevelt, whom the Russians, it was believed, held in great esteem. Ambassador Harriman thought himself disqualified for the task because of his clashes with the Soviets on the Polish Commission. Hopkins, it was thought, could "get through" to Stalin, who was, in the view of American observers, basically friendly toward the United States but was being pulled in the opposite direction by Molotov. This was an old Soviet game, and the Americans fell for it just as the Nazis had before 1941, when Ribbentrop believed Stalin to be pro-German but influenced against Hitler by his foreign minister. The role assigned to Molotov was that of an unyielding and sarcastic diplomat who would contrast with Stalin—affable, understanding, and at the right moment willing to make a concession. That Molotov, who could not even prevent his own wife from being sent into exile, could veto any policy determined by Stalin was, of course, unthinkable.

Hopkins was not well versed in the issues under dispute, for his knowledge of the Polish problem was superficial. He was also a very sick man, and while this made his undertaking such a strenuous mission all the more touching, he could not have the alertness and endurance necessary for successful negotiation with Stalin and Molotov.

In retrospect the choice of Davies must appear even more embarrassing. A corporation lawyer and husband of an heiress, he enjoyed the reputation of being something of a seer on Soviet affairs, and he had spent two years as ambassador to Russia before the war. His arrival in Moscow in 1936 had led the personnel of the embassy, so George Kennan tells us, to contemplate resignation on the spot *en masse*. And indeed Davies displayed considerable independence of his professional advisers. His opinion of the Soviet system (his tenure coincided with the worst purges) was quite favorable. On the day of Hitler's attack on Russia he expressed confidence in a Russian victory—a view in direct contradiction to that of most experts (including, as we learned later, Stalin's). He had become a celebrity, his book *Mission to Moscow* having been made into a popular movie. Both in the book and in the film, Stalin was represented as a fatherly and genial figure, while Soviet victims of the purges, especially professional diplomats, were skulking and cowardly traitors.

Roosevelt had dispatched Davies on a special mission to Stalin in 1943, but he did not feel it possible to entrust his "old friend" with any specific job vis-à-vis Stalin. Davies "was not acquainted with our military activities nor with the postwar plans of our Government." [4] Now as a Soviet expert he was to brief Churchill on President Truman's decision to try a conciliatory approach. As if that were not enough, Davies was to convey Truman's desire to have a private meeting with Stalin before the Big Three conference.[5] Thus the Russians would not have reason to fear that the United States and Britain were ganging up on them.

It tells a great deal about Churchill's stamina that the message and personality of this emissary did not have a serious effect on his health. His whole scheme for bargaining with the Russians was collapsing. The only way of extracting anything from Stalin was precisely to convey to him that the United States and Britain *were* "ganging up." The

---

[4] *Ibid.*, p. 63.
[5] Truman was to claim that there had been a misunderstanding: all he sought was a private meeting *during* the conference. But he writes of the whole episode with some embarrassment.

Americans were now backsliding into their pre-Yalta attitude. Churchill evidently became quite violent on the subject with Davies, and the latter, if his account is to be believed, had the impudence to tell the Prime Minister that his views now coincided with those of Goebbels. The Prime Minister's own account of the encounter is amazingly restrained. He notified Truman that he could not countenance a Big Three meeting which would be preceded by a private meeting between the President and Stalin.

The Davies-Hopkins missions destroyed effectively any hope that Stalin might relax his grip on Poland and Eastern Europe. To Hopkins, Stalin spoke courteously but in a way that indicated his confidence that he had won the day. He freely indulged in anti-British innuendos (the British desired a *cordon sanitaire* around Russia; they had encouraged the London Poles in their obstinacy) which brought no protests from the Americans, although they knew them to be contrary to the facts.

Stalin was amiable and discursive. He volunteered that the defeat of Germany would have been impossible without America. "In fact the United States had more reason to be a world power than any other state." [6] If so, why were the Americans so afraid that the Russians would pull a fast one on Poland? He showed his erudition on subjects not remotely touching on the conversation: he knew the Defense of the Realm Regulations which empowered the British during the war to arrest suspects and hold them without a trial. That, needless to say, led to the case of the sixteen Poles and how, regrettably, in wartime one had to abrogate democratic freedom unless a country was as fortunately situated as the United States. The Soviet Union did not mean to export her system. Communism, for instance, was not suitable to the national character and specific social conditions of Poland. In all this sensible talk, with its frankness, common sense, and handsome but not excessive flattery, it was difficult to perceive those undertones of trickery and calculation which were uppermost in Stalin's mind.

The Polish problem now loomed very small. Stalin gave precise (and, they turned out, truthful) dates for the Soviet entry into the war against Japan. He could not let the occasion pass without again sinking a harpoon into the British. He had heard rumors, he said, that the latter were secretly negotiating with the Japanese to enable them to capitulate on terms short of unconditional surrender. He himself favored unconditional surrender for Japan. But there was not that much difference

[6] Robert E. Sherwood, *Roosevelt and Hopkins* (New York, 1950), p. 900.

between a conditional and unconditional surrender: it would be possible "to accept a conditional surrender and then subsequently to impose in stages successively harsh terms . . . in other words, unconditional surrender by stages." [7] It is odd that this prudent advice should not have led Hopkins even in his weakened condition to some far-reaching reflections and conclusions. In addition to the Soviet conditions for entering the Pacific war stated at Yalta, Stalin now mentioned that he expected the U.S.S.R. to have an occupation zone in Japan.

The dictator was equally helpful and reassuring on other subjects. He minimized difficulties in the U.N., and supported Chiang Kai-shek as the only man capable of uniting China, there being no Communist leader to equal his ability and prestige. This must have been especially reassuring when relayed to Washington, since there were growing doubts on this subject.

There was considerable satisfaction and relief in Washington over this meeting. The logjam appeared to be broken, and relations with Russia restored to a friendly basis. Once again Stalin's masterful personal diplomacy concealed the fact that he yielded nothing but, on the contrary, had claimed and obtained more than ever before.

The Polish question was now resolved entirely according to Russian demands. A few outsiders were allowed to join the Provisional Government. The chief of them, Mikolajczyk, was appointed Deputy Prime Minister, a position with virtually no powers and soon with no influence. A few months before, the Russians would readily have agreed to have him as Prime Minister. It had been forgotten in Washington what Hopkins had said to Stalin: "Poland had become a symbol in the sense that it bore a direct relation to the willingness of the United States to participate in international affairs." [8] And yet there was special significance and eloquence in one small detail: when Churchill, pressed by Truman to hurry the date when the two Western Allies should repudiate the London regime and recognize the new one, proposed July 4, Truman asked for a postponement: July 4, he telegraphed, was inappropriate.

In Britain there was also some embarrassment. In 1939, Britain went to war on behalf of a semi-authoritarian Polish regime; now she was repudiating one which comprised all the major democratic parties. The rationale for the British action in 1939 was to prevent the domination

[7] *Foreign Relations of the United States, Diplomatic Papers: The Conference of Berlin (Potsdam)* (Washington, 1960), I, 44.
[8] *Ibid.,* p. 38.

of East and Central Europe by a totalitarian power and now. . . . One junior minister resigned in protest from Churchill's government.

It was with a heavy heart that the Prime Minister acquiesced in an almost complete collapse of his scheme of containing the Russians. He had wanted a Big Three meeting to show the Soviets "how much we have to offer or withhold" and that "we have several powerful bargaining counters on our side." Now those counters had vanished. In a message to the President of June 4 he spoke with alarm bordering on despair, using for the first time a now famous simile: "I view with profound misgivings the retreat of the American army to our line of occupation in the Central sector, thus bringing Soviet power into the heart of Western Europe and the descent of an iron curtain between us and everything to the eastward." [9]

Despondency was one feeling the old warrior would not indulge in for long. In the same message he indicated that he still hoped for something to be saved at and through the Big Three meeting. Whether because of a desire to capitalize on the still fluid situation or because of a premonition that with a delay he might be (as he was) replaced in the midst of the conference, Churchill was in a frantic hurry, and it was with great reluctance that he agreed to its postponement to July 15.

On the American side there was at first some reluctance and then lack of hurry in scheduling the meeting. Truman pleaded rather unconvincingly that he could not leave Washington before the end of the fiscal year. For all his self-assurance it was natural to feel some anxiety about an encounter with two renowned, already semilegendary figures. It was equally natural to try to avoid being in the middle of a raging controversy between the British and the Russians. Hence it was thought more prudent to await partial solution to some of the thorniest issues: the new Polish government to be recognized, the pullback of the American troops to be in progress. By mid-July the President would have as his new Secretary of State his *then* great friend James Byrnes, a man of greater experience than he in affairs of state. Churchill had to restrain his impatience, and his consequent bad mood undoubtedly contributed to his unfortunate tactics during the general election, a factor of some importance in the Conservatives' unexpected and crushing defeat.[10]

On the way to Potsdam, the American delegation did not stop in

[9] *Ibid.,* p. 92.
[10] With V-E Day, the coalition government was dissolved, Churchill forming a Conservative one which went down to defeat in July.

Britain, another gesture to appease the Russians. It is likely that the President's advisers also felt that in a lengthy interview with Churchill Truman might succumb to the Britisher's charm and persuasiveness, and even at this late moment fall in with some anti-Russian scheme. This was possibly on Truman's mind when one year later, against the protocol and warnings of some advisers, he accompanied the British hero, then a private person, on his trip to Westminster, Missouri.

The Potsdam meeting received the code name Terminal. With the end of war in Europe, there was really no need for strict secrecy and code names, but Churchill took a rather childish delight in such things. And indeed, the conference marked the end of that tempestuous collaboration between the virtual triumvirs. But it also marked the transition to the rather disorderly diplomacy of the "neither war nor peace" period. Considerations of domestic politics impinged increasingly on the mind of the leaders. With the major part of the war over, the President and the Prime Minister were rapidly transformed from virtual dictators of military and foreign policies into politicians whose actions were under constant scrutiny. And in a quite different way domestic considerations were becoming more important also for Stalin. No longer were the three leaders required to discuss only the broad outlines of policy and strategy, leaving details for subordinates. At Potsdam, questions of frontiers, reparations, etc., in all parts of the globe crowded the agenda. There seemed to be no occasion, no room for that dramatic showdown for which Churchill hoped, followed by a clarification of relations between the great powers.

Truman's account of the conference conveys the impression that he was rather oppressed by the number and variety of international issues with which he had only recently begun to familiarize himself. Predictably enough, he fell under Churchill's spell, and his admiration for the Prime Minister was never complicated by the rather involved complex his predecessor had had vis-à-vis the British. (Yet, as Truman reported to his aged mother in Independence, Missouri, the Englishman had one great defect: he did not care for music, at least Truman's kind of music.) The main target of his dislike was Molotov, whom he suspected of withholding information from Stalin. As this implies, the President had fallen for the common Anglo-American notion of Stalin as an essentially reasonable and genial if obstinate politician.

There was, however, a perceptible though subtle change in Stalin's tactics. He no longer pleaded his case with arguments designed to mollify the United States. This may have reflected not a lesser respect for Truman but the feeling that the game had been won. Eastern Europe was his. The dictator had every reason for satisfaction. He had promoted himself to Generalissimo of the Soviet Armed Forces, unmindful that this pompous title was associated with Chiang Kai-shek, for whom he had no high regard, not to mention its Latin connotations. Soviet military and naval personnel were decked out in handsome new uniforms with epaulettes. Even officials of the Foreign Ministry wore special uniforms. The Soviet Union was putting its diplomats in uniforms just as the British were abandoning theirs.

The Soviet sphere in East Europe and Germany was not a *fait accompli*. The American delegation arrived in Potsdam burdened with a mass of position papers, diplomatic reports, etc., bearing on Soviet exactions and moves in the countries occupied by the Red Army. A typical document contained a plaintive report from the American member of the Allied Control Commission in Bulgaria: not only was he not informed of what was being done in the name of the Commission, but he was a virtual prisoner, isolated and spied upon; anti-Communist Bulgarians were being imprisoned or worse; an attempt to get in touch with the British or Americans was considered in itself a political crime. Attempts to turn the discussion to such subjects proved futile: Stalin brusquely asserted that the Bulgarians, Rumanians, etc., now had their own democratic governments and it would be inappropriate for the conferees to interfere with the affairs of those nations. Any allusion to the role of the Russians was met by counterinquiries: What were the British doing in Greece? What were these rumors of German units in the British zone still under arms? Not only was there no opportunity for Churchill to bring up the "fundamental questions" which he had hoped so strongly to decide at the conference, it was no longer clear what those "fundamental questions" might be. By their previous compromises, concessions, and confusions of declarations of principles with political facts, the Western powers had hopelessly tangled the issues. If there was one fundamental issue, it was the obvious one that the Soviet Union was not Britain or the United States, but what could be done about that?

The issue of Germany's future could not in its nature be settled at Potsdam. The three powers had agreed that the final peace settlement be postponed: the example of hurried peacemaking at Versailles was not an encouraging one. The general principle of division into zones of occupation and of a similar scheme for Berlin had likewise been accepted before. No one at the time, including the Russians, would have believed that in the main this provisional arrangement would endure as long as it has. It was expected that a final peace treaty with Germany could be signed within four or five years.

The idea of partitioning Germany now lapsed. The Russians had never been really committed to it. If Germany was going to be occupied under a zonal arrangement, this meant effective partitioning for the time being. The British, with their faint hopes of restoring some semblance of a balance of power on the Continent, were certainly not going to press for dismemberment, though Churchill had at one time entertained the notion of a southern German state comprising Bavaria, Austria, etc., which due to its mainly Catholic population in those pre-ecumenical days would be likely to be monarchist and traditionalist. President Roosevelt had been a strong proponent of partition, but his successor had a less emotional approach to the German question. The most enthusiastic proponent (or at least exponent) of a Carthaginian peace on the American side, Secretary of the Treasury Henry Morgenthau, was no longer in the councils of the nation. Some time before, he had informed Truman that he could not keep his office unless he was included in the American delegation to Potsdam, whereupon the President, glad of the opportunity, fired him on the spot. The whole issue of economic punishment for Germany seemed now irrelevant, with misery and destruction literally surrounding the conference. Only a most prescient man could have predicted that in just ten years, *West* Germany would be among the greatest economic powers in the world.

The conference thus centered on two problems: reparations to be exacted from Germany; and how much German territory was to go to Poland in compensation for her eastern lands lost to Russia.

At Yalta the Americans had accepted as the basis for further discussion the Russian figure of $20 billion in reparations, half of it to go to the U.S.S.R. This, needless to say, enabled Stalin and Molotov to claim now that the Americans had agreed to Russia receiving $10 billion worth of reparations from the *Western* zones. The British with their memories of the folly of the reparations settlement after World War I strongly opposed any set figure. The moral right in this case was, for a change, undeniably on the Russian side: the amount of material destruction alone inflicted upon the U.S.S.R. had been incalculable. But economic common sense argued just as powerfully against the West's agreeing to reparations from its zones. The Russians had been vigorously looting their own zone. If the West was to hand over billions of dollars worth of industrial equipment from the Ruhr, etc., where were millions of German workers to find their livelihood? As it was, the mere task of providing food and fuel for the population of the Western zones, swollen by escapees from the east, verged on the impossible. The issue ranged from high drama of the Russian delegates recalling the incredible sufferings and privations of their people to the low comedy of junior members of the American delegation sent around to peek into various factories and railway yards to observe the removal of equipment and being shooed off by Russian guards.

In the end, much as it ran against the grain, the Soviets agreed that each power would exact reparations from its own zone. In addition, the Russians were to receive 25 per cent of the industrial equipment removed from the Western zones—15 per cent in exchange for raw materials and foodstuffs they would provide from their own zone, and 10 per cent without any counterdeliveries. That they agreed to such an—from their point of view—unsatisfactory solution was largely because of the intimation from the American side that without it the United States would not countenance any recognition of the Polish territorial claims.

At Teheran, it seemed ages ago, it had been Churchill who proposed to "move Poland westward." Now he fought strenuously to limit the extent of this move. Stalin was equally obdurate on the other side. In retrospect, the whole debate appears of less consequence than thought at the moment: Poland's loss was to be Communist East Germany's gain. But at the time no one forsaw how permanent the provisional arrangements would prove. Had he been retained in office, the Prime Minister assures us, he would never have agreed to the solution: the German territories claimed by Poland to be retained under Polish administration until the peace conference. But when that moment comes in our or our children's time, it is unlikely that this result will be reversed: through a strange configuration of modern politics and ideologies, the western frontiers of Poland have reverted to where they were in the thirteenth century, and Hitler's war, allegedly embarked on to secure living space for his nation, undid six centuries of expansion by the German people.

There was little disposition on the American side to follow the British and to haggle over territorial details. There was a comforting if (as things were to turn out) unrealistic thought that this was all provisional. The thing uppermost in American minds was the forthcoming final blow against Japan. For all the tremendous news flashed from New Mexico on the day the conference opened—the first explosion of an atomic bomb at Los Alamos—it was still believed imperative to secure Soviet cooperation in the struggle against Japan.

If one sees American diplomacy as being at times naïve, what is one to say of the Japanese government, which still held to the ludicrous hope that it could secure Soviet help in reaching an agreement with the United States? Its ambassador in Moscow, a gentleman with some sense of reality, kept warning Tokyo that proposals to send special envoys were tomfoolery and a dangerous waste of time. There was absolutely no reason for the Russians to favor an end of hostilities between America and Japan. Stalin on his part kept his allies loyally informed of the Japanese overtures, though one must uncharitably wonder whether he realized that the Americans, having cracked the Japanese code, were well aware of the communication.

From Potsdam, Truman and Churchill once more addressed a warning to Japan to heed the call for an unconditional surrender. They sought to have Chiang associate himself with the declaration, which he did, but not before putting on some airs.[11] Like de Gaulle, he was deeply embittered by not being admitted to the intimacy of the Big Three meetings, and having decisions concerning his country being made in his absence.

The news of the successful testing of the atom bomb was conveyed, after some hesitation, to Stalin by Truman. During a break in one of the sessions, the President simply approached Stalin to say that the United States had a weapon of unusual force. It would have dearly pleased Churchill, avidly watching the scene from some distance, if Stalin had blanched or in a broken voice asked for details. But none of that. He was pleased to hear the news and hoped the Americans would use the new weapon against Japan, said Stalin. Churchill and Truman, the wish being father to the thought, concluded that this was the first Stalin had heard about the atomic bomb. Some Soviet accounts embellish the occasion. According to Marshal Zhukov's memoirs, published in 1969, which strive to rehabilitate Stalin, the dictator reported wrathfully upon his return to Russian headquarters how gleefully

---

[11] The Generalissimo was displeased first that his advice had not been sought and then that his name on the document was to follow that of Churchill. As president of China, he ranked before the Prime Minister. The American ambassador's dispatch threw some interesting light on conditions prevailing in Chunking. He had difficulty in procuring a boat to cross the Yangtze to the Chinese leader's residence. After Chiang's concurrence in the declaration was finally obtained, there was further delay, since the telephone in the residence of the President of the Chinese Republic and the Generalissimo of its forces was not working(!).

Churchill had watched the encounter, and ordered an immediate speed-up in Soviet nuclear research. We know from more reliable sources, however, that Soviet nuclear research had begun on a modest scale in 1942 and gathered momentum after January 1945, when Soviet espionage reported that the Americans were making progress on the weapon. It is unlikely that Stalin was entirely surprised and equally unlikely that he realized fully the awesome potentialities of the bomb.

Churchill's joy at the news was great. He felt that the bomb would at least neutralize the Russians' military preponderance in Europe and might yet save the Continent from Soviet domination. This excessive joy now warped his political judgment. He claims to have perceived a new air of determination and strength in Truman's behavior at the conference. He believed that the Americans no longer wished for Soviet participation in the Pacific war. This was largely wishful thinking. There had been no abrupt turn-about in American policy. It was still thought likely that a speedy end to the war might require an invasion of Japan, and hence Soviet assistance was still needed. It will be argued below that possession of the atomic bomb had in fact a debilitating effect on American foreign policy vis-à-vis Russia. For a dictator, a special advantage in military technology is a spur to action; for a democracy, it is a convenient rationalization for inaction.

Certainly, Truman's behavior at the conference did not bear out Churchill's impression. He was neither overbearing nor unusually self-assertive. During a social hour he avowed charmingly that it was a great thing for a country boy like himself to be together with Stalin and Churchill. If the President displayed some immodesty, it was not in his capacity as war chieftain but as a philosopher of history. His study of history had convinced him that all great international conflicts had taken place over waterways—hence the need, he proclaimed, of internationalizing them and removing this source of friction. These incursions into history secretly amused some members of his delegation, but brought forth a response from Stalin. He had in mind a peculiar type of internationalization for the Dardanelles: since Turkey was too weak to protect the entrance to the Black Sea, the U.S.S.R. demanded a military and naval base there as well as unrestrained rights of passage. The war in Europe had barely concluded when a great propaganda campaign was started in Russia against Turkey for a return of the Caucasian districts which Turkey had reclaimed from Russia after World War I and for a base in the sea of Marmora. That this demand was now and for some time to come pursued strenuously is a good commentary on the assertion that the Russian diplomacy was inhibited by the knowledge of the atom bomb. Truman was embarrassed: he had in mind international control of the Rhine and the Danube. The two Western statesmen agreed to support a change in the conventions regulating the passage through the Straits, yet they could not agree with Stalin's vindictive demands on Turkey, a nonbelligerent. For the moment, this Soviet thrust toward the Mediterranean was repulsed. The Soviet Union would not get trusteeship of the former Italian colonies, neither would she get a base or territorial concessions from the Turks. But it was an omen for the future. And Truman's excursion into history served the impossible Molotov with opportunities to rail at Churchill: if international control for waterways was such an excellent thing, how about Suez? The question has not been raised, said the Prime Minister, with what feelings one can imagine. *He* was raising it, said Molotov.[12] Truman was fortunate that nobody mentioned Panama.

This was the last of the Big Three conferences. Stalin drank gaily to the next meeting in Tokyo; Truman hoped they would meet in Washington. But the Big Three meetings could not really be prolonged into peacetime. Their main usefulness lay in what the Americans traditionally abhorred—secret diplomacy—and this simply could not be accepted in the United States once the guns were silenced. Already in Potsdam, to Stalin's irritation, newspapermen were hovering nearby—a startling change from Yalta and Teheran.

Churchill, the main proponent of personal diplomacy on the highest level, was abruptly overturned while the Potsdam Conference was still going on. The Conservatives' defeat in the general elections was eloquent proof that Churchill's notions of the primacy of imperial and foreign policy were unacceptable to the majority of the British electorate. And by the same token, it shows how difficult, virtually impossible, it would have been to convince the public about the necessity of tough policies vis-à-vis the Soviet Union.

Now there was no branch of the socialist movement for which the Communists historically had more contempt than the British Labour Party. During the elections it had been believed in Labour circles that a socialist British government would find it easier to get along with socialist Russia. But Stalin's behavior soon indicated how fatuous such expectations were. Churchill's personal prestige and the influence he enjoyed in America even at this late date obscured and minimized

12 *The Conference of Berlin,* II, 365.

the otherwise obvious decline in the power of the British Empire, but the Russians no longer found it necessary to conceal their conviction that Britain had become a second-rate power.

On August 2 Truman adjourned the conference. He expressed the hope that the Big Three meeting take place in Washington. "May God grant this," said the former pupil of the Tiflis Theological Seminary, which astounded the American, as Stalin's not infrequent references to the divinity usually did. To his mother Truman expressed his real feelings: he wished he had seen the last of the Russians, yet of course there would have to be other meetings. However, God was not willing.

Within two weeks of the end of the Potsdam conference, Japan capitulated. A dazzling series of events crowded into those two weeks: Hiroshima and Nagasaki, Russia's entrance into the war, her occupation of Manchuria and North Korea, and the collapse of Japan. And the legacy of those August weeks still lies heavy upon us: it is largely because of them that American soldiers are today in Vietnam and that Communist China and the Soviet Union are hovering on the brink of war.

The events themselves were triggered by a decision which represented probably the most basic and unnecessary error of American policy during the war: the demand for Japan's unconditional surrender.

The analogous demand in relation to Germany may well have been a psychological error, but at least it could be justified on several grounds not applicable in the case of Japan. In 1943, when this demand was voiced at the Casablanca conference, Russia was still bearing the brunt of land war against Germany; without such a definite pledge it was thought (erroneously) that Russia might still seek a separate peace. In two world wars Germany had come close to a victory and to transforming Europe into an unconquerable fortress and economic base for her military power. Nothing short of a shattering defeat, it could be argued, would prevent the recurrence of the danger. Hitlerism was so deeply ingrained in German society, it was also said, that only total defeat and occupation could lead to its eradication.

But was Japan's case similar? Her dazzling successes and conquests in 1941–42 obscured the fact that simple geography rendered her incapable of conquering a major country. She could control parts of China, but complete control of that huge country and its vast population was beyond Japan's resources. Her attack in 1941 was an act of folly, but that it was undertaken at all was due to the conviction of the Japanese war party that the struggle in Europe was as good as won by Germany. In 1945, with Germany defeated and with Japan's naval power smashed, it was difficult to see how this country could in the foreseeable future become a threat to the United States.

Complete elimination of Japan as a factor in Far Eastern politics was at the time in the interests of one great power—the U.S.S.R. No one in 1945, including Stalin, could foresee how swift and all-embracing would be the victory of the Chinese Communists. But it was at least possible that the civil war would be renewed and long-lasting, and that the Soviet Union would be in an excellent position to have its help invoked by both sides. She might then, already entrenched in Manchuria under the Yalta agreements, be able to transform this area into another Mongolia—a Soviet satellite. The Soviet Far East, traditionally a vulnerable area and on a war-footing since at least 1931, would thus become an expanding frontier. Similar opportunities might arise in other border areas of China, such as Sinkiang, which Chiang had recently reclaimed from Soviet control. History was to deal with special irony with such speculations, but Russia's discomfiture has not been America's gain.

Unconditional surrender carried with it the implication that Japan's political and social order would be overthrown, especially if the emperor were held responsible for the war crimes and the imperial institution itself abolished, as some American policy-makers insisted it should be.[13] If so, the subsequent social turbulence combined with postwar economic distress might well open special opportunities to Japanese Communism, opportunities which would be enhanced if the Russians, as Stalin demanded in May from Hopkins, were allowed an occupation zone in Japan.

All those considerations indicate how important and profitable a Draconian settlement of the Japanese problem appeared from the *Soviet* point of view. In Stalin's conversations with the American officials, one can detect an undertone of amazement at the American insistence that Japan surrender unconditionally and be treated as harshly as Germany. A negotiated settlement could have secured all the reasonable American objectives in the Far East and would have avoided Soviet intervention in the final phase of the conflict.

---

[13] Minuted the then Assistant Secretary of State MacLeish to Byrnes on July 6, 1945: "What has made Japan dangerous in the past and will make her dangerous in the future . . . is in large part, the Japanese cult of emperor worship which gives the ruling groups in Japan . . . their control over the Japanese society . . . to leave that institution intact is to run the grave risk that it will be used in the future as it has been used in the past." *The Conference of Berlin*, I, 896.

But in regard to Japan, much more than Germany, American policy was prompted by vindictiveness and impatience. Japan had struck the treacherous blow at Pearl Harbor and inflicted the humiliations of the defeat in the Philippines. Hostility against the Japanese was fed by stories of atrocities they had inflicted upon American prisoners and of their fanaticism in combat. It was the combination of Hitler's imbecility in declaring war and of Roosevelt's political skill which made it possible to persuade the American people that most of the American land and air effort should be employed against the Germans rather than the treacherous Asiatics. If political faults committed in connection with the European war were primarily those of judgment, then in the case of Japan emotion crowded out political calculation. When Churchill at Potsdam hinted that the Japanese might be allowed to lay down arms in a way which would not impair their notions of honor, Truman replied heatedly that Pearl Harbor had shown that Japan had no honor. Popular outcry would have chased out of public life any politician who claimed that a reasonably strong Japan was a necessary component of balance of power in the Far East and hence in America's interest.

American vindictiveness was, to be sure, facilitated by the clumsiness of Japanese diplomacy, which continued to try to negotiate through the Russians and clung to the hope of saving Japan's pre-1931 territorial conquests (and perhaps Manchuria and Korea). Impatience in turn dictated the American strategy for a huge land invasion of the Japanese homeland, an invasion which, were it to take place, was bound to bring American casualties on a scale unprecedented in the war. From a twenty years' perspective, we may well point out the folly of even *contemplating* a land invasion. Japan had already been defeated and was pleading for peace; even if unconditional surrender was desirable, a naval blockade and conventional bombing might eventually do the job. But the word "eventually" is not easily tolerated by a democracy at war. (What will a historian some years hence say about American policies in Vietnam?)

Granted this passion, both decisions—to seek Soviet help and to employ the atom bomb—were almost inevitable. Even with both a Soviet intervention and use of the bomb, the Joint Chiefs of Staff thought, the invasion would be necessary, although they hoped the struggle would not be so protracted and American casualties so cataclysmic as without them.

Few historical arguments are more fallacious than the one advanced by "revisionist" historians concerning the use of the atom bomb. Its thesis [14] is that the first bomb was dropped not in the hope of speeding Japan's surrender, but to scare the Russians and to wrest political concessions from them. As such, it cannot withstand the test of simple logic, not to mention the facts. If the bomb was used in order to rob the Russians of some political advantages, if the Americans knew that Japan would collapse without Hiroshima, why did they still require Soviet help against Japan? Why did they not cancel the whole Yalta bargain, under which Soviet help was to be paid for by substantial Chinese concessions?

In fact this would have been a most sensible as well as fair policy: you tell your ally his help is no longer needed, he no longer has to incur casualties, expenses, etc. Hardly atomic blackmail. But as we have seen, even at Potsdam *after* the new weapon had been fully tested, it was a firm decision of the American leaders that Soviet help would still be needed, and that the price for it should be paid in full.

We shall revert to the revisionist argument, since it has become an important part of the argument concerning the Cold War. As a matter of fact, what *is* astounding is that *no* attempt was made by the United States to exploit politically the monopoly of this weapon of unique destructiveness when it came to the peace settlement in Europe or Asia. *Even Soviet sources,* while freely accusing the United States of practicing atomic diplomacy during the Cold War, and assailing the atomic bombing of Hiroshima and Nagasaki as both unnecessary and barbarous, do not accuse the United States of threatening the Soviet Union in 1945. Indeed, the Russians would be hard put to specify what more the U.S.S.R. would have gotten had the United States *not* had the bomb.

The prospect of Soviet aid in the Pacific was resented by some American military and naval figures, but out of professional pride rather than for political reasons and apprehensions. This had been America's war, and it should have been up to the Americans to deliver the final blow rather than to share the glory with others. Yet it was not *Russian* help which was resisted most strenuously. The initial plans to have the British fleet and the Royal Air Force operate against Japan, and to have an imperial contingent participate in the actual invasion, were strongly opposed by General MacArthur and Admiral Nimitz. It took a determined stance by Churchill and orders by

[14] Most succinctly stated in Gar Alperovitz, *Atomic Diplomacy, Hiroshima and Potsdam* (New York, 1965).

Roosevelt and Truman to make the recalcitrant commanders acquiesce in this unwelcome prospect of British assistance and presumably lower American casualties. MacArthur credited the British with designs on the Netherlands East Indies. Among American diplomats in China there was deep suspicion that the perfidious English desired perpetuation of China's disunity while having Chiang "as a quasi puppet in the area; between the Yangtze Valley and the Indo-China border." [15] It throws a strange light on the mentality of the American leaders and officials that Great Britain was credited with the desire and *ability* for such vast imperial expansion. A strange masochistic streak in the American political mind has often subjected countries closest to the United States in political tradition and interest to the most suspicious scrutiny by public opinion and the most vigorous pressure by American officials to be more virtuous in their foreign policies. Thus, at the end of the Pacific war, American officials—including people with as little sympathy for the traditional Left, not to mention Communism, as General MacArthur—viewed with chagrin the prospect of the Dutch and the French returning to the colonial possessions the Japanese had wrested from them, while the British were repeatedly urged to demonstrate their democratic virtue and to foresake their imperialist ways by granting independence to India, by returning Hongkong to China, etc. "I had always been opposed to colonialism. . . . Colonialism in any form is hateful to Americans," wrote Truman. [16]

Yet while other Western nations were supposed to emulate and even surpass American anticolonialism, no such selfless position was expected of *nondemocratic* allies of the United States, in this case the Soviet Union. Roosevelt had pressed the British to return Hongkong, which had been theirs for a century, to China. [17] On the other hand the Americans agreed without too much ado that the base of Port Arthur and a neighboring area which had not been Russian for decades should go to the Russians, who, also at the expense of the Chinese, were to obtain the huge industrial complex of the Manchurian railway, which they had sold in 1935.

We must digress. The case of Hongkong epitomizes the ironies of international politics of our century. On Japan's collapse, Chiang Kai-shek wanted the Japanese garrison there to surrender to him, and he

---

[15] *Foreign Relations of the United States, Diplomatic Papers 1944: China* (Washington, 1967), VI, 697.
[16] *Memoirs* (New York, 1955), I, 275.
[17] At one time, according to Lord Halifax, he threatened to take this up with the King if Churchill persisted in being stubborn.

evidently planned, though he had plenty of other worries, to reclaim the port for China. But despite American backing and the fact that the Labour rather than Conservative party was in power, the residue of imperial pride was strong enough for the British to demand and obtain the return of Hongkong. That they should have done so turned out to be a piece of good luck—for the Chinese Communists. The British Crown Colony became their main avenue of commercial and financial intercourse with the West, the main source likewise of their dollar and other hard-currency earnings, hence not an inconsiderable factor in the industrial and technological progress of Communist China. All this would have been impossible had Hongkong been returned to China in 1945. As the years passed the British government felt it could not provoke the Chinese Communists by *returning* to them this part of their ancient patrimony, this relic of the day when the West lorded over China. And so today Hongkong remains the only British colonial possession of any importance. Mauritius and Swaziland have been granted independence, but this thriving and populous bit of China must remain under British sovereignty as long as it is in the interests of Mao. What would Churchill and Roosevelt make of this?

The Japanese capitulation on August 14 was expedited by the Americans bowing to common sense and allowing the Japanese to retain their Emperor. The Russians had entered the war on the date they had specified, and Soviet historians have a legitimate grievance against those who insinuate that the Soviet Union hurried into the war because of the news of Hiroshima. The announcement of the Japanese capitulation on August 14 did not lead the Soviets to stop their offensive. To be sure, some local Japanese units were still fighting, but the situation was bound to be clarified within a few days, and by curtailing their action the Soviets would have spared many Russian as well as Japanese lives. But Stalin was in a hurry, eager to cash in the gains promised under Yalta and confirmed on the very day of the Japanese capitulation by the Soviet-Chinese treaty.

The dramatic climax of the war threw Stalin into one of his atypical public displays of anxiety complicated by cupidity. Both motifs were present in the message Stalin addressed to Truman on August 16. MacArthur's order of the preceding day specified that Japanese units in Manchuria, Sakhalin, and North Korea surrender to the Soviet command. Now, Stalin reminded Truman, according to Yalta the Kuril Islands were to go to the U.S.S.R., and consequently the Japanese there should also surrender to the Russians rather than the Americans. But then the dictator tried to slip in something which had *not* been provided for: half of the northernmost Japanese island of Hokkaido should also be occupied by the Soviet Union; this, pleaded Stalin, was very important for Russian public opinion, which remembered bitterly how between 1919 and 1921 the Japanese had occupied the Soviet Far East—an argument in direct contradiction to his statement at Yalta that the Russians had no grievances against the Japanese and hence had to be rewarded for going to war.

Truman agreed to the Kurils, though he indicated that the Americans would like to have an air base there. As to a Soviet occupation zone in Japan proper, he did not meet Stalin's "modest wish." Soviet troops were welcome to participate in the occupation of Japan, but only under the over-all command of General MacArthur.

The vision of Soviet soldiers being commanded by an American general made Stalin hastily drop any plans for Soviet participation in the occupation. His rejoinder was plaintive rather than indignant: "I and my colleagues did not expect such an answer from you." [18] When it came to an American base in the Kurils, his plaintiveness was mixed with suspicion. Why do the Americans need it? Only *defeated* states grant bases on their territory to a foreign power. (The U.S.S.R. was currently demanding such bases from Turkey.) He was careful, however, not to imply a categorical refusal.

Surely, had there been the slightest inclination on the American side to practice nuclear diplomacy this was an excellent occasion. Stalin could have been told that the Americans get the base or the Soviets do not get the Kurils. Instead, Truman's rejoinder contained a reassuring explanation that the Americans just wanted landing rights; the Kuril Islands were after all not yet Soviet territory. Stalin, in turn, was all sweetness and light: of course the Soviets would be glad to grant landing rights, but could not the Americans grant reciprocal rights to the Soviets in the Aleutians? Soviet commercial aviation was very eager to establish a speedy route to Seattle. This sudden Soviet interest in the American Northwest was rather inexplicable; no Soviet commercial plane is known to have landed in Seattle before or since. But Stalin, as always, was eager to cover up traces of weakness or fear, to remove any suggestion that Russia could be pressured into granting something for nothing.

For its brief intervention in the Japanese war the Soviet Union was paid in full. Port Arthur and a neighboring area large enough to contain

[18] *Correspondence*, II, 265.

a whole army went to the Soviet Union. The Manchurian Railroad, a complex comprising mines and factories as well as rail lines, came under predominant Soviet control. Special rights were allotted the U.S.S.R. in Dairen. From Japan the Russians reclaimed southern Sakhalin and the Kurils and occupied Korea north of the 38th parallel. The Western powers had previously renounced their extraterritorial rights in China. Now the Russians in effect reclaimed them.

In their vindictiveness against Japan, the Americans appeared to have forgotten why they had found themselves in a war with Japan in the first place: to preserve the Open Door policy in China and to prevent domination of that country by a foreign power. Now this door was effectively shut, certainly in the most industrialized part of China, i.e., Manchuria. In 1945 it could not be foreseen—let us repeat, not even by the Russians—that all of China would go to the Communists in four years. But what was foreseeable was a long Soviet economic and probably political domination of Manchuria. Soviet hopes probably went further: a satellite Communist state in Manchuria and in part of northeast China.

The Americans obtained their most immediate objective: complete control of Japan. None of the interallied control or advisory commissions set up after the armistice were allowed, despite feeble protests by the Russians, to interfere with General MacArthur's powers. Japan seemingly reverted between 1945 and 1951 to the form of government she had had before 1868: there was a rubber-stamp emperor and the Shogun, who happened to be an American general who exercised real powers. But ironically enough the Russians were partial beneficiaries of the American general's imperiousness: Japan was thoroughly demilitarized both in fact and spirit. The people's dynamism and skills were turned entirely to peaceful economic pursuits (about which the Americans and, especially, British industrial interests were not exactly overjoyed a decade or two later). In a few years American officials were to ponder ruefully whether they had not done too good a job! Communist activities in Japan were curbed but certainly not to the extent that anti-Communist parties were suppressed in East European countries controlled by the Soviet Union.

The peace settlement in the Far East, where the United States had a traditional and intense interest, unlike its sporadic and recent entanglements in European affairs, thus served the real interests of the United States even worse than the one in Europe.

The central event of the Far East drama was, of course, the later collapse of Nationalist China, the consequences of which may well be ranged, along with those of the Russian Revolution of 1917, among the most momentous political developments of the twentieth century. Here we shall look at events in China in the setting of 1945.

Not long before his death in August, 1945, Harry Hopkins, then out of office, put on paper his ideas about the future of U.S. relations with other great powers. Collaboration with Britain would be very important. America's debt to that country was great: "The British have saved our skins twice, once in 1914 and again in 1940 [but] the American people simply do not like British colonial policy." As to the Russians, Americans had serious ideological and political differences with them: "The American people want not only freedom for themselves but they want freedom for other people as well." But on balance the Russians "trust the United States more than they trust any other power in the world . . . are determined to take their place in world affairs in an international organization, and above all want to maintain friendly relations with us." But, concluded Hopkins, it was China with whom the United States would probably have the closest ties: "If I were to indicate a country in which the United States for the next hundred years had the greatest interest from political and economic points of view, I would name the Republic of China. . . . China will become one of the greatest land powers on earth. . . . We hope that there will arise out of the welter of war a unified China." [19]

Hopkins was not an ideologue, nor at the time he sorted those notes, capable ever again of seeking political office or influence. Hence his testimony is valuable not only as that of a man who was close to the center of power during the war, but as a fairly representative specimen of American thinking on international affairs. As such it is striking in its confusion between peoples and governments, in its inability to see that in the foreseeable future it was not with "the Russians" that the United States was going to deal but with Stalin and the Communist hierarchy, that it was not the traditional virtues of the Chinese people which were of immediate importance but the ability and efficiency of Chiang Kai-shek and the Kuomintang government. The most fundamental illusion was the notion that the country which had been in a practically uninterrupted state of chaos and civil war and partial foreign occupation for more than a century could speedily achieve unity, and that not through military conquest or one party rule but through elections, party coalitions, and other democratic means.

[19] Sherwood, *op. cit.*, pp. 924–25.

But the most interesting aspect of Hopkins' meditations was their expression of a perennial American penchant for assessing a given country's capacity and desirability as an American ally according to its alleged democratic virtue: China was bound to be of greatest importance not only because she was the world's largest nation, but because she was not tainted by imperialism or communism. This last argument, plus a traditional protective feeling toward China, colored much of official American thinking during the war. A country which had never known parliamentary institutions and representative government, even in the limited sense in which Japan had possessed them for over half a century, was assumed to be capable of instant democracy once the war was over. Along with democracy, China would advance toward the status of a great power, the emblems of this expectation being China's permanent membership on the Security Council of the U.N., which Roosevelt had fought for and won over Churchill's and Stalin's skepticism.

As a result of those assumptions, American policy during the war had to deal with two Chinas: one was the China of their hopes—nominal member of the Big Four, "policeman" of Asia, embattled democracy—the other was the real China of increasing governmental corruption and economic chaos, unable, even with American equipment and advisers, to produce a sizable modern army. The crushing burden of expectations put upon the Generalissimo's government and the Kuomintang was in itself, it is fair to say, a cause of the decline of the real China, i.e., the growing incompetence and final paralysis of the Kuomintang government. American officials in China, whether amateur diplomats such as General Hurley or "old China hands" on the staff of the embassy in Chungking, were appalled at the extent of corruption and at Chiang's all too obvious reluctance to expend his best troops against the Japanese, since with the expansion of the war he held, entirely logically from his point of view, that the Japanese would eventually be beaten anyway and he should preserve his best troops in case of a conflict with the Communists.

Some American observers extolled the Chinese Communists, in contrast to Chiang, for their willingness to fight the Japanese, their efficiency in making the best of the very limited resources of their areas, and the refreshingly Spartan ways of their leaders. It was sometimes argued that the United States should establish closer relations and provide help to the Communist-held areas, partly because of the Communists' superior democratic virtue, partly as the means of pressuring Chiang to mend his ways. A typical diplomatic dispatch from China to Washington in 1944 urged that the United States "show a sympathetic interest in the Communists and liberal groups in China . . . limit American aid to China to direct prosecution of the war against Japan . . . use our tremendous and as yet unexploited influence with the Kuomintang to promote internal Chinese unity." [20] More outspoken American officers at the embassy wrote already then about the "fascist" character of Chiang's government and the hopelessness of any regeneration of China under his leadership.

The effect of such public and private criticism is poignantly hinted at by a dispatch in March, 1944, from the American ambassador, Gauss, to the Secretary of State: "Adverse criticism of China . . . has perhaps caused resentment among Kuomintang reactionaries; but many Chinese Government leaders and all Chinese liberals are believed to be sensible of the justification of that criticism . . . viewing such criticism as a means of prodding the Kuomintang into action. . . . General Chiang is believed to be increasingly conscious and resentful of and bewildered by the continued American published criticism of China and is quoted as having asked recently 'What is there about China that the Americans do not like?' " [21] The question "What is it that the Americans really want?" would be asked repeatedly by many of America's allies and protégés in Asia. It was the manner rather than the substance of American criticism and interference which was making Chiang lose face, encouraging intrigues in his entourage, and in general weakening his regime without making it any more democratic.

In retrospect it is clear that American favor as well as criticism contributed to his downfall. The image of Chiang as a Chinese George Washington, publicly maintained even in the face of the countercurrent of criticisms, weakened the Generalissimo's sense of political reality. He now contemplated territorial expansion—Hongkong, perhaps French Indochina—at the same time that the ground was slipping from under his feet. For all of the carping, it appeared inconceivable to him (as it did to the Russians) that the Americans would resign themselves to China's becoming Communist. His previous successes were due to assiduity and skill in making arrangements with various provincial warlords and in respecting regional autonomy and susceptibilities, but he began to be impatient of such caution and subtlety: he had behind him the world's greatest power, which would not allow him to be defeated. Under American tutelage Chiang thus lost his skills

20 *Diplomatic Papers: China*, VI, 781.
21 *Ibid.*, p. 386.

as a warlord without acquiring those of a democratic politician.

None of the above was foreordained, however, nor foreseeable in 1945.[22] The Soviet government and the Republic of China signed on August 14, 1945, the Treaty of Alliance and Friendship, confirming in the main the relevant provisions of Yalta. Though some of them were painful to Chinese national pride, it did not require any undue pressure by Washington to make Chiang agree.[23] What made the treaty most worthwhile and probably would have inclined Chiang to agree to its provisions even without the previous American commitment was the Soviet pledge not to deal with or help any Chinese faction except that of his government. The Russians also promised to withdraw from Manchuria after completing military operations against the Japanese.

Chiang's own instincts and previous experiences with the Russians could not inspire him with excessive faith in their paper guarantees and promises. Yet politically and psychologically it was not an inconsiderable asset to have such a public repudiation of the Chinese Communists and promise of noninterference in Chinese internal affairs. On the Soviet side the treaty testified to the belief in Moscow that Chiang and his regime would remain the decisive factor in Chinese politics for a long time to come.

As to the Chinese Communists, they could not have been entirely absent from the Russians' calculations. They certainly did not discourage the then widely held opinion in the West, and by no means only in left-wing circles, that they were a home-grown radical movement rather than "real" Communists. Stalin and Molotov also applauded American efforts to bring about a reconciliation between Chiang and the Communists, which would culminate in a coalition government and thus prevent a civil war which otherwise was bound to erupt once Japan was defeated.

In fact, the Soviets were most generous in delegating to the Americans the leadership in solving China's political, economic, and military problems and in reassuring them about Chiang. It was a clever—though, one might think, rather transparent—maneuver: to bring about an enduring reconciliation between the Nationalists and the Communists was about

[22] Much of the American attitude on international affairs is tinged with fatalism, and the treatment of China is a good example. Many books on the tragedy of the Kuomintang see its downfall predetermined at an early date and usually in terms of a single factor, this being, according to the author's interest and orientation, corruption, inflation, the "Communists in the State Department," etc.

[23] Characteristically, the vainglorious Generalissimo raised the strongest objections to the provision which merely recognized a *fait accompli* of long standing, i.e., independence from China for Outer Mongolia, ever since the mid-1920s a satellite of the U.S.S.R.

as hopeless a task as one could imagine prior to the effort at mediation between the Arabs and Israel. In washing his hands of the Chinese Communists, Stalin was spared what would have been a natural American demand that he use his influence with them while the Americans "worked on" Chiang. But this maneuver reflected also the awareness that the Americans were very sensitive about the Far East, that they considered it their sphere of interest (much as it would horrify them to call it so). Hence Russia had to be very cautious, and its expectations as well as those of the Chinese Communists could not be excessive. *In private* the Chinese Communists were undoubtedly being urged to be circumspect and modest.

That the latter contained both their ambitions and what must have been rising bitterness against their Soviet mentors must be taken as a sign of docility. But this was not surprising: no other Communist party, with the exception perhaps of the German one in the 1930s, was so brutally used by the Soviets for their own purposes without the slightest *public* protest on their part. To minimize the chance of Japan's moving against the Soviet Far East they fought the Japanese in the early 1930s. Then, in 1937, they entered into an agreement with Chiang, which while it was possibly in their interest, corresponded to the official Comintern policy of the Popular Front. No protests came when Russia concluded a nonaggression treaty with Japan in 1941, nor when, with Japan vanquished, the Soviet Union once more ostensibly turned its back by concluding the treaty with Chiang.

The Soviet Union, to be sure, was soon to put its own interpretation on the treaty: the Chinese Communists would receive the Japanese stores of arms the U.S.S.R. captured in Manchuria, and their initial successes there were undoubtedly facilitated by Soviet help. But in mid-1945 this could not yet be foreseen: the Russians were fashioning their Chinese policy according to their own interest and according to their views on what the American response would be to various options. They might leave the Communists to fight a protracted civil war on their own; they might help them carve out a state in northeast China, which for obvious reasons would have to be their satellite; or—and this could not be entirely inconceivable—were Chiang ready to get rid of the Americans with their constant sermons about democracy and reform, were he ready to pay an additional price in Manchuria and perhaps Sinkiang, they might decide to help him.

Mao tried to cheer up his comrades. In a speech in Yenan on August 13, 1945, he said, "Relying on the forces we ourselves organize we can defeat all Chinese and foreign reactionaries." [24] American policy-makers lacked foresight and endurance to achieve their goals, he went on, as if to answer objections to what seemed like empty boasting. "U.S. imperialism while outwardly strong is inwardly weak." This was something the Russians were not yet sure of. But the best prophecy of all was, surprisingly enough, uttered by Chiang, even though at the time he thought it was a joke. In 1944, when he entertained Vice President Wallace, he had been subjected to yet another lecture on the need for reforms; the Generalissimo, to relieve the tension, "laughingly remarked that the Chinese Communists were more communistic than the Russians are." [25]

World War II ended officially with the signing of Japan's surrender on September 2, 1945. The date also marks the end of the period when American power could have, if intelligently used, dictated a viable international order for generations to come. But the United States' ability to influence world events was suddenly and drastically reduced by the passage from war to peace. This diminution was not caused simply or mainly by the rapid demobilization and an almost equally rapid retooling of the war economy to peaceful pursuits, or by the waning of the atomic monopoly. Rather, it was due to a drastic shift in the psychology of the American people. They did not turn back to isolationism as they had done after World War I. But with the end of the war, it was naturally though erroneously assumed that peace and the restoration of international stability would not require sacrifices even remotely approximating those of the wartime. It took two years before the idea of large-scale economic aid to Europe in peacetime could be accepted by the public, five years before a deeply divided country could acquiesce in American commitment in Korea. Any such commitments were inconceivable on September 3, 1945, and history was to move very fast.

The end of the war also meant that the President of the United States could no longer conduct secret diplomacy or commit his country to strategies which might result in huge American casualties. Before the fall of Japan, Truman had approved plans for an invasion of that country by vast American armies. It is unlikely that in 1946 he could have gotten away with ordering even one American division to take an active part in the struggle for China had the destiny of the whole country depended upon it. And yet basically the United States had found itself

[24] Quoted in Tang Tsou, *America's Failure in China* (Chicago, 1963), p. 304.
[25] *United States Relations with China* (referred to hereafter as *China Paper*) (Washington, 1949), p. 553.

at war with Japan because of its determination that China should not pass into unfriendly hands.

Any critique of American diplomacy and assessment of responsibility for the Cold War ought, then, to distinguish between the periods before and after 1945. Much could have been achieved by intelligent diplomacy after 1945, but the period of 1944-45 was one of considerably greater opportunities, the period of virtual American omnipotence. Had the United States been ruled by a dictator or an oligarchy, or had the American people been permeated by a spirit of aggressive nationalism, there was little that it could not have accomplished without war and merely through diplomatic and economic pressure. But one cannot regret that the American people were not possessed by the passion to rule the world, for certainly such a passion *is* incompatible with democratic institutions and with that pleasant life which the American people have enjoyed, or at least believed they did until quite recently.

When it comes to political disasters Americans are strangely unwilling to accept an error of judgment as an explanation. They tend to seek the answer in moral guilt. Policy mistakes are assumed to have their source in sin (a striking parallel to Stalin's Russia, where an official was seldom discharged for incompetence, administrative or political failure being attributed to treason, Trotskyism, etc.). When it soon became obvious that the peace settlement was both imperfect and precarious, the public inquest addressed itself to the question: Who is guilty? It was easy to answer by attributing moral depravity and evil designs to the rulers of the Soviet Union. Few have the patience to probe for more subtle historical explanations, and fewer still to follow such reasoning. Then the inquiry shifted inevitably to the American scene and asked: Who betrayed? The American people were unwilling to recognize themselves as having been naïve and historically unsophisticated, but they were ready to accept that they had been intentionally deceived. Their officials, especially those entrusted with foreign affairs, were accused, in turn, not so much of being misinformed or unsubtle, as, in some crucial cases, being guilty of virtual treason. The United States, then, with its idealism in world affairs, was confronted with the bad will of its partners, primarily the Soviet Union, its policies constantly frustrated or betrayed not through the incompetence or unrealism of their executors but because of their Communist leanings or ties.

A reaction to these simplistic views of the late 1940s and '50s made its debut when the American people tired in turn of these undifferentiated anti-Communist policies and were frustrated in their exertions and sacrifices on behalf of what had long been known as the free world. But what the "revisionists" revise is not so much the plot as the cast of characters. The villain is no longer the Soviet Union or "godless Communism," but American capitalism, or that equally murky entity, the American Establishment and especially that branch referred to (the term having been spawned in a fateful moment by General Eisenhower's speech writer) as the "military-industrial complex." And as a large part of the American public had confessed to having sinned by accepting the notion of a peaceful and progressive Russia, so now the society was accused of having indulged in unpardonable "arrogance of power." Historical revisionism is thus one expression of that intellectual masochism which has colored the discussion of so many problems in American society. With this broader phenomenon we shall have to deal later. Here we must address ourselves to the immediate problem: Do the views propounded by so-called revisionist historians illuminate or obscure American policy in the period under discussion?

Some of their arguments, as we have seen in the case of the alleged practice of atomic diplomacy, fall of their own weight. But there is an extension of the atomic-diplomacy argument which is sometimes used: that the mere fact of the United States' monopoly of the weapon, even if Russia was not explicitly threatened, was bound to have upsetting effects on the U.S.S.R. and to make Stalin more insistent about Russia's security—hence about having his way in Eastern Europe, etc.; that the best way of disarming Russia's suspicions, of moderating her rule in East Europe, and of securing her collaboration within the U.N. would have been a generous American offer to share atomic technology. This view is, in fact, close to the one expounded after the war by Henry Wallace. What is more surprising, something similar was urged by Henry Stimson, then U.S. Secretary of War, shortly before he left office in 1945. In his memorandums to Truman, the aged American statesman had never been clear as to what exactly he proposed should be done concerning the U.S.S.R. and the bomb—at one time suggesting that the secrets of the bomb could not be shared until Stalin put in effect the 1936 constitution and granted democracy to the Russian people, at another time thinking of offering to trade the weapon for introduction of democratic freedoms in Russia. Finally, in a memorandum dated September 11, 1945, Stimson seemed to lean (his language is not very clear) to an outright sharing of atomic technology with Russia. The letter is full of qualifications and hypothetical cases, but in a key sentence Stimson says: "The chief lesson I have learned in a long life is that the only way you make a man trustworthy is to trust him, and the surest way to make him untrustworthy is to distrust him and show your distrust." [26] It is a heartening sentiment, especially coming from a hardheaded man of affairs, a lifelong Republican, and a lawyer. Stimson can be pardoned for not being familiar with Stalin's biography. But he ought to have remembered the consequences of Neville Chamberlain's applying the principle he recommends in dealing with Hitler.

The letter is valuable testimony to the embarrassment widely felt in some American circles about possession of the atom bomb, the feeling that somehow it was not fair for the U.S. to enjoy a monopoly of this weapon. Stimson deplored that the bomb was viewed by some "as a substantial offset to the growth of Russian influence on the continent"— that growth in influence presumably being, in contrast to the American bomb, natural and justifiable. Furthermore, we know that his views on some form of collaboration with the Russians in the nuclear field were shared by a number of high American officials. Hardly atomic diplomacy.

But the main fallacy of Stimson in 1945 and the revisionists today is to believe, as Stimson wrote, that satisfactory relations with Russia were "not merely connected with but virtually dominated by the problem of the atomic bomb." Absolutely nothing suggests that Soviet policies in 1945 were dominated by the fear of or were a reaction to America's possession of the atom bomb. Stalin's policies toward the United States were dominated by two feelings: one of great respect for the United States' vast economic and hence military potential, quite apart from the bomb; and the other of scant respect for the American capacity to translate this potential into political gains. There was thus no immediate fear, but only vague apprehension that sometime in the future America's resources *might* be mobilized and employed against the U.S.S.R. But to begin to remove these apprehensions, Russia would have had to become as strong economically as the United States.

Another tack the revisionist critique takes is to attribute the postwar tension to the generally reactionary character of American liberation policies: favoring, in various countries in Europe or Asia, status-quo parties and politicians, sometimes those tinged with a reputation for collaboration with the Germans or Japanese. It is undeniable that most American policy-makers looked with disfavor upon, say, the French Communist Party, or the Communist-led guerrillas in the Philippines; it would have been sheer imbecility to do otherwise. But apart from the ludicrous nature of the argument that it is somehow noble to support those movements which are declared enemies of your institutions and interests and the scarcely less ludicrous one that in doing so you turn them into your friends, there is not an iota of evidence that lack of solicitude for such movements had anything to do with the worsening of U.S.–U.S.S.R. relations. Nor, in the many discordant strains of American policy, is there evidence to support the notion of a consistent attitude reflecting interests of ruling economic circles, much less of a *plot* to destroy the U.S.S.R. One revisionist historian, however, has gone so far as to argue that the minimum U.S. objectives were, if you please, "to deny Russia the influence she had won in Europe . . . *to compel* Russia to relinquish her position in Eastern Europe." And the maximum objectives? The United States looked "to the break-up of Soviet power itself and beyond that to the collapse of the Russian Revolution." [27] We are in the realm of sheer fantasy.

While the revisionist critics must sooner or later in their argument ascribe to American policy a purposiveness and clan orientation which it simply did not have, then the opposite school of analysts of the Cold War—shall we call them the orthodox?—has its own weaknesses. Its main point, that American policies toward Russia were wrong because they were based on unrealistic assumptions about the Soviet system, is well taken. But the orthodox historians are hard pressed to describe policies which could have worked. Winston Churchill, the founder and certainly the patron saint of the school, believed, as we know, that if American and British armies had held their lines instead of retreating to their zones in Germany in the spring of 1945, this could have led to the Russians' living up to their pledges on Poland, Rumania, etc. But, as we also observed, the proponents of such a thesis that "tougher" policies could have worked fail to take into consideration the mood of the American people at the time, and the predictable disillusion with and then opposition to such policies.

Are we then left with the fatalistic conclusion that things could not have been much different? Such a verdict would be unwarranted. Within the limits circumscribed by the character of both societies, there was still a great deal that skillful, well-informed, and alert diplomacy could have accomplished. Successful diplomacy is very often not the matter of dramatically drawing the line over an issue or a territory, or of conjuring up magic solutions, but of endurance and patient attention to detail. Stalin and Molotov were extremely clever at bargaining and deception,

[27] David Horowitz, *The Free World Colossus* (London, 1965), p. 278.

but they were not superhuman. They seldom mounted a diplomatic offensive without ascertaining that it had a good chance of succeeding and directing it against a vulnerable spot. On Poland, a key problem in interallied diplomacy in 1944–45, the Western leaders and often their diplomatic advisers were abysmally ignorant, while Stalin was excellently informed. At each phase of the unfolding drama, the Westerners were confronted with their previous concessions and asked, in effect, "Is it worth threatening Allied unity by refusing to give us a little bit more?" Nor were they sensitive enough to perceive the near panic which seized Stalin whenever he thought that they were doing things *he* might have done were he in Churchill's or Roosevelt's shoes. They were hypnotized by the notion of allegedly limitless Soviet manpower at a time when the Soviet Union (as we now know, and as common sense should have informed us in 1945) had fewer men under arms than the United States. In the summer of 1944 the Secretary of State received an official analysis of the U.S. general staff to the effect that Russia's military power after the war would be dominant in Eastern Europe, the Middle East (rather surprisingly), and northeast Asia. The survey concluded that the United States and the Soviet Union would be the only two superpowers and that "the relative strength and geographic positions of these two powers preclude the military defeat of one of these powers by the other even if that power were allied with the British Empire." [28] Military men had to think in such terms and rightly refused to contemplate the possibility of Americans marching through the Russian plains or Soviet armies deployed in California. But statesmen should have realized that Russia would undergo a period of great economic weakness and vulnerability.

In their bafflement, some American officials did think of economics, but as yet without that perspicacity which in 1947 was to lead to the Marshall Plan. Would the prospect of American help to persuade the Soviets to soften their demands, could a large American loan be used as a lever to assure Russia's collaboration and good behavior? The full story of tentative offers of and tentative approaches for large-scale American credits for Russia's postwar reconstruction does not belong here. But one aspect of the story has to be discussed, for it throws light on the almost insoluble dilemma of American-Soviet relations at that point.

Ambassador Harriman reported in 1945 with some indignation that Molotov proposed a huge American loan (the figure mentioned was $6 billion for thirty years at 2.25 per cent) in terms suggesting that

---

[28] Maurice Matloff, *Strategic Planning for Coalition Warfare 1943–1944* (Washington, 1959), p. 524.

Russia would be doing a great favor to the United States. There was great fear of a postwar depression in the United States, said the Soviet foreign minister (quite correctly), and the depression might be avoided or alleviated if the U.S.S.R. condescended to take American goods for credit. Molotov was guided in this strange approach not by insolence but rather by a pathetic desire to conceal how desperate was Russia's need.

The dilemma which the Soviets faced went much deeper than the problem of economic aid, and of not revealing Russia's weaknesses. The main question was the political one: Can the Soviet system afford a degree of dependence on the United States, freer intercourse with the West, real collaboration in world affairs? This question is still being asked in the Kremlin today. In wartime the Americans were indispensable allies; in peacetime close contacts with them might prove demoralizing. Stalin must have studied Chiang's experiences with them from a professional—i.e., fellow autocrat's—point of view. And in China the Americans were ceaselessly interfering, criticizing, demanding constant proofs of democratization. To a dictator of even less suspicious turn of mind than Stalin, it would have appeared that a close relationship with the United States, even a hint of dependence, would endanger the regimented and monolithic society that he believed Russia had to be after the war.

We have not mentioned one obstacle to a collaboration of the two countries which to many would appear as the basic one: the fact that the U.S.S.R. had a socialist and America a capitalist system. Without discounting the ideological element, this was in the period under discussion the least important of all bars to a U.S.–Soviet understanding. One may go even further and venture an opinion that in some ways the Russians would have found themselves more at ease with a truly capitalistic, oligarchic America such as they were soon again to portray in their propaganda: it would have been more likely to agree to spheres of influence, and its leaders would not indulge in sermonizing.[29]

Solzhenitsyn in his *First Circle* has Stalin say that Hitler was the only man he trusted. The great writer undoubtedly exaggerates, but there was an undercurrent of exasperation in Stalin's usually patient and crafty handling of the Americans. Later on Mao was to express this almost

---

[29] "I will not hide behind Soviet public opinion," said Stalin in an undiplomatic moment to Harry Hopkins, when the latter for the nth time repeated the objection that American public opinion would not accept something. And Vyshinsky at Yalta erupted that the American people should obey their rulers.

esthetic and snobbish repugnance for American diplomacy when he described the American imperialists as "newly arrived upstarts and neurotics" [30] incapable of the sophistication of the British or even of minor imperialist powers. One cannot escape the sense that the primary defect of American diplomacy was its failure to make itself respected.

The Americans thus could not change Russian policies through friendship, fear, or skillful and realistic diplomacy. The Russians, on the other hand, who despite their relatively weak position gained through clever diplomacy on most disputed issues, could not alter the central fact in the world of 1945—the enormous power of the United States—or banish the possibility that in future this power might be turned against them.

The gradual estrangement of the United States and Russia did not yet mean open hostility: it was not until 1947 that the Soviets became convinced through a most amazing misunderstanding that the United States had an elaborate plan to undermine the Soviet empire. But what had remained a bond of union even during the last strained year of the Grand Alliance was soon dissipated. Soviet "pig-headedness," as Truman put it, became accepted by the Americans as a fact of life, as well as their inability to do much about it. There was haggling—about when troops of a given power would be withdrawn from this or that country, when America would recognize this or that satellite government—but there was no longer any thoroughgoing attempt, such as still might have been undertaken had Roosevelt been alive, to win the Russians over or to make them comply with their obligations. His successor had no ambitions to change history through personal diplomacy, and was rather glad to stay away from the Russians. Churchill would have undoubtedly urged a continuation of the Big Three encounters or some dramatic improvisation to assert the drift of world affairs. But the Labour Government was busy dismantling the Empire and establishing the welfare state. There was no reason for Stalin to seek the old quarrelsome cordiality of the Big Three meetings. There *should* have been a Big Four meeting after the sudden collapse of Japan,[31] but evidently nobody thought of it or remembered how at Potsdam Stalin proposed it should take place in Tokyo. (Thus passed the opportunity to have a record of conversations between Stalin, MacArthur, and Chiang!)

How ironic the effect of American sins of omission and commission

---

[30] *Selected Works of Mao Tse-tung* (in English) (Peking, 1961), IV, 442.
[31] In his order on the Day of Victory, September 2, Stalin hailed the armed forces of the Soviet Union, U.S., *China,* and Britain as having procured the victory.

looks after twenty-five years! A Soviet official might well conclude that his country would be in a better position had the Americans blocked some of its designs in those distant days. The greatest triumph of Communism since 1917—the victory of the Chinese Communists—is today Russia's greatest problem, as Chiang's China would hardly be. Even the Soviet domination of East European states must now appear of dubious and ephemeral value. After their merciless exploitation and brutal subjugation under Stalin, these states have become the source of constant headaches. Had the Russians been more tolerant in 1945, had American diplomacy been more resourceful, they would still be within the Russian sphere of influence, but in the style of Finland, pursuing foreign policies agreeable to the U.S.S.R., not requiring constant attention.

But Russian troubles have not meant American gains. The world community as a whole, as well as whole nations and countless individuals, have suffered as the result of America's errors. One cannot say that this would be a world without grave problems and conflicts. After all, how disproportionately little this power achieved when it came to making peace rather than war. Many of America's bargaining assets were frittered away for the sake of getting Soviet support for various features of the United Nations. Certainly an excessive price was paid to secure an organization which predictably, in view of the widening chasm between the two superpowers, though useful and convenient in small things, has proved ineffective in dealing with major crises. In politics anything which feeds unrealism, which strengthens the tendency (so strong anyway among democracies) that "somehow" things will get settled without facing squarely the unpalatable facts, usually produces harm.[32]

In addition to the Soviet Union and the United Nations, the fate of defeated Germany and Japan preoccupied U.S. diplomacy during the last year of the war. Even China, the traditional object of American solicitude and still of considerable hope, was considered of secondary importance. And yet, as the history of the next twenty-five years was to show, most of the dangerous conflicts came in connection with areas and issues not *directly* connected with Soviet-American relations. The crucial error was not to perceive how crucial were economically and politically strong Britain and France. This realization came only in 1947,

---

[32] I say "usually" because there are always examples like that of the British, who in 1940 with splendid unrealism refused to come to terms with Hitler.

and the intervening two years were long indeed in terms of their unfortunate effects on the future.

In the last analysis, it is both easy and unfair to argue that this should have been done rather than that, to expect that sorely tried and overburdened men from the President on down, confronting a situation unprecedented in American and world history and having to respond as well to the pressures of domestic politics, should have on each and every occasion correctly gauged the political and economic effects of each policy. There was one unpardonable dereliction and that was *not to know*. Common sense even without any specialized knowledge should have instructed as to the vast unprecedented power of America, the general character of the Soviet regime, the desperate need for democratic nations like France and Britain to become as strong as possible as soon as possible. Rhetoric and moralistic self-questioning obscured the realities of the world as it emerged from the war, thus ruining the prospects for a better peace.

4

Neither Alliance
nor Cold War

Soviet-American relations in the postwar years arrange themselves logically into several periods. The year 1953 forms a natural break—marking the death of Stalin, the inauguration of Eisenhower, the Korean armistice, the development of hydrogen devices by both superpowers. It is more difficult to determine where the next break comes. Perhaps 1959, when the Soviets turned a corner in their relations with Communist China and decided to arrive at a grand settlement with the United States. This praiseworthy effort was, however, handled by Khrushchev with such oversubtlety that it brought the two nations to the brink of nuclear confrontation. By 1964, this period of what might be called intimate hostility was over, with the fall of Khrushchev and the beginning of the massive and disastrous phase of American involvement in Vietnam.

The immediate postwar period 1945–47 may be described as one of gradual disengagement. Stalin had no need to fear American hostility if he simply exploited his wartime gains, and no need or desire for American friendship. The United States after several frustrating attempts had to give up the hope of resolving any basic problem through direct negotiations with Russia. In 1947, the new approach of America to world problems crystallized with the Truman Doctrine and the Marshall Plan: to try to counter the threat of Communism through economic help to Western Europe and with the extension of American protection to the periphery of the "free world."

The Soviet attitude during the period was best conveyed by Stalin in an interview with a United Press correspondent on October 23, 1946. Question: "Are you in agreement with the opinion of State Secretary Byrnes . . . about the growing strain in relations between the U.S.S.R. and the United States?" Stalin: "No." The correspondent then asked what, if such tension did exist, could be the reason for it? Stalin: "No need to answer in view of my previous statement." The poor correspondent kept on asking lengthy and involved questions. How did Russia view the presence of British soldiers in Greece? Stalin: "As unnecessary." What are the relations between Russia and Norway (!)? Stalin: "As yet hard to say." What is needed in the field of atomic energy? Stalin: "Strict international control." [1]

Would the Russians take an American loan? Stalin: "Yes." What did he think of the atom bomb? (i.e. "Aren't your people really scared?"). Stalin imperturbably referred to a dictum uttered on another occasion, when he had said: "Atom bombs are designed to scare those with weak nerves, but they cannot decide wars because there are not enough of them. To be sure, atomic monopoly is a threat, but against it are two remedies: (a) monopoly of the bomb will not last, (b) the use of the bomb will be forbidden." [2] This was excellent casuistry reflecting his early theological training—answers well designed to reassure the Russians and baffle the Westerners. Only the most well-prepared critic would have pursued the subject and punched holes in the argument: If the Americans had *enough* bombs, would they then decide wars? And *who* will forbid the use of the weapon?

The style of this encounter shows a conscious effort on the part of the Russians to produce the impression of chilling distance, not of unfriendliness but of scant interest and no fear of the Americans with their bombs and billions. One must respect this intuitive grasp of the psychology of the people Stalin was dealing with. How distant we are from Hitler, with his long tirades about American lack of culture and cowardice!

The problem of the bomb of course increasingly dominated American thinking on world affairs, and eventually, with the development of the hydrogen bomb and intercontinental missiles, it posed a basic challenge to the very possibility of a rational conduct of foreign relations.

Paradoxical though it sounds, however, the early monopoly of the new weapon debilitated rather than helped American foreign policy.

1 J. V. Stalin, *Works* (in Russian), (Stanford, Calif., 1967), III, 567–58.
2 *Ibid.,* p. 56.

In peacetime, democracies are prone to indolence and procrastination in international affairs, and the bomb was a powerful inducement in that direction. It encouraged, in short, a Maginot Line psychology.

We have also seen that with some representatives of the American government, among them a man as unimpeachably conservative in background as Stimson, possession of the atomic bomb led to a feeling of national guilt. Push it farther and you would get arguments that somehow it was not "fair" for the United States to have this advantage; as long as it did, wasn't it fair for the Russians to have Eastern Europe? Wasn't Communist distrust of the United States and its intentions somehow justified?

Such internal wrestling was not of course universal. Certainly there were Air Force generals [3] and politicians who believed that the bomb should be used to show the Russians what's what. But here precisely lay the trouble: *What* were the Russians to be shown, and how? It was just not possible for the United States to employ first ominous hints, then mounting pressure, and finally overt threats—a technique which Khrushchev applied with *his* bomb and missiles in the fifties. The only person of note who in 1945–47 openly declared that the Russians should behave or otherwise a bomb should be delivered squarely on the Kremlin was Bertrand Russell. The venerable philosopher had always been stoutly anti-American, even before his first marriage to an American lady, and as an occasional anarchist he disliked the U.S.S.R. almost as much.[4] Stalin's assessment of American psychology was to prove correct.

The bomb could not be used as a threat or as a means of pressure (there is a difference between the two), but it might have made sense to use it as a bargaining counter—not, to be sure, as poor Stimson speculated to entice Stalin into democratic ways, but to secure some concrete political advantage: genuine democratic elections for an all-German government in 1947, a free political life for Poland, etc. Scientists after all were warning that the American monopoly would not last long. Even before 1950 and the apprehension of Klaus Fuchs, it was realized that the Russians had secured valuable information through espionage;

[3] This arm is specified because in the Army, and especially in the Navy, the awesome invention was viewed with almost as little sympathy as by the Russians; an admiral contemplating his beautiful battleships sharing the fate of the U.S. cavalry had an irresistible incentive to belittle the bomb's effectiveness.
[4] Even this dislike seems to be connected with his anti-Americanism. On his first visit to the Soviet Union soon after the Revolution, Lord Russell tells us he concluded that Russia was ruled by *American* Jews.

and probabilities are that Stalin would have spurned any bargains, so confident was he that he could wait out the Americans and get his own bomb without paying for it. But at least it could have been tried and the offer would have been of great psychological value as demonstrating the *right kind* of idealism: the Americans were willing to share the awesome secret, not to obtain Russian signature on a sonorous declaration, not because it would bring tears of gratitude and trust from the Soviets, but to secure real freedom for real people. But no public figure made such a proposal, in fact it does not seem to have occurred to anybody. Like a miser with a treasure, so America hugged the evanescent atom monopoly to its bosom, equally unable to exploit it or to exchange it for something useful.

The last may not seem quite fair in view of the United States' offer to give up its monopoly in favor of international control of atomic energy. This was elaborated in the Baruch Plan, the document put forward by the American government in 1946 proposing an international atomic development authority to be set up under the auspices of the United Nations and endowed with a virtual monopoly on all forms of atomic-energy production. It would be armed with the power of sanctions against any state violating the agreement, which sanctions were to be imposed by a majority vote (thus the right of veto reserved to the Security Council's permanent members would be given up in this case). Once the authority was established and effectively functioning, the United States pledged, she would dispose of her stock of bombs and cease their production.

The American plan reflected several strains in American thinking at the time of its unveiling in 1946. The beginning of the Atomic Age gave rise among many, especially within the intellectual community, to the feeling epitomized by the phrase "one world or none." Time is running out on mankind, was the theme of many editorials. Cartoonists delighted in variations of the same theme with clocks set at five minutes to twelve. "It is no reflection on the [U.N.] Charter," wrote one commentator, "to say it has become a feeble and antiquated instrument for dealing with the problems of an Atomic Age. . . . Time today works against peace. . . . Once the nature and imminency of the peril are clearly understood by the peoples of the world their differences will not be a bar but an incentive to common government." [5] All the old complaints against the U.N. Charter's preservation of the veto power, hence of the obsolete notion of state sovereignty, were revived to

[5] Norman Corwin, *Modern Man Is Obsolete* (New York, 1945), pp. 41–42.

nourish a myriad of new plans for world government. Understandable anxiety lay behind such agitation, and in many ways the sentiments in favor of a fundamentally new approach toward peace were commendable. Still, this burst of despair over one's own country acquiring such a decisive weapon was a remarkable phenomenon. The shock was not nearly so great nor the response so emotional at the subsequent news in 1949 of Russia's first nuclear weapon and in 1964 of China's. Time, of course, dulls sensitivity to danger.

The Baruch Plan was a carefully prepared official document, not an agonized plea for mankind to repent and set up a world government. But the international authority it proposed was bound to become a sort of superstate. As such, it was simply out of the question that the U.S.S.R. would even in principle agree to the plan. They might well, for tactical reasons, have pretended to agree, quibbled about details, and prolonged the discussion as much as possible. But Andrei Gromyko, then Soviet delegate to the U.N. Atomic Commission, made crystal-clear that the Soviets would never agree to a renunciation of the veto power. All that the Soviets proposed was a simple convention prohibiting the production or use of atomic weapons and requiring the destruction of existing ones. This position in turn was of course unacceptable to the Americans, who would not surrender the monopoly without what was being described as proper safeguards: sanctions against violators, inspection, etc.

Apart from the sanctions, the mere idea of inspection ran against the grain of the entire Soviet government. At about this time, Soviet authorities were refusing a handful of Russian women married to Britons and Americans during the war permission to leave the U.S.S.R. If what those few women could tell about life in Russia was considered to be a danger justifying this extraordinary inhumanity and pettiness, what of inspection of bomb installations and research facilities?

Western ignorance about the real condition of Russia was deemed by the regime, quite logically from its point of view, as one of the greatest assets it had in its conduct of foreign relations. Access to the U.S.S.R. was never so difficult—i.e., virtually impossible—for a foreigner who was not a diplomat or Communist, travel throughout the country never so limited as between 1946 and 1954. Not even during the Great Purge of the 1930s were restrictions so all-encompassing. The fear which this restrictive behavior suggests cannot have been simply a concern over revelations about the police-state aspects of Soviet life. By 1947, only Communists, fellow travelers, and the most naïve of Western liberals denied that aspect of Soviet reality. Much more dangerous was any revelation of Russian *weakness,* of the magnitude of the tasks of industrial reconstruction and rapid demobilization lying ahead of this still primitive society. A truer picture of Russia's strengths and weaknesses might induce some new and unwelcome thinking in the State Department and the Pentagon.

Meanwhile, the vision of millions of Russian soldiers ready to push on through Europe to the English Channel fascinated and horrified the West. At the same time, Stalin was probably telling the truth when in October, 1946, he told that same U.P. correspondent that Russia had but sixty divisions, most of them incomplete, in the vast area comprising East Germany, Austria, Bulgaria, Rumania, and Poland and that their number would soon be reduced to forty.[6] Stalin must have calculated that no hardheaded Western general or statesman was going to believe this, coming as it did from the man who in the same interview had the audacity to deny that the Soviet Union had any influence on the Western Communist parties.

The other side of the Soviet coin was fear of ideological contamination. During the war official propaganda had warned Soviet soldiers not to be impressed by the superior material culture they would encounter beyond the frontiers of the U.S.S.R. If it was feared that ruined Polish and German cities and villages were capable of inspiring sinful reflections among the soldiers, how could the regime even consider the possibility of intercourse and cultural exchange with the West?

All the labor and ingenuity which went into the Baruch Plan were thus wasted. From the American point of view, it must have appeared a small price for the Soviets to pay—to waive the veto and agree on some minimal inspection—in order to lift what must have been an intolerable burden of anxiety about the American monopoly of the frightful weapon. But Soviet logic was different. Apart from the considerations given above, the U.S.S.R. could not possibly admit that any agency was impartial, or more fundamentally that there *was* such a thing as an international agency. In their eyes the United Nations meant basically two powers: the United States and its clients, and the U.S.S.R. and its satellites. To entrust such a body with jurisdiction over a vital aspect of national policy, to remove the one element in the organization that nullified the West's numerical superiority—the veto—was unthinkable, and would have been whether Stalin or any other Communist was at the helm.

[6] A full Russian division then was composed of about 10,000 men.

The phrase "inability to find a common language" is not just a platitude but a concrete description of a very basic difficulty attending Soviet-American relations, then as now. We shall see how various hints conveyed at various times by either of the two protagonists for a resolution of a basic conflict failed to be taken up or were misunderstood, so that even solutions desired by and in the interest of both sides were frustrated.[7]

During these years, the Soviet Union concentrated on internal tasks. The main one was clearly economic reconstruction and then a "big leap forward" of the Soviet economy, especially heavy industry. In his speech of February 9, 1946, Stalin set ambitious goals—a threefold increase in heavy industrial production within fifteen years from the prewar level —18 million tons of steel in 1940, and a projected target of 60 million by 1960. "Only then will our country be safeguarded against all kinds of eventualities," [8] said Stalin in a significant slip of tongue—the phrase implying both that Russia was then unprepared for a major conflict, and that Stalin judged the chances of one occurring for a decade or so as extremely small.

The Soviet consumer, sustained through his incredible hardships during the war by the hope that victory would bring with it a more abundant life, once more had to tighten his belt and defer his hopes for a higher standard of living. Those who hoped with a wartime poet that "After victory we will make a halt, Drink a cup, and rest to our heart's content," [9] were in for a cruel disappointment. The hardest hit was as usual the peasant. In 1947, the government adopted a financial reform of a kind that not even an *ordinary* totalitarian state could have put into effect without leading to widespread disorders if not indeed revolution. The ruble was revalued in a way that brutally punished those who kept their money in cash, i.e., mainly the peasants. Inflationary pressures were wiped out, but with them the life savings and resources of a considerable segment of the Soviet population.

[7] In contrast, when in the summer of 1939 Nazi Germany and Russia decided it was in their interest to reach an agreement, how speedily mortal hostility between the two was laid aside, how easily and efficiently they came to terms, and with what delicacy of language! None of "I take this, you take that." Primly, Nazi Germany "disinterested" itself in eastern Poland and the Baltic states, and with equal delicacy Russia conceded that in the hypothetical case of "territorial rearrangement" taking place in Poland she would not be interested in the western part.

[8] Stalin, *op. cit.*, III, 20.

[9] Alexei Surkov, quoted in Harold Swayze, *Political Control of Literature in the U.S.S.R. 1946–1959* (Cambridge, 1962), p. 35.

Alongside the ceaseless ritual of sacrificing practically every other social objective at the altar of industrialization, the regime had traditionally exhorted its people to vigilance against enemies both foreign and domestic. Stalin's actions betrayed a conviction, whether conscious or unconscious, that the mere expectation on the part of the Soviet citizen that his regime might become more liberal was a political threat. The last Czar, on his ascent to the throne, had warned the people not to indulge in "senseless dreams" of constitutional freedoms; Stalin was too clever to say this, but his regime's practical measures made clear that any secret wartime hopes in that direction had been senseless. Moreover, the government had to undo much of its own propaganda about Britain and the United States. It is sometimes asserted that Stalin in 1946 reverted to the assertion that eventual war was inevitable in view of the persistence of capitalism. This is not correct. In fact both then and later the Soviets continued to point out that peaceful coexistence between states with different social systems was possible and desirable. But the stress in propaganda now shifted to allegations of hostile designs by the *ruling circles* of Britain and the United States, designs which were being held in check by the growing might of the U.S.S.R. and the desire for peace among the working masses of the capitalist countries. In brief, the Soviet citizen was being told what he has always been told about main capitalist powers: they would like to make war on the U.S.S.R. but they don't dare [10]—a shrewd approach designed to keep a true believer both vigilant and confident.

Special efforts were devoted to dismantling the wartime image of America as an enormous economic and military power. Now it was being taught that the war had been won *mainly* by Soviet armies. An elaborate campaign was embarked on to present *Russians* (and now we use the term in the ethnic sense and not as a convenient abbreviation for the inhabitants of the Soviet Union regardless of their nationality) as having made every major invention in modern times, pioneered principal scientific techniques, initiated every notable cultural and artistic trend. A foreign observer could only gasp at a society where it was considered close to treason to assert that an American invented the telephone; at a country ruled by a party and in the name of an ideology which proclaimed themselves above nationalities but where one of the

[10] The only case where a major capitalist power was portrayed by official Soviet propaganda as friendly and hence with no warlike designs on the U.S.S.R. was that of Germany between 1939 and 1941.

most severe derogations was to be accused of "cosmopolitanism" and lack of respect for *traditional Russian customs and values*. It was an atmosphere favorable to scientific quacks and empire builders.

As with related phenomena years later in China, so this campaign against cosmopolitanism and for glorifications of things Russian may have been rationally conceived, but once launched it soon turned into a wave of hysterical denunciation and witch-hunting, which by excessive pressure inflicted upon various segments of the scientific community was bound to impair its efficiency and thus in the end harm the state. What price did Soviet agriculture pay for the restraints placed upon free biological research consequent to the rule of Lysenko and other bureaucrats and quacks? Official dogmas and decrees could not deal easily with complex issues in mathematics and theoretical physics, but even there damage was done by occasional campaigns against such "cosmopolitan" products as the theory of relativity. The obsessive passion for conformity and for regulation cost Soviet society dearly not only in science and education, but in those indirect but enormously important benefits which free scientific activity contributes toward the growth of the economy and general progress. Only in fields directly related to the imperative needs of state security, such as atomic and missile research, was the system able by its power to mobilize resources and to overcome the detrimental effects of fettering free scientific inquiry.

The theme of Soviet and especially Russian chauvinism was sounded even more insistently in the arts. Certainly when it comes to his literary inheritance, no Russian need feel inferiority to any other nation. But this justifiable pride was soon turned into xenophobic outbursts against foreign influences and use of foreign themes, into demands that *all* symphonic music be based on folk tunes, etc. Official censure or worse now awaited those non-Russian Soviet composers, artists, and historians who displayed or seemed to exhibit too warm an attachment to their national or local traditions. One had to point out repeatedly how the cultural and social life of the Ukrainian nation, say, *always* benefited from the warm interest and support of the paternal Russian nation.

Andrei Zhdanov, then reputedly the most influential man next to Stalin and until his death in 1948 one of the two putative candidates for succession, launched the campaign of cultural regimentation required of the arts: socialist realism demanded the correct ideological attitude, a positive and optimistic approach toward the Soviet reality, rejection of morbid themes and of individual introspection. This by definition precluded any of the modern trends in the arts and literature. The two greatest poets of Soviet Russia were thus silenced: Boris Pasternak had for some time prudently confined himself to translation; Anna Akhmatova was specifically and savagely attacked by the satrap.

The campaign against cosmopolitanism found an almost inevitable reflection in officially sponsored anti-Semitism. Right after the war it became fairly clear that the regime was consciously restricting the number of Jews in strategic political and other occupations. Stalin, as his daughter's memoirs confirm, had always had anti-Jewish proclivities, and after the war the Jews became a national target for suspicion and veiled or not so veiled attacks.[11]

This cruel and stupid campaign, with its countless human tragedies, was greeted first with incomprehension, then with disgust in the West. But there was little reason for foreign observers to be surprised over the concept of artistic and intellectual repressions and regimentation. How could it be otherwise? The end of the war marked the beginning of a veritable world-wide revolution, the essence of which was the eventual victory of the "American style" over older civilizations and ways of life. It was not only a matter of refrigerators or automobiles or that disregard of customs and traditions which resentful Frenchmen dubbed "coca-colonization," but the whole individualist and secularist thrust of American culture. This unconscious cultural domination was to prove of perhaps greater significance than the economic one, for in many countries it destroyed traditional elements of social cohesion without providing new ones, and resentment against the people who carelessly destroyed customs and values of an older civilization, who by their wealth set up standards which less fortunate nations could not meet, often united the conservative and radical. And when this enormous country failed to provide that which is always expected of the leader—stability and a sense of direction—this resentment turned into a bitter conviction that the gods worshiped all along had been false ones. Anti-Americanism was

11 Most everyone understood who was meant by the *"rootless cosmopolites"* so frequently denounced by official spokesmen. The atmosphere of the times is well portrayed in a story about Ilya Ehrenburg. A well-known if not really distinguished writer, he had been during the war an extremely popular newspaper correspondent and columnist. After the war, Ehrenburg found himself in official disfavor: he was a Jew, he was well known to be close to the quintessence of "cosmopolitanism." Friends shunned him, his writings were criticized in increasingly ominous terms, his acquaintances could not conceal their surprise that he was still at large. He appealed personally to the Kremlin. And then, at a meeting of the Writers' Union, his work was subjected to a predictable chorus of criticism. Ehrenburg then spoke; while admitting that many did not like his work, he protested that he still received some fan letters and begged permission to read one—signed J. V. Stalin. Not many in his predicament were so fortunate.

to become a potent ideology, though these perspectives were hidden in the immediate postwar years.

In the face of this Americanization, the Communist Party of the Soviet Union since the 1930s had propagated and enforced an essentially traditionalist system of values and morals. Hard work, obedience to constituted authority, eschewing of individual preferences when they came into conflict with those of the collective or the state—those were the official injunctions. Divorce was expensive to obtain; large families were encouraged. Except for the socialist label and the discouragement of religion, there was little in the required morals and motivations that a Victorian businessman with no democratic sympathies could have objected to in Stalin's Russia. Indeed, sometimes the most hardened capitalists would return with favorable impressions from a visit to the country where the labor unions' primary task was to strive for higher productivity and where any idea of economic equality was banned as "not socialism but petty-bourgeois anarcho-syndicalism."

Modernism of any kind was held to be baneful. Soviet propagandists were proud of how widely Soviet translations of Western literary *classics* were circulated; but a large printing of, say, Joyce or D. H. Lawrence was unthinkable. Nonobjectivism, like any "undue" stress on sex in literature, was deemed unhealthy and psychologically disturbing for men and women building a socialist society. And since the Soviet people did not suffer from decadence and morbid capitalist influences, they were in no need of Freudian psychology. Both Marxism and the traditions of Russian psychology associated with names like Korchakov and Pavlov decried the main thrust of Freudianism, holding that the whole psychoanalytic school was a sham science designed to cover up the ills of capitalist society by attributing them to the human psyche rather than to the environment.

The barrier erected, or, more properly speaking, restored, against Western influences was then a reflection of the conservative outlook which Stalin and his successors up to this day have shared. It also betrayed the rulers' conviction about the impressionability of their people and the fragility of their devotion to the Soviet ideal. Even a more liberally inclined Soviet bureaucrat may well argue: "The American can afford Freud, nonobjective art, novels with morbid and pessimistic themes, pornography masquerading as stage and cinema art. But the whole history of the Russian people is a lesson that there is no middle road between authoritarianism and anarchy. Anything that even intellectually damages the principle of authority and unquestioning obedience to the leader, to the officially imposed dogmas on art, science, and morals will lead eventually not to a more liberal form of authoritarianism and communism but to complete disaster and to the undoing of that national greatness for which so great a price has been paid." But in 1946 or 1947 it is unlikely that the question of liberalization was even raised.

Full details of what was happening within the ruling apparatus in those years are still unavailable. But evidently advancing years were making it difficult for Stalin to stick to his old style, one which required constant and detailed attention to all the major and sometimes minor details of governance of the vast empire. But he took care that no single satrap would entrench himself in any important branch of government. Marshal Georgi Zhukov was the outstanding military hero of the war, and as deputy supreme commander to Stalin and in the prime of his life, he was the logical candidate now that the war was over to relieve his aging chief of his military duties. (On his visit to Moscow in 1945, General Eisenhower received the impression, he tells us, that Zhukov was second man in Russia and personally close to the dictator. And the Marshal himself, as it appears from his memoirs—granted that he received official "help" to insure what in 1969 was considered the proper image of Stalin—evidently shared that impression or illusion.) But after a rather brief stint as Soviet commander in Germany, Zhukov was removed from the public eye and from contacts with foreigners and confined to the obscurity of a provincial garrison. The Ministry of War went to a party bureaucrat, Nicolai Bulganin. In the all-important party secretariat, two potential rivals for succession, Zhdanov and Malenkov, now balanced each other. The faithful Molotov still held the Foreign Ministry. On the Victory Day celebration Stalin had singled him out for praise, saying typically that a good foreign minister is worth two army groups and raising his glass to "our Vyacheslav." Now "our Vyacheslav" was progressively stripped of any importance in *internal* politics, and his wife was soon to be exiled. More drastic was the fate of secondary figures who were thought to have been contaminated by too close contacts with the West. Maisky and Litvinov were dismissed as deputy foreign ministers; the latter, through whose skillful diplomacy the Soviet Union owed so much of the West's favorable attitude toward Russia, was denied a pension!

To illustrate the atmosphere within the Kremlin in the postwar period, one may repeat a story told by Khrushchev shortly before his dismissal. A draft of the new economic plan was submitted for discussion by the

Council of Ministers. It was known that several ministers were going to object that production goals in some branches of the economy were unrealistically high and had to be modified, appropriations for their ministries insufficient to meet the targets, etc. There was consequently some consternation when Stalin, who though still Chairman seldom bothered to attend the Council's meeting, suddenly appeared and took the chair. Pointing at the document, he said that here was the plan and asked who had any objections. Ministers looked at each other and remained silent. Since there was no need for discussion, let them all go and see a movie, said Stalin grinning. Thus was Russia governed and decisions reached affecting the everyday lives of millions.

As against this picture, America reverted with the armistice to the raucous ways of democracy. The great wartime fear of an impulsive relapse into isolationism never materialized. American participation in the war had been longer and more intense than her experience of World War I, and the country was accustomed to an international role. Even for conservatives and traditionally conservative politicians like Senator Vandenberg the combination of long-range aircraft and the atomic bomb, which would become available to Russia as well, meant that a return to the good old days was unthinkable. The interest in world affairs, especially European, which for so long had been concentrated along the Eastern seaboard became generalized.

In fact, since in the United States things are seldom done in moderation, internationalism was to become as popular as isolationism had once been. In the past, the disenchantment over "Europe" not paying its debts crystallized in a popular mythology of a virtuous and inexperienced America having been tricked in World War I to join the futile and immoral squabbles of the Old World.

The mood had shifted in 1946, and with it interpretations of the past. Isolationism now was said to have contributed to (in some versions caused) the evils of Hitlerism and fascism. Internationalism and faith in the United Nations was extolled not so much as a wise policy in America's interest but as an act of penance for past sins and as a repudiation of the immoral stress on national sovereignty. The American Legion and the D.A.R. might grumble, but much of the opinion-molding element propagated the new faith. The mass of the people remained unaffected by this passion, but in the opinion-forming circles it was now decidedly unfashionable to be isolationist or skeptical about the importance and benevolent potentialities of the U.N. And this attitude tended in turn to erode Congressional doubts and the professional diplomats' more realistic approach to the complexities of the world situation. The United Nations became a part of the American scene also in the physical sense of the word. It would have been unimaginable certainly to F.D.R. and his advisers that it should have been otherwise, that this dearly fought for institution should be situated elsewhere.[12]

The drastic shift in the American view of the U.S.S.R. was due in large measure to what the public considered Soviet sabotage of the United Nations—as expressed by its repeated exercise of the veto in the Security Council, obstruction of progress on international control of atomic energy, etc. To Henry Wallace and his supporters, this was the United States' fault, the reasoning being that her hostile acts and pronouncements forced Russia to overract both in its policies in the U.N. and in Eastern Europe. But this line of argument steadily lost ground even among those who were tolerant if not friendly toward the U.S.S.R. It was difficult for most people to form a correct picture of events in distant lands—to know whether the people being executed and imprisoned in Poland, Yugoslavia, etc., were in fact fascists and war criminals as charged or genuine democrats—but the picture of the stony-faced Soviet delegate pronouncing the ritualistic *"nyet"* in the Security Council became a familiar and hated theme, repeatedly arousing the wrath of newspaper editorials, churchmen, and lecturers.

The U.S. government found it both convenient and politic to stress this Soviet misbehavior. It in a large measure absolved the administration from criticism of not doing something about Soviet policy in Eastern Europe. It could always be argued that the United States had carried a matter to the Security Council and there, having denounced the wanton acts of oppression and having been joined in these sentiments by other states, isolated the U.S.S.R. within the community of nations by forcing it to take ignoble recourse in the veto. It must have occasioned considerable and pleasant surprise in the State Department when in 1946 such wrangling within the Security Council did *not* have the predictable outcome and the Russians *did* pull out their troops from

---

[12] It is surprising that the Russians had not chosen to bargain over the location. But then they might have been dissuaded by the possibility that if they did, the U.N. might end up in the *U.S.S.R.* The mere thought of such a situation would have panicked any Soviet official. Years later, Khrushchev was to suggest that the U.N. leave the shores of the Hudson for Vienna, Geneva, or Moscow. It is symptomatic of the lack of alertness of American diplomacy that the invitation to Moscow was not immediately and warmly espoused. Most likely the world body would have witnessed embarrassed explanations by the impulsive Soviet statesman that he really did not mean that, that the housing problem in Moscow, alas, forbade it, etc. . . . .

Iran. But, as we shall see, the reason for this uncharacteristic Soviet action lay elsewhere than in the fear of world public opinion.

The U.N., then, enabled the U.S. government to shout at the Russians, so to speak, while freeing it from much of that face-to-face, note-after-note, strenuous diplomacy which the President dreaded and which exhausted and infuriated his subordinates. Yet harrowing and exasperating as the latter method is, it was necessary and on occasions could be effective. The illusion of the United States' being protected by two oceans was replaced by another one of peace being secured by the United Nations.

Some of the dangers inherent in accepting the United Nations as something it was not and could not be were foreshadowed by an American scholar when he wrote shortly after the war:

> What collective security demands of the individual nations is to foresake national egotisms and the national policies serving them. . . . This . . . assumption is really tantamount to the assumption of a moral revolution infinitely more fundamental than any moral change that has occurred in the history of western civilization. . . . By the very logic of its assumptions the diplomacy of collective security must aim at transforming all local conflicts into world conflicts. . . . Instead of preserving peace between two nations, collective security, as it must actually operate in the contemporary world, is bound to destroy peace among all nations.[13]

The last assertion has not been borne out: the U.N. has been *unable* to provide collective security and its *apparent* successes in this field have been due to agreement or tacit understanding between the two superpowers.[14]

American diplomacy vis-à-vis the Soviet Union during the period was characterized by a certain fatalism, epitomized by the question General Walter Bedell Smith, the newly appointed ambassador to Moscow, asked in his first audience with Stalin in April, 1946: "What does the Soviet Union want and how far is Russia going to go?"[15] There was still considerable hesitation about what could be done to areas peripheral to those under Soviet pressure: Greece, where a full-fledged civil war now erupted; Turkey; and Iran. Foreign ministers' conferences adjourned after inconclusive wrangling, and even those

---

[13] Hans J. Morgenthau, *Politics among Nations* (New York, 1949), pp. 333–335.
[14] The only major exception is Korea, which will be considered below. Mr. Morgenthau wrote at the time the idea of a *standing and sizable* United Nations Armed Force was still under discussion. No one would deny the U.N.'s usefulness on some *minor* crises, say, in the Congo in 1960 or in Cyprus.
[15] Walter Bedell Smith, *My Three Years in Moscow* (New York, 1950), p. 50.

where a friendlier atmosphere prevailed, like the December, 1945, one in Moscow, were barren of major results,[16] though for some mysterious reason Secretary Byrnes in a book of memoirs entitled his chapter on the conference "Moscow Ends an Impasse." [17] By the end of 1946, the Big Three finally agreed on peace treaties with the minor enemy states. This meant that Soviet and the local Communist actions in Rumania, Bulgaria, and Hungary would no longer be embarrassed by the existence of Allied Control Commissions whose Western members (to be sure under virtual house arrest) might suddenly prove bothersome, and also that the remaining Western troops would pull out of Italy, where the Communists were thought to have a fair chance of winning the forthcoming elections.

The huge problems of Germany and China appeared untractable. Germany was being split in two. In China, the Russians looted Manchuria and turned stockpiles of Japanese arms over to the Communists. They were then content to contemplate General Marshall attempting in politics what would have been equivalent to squaring the circle, i.e., to bring about a "unified and democratic China" through a lasting reconciliation between Chiang and the Communists.

It was in order to stop this policy of drift, this fruitless haggling followed by partial concessions, that Churchill made his speech at Fulton, Missouri, on March 5. Repudiating the notion that a new war was inevitable, he argued that if it was to be avoided, democracies had to maintain their strength and above all unity. The Russians respected strength and despised weakness. He astutely phrased his plea for the continuation of intimate British-American collaboration in the idiom designed to appeal to the new American passion: he wanted the Western democracies to "stand together in strict adherence to the principles of the United Nations Charter."

Churchill's speech, largely because of the locale and audience, created a world-wide sensation. Yet there was little in it that was new or that had not been said by him before. But in both America and Britain there was plenty of adverse criticism of the speech. The view that it was an old imperialist's plea for the United States to pull British chestnuts out

16 It was at a banquet during this conference that Stalin sharply admonished Molotov before his foreign visitors. "Our Vyacheslav," with his quaint sense of humor, enquired of Dr. James Conant, who had accompanied Secretary of State Byrnes, whether he carried an atom bomb in his pocket. "No need to joke about the achievements of American science," said Stalin. He may have thought of a Ukrainian proverb: "Do not tempt a wolf out of the woods."

17 *Speaking Frankly* (New York, 1947).

of the fire was expressed most forcefully by Wallace, who on September 12 made a speech in which he said, "To make Britain the key to our foreign policy would be a height of folly. . . . We must not let British balance of power politics determine whether and when the United States gets into war." [18] Wallace was subsequently, at Secretary Byrnes' request, fired by Truman from the Cabinet, but his sentiments were reflected in wide circles. And in Labor-ruled Britain, public reaction was also mixed. *The Times* chided Churchill: instead of talking about things that divided the West from Russia, it said, one should seek common ground; the democracies could learn from Russia in "the development of economic and social planning." [19] *The Times* tended to reflect editorially the views of the party in power, and these sentiments were those of the majority of the Labour movement, even though Foreign Secretary Bevin was disenchanted with Moscow.

But the basic fear was more widely felt than by those with certain doctrinal preferences: Wasn't war being brought *closer* by speeches like Churchill's? It was to exploit this feeling that Stalin professed to read into the Fulton speech instigation to a crusade against the U.S.S.R. In a special interview in *Pravda* on March 13, his language was brutal: Churchill was compared to Hitler. His call "for armed intervention in Russia" on the order of the one organized by Britain and France after World War I was not likely to succeed, but if it did, the invaders would be beaten back as they had been then.

Yet while exuding this confidence and execrating his wartime partner, Stalin's policy did not remain unaffected: within a few weeks of the speech Soviet policy executed a significant retreat. The U.S.S.R. had retained her troops in Iran beyond the period agreed by the Big Three during the war, while Britain and the United States had withdrawn theirs as scheduled, and had set up two puppet governments in northern Iran which were pressuring the central Iran government for a variety of concessions. Previous American requests for the withdrawal of these Soviet troops had been ignored or answered in provocative terms: Stalin in December, 1945, assured Byrnes that the troops were needed because of the danger of an Iranian armed incursion into the oil fields of the Caucasus. At the time of Churchill's speech, the dispute was in the Security Council, with British and American complaints delivered to Moscow on March 4 and 8. On March 26, however, the Soviet government suddenly reversed its position and announced that

[18] *Survey of International Affairs, 1939–1946* (London, 1953), V, 658.
[19] *The Times* (London), March 6, 1946.

all troops would be withdrawn within six weeks! Throughout the rest of the year, the Soviets watched passively while the Iranian government liquidated the separatist regimes and executed their leaders, the Iranian parliament rejected any concessions to the Soviets, and the pro-Soviet party was suppressed. What the United Nations failed to achieve through any of its numerous debates on East European problems it *seemingly* succeeded in doing in Iran. The country was miraculously, it seemed, snatched out of the jaws of Soviet imperialism. But the presumption is overwhelming that it was Churchill's speech that did the trick. With all the debate going on about that speech, the Russians were loath to present additional evidence that its main thesis was sound: the chances that Britain and the United States would *do* something about the Soviet occupation of northern Iran were small, but prudence advised a withdrawal that would allow time for passions to cool and anti-Soviet impulses in the West to dissipate.

Nobody in the West seemed to have noticed the coincidence of the Iron Curtain speech and the Soviet's relinquishing a fair and beckoning prize (far more valuable, in view of its oil wealth and the traditional Soviet interest in the area, than, say, Bulgaria). Yet the event was a suggestive example of how an enlightened and patient Western diplomacy could have worked. Nonrecognition, constant harassment through notes, and keeping the issue in the spotlight—these techniques were not negligible if they produced in the Russians the impression that they *might* lead to concrete steps. What Stalin in 1946 feared might be the result of his continued obduracy in Iran was probably increased American and British armaments and something on the order of a NATO, which did not in fact appear until 1949. The most effective means the West had to pressure Russia in the *immediate* postwar years was to force her to maintain a large army, but the pressure was not employed. By the time NATO came off the drafting board and became operative, the Russian economy had substantially advanced, China was conquered by the Communists, and the United States was involved in Korea. Time is a very precious commodity, especially in diplomacy, particularly in the atomic age.

If Iran was an example of a Soviet retreat, Finland was one of Soviet restraint. Few in 1945 expected that small country to escape either absorption by Russia, like Latvia and Estonia, or introduction of the satellite pattern, of the type the Soviet Union was establishing throughout Eastern Europe. Finland was geographically close to the second center of the U.S.S.R., Leningrad; she had been Russia's for a century before 1918; the war with her cost the Russians dearly in 1939–40, and she then was an ally of Germany; she had a not inconsiderable Communist party. (In a story of Conan Doyle's the fact that the dog did *not* bark at the intruder suggests to Holmes a correct solution of the mystery. The fact that the Soviets did *not* absorb Finland, while it does not offer a clue to Soviet foreign policy as a whole, certainly throws some interesting light on it.) Presumably the Russians had every reason to be satisfied with the Finns' scrupulous observance of the peace treaty and its general deference to the U.S.S.R.—yet these same factors did not save the Czechs in 1948. There were tense moments in 1947–48, when the Russians pressured for a treaty of alliance with Finland, but after it was concluded, the Finnish government got rid of its Communist members and the lightning still did not strike.

Two reasons undoubtedly contributed to Russian forbearance. First, the Finns gave every indication that they would fight to oppose complete absorption. Secondly, American interest in Finland was of a sentimental nature: it went back to the 1930s, when the small country was the only one of the United States' European debtors to meet its obligations, and to the memories of the heroic stance of the Finns in the Winter War.

These lessons do not appear to have been pondered very deeply by American diplomacy of the period. Both the government and the people were groping for some form of a handle on the Soviet Union, some sort of a general formula to understand and cope with the "Russian problem." There was the usual American impotent approach to elaborate and historical explanations. Were they acting out of fear and genuine grievance against the United States, as Wallace and his supporters alleged; or were they about to sweep to the Channel; or could they somehow be induced to "play ball" within the United Nations? The feeling of fatalism about Soviet encroachments was beginning to give way to irritation. The Russian problem was the main disturbing factor in that generally and rather unexpectedly pleasant world in which the Americans now found themselves. The wartime fears of depression and massive unemployment had been confounded, shortages of goods and labor disputes were receding. The prosperity which many an academic prophet had warned would be impossible unless the United States took a path similar to that taken by Britain in 1945 now seemed to be occurring under an eclectic system which combined features of old-fashioned capitalism with state intervention and planning. Their domestic anxieties for the moment allayed, people naturally worried about how long their well-being could continue and improve in view of what politicians and newspapers warned were the somber potentialities of the world situation.

The year 1947 was one that saw a basic shift in American foreign policy. In July of that year, George Kennan, then a leading State Department expert on Russia, formulated what was the theoretical basis of the new approach in an article which made "containment" a household term.[20]

The Truman Doctrine, enunciated in March, and the Marshall Plan, announced in early June, revealed drastic departures from the traditional practices of American policy. Though the U.S.S.R. was a *direct* objective of neither, it is also certain that neither would have been adopted without the underlying belief that (a) the U.S.S.R. was continuing to display expansionist ambitions which the United Nations could not by itself stop; and (b) direct negotiations with the U.S.S.R. were now fruitless and the advance of Communism must be stopped by an active policy of the United States.

Hence the formula which had dominated American foreign policy since 1943, albeit with diminishing force—that of bringing about a satisfactory world order through direct negotiations with Russia and through the U.N.—was changed, its first part abandoned, its second refined by a degree of skepticism. One would still sit at the same table with the Russians and talk, still introduce resolutions in the U.N., but one would not expect much from either. The main emphasis was now to be on *containment* (though Kennan was later to claim that his idea was imperfectly understood and applied), on the creation of a global environment which would defeat Russia's attempts to exploit economic weakness and social anarchy. Thwarted in their expectations that economic crises would bring the capitalist world to its knees, the Soviets would eventually be forced to negotiate in *good faith*.

There are *some* signs that at this very time the Russians, alarmed at the indications of an impending shift in American foreign policy, were ready to negotiate with a view to a solution of some basic problems separating the two worlds. The period between March 12 and the summer may well be one of those tragic times where, through mutual misunderstanding, an opportunity was missed not indeed to solve all problems but to take an important step in that direction.

On March 12, the Truman Doctrine was enunciated. In April, Stalin

[20] This was in *Foreign Affairs*, July, 1947, under the pseudonym "X," and subsequently repeated in his *American Diplomacy 1900–1950* (Chicago, 1951).

received Governor Harold Stassen in Moscow. The reception accorded to the American visitor was different from the brusque and ominous technique Stalin had used in his interview with the U.P. correspondent five months before, just as it was distinct from the mere reassurances given critics of American policy such as Henry Wallace and Elliott Roosevelt: it was the "old Stalin" of the wartime interviews with Western visitors—affable, discursive, not seeking merely to "take in" his visitor but evidently trying to make a point. He inquired politely of Stassen whether he thought a major depression was likely in the United States (something that Soviet economists were divided about). There were revealing glimpses of his philosophy: America was lucky to have *weak* neighbors like Mexico and Canada, "so you need not be afraid of them." [21] He was ready with advice on how the United States might avoid a crisis: the government must be armed with broad powers; but would businessmen be prepared "to be regulated and restrained"? (The United States then had a Republican Congress.) The whole tone was relaxed, that of a man weighing possibilities and collecting impressions.

Stalin's amiabilities would not be significant except that they came *after* the United States' pledge to help Greece and Turkey and *during* the Moscow conference of foreign ministers of the Big Four, where the problems of a peace treaty and German unity were once more being discussed. The usual complement of discordant claims and mutual accusations was still there, but Molotov's oratory was free of the usual harsh charges against the West. The Russian proposal looked to the formation of a central German government and termination of occupation once the basic aims of demilitarization had been secured, but Molotov also reverted to the old demand for $10 billion reparations and Four Power supervision of the Ruhr. The West, having been bitten several times, was now morbidly shy: Weren't the Russians once more offering vague promises while demanding concrete concessions? General Marshall professed to read sinister implications into the Soviet proposal for a centralized government, the Russians on the contrary prophesying dire consequences were Germany to be set up on a federal basis. The conference broke down amidst the clashing oratory.

Were the Russians trying to "signal" to the Americans that for certain guarantees and reparations they would be willing to release

---

[21] *Documents on International Affairs, 1947–1948* (London, 1952), p. 119. At the time, Soviet propaganda presented the fictitious possibilities of fascism in such weak neighbors as Poland and Rumania as mortal dangers to the U.S.S.R.

East Germany from their grasp? Possibly. It was evident that the Western zones would be united and that the new West German state would become an industrial and perhaps military power sooner than had seemed possible. (Production was still very low, but the chaos foreseen under the Potsdam decisions did not develop.) The Soviet zone, in contrast, could never offset such a power. In a conversation with Marshall, Stalin hinted strongly at the need for a summit conference.

Would a united but disarmed and neutral Germany have been in the West's interest? Quite apart from saving 16 million or so people from the misery of Communist rule, anything which contributed to the rollback of the Soviet sphere of influence would have been a net gain, an omen of hope for the still not fully "satellized" countries of Eastern Europe, a step toward a give-and-take coexistence with the Soviet Union.[22] The price would presumably have included formal recognition of Polish acquisitions at the expense of Germany as *provisionally* agreed on at Potsdam. Reviewing the history of the last twenty-five years, one must conclude that it would have been a sound bargain. The military potential of West Germany was to be utilized too late and too ineptly to wrest any concessions or to achieve additional ones for the West. And today no one really believes that the Potsdam decision on behalf of Poland can be undone or substantially modified. Years later the expression "negotiating from strength" was to acquire wide currency. In the spring of 1947, the West was in the position to negotiate from strength, but the tragedy was, just as in 1944–45, that it did not know it.

[22] Give and take of the right kind, and not the kind described in the House of Commons by Harold Nicolson, when, responding to Chamberlain's defense of Munich as an example of give and take, he said that indeed Britain and France gave and Hitler took.

5

Great Decisions—Great Misunderstandings

Containment, the Truman Doctrine, the Marshall Plan: within the space of a few weeks American foreign policy turned into new channels —not unexpectedly, for pressures had been building in that direction for some time—with all that energy and impulsiveness of which the United States is capable once doubts and hesitations are overcome and the course of action seems clear. Some of the old doubts and divisions of course remained. The residue of isolationism persisted, and a sizable element—nobody could be sure until the election of 1948 how strong it was—held to Wallace's position that U.S. policies were wrong because of their basic anti-Soviet motivations. But to the great majority, the new initiatives brought a sense of relief. *Something* was being done about the Soviet and Communist threat, and the plan for massive amounts of economic aid tended to assuage the abashment many an American felt in comparing his own growing abundance with the chaotic and still desperate economic conditions in Europe.

Containment as it became popularly understood was highly acceptable to the vital center of American politics (to borrow Arthur Schlesinger's expression), that broad spectrum which extended from the proverbial "enlightened businessman" to the New Deal liberal, and thus excluded the old-fashioned isolationist, whose attitudes appeared antediluvian, and the fellow traveler, whose views clashed with what newspapers daily reported from Russia and East Europe. For containment preached patience but not passivity. One did not have to threaten the Russians with the atomic bomb or increase armaments: all that was needed was that the democracies preserve their economic good health and help those who wanted to help themselves. Confounded by the collapse of their Marxian prophecies about cyclical depressions, the Soviets would in the long run have to abandon their Messianic urge to communize the world.

The Truman Doctrine ran more against the grain: it meant not only economic but military aid (observers and equipment) to foreign countries. In Greece, where the guerrillas fighting the central government claimed they represented a broad democratic front, was the United States propping up a reactionary and corrupt monarchy? (There was less reluctance in the case of Turkey, probably because she did not have a king and the menace was a Soviet rather than a domestic one.) By the same token, the Truman Doctrine was more popular on the more conservative wing of the vital center: it meant getting directly at Communist forces rather than indirectly propping up socialist Britain and France (which lately, with de Gaulle gone, had reverted to the hopeless prewar pattern of continuous political crises).

Still, an impartial observer could well conclude in the autumn of 1947 that the American people and their representatives were displaying amazing maturity and boldness in restructuring their foreign policy. He could also add that in their enlightened self-interest they were striking the right balance between the extremes of bellicosity toward the Soviet Union and supine acquiescence in the face of Communist encroachment. This judgment, with qualifications to be developed below, still stands.

The Truman Doctrine, expounded by the President before a joint session of the Congress on March 12, was in its essence an undramatic and modest measure. Great Britain could no longer afford to help Greece fight internal subversion (assisted and made possible by Greece's Communist neighbors) nor Turkey to modernize and re-equip its army. If those two countries, and especially Greece, were to be saved, the United States had to step in. But it was thought (and perhaps correctly) that it was hopeless to explain this policy to the American people in those dispassionate terms, for it appeared to bypass the United Nations. (Those who argued thus had little objection to the *British* "bypassing" the U.N., but then the British were old imperialists.) The decision then had to be justified by a recourse to rhetoric: the civil war in Greece and Soviet pressure on Turkey to be presented as part of a world-wide struggle between light and darkness. Thus the President said that "it must be the policy of the United States to support free peoples who are resisting subjugation by armed minorities or by outside pressures."

This rhetoric may have been thought to be both good politics and harmless. But some of the more farseeing officials of the State Department, such as Kennan, were disturbed by it. And in retrospect it would have been vastly preferable had Truman been able to present the grim realities of the postwar world more frankly: to say that it was in the interest of the United States that Greece and Turkey not be Communist powers; and that while the Greek and Turkish governments did not conform to the concept of democracy as understood in Britain and the United States, they still were preferable for their own people and for the world to Communism as practiced by Stalin or (then) Tito. Perhaps much of the ensuing confusion could have been avoided as to which nation the United States should help and why. The United States government would not have had the impulse to rush in each time Communists threatened to take over a country. The American people would not have been led to expect credentials of impeccable democratic virtue from every government requesting aid from the United States. Is it excessive to expect such intelligence from one's leaders and such rationality from the public? The tragedy of American policy in Asia offers abundant proof of what happens if we acquiesce in less.

Some experts and commentators (Walter Lippmann, for one) felt at the time that the Truman Doctrine was unduly provocative, that the Russians would not take it lying down. Yet, as we have seen, if it disturbed the Soviets it disturbed them in the right way, i.e., in the sense of making them grope for an accommodation with the United States on another and major issue in the hopes of preventing further anti-Soviet moves.

Even the dramatic success of the first application of the Truman Doctrine was to be deceiving. Greece was saved from Communism, but the Americans (and to be sure the Greeks) must share the credit for this happy development with Marshals Stalin and Tito, for it happened only when those two potentates fell out among themselves. Tito was soon to close his frontiers to the Greek guerrillas; Stalin to decimate the Greek Communist leadership, charging them as tainted with Titoism and demanding that the rebels make cession of Greek Macedonia to Bulgaria one of their postulates. Thus the civil war in Greece came to an end.

The Marshall Plan represented a much greater and more fundamental change in American foreign policy. Where in human history does one find an example of economic help extended on so vast a scale? The closest approximation is the massive export of British capital in the nineteenth century, which built railways and factories throughout the world. This was done primarily for reasons of profit, and would by future generations be called economic imperialism and exploitation. But with the British investments went the ideas of free enterprise, and they in turn planted, as the advocates of free trade had hoped, seeds of parliamentarism and political reform.[1] Until around the turn of the century, when the teachings of Karl Marx gained currency, it was extreme nationalist and reactionary elements, whether in Russia or Argentina, who resented the foreign investor and accused him of exploitation.

The Marshall Plan was designed to restore economic good health to Europe, remedy the immediate shortages of essential commodities, provide the sinews of expanded industrial and agricultural production. It involved an act of self-denial on the part of the American taxpayer (just as it had, in a less obvious sense, on the part of the nineteenth-century British investor). But while the latter had expected immediate and direct returns, the American taxpayer learned that he would benefit only after a while and then only in the indirect form of increased international trade and expanded markets for American exports, etc. Since people are unwilling to make concrete sacrifices for the sake of distant and uncertain benefits, an action so intelligent and so necessary was justified by an appeal not only to generosity but also to fear: without help on so massive a scale, President Truman and Secretary Marshall argued, France and Italy might go under, i.e., fall to Communism. Nobody envisaged the possibility of the red flag over Buckingham Palace, but without help Britain would clearly be unable to meet most of her still considerable foreign obligations. The American voter, required to worry about Turkey and Greece, would be also called upon to assume additionally the burdens of Cyprus, Singapore, etc., etc., although in 1947–48 these perspectives were hidden.

One cannot help wondering how different the course of postwar history might have been if the mentality present behind the Marshall Plan had inspired the administration and lawmakers *in 1945*. At that time it was believed that the United Nations Relief and Rehabilitation Administration would be sufficient to meet immediate relief needs and that institutions such as the International Monetary Fund and the

[1] And of other reforms and movements certainly unintended by the Victorian manufacturers: Marxian socialism in Russia would never have started in the 1890s without massive Western investment in that country. It was a strike in the Thornton factory in St. Petersburg in 1895 which marked the emergence of Marxism on the Russian labor and revolutionary scene.

International Bank would provide long-range stimulants and safeguards for economic recovery and expansion of trade. (The U.S.S.R., of course, joined none of these.) Britain's special needs, it was thought, were provided for by the American loan in 1945 of about $4 billion; but the amount proved inadequate and the condition attached about early convertibility of sterling contributed to Britain's desperate financial crisis of 1947.[2] And it would have been unthinkable then to envisage the extension of comprehensive economic help to Germany as a whole or any part of it. Yet, if by a miracle a version of the European Recovery Program had been possible and adopted in 1945, the political benefits might well have been greatly superior to those which accrued under its later adoption. Notably, an earlier start on economic cooperation amongst the West European powers might have arrested the catastrophic decline in global influence of Britain and France, and strengthened the efforts to achieve a united Western Europe.

The policy planners who drafted the Marshall Plan (among whom Kennan was prominent) thought it desirable to extend the offer of aid to the U.S.S.R. and countries within her sphere. Again, it would be difficult to state precisely how much they really believed that Russia could or would come into the Plan, and if she did, what the chances were of the Congress sanctioning such handsome gifts for Stalin. There was considerable opposition already to a "give-away" program of any kind. It certainly occasioned surprise, not unmixed with apprehension, when the Soviet government accepted the British-French invitation for ministers of the three powers to meet and to examine the Plan as outlined by Secretary Marshall in his famous speech of June 5 at Harvard. Suspense must have heightened when Molotov alighted in Paris accompanied by a good number of economic experts.

That Stalin should have considered Soviet participation seriously appears hard to believe, but such was almost certainly the case, despite Truman's opinion expressed in his memoirs that the Soviets from the beginning wanted to sabotage the Plan. Molotov in his first speech at Paris on June 28, though not very gracious about the American offer ("The United States in its turn is interested to use its credit facilities to enlarge its foreign markets, especially in view of the approaching crisis"[3]) still considered it seriously and appeared to foreshadow Soviet

---

[2] In all fairness it must be remembered that the British had the right to ask for postponement of convertibility, an option which the Labour government most imprudently did not exercise.

[3] *Documents on International Affairs, 1947–1948* (London, 1952), p. 36.

participation. The Kremlin's mind was not made up. An official Soviet communiqué repeated Molotov's thesis, stressed that the Plan should be comprehensive, should include several other countries as well as the three meeting in Paris, and accepted the possibility of Germany benefiting from European cooperation.

All the more shock (and relief?) when, on July 2, Molotov broke off the negotiations and announced that the U.S.S.R. would not participate, since the machinery envisaged under the Plan would infringe on national sovereignty. He also took occasion to warn the British and French governments against participating in the Plan "which has as its goal not to unify nations of Europe in postwar reconstruction, but other things which have nothing in common with their real interests."

There must have been considerable enticement for the Russians to enter the Plan. They were clamoring for resumption of industrial reparations from West Germany. Here was a chance of something much better: the United States supplying vital aid and helping to speed up that industrial advance which was so high on the list of Stalin's priorities. Reasons which in 1945 dictated aloofness from the West were perhaps no longer so pressing; while the economic cooperation envisaged under the Plan could be regarded (and not only from the Soviet point of view) as intrusion upon national sovereignty and opened up the possibility of foreign interference in some of the most jealously guarded prerogatives of economic control and planning,[4] the U.S.S.R. could always agree in principle and then try to interpret those stipulations according to its own lights.

Yet the Plan evidently was a gamble which Stalin could not take. The Soviet system could not afford disclosure of information about its economy, the standard of living of its people, or production norms. For one thing, except when it came to armaments and heavy industry, the government itself had no reliable data. As Khrushchev made clear after Stalin's death, figures relating to agricultural production were systematically falsified at the central as well as local levels, to such a degree that what might be described as statistical anarchy reigned, with neither the Central Committee nor the government really knowing the true state of affairs. But even taking all this into account, what has been revealed was a picture of weakness and misery that could only

---

[4] A typical Economic Cooperation Agreement required of the recipient of aid "to stabilize its currency, establish or maintain a valid rate of exchange, balance its governmental budget as soon as practicable." And the agreement envisaged certain reciprocal benefits for the United States.

encourage an enemy and shock the most inveterate fellow traveler. Khruschev alleged later that the government exported grain while conditions close to starvation prevailed in some areas, that in 1953 agricultural production in absolute as well as average terms was below that of 1913.

The broader problem of the morale of the Soviet citizen and the effect on him of any kind of relationship with the West was equally insuperable. Here was the regime instilling through plays, through speeches, through a continuous din of propaganda the duty to be vigilant, to be hostile to the bourgeois world. At the same time, news would be spread of American billions pouring in to bolster the economy and raise the standard of living. And what of the effect on the satellites? There was one thing which Stalin prized above his country's economic strength, and that was his own political power, and the Plan which promised to advance some of his most cherished goals had to be rejected.[5]

A month or two afterward, Soviet suspicion about the real purpose of the Marshall Plan hardened into conviction. The real goals of the Plan, the Russians argued at the founding meeting of the Cominform in September, 1947, had little to do with economic rehabilitation, not even with stopping the spread of Communism in the West; the real aim was an aggressive one: to lay down the economic base for political and military pressures against Eastern Europe. The *rhetoric* of the later Dulles period of American foreign policy was thus ascribed to the Truman-Marshall-Acheson administration. Stalin did not anticipate war. But the strategy with which he credited the American policy makers was a highly flattering one, such in fact as he himself might have adopted were he in their place. Once a powerful Western bloc was formed, what would prevent it from instigating and helping uprisings in Bulgaria, say, or the Soviet zone of Germany? Restored prosperity in Western Europe would in any case act as a magnet on the population of the satellites. What would then have to be the Soviet response: to attack the West and thus to challenge America as well?

The danger was felt to be real but not imminent. There were still Congressional debates ahead, separate agreements, the setting up of the intricate aid machinery. The restoration of the West European economy would at best take years. The Western zones of Germany, the key to

[5] Poland was also tempted by the Marshall Plan but rejected the offer under strong Soviet pressure. Czechoslovakia accepted, whereupon the Czech leaders were summoned to Moscow and ordered to reverse their decision.

the Americans' Machiavellian plans, had a long way to go: industrial production there was at about one-third of the 1938 level. And it would be a long time, if ever, before the French would agree to German rearmament. Soviet demobilization continued throughout 1947 and 1948, and at the end of that year Soviet armed forces were down to about 2.9 million, hardly an excessive figure in view of Russia's garrisons from Port Arthur to Berlin.

But political urgency was there: the satellites had to be secured; what remained of anti-Communist forces had to be liquidated and their Communist parties had to be purged of those whom the heady sense of power made forget that they were just Soviet satraps. The Communist parties of the West, of France and Italy, had to be reoriented: their primary task was no longer to obtain power through legal means but to disrupt the economy of their countries. Since they controlled most organized labor in their countries, they could be counted upon to sabotage the Marshall Plan. This last was a particularly bitter pill: the French and Italian Communist leaders had begun to fancy themselves being able to accede to power by respectable means. Now they were to embark on a course of action bound to end such expectations. At the same time, they were not given license to work for a seizure of power, for such behavior, it was thought in Moscow, was bound to bring direct American intervention. Years later the concepts of "measured response" and "calculated risk" were to become popular in the Pentagon, but there was little that those social-scientist military advisers could teach Stalin.

To set up an institutional framework for the new policies, the U.S.S.R. improvised the Cominform—an organization uniting the ruling Communist parties of Eastern Europe plus the two great Communist parties of the West.[6] On the surface, the Cominform was not a continuation of the Comintern, dissolved in 1943, but a bureau for exchange of information among the leading parties. But what Moscow really hoped its function would be it is difficult to gauge. The machinery for coordination of European Communism was already within the Central Committee of the Soviet Party. But, it was hoped, the Cominform would provide a convenient shield against "slanders" that decisions as to

[6] The German Party in the Soviet zone was not represented, presumably because East Germany was still thought a negotiable asset for some future bargain over Germany as a whole. Albania was not there because at the time this tiny country was slated for absorption by Tito's Yugoslavia. The Greek, Finnish, et cetera, parties were also not represented at the founding meeting in Poland, in each case the peculiar situation of the given country making their absence desirable.

Communist policies were made in one place by one party and one man. The tasks of disciplining a Tito, of coping with French and Italian grumbles, would be easier and more decorous.

In fact, the short, inglorious history of the Cominform proved the opposite to be the case. That history is reminiscent of nothing so much as the history of those treaty organizations spawned during Dulles' tenure of office, those SEATOS, CENTOS, and Baghdad Pacts which by their very act of creation accentuated the danger they were supposed to combat, and which eventually subsided into ineffectual paper charts and periodic meetings with little or no effect. Within a year of the Cominform's creation it attempted its only significant action: the expulsion of Tito and his associates from the world Communist movement. It then vegetated for a while in Bucharest with its ridiculously named and fantastically dull journal: *For a Lasting Peace, For a People's Democracy*. With Stalin's death, the moribund organization became a source of embarrassment, equivalent to a deranged relative confined in an attic and increasingly ignored by the rest of the family. Finally, to consummate a reconciliation between Tito and the Russians, the Cominform was dissolved. The history is a useful reminder of how cunning men like Stalin are nonetheless capable of making errors at once serious and ridiculous.

The founding meeting had primarily an educational purpose. The two principal Soviet delegates—Zhdanov and Malenkov—were both rivals for succession. The first delivered an appraisal of the world situation, nothing new to those assembled; but just as a performance by a live orchestra may leave a more lasting impression than a recorded one, so this relentless exposition of Soviet policy themes was believed more effective than written communications and private meetings. The Marshall Plan had to be defeated by any and every means. The Soviet Union, said Zhdanov, did not object to the use of foreign credits (this ignored the fact known to all present that much of the Marshall Plan was in forms of grant-in-aid and supplies), but it objected to the "extortionate terms" on which they were to be granted! The Marshall Plan violated the equality of nations. (Compare proposed terms of agreements between the United States and recipient countries with those treaties of mutual aid completed between the U.S.S.R. and the people's democracies! Even the most slavish in the audience could not but reflect how through such treaties Russia was imposing unequal terms of trade, exploiting their countries through "joint stock companies," and robbing its "fraternal allies" in innumerable other ways. The assembled leaders were thus brusquely taught that they were not only to acquiesce in but to praise Soviet exactions.)

An especially brutal lesson was dealt to the French and Italians. To remove any illusions born of the wartime resistance that patriotism and Communism might be combined, they had to confess to grave errors of the recent past: they, the leading element in the resistance, it was said, could have conquered power, but after the liberation sheepishly laid down their arms! This was almost more than they could bear: the obvious truth was that huge Anglo-American armies were then in their countries, and their actions in 1944–45 had been in line with stern Soviet injunctions against selfish adventurism which might undermine Western-Soviet amity! Jacques Duclos, the French Communist leader, tells us that he left the room during one of these attacks upon his party's record and cried in impotent rage. To make this censure more poignant, the main task of chastising the Westerners was assigned to the Yugoslavs, who went at it with special gusto.

But a severe lesson was also in store for the ruling Communist parties. Malenkov detailed measures which the Soviets were adopting to combat "idealistic" and "cosmopolitan" ideas in the arts and science. The moral was unmistakable: the parties had to follow the Soviet model, to extol everything Russian. The Czechs and Poles, because they had been tempted by the Marshall Plan, had to confess special gratitude to the Fatherland of Socialism: only because of Soviet support was Czechoslovakia able to expel the Sudeten Germans; it was only fraternal Soviet help, Poland's Gomulka himself had to say, that guaranteed the country's western frontiers.

In the West, the lesson of the Cominform meeting was misread as a new Russian political and ideological offensive. And thus the struggle was joined. The breach was not absolute, for Russia could not afford it and the United States did not want it. Foreign ministers still met, the United Nations still functioned, albeit in an atmosphere of increasing futility. On some minor issues collaboration between the West and East continued. "We are still allies," said Stalin paradoxically to the British and American ambassadors at the time of the Berlin blockade. But each country went its own way in lack of comprehension of the other's policy. The interallied machinery for governing Germany now had definitely broken down. And in another area, the collapse of any real communication between the two superpowers had fateful results, unwished for by either.

It was not in the Soviet interest, and indications are that Stalin realized it, that *all* of China should come under Communist rule. If the wartime pattern of the summit conferences and secret diplomacy had persisted after the war, it is at least possible that Soviet diplomats might have raised the solution of having two *mainland* Chinas. Throughout 1947 certainly and 1948 probably, Stalin could still have imposed a compromise settlement on the Chinese Communists: one detects a certain nervousness about that possibility in their pronouncements throughout this period. But at the crucial time, not only American but also Soviet preoccupations were with Europe. The decisive turn of events in China took place during the Berlin blockade, June, 1948–May, 1949. When it was lifted, the issue in the Far East was decided. And during the crucial period, Stalin's political intelligence was clouded by bouts of unreasonable suspicion: Tito was showing dangerous independence. Other Communist officials in minor Communist countries were being unmasked as "nationalists." Was this all connected with the master plan concocted by the American imperialists—with the Marshall Plan and with the international Zionist conspiracy, ramifications of which reached into the Soviet Union itself? When these nightmares temporarily subsided, Stalin was faced with another Communist ruler —this time of a country comprising one-fourth of mankind.

In the United States, the launching of the Marshall Plan absorbed much of the public's attention throughout 1947 and 1948. One could see this typically American generation of public pressures in favor of a specific foreign policy, the pressures in turn translating themselves into civic organizations aroused to protect the Plan from the ravages of skeptical and penny-pinching congressmen. Thus the Committee for the Marshall Plan was formed, headed by and including many elder statesmen (its national chairman was Henry Stimson), "enlightened businessmen," and labor leaders with an international outlook. Soon vast resources for publicity and education—what in the U.S.S.R. would be called agitation and propaganda—were marshaled behind the effort. Congressmen were subjected to a barrage of letters and petitions. A registered lobby was set up in Washington. This was an impressive example of how an idea conceived by a few enlightened minds, yet clashing with the long-standing tradition and whole temper of American politics, could gain—through entirely democratic processes and public debate—a decisive hold on the majority of citizens. One was reminded of a similar wave of propaganda (to use this realistic term, although it offends the American ear) sweeping the United States in 1940 in favor of helping Britain and laying the groundwork for the subsequent Lend-

Lease legislation. Public conviction turned into public enthusiasm, and like every great emotion in American political history, the pressure toward enactment of this beneficent and complicated legislation took on at times the appearance of a revivalist meeting or a football rally.[7]

One could not but applaud the mood and its results. But some of the campaign was reminiscent of those which in the past had brought about Prohibition, the Neutrality Acts, and excessive hope in the United Nations. There are unquestionably dangers in arousing quasi-religious emotions, even on behalf of a good cause, and of regarding all rational dissent from a currently popular policy as immoral or foolish. And just as this Dr. Jekyll belief in curing the evils of the world through economic help grew and prospered, soon the Mr. Hyde of the American political personality was to appear—the irrational conviction that treason permeated the Establishment.

On March 1, 1948, the Plan received the expected public support from Senator Vandenberg, who now as much as the Secretary of State was responsible for the general direction of American policy: "This act may well become a welcome beacon in the world's dark night, but if a beacon is to be lighted at all it had better be lighted before it is too late. . . . This legislation . . . seeks peace and stability for free men in a free world." [8] All in all it was an excellent speech. But the Republican leader in his zeal put extravagant hopes in the measure: "It can be the turning point of history for one hundred years to come. If it fails, we will have done our final best." Perhaps this was necessary to "sell" the measure. But no economic measure in itself could effect such a decisive turn in world history.

The Plan became law on April 3, 1948. The American gift for improvisation soon conjured up a whole new organization, the Economic Cooperation Administration, to implement it. By not being subordinated to the State or Treasury Departments, the ECA was supposed to be more than just an extension of the American government; rather, it was seen as an agency international in spirit as well as function. Nonetheless —and even though not a general but an automobile executive, Paul Hoffman, was named as Administrator—the Kremlin was not fooled. Calls went off to the European proletariat to resist. Yet even the initial phase of the Marshall Plan was so successful (not the least propaganda-

[7] The author remembers attending an actual rally on behalf of the Plan while a student at Harvard. It was preceded by a march led by the Harvard Band.
[8] Harry Bayard Price, *The Marshall Plan and Its Meaning* (Ithaca, N.Y., 1953), p. 63.

wise) that it embarrassed Russia. In January, 1949, with great fanfare, the U.S.S.R. and her satellites set up an economic cooperation plan of their own, and the Council of Mutual Economic Assistance (Comecon) was located in Moscow. As a current but realistic witticism had it, the Soviet idea of mutual assistance was to sell Poland machinery for digging coal at an inflated price while buying Polish coal at prices below those of the world market. But with Stalin's death, expanding economic aid, and not only to "socialist countries," was to become a feature of Soviet policy as well. The Soviet taxpayer contemplating his unspeakable roads and bad living conditions would soon be comforted by the thought that his "selfless help," as the official Soviet phrase has it, enabled Afghanistan to construct highways and Sukarno's Indonesia to build luxury hotels. In the early sixties there were reports of riots in some Soviet ports when stevedores balked at loading foodstuffs for Cuba in view of shortages in Russia. But fashion is a strong force even in politics.

Given the Soviet Union's interpretation of the Marshall Plan, it was imperative, in the eyes of its leaders, to strengthen their hold over the East European sphere. In February, 1948, Czechoslovakia was secured when its government, which had previously been a genuine multi-party coalition led by Communists, became Communist-dominated and a coalition only in name.

Czechoslovakia had been virtually conceded to the Soviet sphere in 1946, when the Communists emerged as the most popular party in free elections: their leader, Clement Gottwald, became premier; Communists headed the strategic ministries, including that of the Interior. There was some hope that this halfway house between the East and the West might be allowed to continue. The popularity of the Communists had somewhat waned, and it appeared probable that another free election, scheduled for May, 1948, would bring them defeat and deprive them of the leadership of the government. To deal with this contingency, the Czech Minister of the Interior began to purge the police force of non-Communists. This in turn led to a revolt within the ranks of the Socialist party, and in February, twelve non-Communist ministers resigned from the government, hoping to bring an election before they could be "fixed" by the Communist police. The Communist-led trade unions and the workers' militia then organized country-wide manifestations and strikes to force President Beneš' hand. He could still counter them with the army and dissolve the parliament. But Soviet pressure was applied by a special emissary, Valerian Zorin. There was no countervailing action from the West. And for the second time in his life, Beneš, who had staked his policy on the belief that the U.S.S.R. would be content with a friendly but non-Communist Czechoslovakia, had to consign his country to satellite status. Gottwald was entrusted with the formation of the new government and soon afterward replaced the heartbroken, ailing president.

It is quite possible that a *strong* and prompt reaction by the West could have tilted the scales in favor of Czechoslovakia preserving her limited sovereignty. Britain, the United States, and France condemned the action in a joint declaration on February 26, but there was none of the hue and cry and the fortuitous combination of circumstances which had helped save Iran in 1946. The Security Council was allowed to proceed sluggishly, the decisive vote on whether to investigate the Prague coup not being taken until May 24, when, the matter declared to concern a substantive rather than a procedural point, it was of course vetoed by the U.S.S.R. This sluggishness reflected, it is fair to say, the conviction in the West that nothing could be done, that even undue haggling over Czechoslovakia risked a Soviet armed move.

How the Soviets would have reacted if Beneš held out and if the West had been more concerned must remain conjectural. Czechoslovakia was important to the Soviets and they could not have acquiesced in the ejection of the Communist ministers as easily as they did in the case of Finland. But there were then no Soviet soldiers in Czechoslovakia, the armed forces of the U.S.S.R. having been severely reduced (something which of course was not realized in the West). A few months later, the Yugoslav defection posed a much more basic challenge to the U.S.S.R. and to Stalin personally, and there the Russians could be *sure* that the West would not intervene—yet the Soviets did not move on Yugoslavia even in their ultrasuspicious mood of 1948. In brief, it is difficult to resist the conclusion that Czechoslovakia could have been saved by calling the Russian bluff. A few months later, with Stalin discovering real or fictitious Titoists in every Communist country, the Soviets themselves might well have agreed that a deferential non-Communist regime might be less trouble.

For in the summer of 1948, an event occurred which for once took by surprise not only the capitalist but the Communist world (except for the leaders of the two countries concerned).[9] Yugoslavia challenged the Soviet Union. Yugoslavs who all their adult life had been professional

---

[9] Other parties had been informed by the Russians since March but had no reason to believe that the Yugoslavs would not yield.

agents and fanatical devotees of Stalin defied the man and the system for whom they had been ready to suffer imprisonment and death a few years before. At once one of the main principles underlying the Soviet Union's shrewd and tortuous foreign policy was revealed as being as visionary as that of the One World proponents in the West: Communist expansion was not necessarily in Russia's interest; the day would come when *Communist* encirclement would be more dangerous to the U.S.S.R. than capitalist encirclement had ever been. Simultaneously, the main premise of American policy since 1944 was seen as unrealistically timid: the Soviet Union, when her expansion was blocked, did not immediately send her armies sweeping across frontiers. The Communist chieftain of a primitive Balkan country with a population of only 16 million said "no" to Stalin, chased out Soviet minions, imprisoned Soviet partisans, and dared the Soviet bloc to do its worst.

Such in twenty years' perspective is the lesson and importance of the Soviet-Yugoslav break. In 1948, this lesson was, of course, not seen clearly. Tito and his people clung for some time to the hope that the "geniuslike leader of progressive mankind" simply did not understand them, that Stalin was misled by libel about them, that once he understood what devoted Communists they were, all would be well again. Stalin hoped that the mere announcement of his wrath and the Cominform's anathema would make the walls of Titoism crumble. And in the West, dark suspicions clouded the interpretation of the momentous event. Was it perhaps a "put-up job"? An American diplomat was asked by newspapermen what he thought of the news: Were the Communists simulating a fight so that Yugoslavia would get American credits and supplies and become a conduit for them for the whole Communist bloc? "You've got something there," replied the perceptive official, thus anticipating those who saw no signs of dissension between China and Russia until 1963–64.

More sophisticated analysts in the West were hesitant to dismiss Soviet charges that Tito was being excommunicated for ideological reasons. Perhaps he *was* displaying left-wing deviation by trying to industrialize too fast; or following in the footsteps of right-wing deviators by not collectivising agriculture fast enough. But even such sophisticates could not swallow the charge that the Yugoslav party was not following Communism's democratic precepts, with Tito and a few associates running the party and the state. The charge of "nationalism" was also hard to swallow: its basis was Tito's (not very great) reluctance to pay huge salaries, by Yugoslav standards, to Soviet officers whose main task was to subvert the Yugoslav army, and Soviet economic or other "experts" who in addition to spying were there to devise the most efficient procedures for exploiting the country.

The Yugoslav leaders had been in fact among the most fanatically Communist, the most loyally pro-Soviet of any parallel group in Eastern Europe. Even during the war, Tito had chafed at the non-ideological nationalist role which the Kremlin as well as circumstances dictated. The war was not yet over when he threatened to disrupt Soviet strategy in Eastern Europe by provoking a confrontation with the West over Trieste. At that time, Yugoslavs simply could not understand why the all-powerful Soviet Union could not coerce Britain and the United States to hand over this port to their fellow Communists. In August, 1946, at a tense moment in Soviet-American relations, Yugoslav fighters shot down two unarmed U.S. transport planes for allegedly straying over Yugoslav (i.e., "friendly") territory. Such anti-capitalist zeal was not appreciated in Moscow; by the same token, how could the very same people become, within two years, "agents of the Wall Street"?

For all its picturesque and amusing details, the crisis was serious and epoch-making. Communist leaders who could be counted on as the most docile and self-sacrificing servants of the Soviet Union while fighting for power, once in office were bound to develop viewpoints and interests that brought them into conflict with the Kremlin. With the end of the war, the Yugoslav Communists developed a healthy imperialism of their own. Visions of a United Balkans under Tito's leadership tantalized the Yugoslav dictator, and they were for a time encouraged by Moscow. Yugoslavia was going to "swallow" Albania, as Stalin once put it. Then were to come larger tidbits: Bulgaria, whose Communists viewed the prospect with little enthusiasm; then a generous slice of Greece, once the Communists won there.

In January, 1948, Stalin changed his mind and vetoed the Balkan Union. At the same time, the leaders of Yugoslavia realized that a Soviet-sponsored plot was taking shape, and that Tito and his closest associates were scheduled for that process of gradual liquidation which they themselves had so often witnessed or helped arrange. Just as for years their courage and the (then unconscious) drive for power made them spurn danger as well as any precepts of moderation, so now they were not discouraged by overwhelming odds against them. It was not as yet nationalism: it was a realization that with power they would be surrendering their lives. But then, in reviewing recent Soviet behavior, they began to see how contemptuously Stalin had treated them, how little their devotion and their heroism had mattered. And suddenly Tito, Djilas, and the others who had taken up arms—when not their own country but the Soviet Union was invaded—felt pride in their double heritage as both Slavs and Communists, and refused to subordinate one to the other.

In taking up their stance, the Yugoslavs could not and did not count on help from the West. In fact, throughout 1948 and 1949, they continued to revile Britain and the United States in terms no less harsh than those employed by their Soviet antagonists. Had Soviet troops poured across the Hungarian and Bulgarian borders, it is unlikely that the West would have been much concerned. Britain and the United States did not intervene to preserve what remained of Czech democracy; they would hardly intervene on behalf of a Communist dictator who had liquidated opposition more cruelly, persecuted the Catholic Church more thoroughly than any other satellite regime.

What, then, restrained Stalin? Megalomania and prudence. Megalomania persuaded Stalin that Tito and his miserable partisans would be cast at his feet in chains by their frightened associates. "I shall shake my little finger and there will be no Tito," he is alleged to have said, and though this may not be a literal quotation, that is how he felt. Prudence dictated that Soviet armed intervention be deferred, at least until the situation was ripe. What if the aroused country were to hold out for weeks or months? There might be armed uprisings elsewhere. Could Soviet forces, now less than 3 million, repress them quickly before the West was drawn out of its lassitude and awe of the non-existent Soviet armies?

Thus nicely balanced between hope and fear, the Soviets did nothing to put down the increasingly insolent rebel. Ominous threats and frontier "incidents" did not unnerve the people for whom conspiracy and guerrilla war had been a normal way of life. Dissident pro-Soviet elements were put down with a skill which showed that the Yugoslav secret police was an apt pupil. And to the non-Communist population, their oppressors now became the defenders of national independence, very much as Russians rallied behind their regime from 1942 on.

In other Communist countries, the pace of Communist "reforms" had to be speeded up. Potential Titos were tracked down, demoted, tried, and often executed. In none of the other satellites was there in fact that combination of factors which had enabled Yugoslavia to launch her defiance, but the Soviets were not taking chances. And, again, in their zeal to curb minor or nonexistent opposition—to secure the Communist party of Hungary or the already frantically loyal one of Bulgaria against some horrendous Titoist or Zionist plot—the Russians were neglectful of the fact that by their inactivity they were letting the greatest jinni of all out of the bottle. When all the Rajks and Kostovs had been executed, the Gomulkas and Kadovs put in jail, when all the Communist countries were pervaded by terror and prostrate before the Soviet Union, there were Mao and the Chinese Communists: dwarfing all the satellites, inaccessible to the methods of control the Soviets employed so effectively and so needlessly in Eastern Europe.

One is struck by a certain symmetry in the behavior of the two superpowers in the late 1940s and early '50s: the search for internal subversion as it reflects and explains the vicissitudes of foreign policy became a strong feature of the American political scene in 1948–49. To be sure, McCarthy himself did not enter the lists until 1950, but eschewing pedantry, let us classify the whole phenomenon as McCarthyism. It is a huge and absurd exaggeration to equate McCarthyism with the political persecutions and purges in totalitarian countries, but they did share one important characteristic: the refusal to attribute errors in policy, especially foreign policy, to honest miscalculation, stupidity, or historical circumstances. Rather, McCarthyism required that errors be traced to one master cause—disloyalty, in many cases taking the form of outright treason. Underlying this betrayal, it was argued, was the sin of pride, which made the policy-makers forsake the will of the majority of the people in favor of their own peculiar material or ideological interests. This motif establishes the affinity of McCarthyism not only to the purge trials in the U.S.S.R. in the 1930s and similar phenomena in Eastern Europe between 1948 and 1953, but also to a number of precedents in American political history. One recalls the hearings before the Nye Committee, searching for the culprit who had enticed the American people out of their happy state of innocence and isolation and thrust them into a world war—the culprit then identified as munitions makers and the Eastern financial establishment, with its economic and ideological ties to Great Britain. One may also find a parallel in the present, when to a large segment of the American intellectual community the tragedy of Vietnam has its source not in a series of errors but in *sin,* and to the most frenzied among the New

Left it is within the government that traitors to the American ideal are to be found.

The great postwar disillusionment about the Soviet Union was bound to be reflected in a campaign against domestic Communism. But in 1948 as now, the Communist Party of the United States represented a negligible danger to the institutions of this country. Its ephemeral importance after the war sprang from its power, quite disproportionate to its tiny membership, in certain important labor unions, a tribute to the ability of a small, organized, and disciplined minority to secure commanding positions in large organizations whose membership is in the main apolitical. But this situation soon corrected itself, no so much on account of any legislation, but simply because of the growing maturity and experience of the American labor movement. The inroads of Communism on the American campus, viewed with such horror by the American Legion and Congressional committees, again, while not inconsequential, were hardly dangerous. Viewing from today's perspective the effect of Communism on the students whom it enticed, one may well conclude that it was a tranquilizing one, for it took disturbed and passionate youth and disciplined their emotions by channeling them into the worship of an exacting cult, Marxism, and a distant divinity, Stalin's Russia. The goals of Communism, while unreasonable, were rational—i.e., power: the university was not to be destroyed, any more than General Motors, say, for both were eventually to be taken over and used.

From the psychological point of view, the preoccupation with domestic Communism had a by and large crippling effect on American foreign policy. It diverted the public mind from the important questions to relatively trivial ones, and there was little time and less energy to consider what concrete steps could be taken to solve the admittedly difficult issues of international affairs.

The case of Alger Hiss, which broke in August, 1948, heralded and set in motion much of the development described above. The judicial and factual history of the case need not concern us, for it has been told many times and from many points of view. A veritable flood of similar revelations, some to be substantiated and some not, about Communists and Communist agents (the two categories in the public mind became identical, though in theory and sometimes in fact they are not) in high positions in the Roosevelt Administration provided a seemingly convincing explanation of the United States' diplomatic defeats during and after the war. By the same token, much of what now would be called the "liberal establishment" took an opposite but equally unrealistic attitude: such was the character of the accused on the one hand and the accuser on the other, so unscrupulous was the use of the revelations for political purposes, that the charges were deemed prima facie false and inconceivable; spies were supposed to be people who wore ill-fitting clothes and spoke with accents or, contrariwise, voluptuous females—anyway not graduates of the Columbia or Harvard Law School. Previous stories of Soviet atomic espionage in Canada and the United States had been received with only a mild shock, the American public being both reluctant to accept the facts of international life and entirely believing the myth of the infallibility of the FBI. And now there were lurid stories of Presidential assistants, high State and Treasury Department officials recruited into the Soviet spy network in the 1930s and sitting in on decisions of the greatest importance during the war.

In the Hiss case, the most important question from the point of view of the *public interest* would have been whether the accused was ever in a position (a) to betray information of value to the Soviet Union, or (b) to influence American policies for its benefit. Yet this question was barely asked. The State Department documents which Hiss, according to his accuser Whittaker Chambers, transmitted to him in the thirties (the notorious "Pumpkin Papers") were of slight value. American foreign policy at the time was an open book, and it appears extravagant for the U.S.S.R. to have tried to penetrate it by espionage rather than by reading *The New York Times*! During the war, information as to viewpoints and personalities within the government would have been of great value to the Russians, but it is absurd to ascribe major or even significant shares of the responsibility for the mistakes of Teheran, Yalta, etc., to espionage. If half the State Department had been in the pay of the U.S.S.R., this still would not have warped American foreign policy as much as did Roosevelt's conviction that he could "domesticate" Stalin, or as the unrealistic suspicions about the British shared in varying degrees by the President himself, Secretary Hull, and leading senators. The pro-Chinese Communist bias of some American officials both in China and in Washington again reflects more on their political intelligence than on their loyalty. It was after all General Hurley, a rock-ribbed Republican, who at one time declared that Mao's people were no more Communist than Oklahoma Republicans, and who in resigning as special envoy to China blamed not only Communist but unspecified "imperialist" influences within the State Department for the turn of events there.[10]

Apart from this formidable barrier to a dispassionate assessment of the nation's needs and interests, the task of statemanship became complicated in 1948 through the quadrennial bacchanalia of American politics, i.e., Presidential elections. In normal times (if such exist), an election is not only a time of decision, but also a nationwide spectacle, with profuse and flowery oratory, parades, dramatic circuits through the country by the candidates, a national holiday. *Ostensibly* foreign-policy issues play a subordinate role in most elections, but deep if not perhaps fully conscious anxiety about the world at war undoubtedly contributed to the tradition-breaking third term in 1940, and the war itself made Roosevelt's defeat in 1944 virtually unthinkable.

The dramatic finish of the 1948 campaign, when Truman and his party confounded the Republicans' confidant expectations as well as the public-opinion polls, is usually and probably correctly credited to the President's skillful exploitation of domestic issues and his attacks at the record of the Republican-dominated Eightieth Congress. Divisions over foreign policy, it is held, were insignificant in deciding the election. The Republican candidate, Thomas Dewey, belonged to the "internationalist wing" of the Republican Party, and the only breach in bipartisan foreign policy was—and it was not very definite at that—the Republicans' promises of more vigorous aid to China. But China had not as yet been "lost," and the issue lacked that dramatic intensity which alone makes a foreign-policy dispute of importance in an election. While foreign policy was important for Wallace's Progressive party, it did abysmally badly in the election and soon afterward virtually disintegrated.

United States–Soviet relations and the broader problem of Communism were then not major factors in deciding the outcome. By the same token, it is quite clear that the Soviets appraised Presidential elections at this conjunction of affairs as a period of weakness for U.S. foreign policy, and an opportunity for theirs. This was an entirely logical conclusion, from their point of view, and justified by the subsequent turn of affairs. The United States' over-all strategy and attitude toward world politics was still in transition, which was taking place

---

[10] Of all the officials whose names were alleged as having been involved with the Soviet espionage network, only one had an important policy position during the war. This was Dr. Harry Dexter White, Assistant Secretary of the Treasury.

with that slowness so characteristic of democracies in peacetime. The major outlines of the new policies were, the Soviets thought, already clear in the Truman Doctrine and the Marshall Plan, but what they believed was the most vital and dangerous part of the American scheme, the creation of a West German state and its remilitarization, had not yet been achieved, and perhaps it could be frustrated or delayed.

Soviet propensity to think in such terms was undoubtedly increased by the well-meant but unfortunate initiative of American diplomacy. To counter any *false* impressions and deductions the Soviets might draw from the election, Ambassador Smith made a confidential *démarche* with Molotov on May 4. The Russians were told not to believe any stories that American foreign policy was paralyzed and irresolute in an election year; the course was set firmly and with the backing of both major parties, and the country would not be deflected from it, whatever might be said during the campaign. Nor should the Russians believe that an economic crisis would soon be upon the United States and that it would drastically affect American policy (presumably in the direction of isolationism). At the same time that Ambassador Smith reiterated the friendly sentiments of his government toward the U.S.S.R., he implied its abiding hope that once the Communists stopped their nasty habit of seizing countries by Communist minorities and establishing regimes there "subservient to foreign interest," all could be well between the two powers.[11]

The effect produced on the Russians by such reassurances bore a similarity to the attitude epitomized in a famous East European Jewish story: Two business rivals meet at a railway station, and one after suspicious probing asks point blank where the other is going. Upon being told that the destination is Pinsk, he explodes: "You thief, you swindler, you *are* going to Pinsk, but you are telling me that so I should think you are going to Berdichev!"

Despite the confidential nature of the *démarche,* the Soviet government released its text together with Molotov's sententious rebuttal of its main points. This they knew well would be very embarrassing to the State Department. West Europeans would again start wondering whether the United States was really in earnest about erecting defenses against Communism or whether it would revert to secret diplomacy à la Teheran and Yalta and make deals with the U.S.S.R. Secretary Marshall was forced to some embarrassed explanations.

The truth was that American foreign policy *was* being inhibited by

11 *Documents on International Affairs, 1947–1948,* pp. 153–55.

the elections. It was widely held that the Progressive vote would cut into traditional Democratic majorities in some strategic states and thus be decisive in securing Truman's defeat, even if the expected pro-Republican swing should by some miracle not materialize. Democratic party strategists were thus ready with the usual advice not to "rock the boat," to regain the vote of those who might otherwise support Wallace's pro-Soviet platform. Whether it was because of such advice or on his own, Truman publicly characterized "Uncle Joe" as a man essentially of good will but thwarted by the Politburo, of which he was a prisoner. And on the eve of the election, it was proposed to refute Wallace's charges that Truman had betrayed Roosevelt's heritage of American-Soviet friendship by the dramatic gesture of sending Chief Justice Vinson as Presidential envoy to Stalin. The project was abandoned only because Secretary Marshall threatened to resign.

The incident is no mere humorous footnote to history. In fact, it reveals certain tragic misunderstandings at the root of America's foreign failures. Why should the *Chief Justice* go on the mission? Truman's explanation is of great psychological interest: "If we could only get Stalin to unburden himself to someone on our side he could trust, I thought we could get somewhere." [12] Why, might a foreigner wonder, should Stalin trust Justice Vinson, a man completely unknown to him, of no experience and background in foreign affairs? Well, in the American secular, legalistic system, the judiciary comes closest to what is in other societies the Established Church, and the Chief Justice serves as a symbol of judiciousness, probity, and independence from political considerations. But it did not occur to Truman, who was a man straightforward enough to think of the mission as not *merely* an electoral gimmick, that there was no reason in the world for Stalin or anybody else abroad to view the Chief Justice in that light and to discuss politics with him, let alone unburden himself.

The same incapacity to understand was revealed in Wallace's critique and candidacy. Wallace began his critique with a sensible point—that channels of communication between the two governments should not be closed—but gradually, by the inner impetus of his passionate personality, he was swept into an emotional indictment of the moral iniquities inherent in American policies, primarily foreign but also domestic. To himself and outwardly, Wallace undoubtedly rationalized this indictment of his country on the grounds that he was denouncing *both* superpowers for not collaborating to secure peace. Thus in an open letter to Stalin of

[12] Truman, *op. cit.,* II, 215.

May 11, 1948, Wallace characterized recent notes of Ambassador Smith and Molotov as being equally self-righteous, pleaded that "neither the United States nor the Union of Soviet Socialist Republics should interfere in the internal affairs of other nations," or use economic pressure, espionage, etc., to influence policies of other countries. Apart from the lack of a sense of proportion and realism that such sentiments betray, the most fatuous delusion was the notion that in writing to Stalin one was communicating with the Russian people, that the despot could be convinced by "fairness" and assurances of good intentions of the other side, and that the peoples of the U.S.S.R. could somehow understand and respond to the plea of an American politician. And inevitably, since Wallace and his partisans could not affect the behavior of Stalin and the Russians, their zeal and moral fervor turned increasingly against their own government.[13]

Toward the end of the campaign, the Progressive party was largely captured by Communists and fellow travelers, as Wallace himself was to acknowledge some years later. This could not have been viewed with pleasure in Moscow, where the internal affairs of American Communism were treated with contempt and where the chief value of the Progressive candidacy lay in the possibility of deflecting American foreign policy from a "hard" course. That Wallace might help to elect Dewey was probably felt in the Kremlin to be of little consequence. If the Republicans had none of the illusions about the U.S.S.R. which still lingered among some Democrats, they were by the same token more skeptical about huge aid to and involvement in *Europe*. In the case of a Republican victory, the Taft wing of the party would undoubtedly make its influence felt in that direction. By the same token, they were likely to become more involved on behalf of Chiang Kai-shek, and again from Moscow's point of view this would have been desirable both as a distraction from Europe and because there was neither wish for nor yet expectation of *complete* victory by the Chinese Communists.

We may now indulge in a little historical fantasy. In view of these issues, it would perhaps have been better if Dewey had been elected in 1948 and Stevenson in 1952, reversing the Republican and Democratic victories. Dulles would then have been Secretary of State at a time when his moralistic rigidity would not have been largely obsolete as it was to be after 1953, and when it would have been restrained by a more active

[13] Stalin offered a polite and approving answer to the former Vice-President, though he could not refrain from pointing out that "neither can it be said that some of the formulations and comments in the Open Letter are not in need of improvement." *Documents on International Affairs, 1947–1948*, p. 164.

and perceptive President. Stevenson would in turn have brought to foreign policy a mind more alert to the complexities of the world situation than his opponent's. Both Truman and Eisenhower appealed to the American people because of their undoubted human qualities, one as a plucky fighter, the other because of the sense of reassurance he could convey amidst the troubled times. In contrast, Dewey and Stevenson in their quite different ways clashed with what might be called the sentimental needs of a large part of the American electorate.

The Russian squeeze on Berlin began in the spring of 1948. The three Western powers' determination to organize a West German state, heralded by decisions to establish a joint currency for the Western zones, became very clear, and with it Soviet determination to go very far to block such a step. The vagaries of the Presidential campaign played an undoubted role in the Russians' final decision on June 24 to cut off all passenger and freight traffic to West Berlin. In the past, a drastic foreign threat worked usually in favor of the administration in power: a resolute American move against the threat, such as in this case sending a military convoy through the blockade, might have increased Truman's chances of re-election. But such a step (urged by people as diverse as the American commander in Germany, General Lucius Clay, and the left-wing British Labour minister Aneurin Bevan) was eschewed. It is easy for a historian to argue twenty years later that this would have been the right response: the chances of the Russians initiating an armed conflict were infinitesimally small, the Russian bluff could have been called, the subsequent history of Germany would have been different. But those in power in London and in Washington felt that election or no election, every other avenue had to be explored before making any move which might initiate the catastrophe of World War III.

What was not excusable was the belief in the West that the Soviet Union's principal aim was to force the West out of Berlin. It should have been abundantly clear from everything the Russians said and did that their real objective in the first as well as in every subsequent Berlin crisis was a resolution of the German problem as a whole, more specifically in this case prevention of a rearmed West German state. The three Western powers had just adopted a currency reform for their zones. This was rightly construed as a major step in the setting up of the future Bonn republic. The Berlin blockade was the most efficacious way to reopen the German question as a whole and to force the West to abandon or at least postpone setting up their own West Germany. To have forced the three powers out of West Berlin would have availed the

Russians nothing if the Allies set up a West German state anyway and *immediately* proceeded to organize a West German army. For at its *least ominous,* this would involve a considerable increase of Russian military effectives, something which, with the satellites in turmoil and the needs of economy still fragile, the Soviet Union was determined to avoid.

A cold-blooded diplomacy on the part of Washington would then involve a realization of and a playing upon these Russian fears. It would have involved saying to Moscow: "Yes, you may force us to abandon two million Berliners to you. But this will involve adding that many persons to the disgruntled population of the Soviet zone, two million more to feed and supply, and then you must count on facing in short order a million or so West German soldiers, and who knows what might happen next. Take your choice." There can be little doubt as to what this choice would have been.

But of course such a policy was virtually impossible for the West. Many people, especially in France, were deeply averse to raising at this time even the possibility of a rearmed Germany. It was equally repugnant to consider two million Berliners as a mere counter in a diplomatic game. That the threat to two million individuals who only recently had been citizens of a hostile nation should have evoked such an emotional response was a tribute to both the compassion and the irrationality of democracy: the travails of millions of Poles and Czechoslovaks were on the contrary felt to have been preordained and something about which one could do nothing.

The fear of war on one hand and the need to preserve mobility to counter the Soviet move diplomatically led to the desperate expedient of the airlift to the besieged city. It was an episode as touching as it was appalling: the task of feeding and supplying Berlin through a narrow air corridor wrested a considerable toll in pilots and aircraft. To break a blockade imposed by an ally and in order to save from starvation or oppression people who were technically still enemy nationals, young Americans and Englishmen were risking and some giving their lives.

For all of the West's fears and uncertainties, the blockade involved a grave risk for the Soviet Union. It was brinkmanship of the most desperate kind. An actual armed conflict was unlikely, but who in an atmosphere so charged with emotion and rising tempers could absolutely preclude the possibility of an incident? The Western strategists believed that their stock of atomic bombs could not offset Soviet superiority in combat-ready troops. Yet Stalin even in his then advanced state of megalomania could hardly be reassured by such considerations. Were his armies to advance against the skeleton American and British forces, they would be strained to the utmost. And atom bombs apart, the United States could conjure up armies overnight. War, from the Soviet point of view, could end only in utter disaster.

Yet there were certain factors mitigating the danger. In the first place, the blockade could be lifted instantaneously. In the second place, the Soviets were very careful not to break off the negotiations, never to make it appear that the situation was beyond a diplomatic solution. Stalin himself, who now seldom saw a foreign diplomat, took pains to receive the three Western ambassadors twice in one month—August—and to appear amiable and conciliating. "We are still allies," he said; the Soviets did not mean to push the West out of Berlin, but why should the West try to set up its own German state? Subsequent conversations with Molotov convinced the negotiators that a solution was just around a corner. In fact, having decided fairly early in the game that their principal aim would not be achieved, the Soviets were waiting to see whether they might get something else for their brinkmanship: perhaps simply a joint declaration which by its language rather than substance might lead the West Germans to believe that their statehood was still a negotiable item.

After each act of force by the U.S.S.R., it has been usual for both government officials and journalists in America to console themselves with the reflection that the transgressor has been condemned "by the court of world opinion." Usually such consolations have been hollow: after a few weeks of agitation over Hungary in 1956 or Czechoslovakia in 1968, left-wing circles in Paris, London, and New Delhi would return to their more customary and satisfying practice of denouncing America as the greatest source of evil in world affairs. But in the case of the Berlin blockade, the revulsion felt against Soviet actions was actually translated into political gains for the West. Any lingering feelings in West Germany that neutralism between the East and the West might be the appropriate policy were effectively demolished, and Communist influence there rendered even less significant. In America, while the direct response to the crisis was hesitant and fearful, the general impetus toward mutual security arrangements with Western Europe was strengthened, and on June 11, 1948, the Senate passed the Vandenberg resolution proclaiming American readiness to enter into such arrangements. For the Soviet commentators this was an outrageous betrayal of an American tradition going back to the Founding Fathers: America was entering entangling alliances "in peacetime and a time when in fact nobody threatened the security of either the United States or Western Europe." The strange irony was that the last statement was true: Russia was acting aggressively but was too weak to prove a real threat to the West.

On April 4, 1949, the North Atlantic Treaty was signed in Washington. Stalin had been indicating in his answers to an American correspondent in Germany that the blockade might be lifted and that the German currency question, supposedly the provocation which led the U.S.S.R. to institute the blockade, was not that important. But hope still lingered behind the Kremlin wall: bad weather might render the airlift inoperative, then Americans might be drawn into bilateral negotiations with the U.S.S.R. in which they would be willing to bargain over the West German state. But the interminable discussions between Messrs. Malik and Jessup, representatives of the two powers in the Security Council, revealed no sign that the Americans were catching on.[14] Like a dog unable to eat and unwilling to release the bone it has seized, so did Soviet diplomacy hold on to Berlin long after it became obvious that the original purpose behind the blockade could not be achieved.

Finally, in May, the blockade was lifted. The outcome in a way was a draw. Any appeal Russia might now make to German nationalism would be unavailing for at least two decades; a separate West German state was coming into existence. The United States on the other hand had allowed it to be demonstrated that her rights in Berlin could be challenged with relative impunity, and this dangerous lesson would not be lost upon Stalin's successors. In another way both sides were losers in the Berlin crisis. The struggle over Berlin was a struggle over phantoms which existed in the imaginations of both sides: in the West those phantoms were Soviet soldiers ready to sweep to the English Channel; in Stalin's mind they were millions of West German soldiers who were going to materialize in the near future. Very soon there would be millions of real soldiers who posed a real threat to the security of both the West and Soviet Russia. They were Communist China's.

[14] A few excerpts from a State Department *aide mémoire* of April 16 may be quoted: "Mr. Jessup took occasion in a conversation on February 15 with Mr. Malik . . . to comment on the omission by Premier Stalin of any reference to the currency question. . . . On March 15 Mr. Malik informed Mr. Jessup that Premier Stalin's omission of any reference to the currency question was 'not accidental.' . . . On March 21 Mr. Malik again asked Mr. Jessup to visit him. . . . A statement was read by Mr. Jessup to Mr. Malik on April 5. . . . On April 10 Mr. Malik again asked Mr. Jessup to call upon him . . . further discussions took place between the three governments which have resulted in a more detailed formulation of their position which will be conveyed by Mr. Jessup to Mr. Malik." *Documents on International Affairs, 1949–1950* (London, 1953), pp. 155–56.

II

New Worlds Emerging

6

A Neglected Lesson

Though the realization of it was not to dawn upon the councils of the two superpowers for a decade or so, the year 1950 marked the beginning of the end of the bipolar world which had emerged from the war. Appearances have seemed to refute this assertion: since 1950 the number of places where Soviet power and influence confronted those of the United States has drastically increased. But though it is the Soviet-American conflict which renders these trouble spots and areas a danger to *world* peace, it would be difficult to argue that American interests clashed with those of the Soviet Union in most of these cases. Seemingly the two powers are struggling for power and influence all over the globe and in the process employing the resources of their allies and satellites. Yet in many cases it is the superpowers which are being exploited, and their weak allies and clients (or at least their leaders) are the exploiters.

In the most immediate terms, the Soviet like the American citizen is poorer because their governments use foreign economic aid as a means of making friends and influencing peoples. Perhaps this aspect of the rivalry can be justified as leading to economic progress in the countries thus aided, but the same rationalization can hardly be applied to the vast number of treaties, commitments, and hence dangers assumed by the two powers. Their justification in each case has been that the commitment was necessary because of vital security reasons, and the criticism in each case was that the pledges were in fact expressions of

American or Soviet imperialism. Yet most of these engagements could be neither justified nor attacked on grounds of ideology or interests, legitimate or illegitimate, of America and Russia. The strange dynamic of the Soviet-American conflict has drawn the two nations into expensive and dangerous policies, the beneficiaries of which have been potentates such as Mao, Nasser, Castro, Diem, etc. The danger of war and atomic destruction has come less and less from decisions and policies made and contemplated in Washington and Moscow, and increasingly from those devised or set in motion in Cairo, Saigon, Rhodesia, or Cyprus.

Had the world been still in an era when monarchs and cabinets ruled with a scant regard for public opinion, especially in foreign policy matters, 1949–50 would have been the logical time for the rulers of the United States and the Soviet Union to enter into confidential negotiations with a view to adjusting their differences and relieving tensions. After all, there was a virtual stalemate in Europe: the United States would not and the U.S.S.R. could not change the status quo. The two German states had just been set up. NATO had just been organized on paper, but there would be some time before it could dispose of a sizable military establishment. The U.S.S.R. had just, in the fall of 1949, exploded its first experimental atom bomb, but it would be some time before the Soviets would acquire a stock of the weapons and adequate means of delivery. The United States still had the preponderance of strength, but it was balanced by a democracy's unwillingness to act decisively and in a forceful way unless drastically challenged.

This stalemate should have called for negotiations. Such negotiations still might have provided for a united, demilitarized Germany and for that decrease in tension which would find a tangible expression in arresting military expenditures on both sides. The clash in Korea might have been avoided. It could be argued that such a *détente* would *basically* have solved nothing. But, it may be retorted, long-range solutions can be reached in this sinful world only through short-range and partial accommodations. The tragedy of 1949–50 was that no such negotiations took place. American foreign policy continued to be imprisoned in moralistic rhetoric, and in the unavowed but real sense of inferiority vis-à-vis the Russians when it came to diplomacy. Stalin, on his part, while not entirely free of the influence of Communist dogma, was most of all a prisoner of his fears. Obscure hints and tortuous sessions of the Foreign Ministers of the Four Powers could not by now shake off the West's conviction that serious negotiations with the

U.S.S.R. were at best a waste of time. Messrs. Bevin and Acheson kept repeating that before such dialogue could be reopened, the Russians must offer a proof of their sincerity, tangible guarantees that negotiations would be fruitful. This concept of negotiations was and remains entirely alien to the Soviets.

There was now among American policy-makers a considerable tendency toward a self-congratulation. America, it was believed, finally had a "tough," realistic policy to meet the Soviet challenge. To sit down with the Russians and engage in those interminable negotiations would be to weaken the American people's resolve, make them reluctant to support foreign aid, etc. This air of confidence was well expressed in Secretary of State Dean Acheson's speech of April 22, 1950. He supplemented his recital of the achievements and lessons of the last few years with some high rhetoric: "We are children of freedom. . . . We have in our hearts and minds the most dynamic and revolutionary concept . . . and one which properly strikes terror to every dictator [sic], every tyrant who would attempt to regiment and depress men anywhere." (The American government had just expanded its overseas information service, and through agencies like the Voice of America and through subsidization of various journalistic and radio ventures abroad, had finally begun to compete with Soviet propaganda efforts. Here also a somewhat extravagant note crept in.) "The doctrine of freedom will carry conviction because it comes not out of the government alone but also out of the hearts and souls of the people of the United States . . . freedom will ring around the world." The recent reorganization of the defense establishment also inspired Secretary Acheson with quiet confidence. He was not competent to talk about defense, he said, but added that "we can have complete faith and confidence" in the Secretary of Defense and the service secretaries.[1] This was an unfortunate prediction, for soon, in the wake of the Korean War, Secretary of Defense Johnson was to be subjected to strong criticisms that through his economies he had cut "into the muscle" of American armed strength and was constrained to resign.

Acheson's justifiable pride—What other peacetime administration had done so much for constructive policies abroad?—was thus marred both by overconfidence and by a tone of what might be called moral imperialism. It was not within the power of the United States, nor was it her task, to "sell" the American concept of government throughout

[1] Acheson's speech in *Documents on International Affairs, 1949–1950* (London, 1953), pp. 61–66.

the world. Once again the lessons of the recent past were beclouded. If America's mission was indeed to propagate freedom, why had she helped one dictator against another in the recent war? Why had she acquiesced in the Iron Curtain? Some of those who were children when Acheson spoke grew up to discover that America's policies were not in every case devoted to preservation of virtue and democracy. They were then tempted to conclude that *all* American policies were based on deception, that the society which permitted them must be corrupt.

Application of the principle that virtue is the best policy was relatively easy in Europe. But in the case of Asia this simplicity disappeared. Roosevelt's policy on China had been based on the thesis that Nationalist China was potentially both a great power and a democracy. By the end of the war with Japan, only Chiang was ready to believe in the first part of this fatal fiction. Yet, with what he believed was full American support, such caution appeared unnecessary. He aspired to bring all of China rapidly under his control. That is to say, American support was a vital factor in inducing Chiang to overextend himself; when this support was first limited and then withdrawn, his collapse was all the more prompt.

By the end of 1946, General Marshall had to give up his mission of mediating between the Kuomintang and the Communists, and it became clear to the most optimistic American officials that there was no earthly prospect of China becoming a democracy, and that no form of agreement could be found to enable the main Chinese factions to coexist peacefully.

At that point, one would think, the American government should have undertaken an "agonizing reappraisal" of its policy in Asia. The first and the most inexcusable error was a failure to realize and state that the fate of China was at least as important to American security and world peace as that of Germany. It had been, after all, Japan's actions in China and her domination of a *part* of that country which had initiated the series of events which led to Pearl Harbor. Whatever view one took of Chiang and the Chinese Communists, the notion that the outcome of the struggle between them was of secondary importance to the United States was as unjustifiable as it was to be catastrophic in its consequences.

The most arresting fact about the official American attitude toward China from about the middle of 1947 until 1950 was that, since the situation there was complicated and reactions to it in the United States so contradictory and confusing, the United States had *no* China policy except to hope for the best, and it was far from clear what this best was. On August 3, 1949, in transmitting the famous White Paper on China after the Communist victory, Secretary Acheson wrote, "Ultimately the profound civilization and the democratic individualism of China will reassert themselves and she will throw off the foreign yoke." It would be difficult to crowd more mistakes into one brief statement. Communist rule over China was not a *foreign* yoke; if there were elements of such, they disappeared soon after Stalin's death. But contemplating Chinese history since 1949, and especially the barbarities of the Cultural Revolution, one can hardly credit Communist China's independence to "profound civilization and democratic individualism."

If, however, the American government believed that a Communist victory in China meant a foreign—i.e., Soviet—yoke, one must wonder at the detachment with which the Communists' successes in China were viewed. Secretary Acheson was specific in his introduction to the White Paper: "The Communist leaders have foresworn their Chinese heritage and have publicly announced their subserviance to a foreign power, Russia." [2] But if this was so, it was at least disingenous for the Secretary of State to argue that the "ominous result of the civil war in China . . . was the product of internal Chinese forces" and "that nothing that this country did or could have done within the reasonable limits of its capabilities could have changed that result." It could hardly be claimed that the United States had done everything within its capabilities to prevent the addition of several hundred millions to the Soviet empire, a fact which would decisively alter the balance of power. After all, if the situation in China had been as described in the White Paper, then it paralleled very closely the situation in Greece. However, in that country the United States had been unwilling to leave the resolution of the conflict between the Communists and the government to internal Greek forces, but stepped in with economic help, military equipment and advisers, and, most important, with a pledge to preserve the country from internal yet foreign-controlled subversion.

If the American policy-makers had honestly described their dilemmas concerning China, the story would have run somewhat as follows: Until 1947, we believed that the intermittent civil war was an internal affair; we hoped that the Chinese Communists were not "really" Communists; anyway, there was not much to choose between them and Chiang's reactionary clique. By 1947, when we finally realized that

[2] U.S. Department of State, *United States Relations with China* (hereafter referred to as *China Paper*) (Washington, D.C., 1949), p. xvi.

Mao and his party should be taken at their word, the civil war was in full sway and we hoped that Chiang might still purge his regime of its undesirable elements and win. By 1948, it was widely recognized that Chiang was losing and that the Chinese Communist party was close to Moscow. But by that time we thought that the Kuomintang could not be saved except through *massive* American aid involving the dispatch of troops. American efforts were now centered on Europe, and we believed that additional commitments involving increased risk of a clash with Russia were unacceptable to the Congress and the American public.

But, apart from its other momentous results, the Communist victory in China was a main factor in that erosion of the rational approach to foreign policy which has plagued American society for decades and which currently threatens it with domestic as well as foreign disaster. There has been simply no middle ground between the two most strident views of the causes of the "loss of China." "Treason," said the Right, adducing corroborating testimony from diplomatic reports, professorial and journalistic accounts. "Irresistible forces of history," answered the liberals, echoing Acheson's verdict of 1949, repeating the testimony of Nationalist China's corruption and inefficiency, dipping into sociological wisdom about the Communists' irresistible appeal to peasants and about the Chinese national psychology ordaining that whenever a government or movement begins to lose it forfeits the Mandate of Heaven and is doomed to an irretrievable defeat.[3] The right question—What were the practical possibilities between 1945 and 1949 for a policy which could preserve at least part of mainland China from Communist domination, since such domination was definitely not in the interest of the United States?—was in effect never asked. The main thrust of American policy was to work for a "democratic China," i.e., for a reconciliation between Chiang and Mao and a coalition government. If that attempt could have been rescued from complete fatuity, the primary place to work for it was not in China but in Moscow.

As long as they were not masters in their own country, the Chinese Communists could not afford to incur the displeasure of Stalin. Their eventual success was made possible through Soviet complicity in handing them Japanese stocks of arms and in enabling them to become en-

---

[3] It would be difficult to explain why this Mandate of Heaven did not operate against the Communists when they were being beaten in the mid-1930s, or for that matter in the beginning of 1947.

trenched in Manchuria, where Chiang's subsequent and foolish attempt
to reconquer this province led to the attrition of his best army and his
first decisive defeats. But apart from such tangible Soviet help, no
Communist party in 1946–47 was in a position to reject determined
Soviet "advice." In fact, as one observes the Chinese Communists'
moves between 1945 and 1949, one gets a strong impression that their
main fear was not what the Americans but what the *Soviets* might do.
Hence Mao had a great stake—then as now—in the escalation of U.S.–
U.S.S.R. hostility. But whereas now this stake dictates baiting the
Soviet Union, then it argued for repeated gestures indicating subservi-
ence to the Fatherland of Socialism.

As for the Russians, until 1947 there was no reason for them to
become too involved in Chinese affairs. None of the possibilities looked
displeasing: Chiang might tire of American admonitions and come to
them for help; or the Communists could conquer Manchuria and the
north and then they would become an exemplary satellite state.

By the middle of 1947 it began to look at least possible that the
Communists would conquer all of China. Ordinarily this would have
stirred the Soviets into action: Stalin in his megolomaniac way would
not openly admit the possibility of a Communist country defying him,
but there must have been an inkling, at least, of the fear that here Russia
might be raising a Frankenstein monster. Yet precisely at this point the
Soviet leaders became convinced that the more immediate threat was in
America's role in reconstructing Western Europe. It was, therefore, no
time to pull Chiang's and America's chestnuts out of the fire simply to
ward off some future contingencies.

What assets could the United States have disposed of in bargaining
with Russia over China? The United States, like the character in
Molière who realizes only in his middle age that he has been talking
prose all his life, never realized—or at least no American statesman
would ever concede—that China was within her sphere of influence. At
Yalta the United States undertook to obtain from China certain concessions to the U.S.S.R.; American officers commanded Chinese forces
against the Japanese; after the war the United States undertook to resolve the country's most serious domestic problems. Operations of the
Chinese National Government were subject to constant scrutiny and
sometimes public criticism by American officials. American intercession or support was constantly sought by Chinese politicians, professors, etc. But if anybody had suggested that the most promising way of

solving China's problems was to negotiate with Moscow about a solution acceptable to all four parties, this would have been decried as the height of immorality and an infringement of China's sovereignty.

In fact, the most realistic American appraisal of the situation at the turning point in the Chinese crisis in the summer of 1947, made by General Wedemeyer, foundered exactly on this objection. General Wedemeyer had been delegated by the President to assess the Chinese situation, and his report stressed that the Nationalists' attempt to hang on to Manchuria would prove to be their undoing. Hence, he proposed, the United States should sponsor a United Nations or a Five-Power trusteeship of Manchuria. This was vetoed in Washington because, "It was the conviction of the President and the Secretary of State that any such recommendation, if made public at that time, would be highly offensive to Chinese susceptibilities as an infringement of Chinese sovereignty and representing the Chinese government as incapable of governing Chinese territory." [4] But such delicacy had not prevented American spokesmen in the past from talking in similar terms. General Marshall's *public* statement on the failure of his mission seemed to imply the American right to regulate Chinese affairs: "Between this dominant reactionary group in the Government and the irreconcilable Communists . . . lies the problem of how peace and well-being are to be brought to the long-suffering and currently inarticulate mass of the people of China." [5]

But if late in the game the United States displayed this concern for diplomatic appearances and eschewed bargaining over a territory that effectively was already lost, it still had a huge asset for bargaining over China. This was Japan.

Soviet initial apprehensions over America's intentions in Japan and her exclusive occupation and direction of the country were very clearly revealed in constant Soviet propaganda: the Americans would become reconciled with the Japanese militarists, and a strong Japan would soon resume her traditional role of balancing Soviet power and ambitions in the Far East. By Moscow's standards, such a policy would have been entirely logical once Chiang Kai-shek's weakness was fully realized: a rearmed Japan could only threaten Russian interests in the Far East and any Communist or pro-Russian regime in northeast China. There must have been, then, a considerable apprehension in the Kremlin that sooner or later the Americans would drop the pretense of their demo-

[4] *China Paper,* p. 260.
[5] *Ibid.,* p. 688.

cratic and educational mission in Japan and establish an alliance with the military and big-business interests in that country. But what the Americans *were* doing in that country, which under the most imperious of their statesmen-generals they controlled as absolutely as, say, the Russians did Outer Mongolia, was quite different. An American source not overly friendly to MacArthur lists his achievements between 1945 and 1950: "The Supreme Commander for the Allied Powers gave Japan a new constitution, reformed the distribution of land holdings . . . established a strong labor movement, decreed equality of the sexes, introduced conceptions of civil freedom, abolished the state religion." [6] More to the point, the new Japanese constitution written under American guidance renounced "war as a sovereign right of the nation and the threat or use of force as a means of settling international disputes." Consequently, Japan also renounced any armed establishment whatsoever.

This was a striking demonstration of national earnestness about pacific ideals, all the more so since the man who presided over this total disarmament of a potiential ally was on the right of the American political spectrum and one of the most notable exponents of the military tradition. And while the United States' idealism is usually assumed to be tempered by selfish material considerations, one predictable consequence of the momentous reforms was that Japan's economy became a formidable competitor to American and British industries.

But it does not take a Machiavellian mentality to observe that in their enthusiasm and reforming passion, the Americans lost sight of the simple truth that their goal of a stable peace in Asia could not be secured by dealing with Japan in complete disregard of what was going on all around her in the Far East. Possession of and then alliance with Japan was an invaluable diplomatic asset. The Russians at least could be sounded out as to how much a disarmed Japan was worth to them. One suspects that until well into 1947 it was thought of greater importance than the still problematic and not quite desirable Communist conquest of all of mainland China.

Barring a diplomatic solution of the Chinese problem, the only means of affecting the outcome of the civil war was massive American help to the Nationalists. Such help was correctly held in Washington to be insufficient to "save" Chiang in the sense of enabling him to win

6 Arthur Schlesinger, Jr. and Richard H. Rovere, *The General and the President* (New York, 1951), p. 87.

a complete victory and eliminate the Communists once and for all. But it is arguable that had the United States invested in China in 1947 only a part of the manpower and resources it was to expend in Korea in the 1950s or Vietnam in the 1960s, it could have preserved a large part of China from the Communists. Having two mainland Chinas would not have been a happy or stable situation, any more than it is in Germany or Korea, but who can say that it would not have been preferable and more hopeful both for the Chinese and for world peace than is the actuality?

Nobody, whether on the Right or Left, was ready to argue strongly for a continued and expanded American military presence in China. The United States would not bargain, would not use its Japanese assets, would not apply its power directly to reverse the trend of events in China. There was then by process of elimination one policy left, and that was to detach the United States resolutely from Chiang, to adopt an attitude of neutrality, perhaps with discreet soundings of the Chinese Communists as to their attitude in the event of their full victory. Such a policy seemed indicated at least from the end of 1947. Yet not only was it politically impossible, but the State Department felt it could not press for it since a neutral point of view would alienate influential (mostly Republican) congressmen, possibly jeopardize the Marshall Plan, etc. Throughout 1948, with Chiang's regime obviously crumbling, new economic aid to China was voted by the Congress, the Americans continued to proffer their advice about how to reform the government, and the U.S. military mission still filed recommendations as to the conduct of the civil war (which because of the Nationalist armies' lack of leadership and disintegrating morale Chiang's generals could or would not follow). For Chiang, to the last there was the phantom of the hope of the Americans coming to their senses and providing really massive help and troops. It inhibited him from seeking Soviet intercession at a time when such intercession could still conceivably change the final outcome. At the same time, public disapproval of the Generalissimo's position helped to erode his prestige still further without enabling a new man or men to emerge.

American hopes, hesitations, and blunders were fully revealed in the famous White Paper on China. Primarily designed to quiet political opposition at home, the paper's main theme was a plaintive "what more could we have done?" But someone should have reflected that it would be also read in Moscow, Peking, and other places, where it would justly be taken as a revelation of American ineptitude and incapacity to formulate clearly U.S. goals and interests in Asia. In Communist China, the document was greeted with derision, and Mao himself devoted a series of articles to it where he celebrated the Americans' "loss of face" and virtually admitted what he had argued among his followers and in Moscow in 1946–47: that the United States was a paper tiger and hence the Communists could push ahead without undue fear.

The White Paper also seemed to support the Communists' contention that the United States' intentions, though clumsily pursued, were evil. U.S. capitalism failed to subjugate China not because it did not try, not because, as Truman proclaimed in December, 1946, "We are pledged not to interfere in the internal affairs of China," but simply because it did not know how.

In a sense, most American policies and attitudes toward the Third World—i.e., toward most of the world—have been influenced by this painful experience in the Far East. President Kennedy declared that those who ignore the lessons of history are bound to repeat their mistakes. But whatever lessons China offered were obscured or forgotten, and a confusing and mutually contradictory variety of "lessons" were drawn from the Chinese debacle.

One alleged lesson was that the United States ought not to overextend itself and that it could not protect its friends everywhere in the world. In a speech in January, 1950, Acheson offered his famous and later much-criticized definition of American defense engagements in Asia as running along a perimeter extending from the Aleutians to Japan, Okinawa, and the Philippines, thus excluding South Korea and Formosa. If other countries in the Pacific were attacked, the Secretary of State hastened to add, they ought to seek help "in the commitment of the entire civilized world under the Charter of the United Nations which so far has not proved a weak reed to lean on by any people who are determined to protect their independence against outside aggression." [7] The Communists could justifiably take Acheson's statement as a rhetorical flourish designed to varnish an avowal that the United States would not protect either Formosa or South Korea.

Even so, the picture Acheson drew was far from clear. Did the United States *really* undertake to defend the countries *within* its defense perimeter? The United States would not tolerate "an attack on the Philippines." But the islands, said the Secretary, also faced "serious economic difficulties." In fact, though he did not dwell on it, their government was grappling with a serious Communist-led guerrilla movement. Would the United States help? Acheson was wary: "It is the Philippine Govern-

[7] *Documents on International Affairs, 1949–1950*, p. 104.

ment which must make its own mistakes.[8] What we can do is to advise
and urge, and if help continues to be misused, to stop giving help." [9]
This sounded suspiciously like the case of China and could not have
been of much comfort to the Philippine government. Nobody expected
a Soviet armada to sail into Manila Bay and start landing troops. But
what if the local Communists, or to use Acheson's euphemism "economic
difficulties," brought the local government to the verge of downfall?
Would the U.S. government issue a Philippine White Paper?

In Acheson's presentation it was "economic difficulties" which defeated Chiang's government. As he said, "the almost inexhaustible patience of the Chinese people in their misery ended." Somehow the
Communists exploited this and beat Chiang. Was the Secretary saying
that Asian Communism was then a native Asian phenomenon, an auto-
matic response to social and economic distress? Not quite, for "Communism is the most subtle instrument of Soviet foreign policy . . . the
spearhead of Russian imperialism which would if it could take from
these people . . . their own national independence." In fact, Acheson
was sure that the Soviet Union had already subjugated Manchuria and
was busy detaching Sinkiang and Inner Mongolia from their Chinese
allies.

The relative clarity with which American interests and commitments
were defined in Europe contrasted with the hopeless confusion in which
both friends and protagonists of the United States foundered when it
came to deciding what America would or could do in Asia. This relative
clarity on Europe, let us note, was due to the *tacit* acknowledgment,
much as the phrase would never pass the mouths of the policy-makers,
that Europe was now divided into spheres of influence: while the United
States could not do anything about Poland, the U.S.S.R. would not dare
to intrude into the West. But in Asia there was this weird jumble of crumbling imperial positions, Communists, nationalists, corruption, American
and Soviet bases, all of which seemed to defy any rational approach. One
may forgive America's spokesmen for stressing the complexity of the
situation and the impossibility of defining America's response to *every*
threatening contingency. What could be the U.S. attitude toward an
India-Pakistan war? What should the United States do if *Trotskyite* Communists should seize Burma or Ceylon? (For some strange reason this
exotic ideological offshoot has flourished in those countries!) But one is
much harder pressed to excuse Acheson hailing this appalling and dan-

[8] Another significant slip of the tongue.
[9] *Documents on International Affairs, 1949–1950*, p. 106.

gerous situation as a hopeful start of a new era: "I believe that there is a new day which has dawned in Asia. It is a day in which the Asian people are on their own, and know it, and intend to continue on their own." And he had just finished saying that Asia's largest country had become a dependency of the Soviet Union!

From Moscow, needless to say, the Asian picture looked quite different. Perhaps it was in view of his own experiences with Asian Communists and nationalist potentates in the 1920s that Stalin in his last years adopted a rather conservative and cautious attitude on the chances and potential benefits of victory of Communism in various Asian countries. The prospect of the Red East did not fascinate him as it had Lenin and Trotsky: in each case the question was, what will it be worth to the Soviet Union? To give Acheson his due, there were some indications that the Russians expected the regimes in Manchuria and Sinkiang to be autonomous and tried to deal with them directly. It was publicly announced in Moscow at the time of the Sino-Soviet negotiations in 1949–50 that representatives of those provinces joined them, a needless humiliation one would think to Mao and his friends and one they would not forget. That Stalin made demands on China of a "colonial nature," as Khrushchev was to say, is thus perfectly obvious. Yet in the very same negotiations, the Russians had to promise to release the large industrial complex of the Manchurian Railway, Port Arthur, and Dairen from their greedy grasp. As to the Communist guerrillas fighting in Malaya, the Philippines, etc., Moscow saw their main value in engaging and weakening the West's resources. In January, 1950, the U.S.S.R. acknowledged Ho Chi Minh in Vietnam. This was undoubtedly prompted by the Chinese, who had done so some days *before* Moscow's action. But a continued civil war in Indochina would tie down the bulk of France's best troops. While much of French public opinion would be outraged, an effective Western military force would be still further delayed.

The momentous fact of the passing of the British empire in India in 1947 created little excitement in the U.S.S.R. Anything marking and contributing to the decline of British power, of the British willingness to hold, at least, to the shadow of their former imperial position, was of course very welcome. But the two successor states were viewed as still within the British sphere. Stalin's Russia did not reciprocate the warm feelings some Congress leaders felt toward her, and their ideological antecedents made the Soviets dislike and distrust Gandhi. For the moment, the Soviets were only too content to leave to the United States the task of nudging the colonial powers to grant independence to their colonial possessions. The U.S. attitude was decisive in the Dutch acquiescing in the loss of their Indonesian possessions and in the sequence of events leading to the British withdrawal from Palestine and to the birth of Israel. For American public opinion and government held, to quote Acheson, that the old relationships between East and West "at their worst were exploitation . . . at their best were paternalism." Here again what seemed then and sometimes still does seem harmless and decorous rhetoric was to cost the American people dearly.

Soviet fears and interests were centered on Europe. There, what the Russians believed to be the key part of the American plot was visibly evolving, to be sure with agonizing slowness. In September, 1950, the three Western powers decided to revise the Occupation Statute of Germany and opened the way for eventual West German participation in the NATO defense force. The Federal Republic had been fully launched: it now exhibited political stability, its two major parties were firmly pro-Western, and it had made economic progress and become a major industrial power. Compared with it, the German Democratic Republic was an anemic child. East Germans, especially those in the most sought-after occupations and in their most productive years, were "voting with their feet" [10] by leaving the oppressed and impoverished zone for the West.

From the Soviet viewpoint, then, the fall of 1949 to the spring of 1950 was thus a period of mounting if still not imminent peril. The Russians had just exploded their first atom bomb, thus jostling the Americans out of their complacency. The main danger was still thought to be that of an indirect American response, of a greatly speeded and intensified effort to build a NATO force. Leaders of the main Communist parties in the West were made to declare that in the case of war with the U.S.S.R., they and their followers would oppose the governments of their own countries. This was thought in Moscow as bound to inhibit the willingness of the French and Italian governments to enter upon a massive military build-up and to make Washington think twice about the advisability and expense of equipping their forces. The French and Italian Communist parties accounted for between 20 and 30 per cent of their respective electorates. Presumably one in four recruits in the French and Italian armies would be a Communist sympathizer. Thus one had to ponder the risk that any vigorous effort to arm Italy and France might incur the risk of civil war.

[10] The phrase used before the November, 1917, Revolution about Russian soldiers who were deserting *en masse*.

In 1949, a vast peace movement was also launched to which the European Communist parties were told to devote most of their energies. This world-wide propaganda campaign culminated in the Stockholm Peace Appeal, which demanded "unconditional prohibition of the atomic weapon as a weapon of aggression," and was subsequently signed, according to the managers of the campaign, by more than 500 million people.

All those steps proceeded logically from the conclusion the Soviets had reached more than two years before: that both the Marshall Plan and NATO were instruments for indirect aggression against the Soviet Union, for abetting and helping "wars of liberation" in Russia's European satellites. The average State Department official no doubt simply prayed for a quiet life free from persistent crises erupting suddenly all over the world; certainly the most bumptious American officials still thought in defensive terms, forestalling or reacting to Soviet moves. Typical of them was Secretary of Defense Louis Johnson, who wanted Joe Stalin to know that if he started something at four o'clock, America's power would be on the job at five. (He thus joined illustrious company. Some of its members include the French minister of war who in 1870 announced that his country was entering the war with Prussia with a light heart; Neville Chamberlain who thought aloud in April, 1940, that Herr Hitler had missed the bus; and Walt Rostow, who expressed his belief in 1967 that the lesson of American intervention in Vietnam would make the Communists forswear "wars of national liberation.")

But the Soviets were not fooled by such rhetoric. In various purge trials in East Europe between 1949 and 1952, the scenario of Soviet fears and American villainy was painted in lurid colors: through their Zionist agents and Titoist allies, the American ruling circles were preparing uprisings against local governments, and new Yugoslavias. Those were the plots to which the accused, in some cases until quite recently the highest officials of Communist parties and governments, were compelled to confess before being sent to the gallows. Behind such fantasies there was a real fear of various contingencies the U.S.S.R. might have to face: the spread of Titoism to Bulgaria or Hungary; an anti-Communist plot engulfing Czechoslovakia and proving too strong for the local Communists. The Red Army stood ready to intervene, but what if the United States, with its atomic superiority and with NATO forces no longer merely on paper, declared the intervention an act of war?

European fears also prompted a basic re-examination of policy on Asia. The Chinese Communists became, not for the first or last time, beneficiaries of Soviet fears about what the Americans might do. The treatment accorded to the Chinese Communist delegation when it reached Moscow in December, 1949, still eloquently testified to China's subordinate status: apart from the matter of separate Sinkiang and Manchurian delegations, which stayed on in Moscow for some time after their Chinese superiors left, Mao himself, notwithstanding the multitude of problems he faced at home (especially after so recent a victory), was made to spend two months in Russia, something which could not be of his own preference. For all such galling details, the Chinese did obtain a number of concessions and a small loan. Beginning with the new year, Soviet references to their Chinese allies grew warmer and more respectful. China was obviously treated differently than the small Communist states of Eastern Europe, and obvious as this might seem to us, it was a marked departure for the Soviets.

The Sino-Soviet alliance was finally signed on February 14, and Mao was free to set out on his long journey home, which he did prudently by train.[11] The treaty spelled out clearly the focus of Soviet fears insofar as Asia was concerned. It pledged mutual assistance "in the event of one of the High contracting Parties being attacked by Japan or States allied with it and thus being involved in a state of war." Curious language which could not have been of great assurance and comfort to the Chinese. The most obvious danger facing *them* was that of Chiang's launching, with American help, an attack upon the mainland from the islands of Formosa and Hainan (then still in his hands) and American air and naval units bombing Chinese cities. That would not have been an attack by Japan or technically a state of war and would not have required Stalin to come to Mao's help. The danger to the Soviet Far East, on the other hand, could come only from a rearmed Japan instigated by the United States to attack Vladivostok and Sakhalin. This curious disparity in obligations assumed by the two allies again seems to have passed unnoticed in Washington.

Everything then seems to indicate that Moscow expected that the American response to the Communist conquest of China would be an abrupt reversal of the policy toward Japan. Nothing of the kind happened. In view of this American equanimity over major setbacks to their position in Asia, it must have occurred to some ingenious minds in Moscow that the Americans could be pushed still further. The logical place was Korea.

[11] He had not hesitated, during his abortive negotiations with Chiang, to entrust himself to American-piloted aircraft.

What could the Russians have hoped to accomplish by allowing—indeed if not ordering—their North Korean vassals to attack? It is still very difficult to answer this question. The likeliest explanation is that additional evidence of America's inability to protect its friends and clients in Asia was thought to be a good lesson for Japan. There the Communists late in 1949 increased their militant and disruptive tactics against American occupation. The fall of still another Asian country would have a profound psychological effect even on non-Communist Japanese. Perhaps the Americans would feel constrained to withdraw their forces, sign a peace treaty which would leave Japan defenseless. A Communist Japan would offset the power of Communist China, thus enabling Russia to play the classical balance-of-power role in the Far East. Or conversely, the Americans would desperately cling to Japan. This would mean a considerable increase in their military forces there, which in turn would force the Americans to re-examine their military commitments in Europe.

It would also make Mao think twice about defying the U.S.S.R. In the Sino-Soviet treaty, Moscow promised to release Port Arthur and its properties in Manchuria by the time the Japanese peace treaty was signed, but in no case later than 1952. The latter date was certainly inserted at Mao's insistence, for he could not reasonably hope to live to see the day when the United States and the U.S.S.R. would agree on a treaty short of the United States packing up and leaving Japan. By the same token, the Russians undoubtedly counted on something happening before 1952 which would make the Chinese Communists appreciate the presence of Soviet soldiers on their soil.

The American reaction to the North Koreans' invasion of South Korea on June 25 must have been one of the greatest surprises of Stalin's life. Having acquiesced in the loss of China, these unpredictable people now balked at the loss of a territory they themselves had characterized as unimportant to their political and strategic interests. The Soviet Union was completely unprepared for this: had there been an inkling of it, the Soviet delegate would not have boycotted the Security Council since January (on the grounds that Communist China should be seated there), and Moscow would have been ready with diplomatic notes and propaganda campaigns about South Koreans invading the North, etc. Between June 27 and July 3, the news from Korea was tucked on the back pages of the Soviet press while the Kremlin obviously meditated over what to do. It was not until a week after the Security Council's action and Truman's ordering armed help to South Korea that the Russians recovered their poise and began to denounce the United States in their usual work-manlike fashion.

There is a strong presumption that the Soviets must have been tempted to call off the whole thing. This would have been relatively easy: having chastised the "invaders," the North would virtuously return where they came from. From this temptation the Soviets were probably rescued by the perceptible apprehension and disarray which lay behind the seem-ingly resolute American and U.N. action.

In the first place, the Americans were utterly unprepared. The mis-tress of the seas and air did not have so much as one combat-ready divi-sion to throw immediately into action, and the unprepared units taken from pleasant occupation duty in Japan did not appear capable of stem-ming the North Korean tide. It was not Stalin but Louis Johnson who had to eat crow and make his exit from the Administration and public life.

Two other factors were of greater importance. No sane person could doubt the ultimate Soviet responsibility for the attack.[12] But the first American move vis-à-vis the Russians was so expressive of Washing-ton's fears of an all-out war that it relieved the Soviets of any apprehen-sion of an immediate confrontation. The American "note of record," so labeled to avoid any implication of an ultimatum, asked Moscow to dis-avow its responsibility for the aggression. The Russians, needless to say, were glad to oblige. It also asked them to use their influence with the North Koreans to persuade them to stop the invasion. Moscow gravely declared this was beyond its powers and would constitute meddling in the internal affairs of a sovereign state.

The Soviet rejoinder of June 29 was mild and polite by the usual standard of Soviet behavior on such occasions: no talk about "responsi-bility of the imperialist circles" and "incalculable consequences" which might follow from unleashing aggression.

The other, probably decisive, factor which made the Russians go on with the enterprise was Truman's order for the Seventh Fleet to quaran-tine Formosa, i.e., to bar any invasion from the mainland or in reverse any attack from the island on the Chinese Communists.

No reason of logic or policy could justify that decision as being in any sense connected with the need to save South Korea. On the con-trary, if one assumed that the Chinese were somehow responsible for

---

[12] Thus it would be superfluous to discuss the contention that the North Koreans attacked without explicit Soviet permission or orders, and absurd to deal seriously with the charge that Syngman Rhee's government was responsible, as claimed by official Communist sources.

the North Korean actions then the quarantine increased the chances of their armed intervention in the peninsula. Their best armies were being assembled for the invasion of Formosa; frustrated in that, they would be able to shift to the borders of North Korea. Also and gratuitously, the Seventh Fleet was now protecting them from any forays from the island.

But quite apart from such reflections, there was no reason for the assumption that the responsibility for the June 25 attack rested in Peking. The relations between the Chinese Communists and North Koreans were known to be strained. The main figures in the North Korean regime were clearly Soviet creatures. And it was not until August that an official representative of Communist China arrived to open diplomatic relations with its Communist neighbor. In the summer of 1950, Peking's main objective was to consolidate its rule on the mainland and to conquer Formosa and Tibet. They could not have wished for any major diversion or adventure *at that time* which would interfere with their most urgent tasks.

The real reasons for the strange decision must be sought in the complexities of American domestic politics. Five months earlier, Senator Joseph McCarthy had made his dramatic entrance into world history by declaring that the State Department was teeming with Communist agents.[13]

The hue and cry was on. To a large proportion of the American public, the vicissitudes of American foreign policy during and following World War II were now explained in terms of treason on the part of highly placed officials within the State Department. But prior to the Korean War, this campaign had not constituted a very serious challenge to American foreign policy and its bipartisan underpinnings, although to the occasional shouts of "treason" were joined more serious accusations about blindness of American policies, especially in Asia. It was a real tragedy that following the outbreak of the war the two were to become merged, and that serious critics such as Senator Taft could not resist the temptation of tolerating and profiting from the irresponsible forays of figures like McCarthy and Senator Jenner. Instead of a rational reappraisal of America's policy in Asia, similar to one which in the case of Europe had led to the Truman Doctrine and the Marshall Plan, there was now an emotional outcry against the country's foreign policy as a

[13] Their exact number as given in McCarthy's celebrated speech in Wheeling, West Virginia, in February was to be variously remembered, some adducing the figure to be 57, others, 205. But whatever the number, they were "card-carrying" members of the party. Someone should have told the Senator that it was a capital offense for Soviet spies to advertise their political affiliation.

whole. Instead of a search for and removal of those who had proved incompetent and naïve, there was a frenzied chase after the wicked and the treasonous. Again one finds a melancholy parallel to the debate on Vietnam in the late 1960s. Here, too, those who started a rational inquest could not refrain, when dismayed by the casualty lists and a frustrating war, from blaming the moral depravity rather than the intellectual shortcomings of the policy-makers. A democracy forgets quickly. But does it ever learn?

When the American policy-makers had to decide what to do about the invasion, the shape of the things to come—the fury of the electorate at being thrust into a confusing and distant war—was already discernible. It was also perceived dimly that somehow all the Asian elements were connected. The assumption of the China White Paper of less than a year before that the United States could and should await the working out of the forces of history had just collapsed. The American people who would be fighting Communists over South Korea could not be expected to continue to tolerate the explanation that a *complete* victory of Chinese Communists was of no importance. There was need, it was confusedly felt, for a move against the Chinese Communists, but one which was not likely to bring on an American military confrontation with them.

Thus in the course of a few hours' conferences in the National Security Council on June 25 and 26, the course of American policy in Asia was drastically changed. The President decided also to expand American help to the French in Indochina and to increase American forces in the Philippines.

Historically, the decision on Formosa, thrown in largely for complex domestic reasons, came both to overshadow the one on Korea and to transform the character of the Korean conflict itself. On January 5, President Truman had declared that the United States would not provide military aid or advice to the Chinese forces on Formosa and that it would not interfere in the civil conflict in China. Now on June 27, in his quarantine order, he declared that the occupation of Formosa by "Communist forces would be a direct threat to the security of the Pacific area and to the U.S. forces performing their lawful and necessary functions in that area." [14] It would be foolish to argue that without the American move on Formosa, the Chinese Communists' attitude toward the United States would have been one of friendship and gratitude. But by thus interposing American power between Peking and Formosa and denying the Communists a try at the consummation of their victory,

[14] *Documents on International Affairs, 1949–1950*, p. 632.

Washington gave them a greater stake in the Korean conflict than they had had before, and by the same token the Russians could now, so to speak, sit back and relax.

Yet the Russians could not afford to be entirely complacent. The Americans had surprised once; they might surprise again. The Soviet note of July 4 denounced the American intervention in strong terms but contained no hint of a Soviet counteraction; instead, it called on the Security Council to procure an immediate American withdrawal. The American desk of the Soviet Foreign Ministry distinguished itself in the preparation of the note by its keen historical sense: "The Soviet Government holds that the Koreans have the same right to arrange at their own discretion their internal national affairs in the sphere of uniting South and North Korea into a single national state as the North Americans had in the 'sixties of the last century when they united the South and the North of America into a single national state." [15] But Stalin did not rest content with this appeal to Civil War buffs, and few Americans were ready to identify Kim Il-Sung with Lincoln and Syngman Rhee with Jefferson Davis. It was in the United Nations that the Soviets could find more fruitful ground for their appeals for moderation and restraint.

The fact that the American counterintervention had official blessing from that organization was a handicap as well as an advantage for Truman. As the latter it helped rally public opinion at home and in the first instance was undoubtedly a propaganda asset. But the actual aid in fighting furnished by other U.N. members was of symbolic rather than quantitatively significant value. And it did not take much foresight to predict that the original resolution and virtual unanimity of the U.N. in supporting the American actions would not be long-lasting. Very soon India recalled that in view of her superior virtue she was to be a bridge between the East and West rather than take sides. Britain's Labour government could not conceal its apprehensions about Douglas MacArthur. Europeans in general reflected unhappily about the U.S. preoccupation in Asia and possible repercussions on Western Europe. For the Third World members of the U.N., support for a Western, thus basically imperialist, power ran against the grain. And thus, after the initial exhilaration that the U.N. because of the Americans was proving effective, everybody began reverting (to be sure slowly and rather shamefacedly) to traditional postures.

Apart from the diplomatic and military complexities of the situation, there was another decisive factor in the Korean drama. This was the

[15] *Ibid.*, p. 654.

personality of General MacArthur. To his detractors, MacArthur appeared as the very embodiment of militaristic megalomania, a man who for all his great gifts was a constant threat to the constitutional concept of civilian supremacy. To his admirers, he has remained a unique man of destiny, the tragedy of whose life really was that of America, which, having scorned his advice, was bound to lose Asia and perhaps more to Communism.

Both judgments ignore one trait of the General, which, while it contributed to his greatness as a man and military leader, handicapped him as a statesman. This was his strong emotionalism, which tended to make him concentrate his drive and dedication on the task at hand, and while often this was responsible for his great successes, it made him oblivious of the broader setting of world politics. Even the most thoroughgoing pacifist could not have thrown himself so earnestly into the task of building a new Japan, of transforming that country's society, even the nation's psychology, in the direction of peaceful and democratic pursuits. By the same token, he lacked that dash of cynicism and calculation which in this sinful world remain as necessary ingredients of statesmanship.

With greatly insufficient forces at his disposal, MacArthur was given the task of first stemming and then reversing the North Korean advance. Few generals in his position in June, 1950, would have acquiesced in having troops from their command committed to such a seemingly hopeless venture, let alone have recommended it, as he did. In September, after some near desperate moments, MacArthur, by a brilliant and most dangerous maneuver, landed troops at Inchon, far behind the North Korean lines, and soon the rout of the invader was on.

In the meantime, MacArthur had paid a visit to Formosa. From his "quarantined" island, Chiang on August 1 issued a statement that "the foundations were thus laid for a joint defense of Formosa and for Sino-American military cooperation." This action of MacArthur's created both surprise and dismay in Washington. As Acheson says revealingly, "explicit orders then went to him emphasizing the limits of our policy regarding Formosa, and Harriman followed to enforce them." [16] If MacArthur's trip was unauthorized, then one must still wonder at the disarray of the administration which, having ordered a quarantine, failed for more than a month to explain to the general commanding U.S. and U.N. forces in actual combat in Korea what were "the limits of our policy regarding Formosa." MacArthur then com-

[16] Dean Acheson, *Present at the Creation* (New York, 1969), p. 422.

pounded his error by issuing a grandiloquent statement stressing the importance of Formosa, which was published and later repudiated by the President and at his order withdrawn by MacArthur.

A remarkable document submitted to the U.N. on August 25 purportedly defined the U.S. position on Formosa. Considerations of space forbid a full reproduction, but a few excerpts must be quoted:

> The U.S. has not encroached on the territory of China. . . . The action of the U.S. in regard to Formosa was taken at a time when that island was the scene of conflict with the mainland. More serious conflict was threatened by the public declaration of the Chinese Communist authorities. . . . Formosa is now in peace and will remain so unless someone resorts to force. . . . The actual status of the island is that it is territory taken from Japan by the victory of the Allied Forces in the Pacific. . . . Its legal status cannot be fixed until there is international action to determine its future. The Chinese government was asked to take the surrender of the Japanese forces on the island. That is the reason the Chinese are there now. . . . The U.S. has a record . . . of friendship for the Chinese people. We still feel the friendship and know that millions of Chinese reciprocate it. We took the lead . . . in the last United Nations General Assembly to secure approval of a resolution on the integrity of China.[17]

In his letter to the U.S. delegate to the Security Council Truman threw his authority behind the declaration and repeated, for some bizarre reason, the gist of the statement. He did so, he wrote, "to the end that there be no misunderstanding concerning the position of the Government of the U.S. with respect to Formosa."

With U.N. forces pursuing the utterly defeated and demoralized remnants of the North Korean army north of the 38th Parallel, it became clear that all of Korea would soon be theirs and the world would witness the liquidation of a Soviet satellite without its protector doing anything about it. It was hardly the kind of lesson which Moscow had in mind when it allowed (or ordered) the hapless North Koreans to start the venture.

The repercussions of Korea were undoubtedly seen also in the more vigorous pace of the Western defense effort in Europe. The NATO Council in September issued a statement envisaging West German participation in the planned European army. General Eisenhower left his safe haven (such was a university presidency in those distant times) at Columbia to head once more the combined forces of the Western Alliance. The unforeseen course of the war probably deflected the Russians from an attempt at a military solution of the Yugoslav

17 *Documents on International Affairs, 1949–1950*, pp. 664–65.

problem. By 1950 it was clear that Tito's regime would not collapse because of any internal subversion; at the same time "frontier incidents" with Yugoslavia's Communist neighbors grew in frequency and intensity. There is a strong presumption that had not the world situation become so thoroughly muddled through the Americans' unexpected action, the summer of 1950 would have witnessed yet another invasion across the Hungarian and Bulgarian frontiers.

In fact when it became clear that the Americans not only would not be forced out of Korea but would march beyond the 38th Parallel, the kind of situation rapidly evolved which it had been the cardinal point of Soviet policy ever since 1944 to avoid: the revelation of Soviet caution and bluff, of how behind the tough talk lay a real fear of confrontation with the awesome power of the United States. The relaxed and humorous Soviet diplomacy of a few weeks before was giving way to visible anxiety. In August, the Soviet representative returned to the Security Council. In October, a hastily arranged meeting in Prague of the representatives of the U.S.S.R. and the people's democracies formulated a proposal for a resolution of the German problem which would allow a withdrawal of all occupation forces within a year. For a change the proposal did not contain a single word of abuse of the United States, nor the by now ritualistic phrases about imperialists scheming to rebuild the Wehrmacht and unleash war. It was amazing how, once a danger seemed imminent, the U.S.S.R. would remember its manners and frame its proposals in irreproachably diplomatic language.

The danger was thought to be considerable. For the moment the American mood was one of combined resolution and exasperation, so that no contingency, however drastic, could be precluded. In August there were isolated voices crying that "one should be done with it": the Secretary of the Navy talked of preventive war, an Air Force general stated his readiness to drop atomic bombs on the source of all trouble, Moscow. The politician was banished to the embassy in Ireland and the general was retired, but there must have been some uneasiness in the Kremlin.

One would give a great deal to read even one of the messages which passed in those weeks between Moscow and Peking. From the Russians' point of view, the great consolation was that the American moves were still more threatening to the Chinese than to them. It was being demonstrated how easy it was to beat *Asian* Communists. Who could believe that with U.S. troops on the frontier of Manchuria and Chiang proclaimed an indispensable ally, America would return to its attitude of "wait till the dust settles" in Asia? And Communist rule on the mainland was far from firmly consolidated. Those warlords who had deserted the Kuomintang and who still controlled some provinces might now decide that the Mandate of Heaven worked the other way.

The Chinese Communists could not view the prospect of their intervention in Korea with wild enthusiasm. They were to enter the war with obsolete military equipment (the North Koreans when they attacked had up-to-date Soviet weapons, but only after their struggle with the Americans began did the Soviets *sell* the Chinese modern arms); and the possibility that the Americans would resort to the atom bomb could not be discounted. There was no public commitment from the U.S.S.R. that she would aid Peking in such an eventuality. If there was a secret Soviet stipulation to that effect, Mao and his government must have still been dubious that Stalin's Russia would depart from its peace-loving ways even if Peking were bombed and civil war were rekindled on the mainland. But such unhappy reflections may have been somewhat balanced by the elation, partly nationalist and partly ideological, felt at the prospect of humiliating the American imperialists, and the pride that it was China that had become the forward wall of the Communist world.

In October there were repeated Chinese warnings that if the American troops crossed the Parallel and moved toward their border, Peking would be compelled to intervene. The American reactions were ambivalent. The fact that the warnings had been conveyed through India decreased their credibility. (The State Department was in one of its frequent moods of irritation over the Indians' nervousness combined with Nehru's "holier than thou" attitude.) On the other hand, the possibility of Chinese intervention was not being discounted. Directives to MacArthur suggested that military operations north of the Parallel should be conducted by South Korean units. But the American commander was at the height of his glory and popularity. The Joint Chiefs of Staff—who had been junior officers when MacArthur was already a national figure, whose fears about the Inchon landing had been so recently confounded—could not bring themselves to *order* MacArthur in direct and unambiguous terms. With Congressional elections but a few weeks away, the President had to ponder the repercussions of a public disagreement with the legendary warrior. There was also a natural temptation to crown what had begun as a military and political calamity with a resounding lesson to the aggressor and his sponsor.

(Here one might consider a few "ifs." What if with the crushing defeat of the North Koreans by the end of September the United States had lifted the quarantine of Formosa? What if the response to the Far Eastern aggression had been at least a *threat* of vigorous German rearmament, rather than a halting and uncertain one envisaging German units of batallion strength within a special European total force not surpassing 100,000 soldiers? What if the President had seized this moment of American success and Russian confusion to propose a summit meeting with Stalin?)

It would have been awkward to ask MacArthur to come to Washington: he could plead the impossibility of absenting himeslf from the theater of war; or if he came, his public reception would be tumultuously friendly. Alexander I and Napoleon solved a somewhat similar problem by meeting on a raft in the middle of a river. Truman and MacArthur met in the middle of the Pacific on Wake Island. In terms of clarifying over-all strategy, the meeting could accomplish little. MacArthur's assurance that the Chinese would not intervene and even if they did would be trounced could have been conveyed by telegram. But politically the meeting could be interpreted as a democracy paying overdue tribute to a hero. On his return to Washington, Truman hailed MacArthur as "loyal to the President . . . loyal to the President in his foreign policy," [18] a rather unnecessary statement, one should think, for the President of the United States to make about a soldier on active service.

On October 7, the U.N. Assembly authorized the establishment of a "unified independent and democratic Korea." As to the means of achieving this happy situation, it recommended appropriate steps to assure stability throughout the peninsula. This euphemism, endorsed by a large majority of the Assembly (the Security Council could no longer be relied upon since the Russians were back with their veto), meant a fairly clear mandate for MacArthur to sweep into North Korea and to finish off its army. This he proceeded to do, disregarding the suggestions (or was it orders?) from Washington to employ only South Korean units in the provinces bordering on Chinese and Soviet territories. Washington's policy was in line with a sound and cautious strategy which urged that the neck, or as it is sometimes called with less anatomical justification, the pinched waist of the peninsula, some fifty miles north of Pynzyang, be recognized as an ideal defense line if superior forces were thrown in against the U.N. It would also have been

[18] Rovere and Schlesinger, *op. cit.*, p. 133.

a cautious response to the Communist Chinese intimations that they would not feel it necessary to intervene if only South Koreans would advance beyond the Parallel and toward their border.

It was subsequently to become a heated political issue whether and how far MacArthur violated explicit orders. There were orders, but were they explicit? Washington's views on the subject prior to the November debacle remind one of the considerations which in the old Austro-Hungarian empire governed the award of the Order of Maria Theresa: The military commander who violated his instructions and lost the battle was, of course, court-martialed; but one who won while disobeying a higher authority was given this highest military award of the Empire. (It was but rarely granted, since throughout the nineteenth century and World War I, Austrian commanders invariably both obeyed their orders and were defeated.) The General, on the other hand, believed that he understood Oriental psychology. It was palpably foolish for the Chinese to intervene at this late stage; had they done so in the beginning or at the crucial stage after the Inchon landing, they would have tipped the scales. On grounds of military logic and of the celebrated Oriental psychology those were perhaps sound considerations, but the decisive element was neither. The Chinese venture proceeded from a very complicated relationship between Moscow and Peking. Another factor was the Chinese Communists' understanding of *American* psychology: once North Korea was erased, they believed, the United States would not be able to resist some further temptation.

The Chinese Communists attacked first at the end of October, and in early November inflicted significant setbacks on the U.S. forces. On November 7 they broke off action and insofar as MacArthur and Washington were concerned vanished for about twenty days. Here came the really inexcusable action by MacArthur and the equally inexcusable acquiescence in it by his superiors. The Chinese move should have been interpreted as an unmistakable indication, and such it was, that they planned to make good their threats but still hoped to avoid prolonged armed conflict with the United States. If it were otherwise, why give the United States an opportunity to change its plans? Why destroy the surprise element and hold off *continuous* blows until later? But after momentary hesitations, rather than holding to his positions or withdrawing to more defensible lines, MacArthur unleashed his offensive to the border of North Korea, utterly disregarding the possibility of a new and massive Chinese counterattack. Again, as Acheson feels constrained to admit in his memoirs, the Joint Chiefs urged caution and

did not countermand MacArthur's orders and insist on a tactical withdrawal. On November 26, large Chinese forces fell upon the exposed
and divided U.N. units. It was the beginning of the new war, which
between November 16 and January 25, 1951, resulted in American defeats and a precipitous withdrawal not only from the North but once
again from part of the South and its capital, Seoul.

A democracy often performs more creditably faced with a stark
defeat than in moments of triumph or apparent peace. The initial panic
and deep humiliation felt at the first news of the rout soon gave way in
Washington to what under the circumstances was probably the balanced
and correct response: the determination to hold on to South Korea at
the same time eschewing the temptation to broaden the war with China.

We cannot follow here the subsequent history of the war: the United
States' recovery in the spring of 1951, the sporadic but still bloody
fighting which went on for two years while the armistice negotiations
dragged on, etc. But we may ask, what were and should have been
the lessons of America's near triumph and near catastrophe, and of
the concluding and frustrating settlement which left the 38th Parallel
as one of the leading danger spots in the world? These lessons can
hardly be gleaned from the lengthy hearings before the Senate Armed
Services Committee, which in 1951, following MacArthur's dismissal,
sought to apportion blame for U.S. policies in Asia during and since
World War II. In the most succinct form the clashing viewpoints were
expressed by Generals MacArthur and Bradley. In war there was no
substitute for victory, said the former. What MacArthur wanted, said
the latter, would have led to a war with China—"the wrong war, at the
wrong time, with the wrong enemy."

MacArthur's formula would hardly be borne out by history, but his
sentiments were the reflection of a very basic trait in American psychology: with a job at hand one does not rest until it is completed.
Certainly the U.S. victory over Japan had been as complete as any in history. But it was largely due to the completeness of that victory and to
the disregard of the wider setting of world politics that within a few
years the United States found itself confronted with another and more
intractable danger in the Far East. Moreover, an all-out American effort
against China would not have been viewed in Moscow with undue dismay.
Once the Korean situation became "stabilized" in the spring of 1951,
the U.S.S.R. could view the resulting deadlock with some equanimity.
Considerable U.S. forces were tied down in the Far East. The Soviet
stock of atomic weapons was growing, and since the U.S.S.R. was

ultimately protecting China as well, she obviously had to retain Port Arthur beyond the scheduled time for evacuation. America's European allies were grumbling. It could not be ruled out that the Americans in one of their incalculable moods might raise the specter of actual war, but those agonizingly inconclusive truce negotiations could then suddenly become fruitful and produce a quick settlement. If Stalin had not died in March, 1953, it is quite likely that the impasse would have continued beyond the date of actual signing of the truce on July 27, 1953.

Stalin's successors were not of the same mettle. They had less confidence in their ability to gauge American reactions and were diffident about pushing the United States too hard. The same applied in regard to the Chinese Communists. Hardly were the obsequies over when the Malenkov-Beria regime proceeded to sign a trade and technological agreement with China which pledged considerable technical and economic aid. V. V. Kuznetsov, then high in the Soviet hierarchy, was dispatched to Peking, replacing as ambassador a career diplomat who had been there only a month. These moves had an eloquence of their own. The magic of Soviet dominance was broken: China was now a partner, even if still a junior one.

It is mostly in its effect on the Chinese Communists that the Korean venture must be considered as one of the most profound blunders of postwar Soviet foreign policy. On the surface it appeared as a master stroke to make Peking the lightning rod for America's wrath and frustration while the Soviet Union remained a sympathetic bystander. In fact, those two years when the Chinese had to assume the burden of the fighting marked their psychological emancipation and speeded up the process of equalization between the two states which had begun with the Mao-Stalin negotiations in Moscow. They acquired not only modern equipment but self-confidence and reliance. Their ability to fight the United States to a stalemate brought them dividends of nationalistic exultation and of speedier and firmer consolidation of their rule on the mainland than would otherwise have been the case. From now on, China would be very careful not to lend itself to any situation where she would be required to pull Soviet chestnuts out of the fire, not to be pushed again into the position and danger she endured from 1951 to 1953.

For the United States, the lessons of Korea were ambiguous. The decision to counter Communist aggression appears, in retrospect, both justified and necessary. Soviet hopes of loosening America's hold on

Japan were frustrated. In September, 1951, the United States rushed through the Japanese peace treaty (which Russia did not sign), which then was followed by a security pact between the two countries. The United States retained bases and armed forces and the agreement stipulated that the latter could be used at the request of the Japanese government to suppress any internal revolt instigated by an outside power. The two documents marked a decisive defeat of the Soviet design to have in Japan a Communist or at least a neutralist power to balance Communist China in the Far East.

At one time the Korean War promised to become a heartening demonstration of how the United Nations could be resolute and effective in stopping aggression. By the time of the armistice, little remained of such high hopes. Technically the side fighting the Communists was the United Nations; in fact, the United Nations label was not significantly less fictitious than the volunteer status of the Chinese fighting on the other side. Many nations contributed small units, some of them (notably the Turks and the British) fought most gallantly, yet in numerical terms it was clearly an American force. Even more significant and lamentable, though predictable, was the discord within the U.N., once "its" forces were attacked by the Chinese, and the mounting criticism of American leadership and aims. In fact if a proof was needed that the U.N. could not perform its primary function of guaranteeing international peace and security, then the Korean conflict offered fairly convincing evidence. The original approval of other U.N. members for the American initiative soon turned into a rather ill-humored acquiescence, and that only on the assumption that the predominant share of fighting and casualties would be borne by the United States (apart of course from the South Koreans). There grew on the other hand a bitter feeling among many Americans that countries bearing little or no share of the responsibility and fighting sought to influence or dictate American strategy. There was an element of cruel irony in the drama, and one which was to recur in the years to come. When the responsibility had not been hers, the United States had repeatedly criticized the British, French, Dutch, etc., for their insensitivity to Asian nationalism, their reluctance to make timely concessions to the new and dynamic forces in the Orient. Now this criticism was vented on the United States. The shock of the Chinese intervention brought Prime Minister Clement Attlee to Washington. In his lugubrious manner, he expounded the necessity of appeasement: "He believed," Acheson tells us, "that withdrawal from Korea and Formosa and the Chinese seat in the United Nations for the Communists would not be too high a price. There was nothing, he warned us, more important than retaining the good opinion of Asia." [19] The Americans could not help being chagrined and infuriated. They had borne the burden of fighting, they had poured billions into the recovery of Western Europe, yet their West European allies, some of whom recognized Communist China and traded with her, while clamoring for American help and support showed reluctance even for diplomatic support of the Korean action. American soldiers, it was believed, were providing a defense against new despotisms, while the Europeans assumed the role so recently occupied by the American spokesmen: pleading for an understanding of Asian nationalism, justifying its excesses and its suspicions of the West, calling for patience and sacrifice of Western pride. Nobody could expect Acheson to appreciate the irony of this reversal in the traditional roles. And indeed he did not.

The disappointments and setbacks of the latter phase of the Korean conflict compounded the difficulty of designing and maintaining an over-all policy of containing Communism (or was it the Soviet Union?) throughout the world. The impetus to create an effective NATO force and some form of West German rearmament which appeared so strong in September, 1950, had visibly weakened toward the end of the year. A Soviet note of November 3 proposing yet another meeting of the Big Four ministers to consider the German question, and its rather conciliatory tone, were undoubtedly prompted by the prospect of *imminent* West German rearmament. But at the December meeting of the North Atlantic Council, it became dismally clear that West German rearmament was *not* imminent. Hence it seemed there was no reason for the U.S.S.R. to offer any tangible concessions, and this was to be confirmed at the foreign ministers' deputies' conference which met in March, 1951, and dragged on until June 21, producing absolutely nothing. The American diplomats had by now an almost superstitious fear of negotiations with the Russians: meetings led nowhere, they increased the West European governments' procrastination about defense and produced first false hopes and then exasperation at home. The British and the French clung to the meetings with equally superstitious hope. Negotiations, they felt, decreased the chances of the Americans doing something rash and just *might* produce some dramatic Soviet initiative which would spare them from German rearmament and from increased exertion on behalf of joint defense. The Europeans were for negotiating, the Americans for *doing*

[19] Acheson, *op. cit.*, p. 481.

things. That the two could be combined, that in fact negotiations could be successful only if the European defense effort was proceeding well and rapidly, does not seem to have occurred to either.

The reverberations of the double impasse in Korea and in Europe echoed angrily in the halls of Congress and on public platforms throughout the United States. There was an impulsive reaction on the part of a large part of the public, in many respects resembling that which was to rage some fifteen years later on Vietnam. Much of the debate concerned not logical alternatives but a search for a magical solution and invocation of moral and philosophical verities inherent in each choice. Europe, it was argued, was being ungrateful and unwilling to assume the burden of its own defense. The British and French were criticizing and quibbling while American boys were dying in the Far East. British intrigues were to blame for the restraints put upon MacArthur and, consequently, for the American defeats and the costly stalemate. The United Nations, some argued, was a hoax which was costing the American people dearly. There was more than a grain of truth in such charges. But they tended to disregard the harsh realities and thus contributed to confusion and certain hysteria rather than to a rational re-examination of the U.S. role and capabilities in international affairs. For all the very considerable criticisms which one can make of the Truman-Acheson management of foreign affairs in 1950–52, one must credit it with not allowing itself to be deflected from the goal of organizing a viable West European defense and political system. But this vital enterprise moved slowly compared to the feverish tempo of modern politics and modern technology. What would the Russians not have given in 1949 in order to avoid a sizable West German force! By 1954, with their nuclear arsenal, they were willing to give much less; and the Russia of the 1960s, with its intercontinental missiles, etc., was not unduly concerned, despite all the propaganda campaigns to the contrary, about a West German *land* force.

In addition to an actual war, the Truman administration in its last two years had two other battles on its hands. It had to assault French obduracy and British fears to get a measure of agreement on European defense. At the same time it had to beat off the persistent attacks of conservative critics at home. From them—people as diverse as ex-Ambassador Joseph Kennedy, ex-President Herbert Hoover, and Senator Robert Taft—came insistent voices that the United States was overextending itself by assuming obligations that created inflation at home and would bring about eventual bankruptcy, and most of all by pledging to rush troops into every threatened breach. In 1947, Taft had warned that

America could not help the "free world" unless she remained "solvent and sensible." Korea was a warning and Vietnam was to provide an ample demonstration of how hard it is for a democracy to remain solvent and, even more, sensible when caught in a situation which is neither full-fledged war nor peace. And Taft's call in 1951 for the Congress to reassert itself in foreign-policy matters and to curb the President's powers there, then decried as new isolationism, would be repeated in fifteen years' time.

Caught in the cross fire between faint hearts in Europe and the Republican Jeremiahs at home, the administration at times seemed oblivious that its real antagonist was the Soviet Union and its real aim a diplomatic victory leading to a solution of the German problem. In 1952, yet another Soviet initiative on the latter threw the State Department into a tizzy. The Russians went beyond their previous tantalizing proposals by expressing readiness to have unified Germany free to rearm, and proposing free elections in East Germany under the supervision of the four occupying powers. This was, at least, a hint that in return for having Germany neutral they might be willing to throw the East German Communist regime to the wolves, or rather to its own people. Again there was an imminent threat: the West was about to grant the Bonn Republic sovereignty—a European Defense Community with German participation was to be set up. Another American Presidential election was in the offing, and prudence dictated yet another friendly approach in Europe. But to Washington the Soviet proposal was the ultimate in unsportsmanlike behavior. The Europeans had been cajoled into doing something—the NATO table of organization had been painfully worked out—and now here were the Soviets ready to spoil everything. Acheson, even before studying the Soviet note, was sure that it "had the usual hooks in it." *After* a careful study he described the Soviet moves as "the golden apple of discord tactics . . . tossed over the Iron Curtain in the hope of causing discord among the allies." [20] The apple was never picked up, and once again the Americans failed to ascertain whether they could cash in on Soviet nervousness. The EDC was to crumble within two years.

The effect of the Korean War was thus to expose and enhance the fragility of the Western alliance. Economically the Marshall Plan had contributed to a near miracle of West European recovery and prosperity. That and the heartening prospect of West European political (as well as economic and military) unity appeared as a splendid vindication of

[20] *Ibid.*, p. 632.

American foreign policies. But undermining this success were the baffling problems of the Third World. The French were fighting in Indochina; their position in North Africa was becoming more precarious. The British were in similar troubles in Egypt and Iran. In practically every case the European power was fighting a rear-guard action against local nationalism. The electorates of the Western nations had become weary of their imperial burdens and eager to enjoy the benefits of the welfare state and the American way of life; they did not want their resources and attention diverted to distant affairs in Cyprus or Tunisia. But the American attitude of anticolonial condescension was bound to irritate, and not only those who clung to the shreds of former imperial grandeur. However greatly Acheson had been disenchanted with India, he still somberly lectured the French ministers (with words that have a pathetic ring in the midst of the Vietnam imbroglio) that the Americans could not help feeling sympathy for *any* people which claimed to be oppressed and that it made little difference "whether or not the allegedly oppressed were, in fact, oppressed." The French were gently chided for their reluctance to have their North African troubles aired in the United Nations, though on legal grounds their position was unassailable.

In fact, the refrain ever so discreetly repeated by Washington to its European allies bears a striking resemblance to the lesson read some years later to the United States: there is no disgrace for a major power in making concessions or even capitulating to colonial nationalism, or in giving in to a small state; on the contrary, such admission of political or military defeat would be applauded as a wise and generous step enhancing that power's moral prestige. But the American attitude changed drastically when a conflict involved Communists. There was support for the British action in Malaya against the Communist guerrillas, and the French in Indochina were recipients of considerable U.S. aid. Still, even there American help and support were tinged with condescension and criticism.

It is not that the American attitude was basically wrong or that specific criticisms were not justified. But discretion and restraint are necessary ingredients of a successful alliance. A critical and carping ally in many ways builds up more resentment than a forceful or even bullying one. The United States expected Britain and France to give up longstanding interests and obligations at the same time that it expected them to expend men and resources against every hypothetical Communist threat. It was immoral to use power to protect centuries-old French interests in North Africa or British investments in Iran, yet at the same time the French army was to be expanded and British defense budgets increased to appease an American obsession (as it was being increasingly viewed) about the danger of Communism. Washington stubbornly refused to reconcile itself to the fact that Communist China was now a reality, while every predatory Near Eastern politician, every non-Communist rebel movement, was seen to embody irresistible national aspirations. Thus mutual disenchantment and irritation grew. The Western alliance limped on. But what could have been achieved had there been more unity and expedition!

Mounting frustrations over the European alliance and the Asian war thus ended much of the public enthusiasm and unity behind American foreign policy which had been generated by the inception and success of the Marshall Plan. Continued prosperity (which moved a rueful Democratic politician to observe callowly, after the 1952 election, "We have run out of poor people") did not cancel the effect of continuing casualty lists. A complex and lingering crisis which calls for patience and measured response rather than widely shared sacrifices and all-out effort can be more dangerous to democratic institutions than an all-out war. This was perhaps the most important lesson of Korea, yet it was largely ignored.

Legally, the United States was not at war. The kind of patriotic elation which in "real" war silences partisan criticism could not assert itself. The issue at stake, clear to some, was and had to be puzzling to most of the people. Whom was the United States fighting? Obviously *not* the North Koreans, for they could be and were defeated with little trouble. The Communist Chinese? But then why not bomb their bases and cities? The Soviet Union? But the United States had diplomatic relations with that state, joined with it in international conferences, etc. Was the United States fighting merely as one of the United Nations and at its behest? Why then was the participation of other members at most only token? The principle at stake also appeared fuzzy. The aim of the U.S. actions and sacrifices was to teach the lesson that "aggression does not pay." But then the real instigator of aggression was not affected and it could hardly be claimed that this was the intended lesson.

"There shall always be a Korea," said some wiser and more pessimistic people, implying that just as the British soldiers throughout the nineteenth century intermittently fought at the northwest frontier in India, so in this strange world the American soldier would always have to watch over some border of the non-Communist world. But this threatened to be a shattering psychological if not a material burden.

Britain's little wars of the nineteenth century were fought by a small professional army. A dictatorship, especially a Communist one, is always in a state of emergency, *psychologically* always on a war footing. But America? Korea could not be compared to the Indian Wars, nor was it a "police action," as Truman once incautiously characterized it. "Laws become silent when arms begin to talk" was an old Roman maxim. But that was an insufferable prospect. Politicians, newspapers, and television (still in its infancy) were free to portray horrors of actual fighting, impugning the purpose of the whole enterprise, questioning motivations of the leaders, while *some* young Americans were required to risk and give their lives. Truman's administration was wiser than Johnson's in a similar predicament, when in December, 1950, it proclaimed a state of national emergency and followed with some economic controls, for these at least created the appearance of the nation sharing in the purpose and the sacrifice. Still, this was merely "tokenism."

These troublesome paradoxes were not without their effect on and beyond the battlefield. The American soldier performed creditably, and the Communist expectation of widespread demoralization of the American fighting men, of actual mutinies, etc., was disappointed, whatever the painful facts which were established later on about the behavior of Americans in prisoner-of-war camps.[21] The Soviet and the Chinese managers of the Korean enterprise were too sophisticated to share Hitler's contemptuous delusions about the worthlessness and lack of tenacity of the American soldier. Yet if one studies their moves and propaganda, one gets a clear picture of their hopes that disgruntled soldiers would blame their government for incomprehensible conflict and might become susceptible to revolutionary appeals; that a democratic community would not have the endurance to sustain the "neither war nor peace" situation; that the resulting frustrations, guilt feelings, and disenchantment with the ineffective and undemocratic South Korean regime would turn into dissent and then widespread defeatism, eroding social cohesion and setting the stage for anarchy. At the time, however, the scenario was not to be acted out.

---

[21] Some studies alleged that 13 to 15 per cent of Americans in Communist hands collaborated actively with the enemy. There were instances of American officers and men joining in propaganda broadcasts and appeals, supporting Communist charges about germ warfare, etc. Beyond active collaboration, and in view of the usual Communist treatment of prisoners, it is not surprising that many snatched from civilian life or from comfortable billets in Japan lapsed, once in the camps, into passivity and despondency.

Yet there were portents of things to come. The effect of Korea was apparently to accentuate the swing to the Right, as evidenced in the furore caused by the recall of one general and the election in 1952 of another. But if one searches for the true meaning of McCarthyism, one finds in its appeal some of the same essentially anarchistic feelings which were to become such a prominent feature of the activity of the extreme Left in the late 1960s.

Joseph McCarthy purported to speak for the People deceived and oppressed by the Establishment: the corrupt national administration with its retinue of cynical diplomats and subservient generals. College administrators and professors offer easy targets for attack. Unfortunate individuals were required publicly to atone for and abjure their earlier political affiliations. The manner was that of contrived pseudopopulist vulgarity and contempt for social amenities. McCarthy was thus bound to appeal to the populist instincts of a democracy distrustful and exasperated by the fruits of leadership of suave diplomats of the Acheson type and the sophisticated New Deal bureaucrats produced by the law and graduate schools of the East. Most of all there was the Plot, which was offered as an explanation of all the travails and anxieties visited upon American society since the war. There had been a Great Betrayal by those directing the affairs of the republic.

McCarthyism lacked two important ingredients for a successful political *movement*. First, the Senator failed to provide himself with a political philosophy. To sell even anti-intellectualism, especially to the young, one needs an ideology and a retinue of intellectuals to expound it. One cannot fight the establishment with nothing more than a senatorial or committee staff. Equally fatal was the lack of a comprehensive economic and social program. It was only a question of time before even the most choleric patriots would tire of the parade of real or alleged Communist operatives and of McCarthy's unsubstantiated stories of treason in high places. And, finally, it was McCarthy's fate to encounter, on a television show which purported to be Senate committee hearings, an actor more skillful than himself and to go down to defeat. What had begun some years before as a suspense drama ended as farce.

The impact of McCarthyism on domestic politics and on popular attitudes toward foreign policy was long-lasting and little short of disastrous. Domestically, it set back what had been a growing maturity and sophistication of both the intellectual community and the public at large on the subject of Communism and radical ideologies in general. By 1948, Communism was a most insignificant, even picturesque, feature of the American scene. The broader spectrum of ritualistic radicalism with its toleration and concealed admiration for Communism had suffered what seemed like an irretrievable collapse with the fiasco of the Progressive party that same year. McCarthyism can be charged with restoring some of the respectability of the extreme Left by endowing it with a halo of martyrdom. It is especially on the sensitive ego of the intellectual community that McCarthyism left a scar. The criteria of loyalty and adherence to the American form of government would for many never lose the partly ridiculous and partly sinister connotations they had acquired through the Senator's antics. The time would come when any call for restraint or self-examination brought forth from the academic and information-media community visceral reactions and cries of "McCarthyism." Thus the lasting damage to the thinking processes of a democracy.

Needless to say, neither the diplomatic nor the military services ought to remain sacrosanct or free from constant scrutiny. But ceaseless reprobation visited upon those necessary agencies must impair democratic government as a whole. The American diplomat has always been in an unenviable predicament. His advice is usually impatiently thrust aside whenever it interferes with the politician's needs. The highest preferments in his profession are reserved for the rich amateur (or for the professor). Conservatives view him suspiciously because of his exposure to foreign ways and connections, liberals because he moves among aristocrats and other diplomats rather than among the masses. The logic of the American world position has required that these prejudices and superstitions be cast aside and that a professional and efficient foreign service be built up. With McCarthy, the effort was set back—irretrievably, perhaps. All of postwar history is a testimony to the truth that successful foreign policy not only is a matter of decisions and initiatives reached at the highest level, but depends at least as much on attention to detail, on careful evaluation of facts and portents by rank-and-file officials. This task cannot be performed well by people who are unappreciated as a group or held suspect by their society.

In the inquest over the Korean War, it was said on one hand that America could not afford another Korea, and on the other that this kind of limited war was the only kind this country and the world could afford. Paradoxically, both views were justified. An all-out atomic war was and remains ever more so an unimaginable horror. Hence it was at least predictable that beginning with the fifties, this country would be exposed to local but not necessarily localized conflicts, which, while within the material resources of the United States, would strain the psychological endurance and democratic framework of American society. But in 1953 such somber prospects did not automatically mean despair and acquiescence in visions similar to George Orwell's *1984*. America's power to enforce the peace was still enormous, the possibilities of supplementing it through a revived and united Western Europe still promising. And the now perceptible weakening of Communist unity, the loosening of the link between Russia nationalism and the interests of world Communism, opened new opportunities for an enlightened and alert diplomacy.

7

Almost Peaceful
Coexistence

When it comes to politics, one ought not to ask "What's in a name?" The course of modern history answers: a great deal. Before 1914, terms like socialism and capitalism had fairly precise meanings. After 1918, they became less clear, and certainly following World War II, neither term could be employed to describe any actual social and political system without such a mass of reservations and qualifications as to render their use uneconomic if not senseless. Yet current history has been powerfully affected by the fact that the Soviet Union proclaims itself proudly to be a socialist society, while most Americans, Britons, Frenchmen, etc., will hem and haw but eventually grant that they live under capitalism. Terms like "welfare state" and "mixed economy" may be insisted upon by specialists, but they do not appeal to or persuade the public at large. Egypt, while trying to conquer or absorb other countries—activities which in a simpler age were "imperialist"—accused Great Britain, then in hasty retreat from its overseas possessions and anxious that this retreat preserve a modicum of decorum and orderliness, of being imperialistic. "Neocolonialism" appears to be a term admirably designed to describe some of the policies and activities of the Soviet Union, but it is used to describe mysterious iniquities of the ex-colonial powers. "One-party democracy" would appear an apt description of Nazi Germany, for alas there can be no doubt that a great majority of Germans in 1935 or 1938 would have voted for the Fuehrer even in free elections. But democracy is good and Hitler was bad, and so the phrase is not used in this instance. But Western help and understanding were obviously required for the new underdeveloped countries, and equally obviously the form of government in Ben Bella's Algeria or Nkrumah's Ghana could not be described as *simply* democracy, so the American social scientists came up with the new term of one-party democracy.

One seeks in vain for a term that would describe adequately the system and method of governance of Stalin's Russia. Dictatorship seems pallid and insufficient: the extent of oppression cannot be compared with that of Franco's Spain or Salazar's Portugal. Even Oriental despotism does not fit: Tamerlane's subjects were not required to attend constant meetings and subjected to indoctrination. Nor, as long as Stalin lived, could the system be recognized as conforming to the classical type of oligarchy. The Molotovs, Malenkovs, and Khrushchevs enjoyed powers undreamed of by a Venetian nobleman or a Whig potentate of the eighteenth century, but they and their families were no more secure than the average citizens, possibly less so, when it became a matter of sudden dismissal from a job, imprisonment, or worse.

It is in this last respect that Stalin's death brought a significant change. After a brief transitional period, the party hierarchy liquidated the leadership of its rival—the security organization—by dispatching Beria and some associates to their amply deserved fates, and thrust aside what could have developed into a military challenge to their supremacy by firing Zhukov. There began the rule of party secretaries, middle-aged men who had made their careers under Stalin. They appreciated the positive side of Stalinism—the fact that they made their dazzling careers under it, and the way the ordinary citizen had to "shape up" or else—but understandably they did not appreciate those constraints it had placed on their enjoyment of power and of life in general. Khrushchev had their endorsement so long as he did not challenge their vested interests. They supported him when he fought against the cream of the Stalinist old guard, but when he continued harping on the bad old times and became ill-tempered and impatient, he became a menace and had to go. To the party managers, 1953 marked the promise and 1964 was to signify the consummation of the bureaucratic paradise: the evil old man was gone, but the useful habits he had instilled in the population remained; then once you got rid of a choleric and unreliable boss you had the best of all possible worlds.

In the spring of 1953, this outcome of the intraparty struggles could not be predicted. To the ten or twelve people on whom the government of the enormous empire devolved, the death of their boss must have been both a relief and a threat. Most of them had evidently been slated to be victims of a new purge which had been presaged by such baffling and ominous developments as the celebrated "Doctors' Plot." Now they could breathe more freely. But apart from their personal interests and rivalries, Stalin's successors shared the task of holding together Soviet society, which—in view of the enormous cruelties and miseries inflicted upon the people, the inefficiencies built into its administrative structures, the hazardous foreign policies—probably seemed to many of them to have been functioning only because of the magic and awe exerted by the tyrant. That they must hang together for fear of hanging separately appeared to members of the Presidium of the Central Committee of the Communist party as much more than just a figure of speech.

Ejected from that august body were the newcomers the 19th Party Congress had placed there only five months before (probably to enable them to get some training on the job before their senior colleagues were removed and liquidated). Hasty arrangements were made to conceal, not entirely successfully, the apprehension and dissonances among the oligarchs. Malenkov succeeded to the presidency of the Council of Ministers but was made to surrender his position on the party secretariat. Beria reunited the security agencies under his direction. Molotov returned to the Foreign Ministry, nothing spectacular in the way of a power base, but a high-ranking party man was needed to replace the loathsome Vyshinsky. Two less important appointments illustrated the new leadership's anxiety for popularity and appearance of national unity. Marshal Voroshilov, Stalin's old crony, much mistreated by him during the last years but enjoying a measure of public appeal because of his military bearing and folksy ways, was installed as the nominal head of the state.[1] Even more characteristic was the prominence given to Marshal Zhukov's appointment as Deputy Minister of War. Russia's most prestigious and successful war commander had been kept by Stalin in the obscurity of a provincial command. His new appointment was an obvious bid for the support of professional army men.

[1] During the war he gave proof of both personal bravery and lack of fitness for command. He fought in the front lines during the first phase of the siege of Leningrad. Some time later an episode took place recounted by General Shtemenko in his delightful memoirs. Voroshilov, sent as a delegate of the High Command to the Crimea, insisted on conducting a tour of inspection in the vicinity of the front on horseback. Such a gesture, he argued with members of his staff horrified at both the delay and the risks involved, was good for the soldiers' morale.

What were the leaders afraid of? First, of the people, then, of each other. To them it was not inconceivable that freed of Stalin, the Russian people would remember their *revolutionary* tradition. Riots, demonstrations, and even armed uprisings had been, after all, not so many years before a constant feature of the Russian scene. As late as 1927, Trotsky's supporters had taken to the streets in demonstrations against Stalin's tightening grip. On the day of the tyrant's death, security forces ringed the center of Moscow, possibly to block a bid for power by a single oligarch or, as in the days of ancient Muscovy, a mob surging on the seat of the government. A modern totalitarian system could not thus be overthrown, but the workers' uprising in East Germany three months later was to demonstrate the dangerous potential of a fusion of people's sufferings and suddenly aroused hopes. Constant repetition of the theme of unity and firmness incongruously combined with a plea for "prevention of any kind of disorder and panic" contained in the official announcement about the reorganization of the leading organs of the government and the party.

The air of secrecy surrounding the moves and intrigues at the highest level could not quite conceal the bitter rivalries and hatreds. It was known that Malenkov and Molotov had been personal enemies—Molotov, for so long second man in the regime, had been replaced by Malenkov during the last years of Stalin's life as his closest adviser and intended successor. The third, Beria, did not let grass grow under his feet: consolidating his grip on the security agencies and at the same time courting popularity, he sought credit for the regime's decision to abolish the worst features of the Stalinist terror and reassured the citizenry that they were now entering the era of "socialist legality" and national equality, with terror and intensive ramifications of the last few years forever in the past. . . . Whether it was or was not so, this was interpreted by Beria's colleagues as a bid for supreme power. In July he was dismissed and "unmasked" as an "enemy of the people." In December he and his closest associates met the fate they had so often arranged for other dignitaries: a secret trial followed by death before a firing squad.[2]

---

[2] There were to be several versions of Beria's fall, encouraged and some authored by the irrepressible Khrushchev. One had him arrested by two marshals while trying to storm into a Presidium meeting. In another, Malenkov was authorized to summon the guard, but the trembling leader was unable to press the button(!), so Khrushchev did the honors and subsequently Beria was carried out and shot there and then. For all the symbolic value of the story during the period of Khrushchev's primacy, one must doubt its authenticity: a person could not advance to the pinnacle of Soviet power if he lacked the nerve to call for the executioner.

Whatever the real story behind the measures, the regime moved rapidly to relieve sufferings and to avoid the wrath of its people. The vast network of forced labor camps began to disgorge its preys. Great numbers of men and women began their trek from the north of Russia, from Siberia, to find their way back, perhaps after years of imprisonment, to normal life. Another equally numerous category now pardoned was that of the people exiled without "deprivation of freedom," as the Soviet law quaintly puts it. They now could return to their families. Among these fortunate ones were Molotov's wife, Mikoyan's son, and the widow of Maxim Litvinov.

The full horror of *everyday* life in Russia before March 5, 1953, is best brought to mind by another and on its face prosaic provision of the amnesty decree of March 27. Amnesties had traditionally been proclaimed on occasions of official rejoicing, such as the Czar's coronation or birth of an heir to the throne and after 1917 on major anniversaries of the Revolution. Now the amnesty coincided with the period of official mourning for "Comrade Stalin, whom we all have loved so much and who will live in our hearts forever." The amnesty canceled forthwith all investigations and proceedings concerning a large number of "malfeasance and economic as well . . . as military crimes": these included such "crimes" as lateness to work, alleged inefficiency in production, desertion as proved by having been a prisoner of war, etc. How urgent was thought the need to correct the abuses and how readily the law bent to political expediency was demonstrated by another stipulation: the Ministry of Justice was to revise the criminal code concerning the above crimes *within one month*—thirty days to reform or abrogate the entire system of laws and sanctions in the shadow of which every Soviet citizen had lived for so many years.

Even a superficial analysis of these steps taken in the wake of March 5 should suggest that the rulers viewed the problem of succession with apprehension and that their moves were an eloquent testimony as to their feeling of how vulnerable was the whole edifice of power and oppression. Yet in the West, the reaction to Stalin's death was one of gloomy forebodings. To some extent this reflected a preference for familiar rather than unfamiliar evils, and there was still a lingering trace of the belief that Stalin had been a "prisoner" of even more evil forces in the Politburo. Once again, more attention was being paid to what the Communists were saying than to what they were doing.

The immediate need was not only for an appearance of unity within the ruling team but within the Communist family of nations. "Let the imperialist aggressors and warmongers tremble in the face of our great friendship," wrote Mao Tse-tung, though he undoubtedly shared the relief and some of the apprehension of his Soviet colleagues at the historic event. The Chinese position vis-à-vis the Soviet Union was now even farther advanced, for Mao's approval, desperately needed by Stalin's heirs—though much as it was also in his interest to conceal any dissonances and conflicts—did not come free. The obsequies were hardly finished when a new and extensive trade and technical agreement was signed with China. Peking's delegation had been in Moscow for several months and nothing prior to Stalin's death indicated that an agreement was imminent. Now it was expedited. The Soviet Union undertook, in addition to credits, to dispatch experts to guide Chinese industrialization and to train Chinese personnel.

China was, in fact, to be the main beneficiary of Stalin's death. Soviet leaders were for the moment eager to advertise the new status of China even to their own people. Any tendency for a violent popular reaction against the Soviet system would be restrained by the reflection that China, that giant country of several hundred million people, was a close ally and a powerful testimony that Communism was the wave of the future. The Soviet press printed a picture of Malenkov with Stalin and Mao, thus implying a kind of apostolic succession and Mao's blessing of the new chief. In fact, it was a clumsy fake; a composograph made of the photograph at the time of the signing of the Sino-Soviet alliance in February, 1950, when Malenkov was one of many officials surrounding Mao and Stalin. It is difficult to decide which is more astounding, the brazenness of the propaganda fraud and the assumption that most people would not remember a photograph printed and widely distributed only three years before or the lack of self-assurance of a regime which felt compelled to invoke the moral support of a foreigner.

The most immediate substantial gain by China was undoubtedly Soviet agreement to the Korean truce. The stalemate which had prevailed in the peninsula since the spring of 1951 had taxed American patience and exacted not inconsiderable casualties, but it had been even more costly and above all dangerous to Communist China. On his inauguration, President Eisenhower undid *half* of Truman's error vis-à-vis Formosa by "unleashing Chiang Kai-shek," as it was melodramatically expressed at the time: i.e., by announcing that the United

States would no longer object to or prevent a descent from the island on the mainland. And he let drop hints through diplomatic channels that if a truce were not forthcoming, "we intended to move decisively without inhibition in our use of weapons, and would no longer be responsible for confining hostilities to the Korean Peninsula." [3] It is still not clear how seriously this threat to use nuclear weapons was meant. But it is unlikely that it scared *Stalin*. The prospect of the United States becoming more deeply involved in the Far East was far from disturbing to the equanimity of the Soviet leadership. On the other hand, the Chinese had every reason to wish for a speedy termination of the fighting. They had extracted maximum gains in prestige from their Korean involvement, but its continuation threatened them with disaster. The last phase of the Korean conflict makes an interesting story. The Chinese agreed in June to voluntary repatriation of prisoners of war, previously the biggest stumbling block to a settlement. Syngman Rhee's moves to sabotage the negotiations, such as his engineered "escape" of North Koreans held in his prison camp, the step which it was feared in Washington would close the door to an armistice, brought a very mild Communist reaction. Chinese military operations in the last weeks seemed designed to help the Americans' efforts to cajole the tenacious South Korean leader to a settlement which would leave his country divided. Thus in their attacks in July, the Peking forces attacked those salients of the U.N. front held by the South Korean units and mauled them badly, which made Rhee see the light and desist from his threat not to abide by any truce even if signed by the United States.

The truce which materialized in July, 1953, enabled the Peking regime to turn its energies to the task of internal construction, industrialization, and an over-all development of the economy which would enable China, it was hoped, within a few years to free herself of dependence on Russia. On the other hand, the armistice brought to an end a situation which from the Kremlin's point of view offered many advantages, promised even greater ones, and did not expose the Fatherland of Socialism to direct danger.

With a precarious peace returning to the Far East, the Soviet leaders faced the unwelcome prospect of the United States' now being able to concentrate on European affairs. In Washington, the Eisenhower administration had just taken over amidst resounding declarations

[3] Dwight D. Eisenhower, *Mandate for Change: 1953-1956* (New York, 1963), p. 181.

that the policy of containment would give way to the brave new world of "liberation" and "roll-back." Such at least had been promised by John Foster Dulles during the campaign. The new Secretary of State was held by the Soviets in considerable respect, more perhaps than any of America's postwar makers of foreign policy. Though his background was strikingly similar to Acheson's, and though in retrospect it is difficult to discern a major difference in the substance of their policies (campaign oratory aside), somehow Dulles was believed by Moscow to be a more authentic specimen of the genus "capitalist," for which the Soviets always had considerable respect. With General Eisenhower being able to secure the kind of national consensus and support which Truman never had been able to elicit, with Dulles imparting his experience and indefatigable energy to the design and execution of policies, it was, at least on paper, a formidable combination.

Alas, these formidable assets were not translated into solid diplomatic gains; the brave slogans did not turn into dynamic initiatives and new policies. Partly, the new administration found itself in a familiar predicament, not unlike Truman's during its last two years: political harassment at home and dissonances within the Western alliance were continuing to cripple American policies. Senator McCarthy's attack was no longer frontal—the charge of heinous if vague and unspecified treason could not profitably be pursued against a Republican administration headed by the enormously popular General and by Dulles, with his lay Presbyterian and Wall Street background. But sniping attacks at isolated State Department officials, the United States Information Service, etc., continued. In fending them off, the administration had to expend much of the attention, time, and energy desperately needed to deal with other issues. During its first eighteen months, the new leadership went through a gamut of diplomatic moves to contain the impossible Senator from Wisconsin. There were efforts to appease, as usual unavailing and leading to new demands; there were near summit meetings with Vice-President Nixon and Secretary Dulles appealing to reason and common interests; there was the unavoidable confrontation in the form of televised meetings of McCarthy's Congressional committee. Then there was massive retaliation: the Senate censure of its maverick member; Eisenhower stopped inviting Mrs. McCarthy to the White House.

To domestic irritation were joined foreign complexities. Here again the factor of timing intrudes with its ironic and baneful repercussions.

In 1953, a multitude of problems not directly related to Russia, though vitally affected by the existence and policies of the U.S.S.R., claimed the attention of American policy-makers. There was Britain's conflicts with Egypt and Iran, France's drastic predicament in Indochina and her increasingly precarious position in North Africa. The position of the Western powers had become both much stronger and much weaker. They had recovered economically, the danger of Communism acceding to power in France and Italy was past, the West German state was a reality and in the midst of its economic miracle. But the sense of danger and the feeling of urgency in working toward military and political unity had been dampened by economic recovery and the passage of time. Most of all, there was now the seemingly intractable problem of liquidating colonialism. To farseeing Europeans, even those acknowledging the inevitable end of empires, the Communist threat was no longer a direct one: no fear of Soviet armies on the English Channel or a Communist government in Rome. But Communism could enter through the breach made in retreating Western power: Soviet influence could replace British presence and ties in Egypt or Iraq and France's influence in Algeria. The distinctions drawn by the Americans— France was urged to hold on to Indochina because the nationalist movement there was Communist-dominated, while she was to concede in North Africa because resistance to legitimate nationalist aspirations inevitably breeds Communism—seemed unreal and nearsighted. Even more jarring was the basic inconsistency in expecting Britain and France to stop acting as great powers in one respect when it came to dealing with their overseas possessions and interests, and to continue and increase their world-wide role in defense commitments and expenditures whenever it came to countering Communism and the U.S.S.R. Inevitably the feeling grew that if the United States was so good at giving advice it might as well assume the responsibility for those areas and problems.

The main consequence of all this was that at first the Eisenhower administration had relatively little time and opportunity to devote to U.S.–Soviet relations. Time was taken up by a variety of important but secondary issues. There were intricate problems of intra-alliance diplomacy: for instance, how to deal with the masterful and wily German, Adenauer, who was determined that his country should not foot the bill for any U.S.–Soviet bargain. If the stability of the West German government was at times an embarrassment, then the instability of the French one was a veritable curse: you would reach an agreement with a Mayer, but before it could be implemented a Laniel or Bidault would be in his place, shrugging his shoulders and expostulating. Churchill was back in office but, like the British Empire, was but a reflection of his past, and his foreign minister and successor, Anthony Eden, found it more difficult to get along with Dulles than with Molotov.

And thus it was that the U.S.S.R. and Communism somehow receded into the background of the United States' day-to-day diplomacy. Unless the Russians made a move in some part of the world, the "Soviet problem" did not appear so urgent as the constant alarums elsewhere. "Rollback" and "liberation" gradually receded as American foreign policy settled back into familiar and comfortable routines of "containment."

But all this campaign oratory was to have an ironic sequence. True, American policy achieved modest successes in preventing new gains by Communism. The CIA discreetly assisted in removing a potential Nasser—Iran's Mossadegh; once this frantic old man was overthrown by the Shah and the army, the United States extended help and its good offices in solving the Anglo-Iranian dispute. Not so discreetly, the same agency helped to remove the leftist Guatemalan government in 1954. But the most important "rollback" effected was to be not of any Communist sphere of influence but of the Western one. Irresolute and inconsistent policies in the Near East contributed to Egyptian and Anglo-French exasperation, prompting the desperate and clumsy Suez venture in 1956.

As against the occasional severity with her allies, American policy under Dulles exhibited considerable hesitation and uncertainty during Soviet Russia's moments of crisis or embarrassment. Such an occasion arose shortly after Stalin's death when widespread riots erupted in East Germany in June, 1953.

There, as well as in other Soviet satellites, Moscow's policies had for some time displayed a degree of confusion and hesitation undoubtedly connected with the event of March 5. The leaders of the satellite states had been urged to proceed with de-Stalinization; to follow the Soviet example by separating the supreme authority in the party from that in the government; and most of all to initiate a program of economic reforms and concessions to alleviate popular discontent and avert riots and revolts. To the Ulbrichts, Bieruts, Rakosis, et al., there thus opened up the possibility of their own demotion from the status of little Stalins and of the necessity of sharing power. Equally disturbing was the lack of assurance and direction which they sensed in their

Soviet superiors and which in turn made them apprehensive and indecisive.

The Kremlin viewed East Germany with particular concern. Because of Berlin, it was not as isolated from the West as other satellites, and the contrast with the already prosperous West Germany could not be concealed. An explosion in East Germany would have grave repercussions elsewhere. Subsequent to the events of June there were rumors, never satisfactorily traced, that Beria and some other Soviet leaders were in favor of abandoning East Germany.

In late May and early June, the Ulbricht regime embarked on a series of far-reaching reforms and promises of relief to its sorely tried people. It acknowledged errors in connection with hasty collectivization, nationalization of small industry, retail trade, etc., and promised to undo them. And it also promised to stop the political persecution of high-school and university students. With remarkable candor, the government and party acknowledged that these "errors" were responsible for "numerous persons having left the Republic." Of special interest was the assertion of the regime's desire for greater intercourse and eventual unification with West Germany. "In its resolution the Politburo has been guided by the great aim of German unification, which demands from both sides concrete measures that facilitate drawing together. . . . The Politburo decided . . . to facilitate traffic between the German Democratic Republic and Western Germany. . . . Scientists and artists in particular are to be enabled to attend conferences in Western Germany." [4]

These far-reaching economic and social concessions and appeals to national sentiment coincided with a change in the structure of the Soviet authority in East Germany. The Commander in Chief was divested of political authority, which was assumed by a newly appointed civilian High Commissioner. The announcement of the change included for the first time in quite a while reference to the association of the U.S.S.R. with the West in the occupation of Germany. "It will be the duty of the High Commissioner to maintain relations with the representatives of the occupation authorities of the U.S.A., Great Britain, and France in all questions of an all-Germany character arising out of the agreed decisions of the Four Powers on Germany." [5]

Altogether, it was a remarkable series of moves. The U.S.S.R. was certainly not going suddenly to quit East Germany, but everything in-

---

[4] *Documents on International Affairs, 1953* (London, 1956), pp. 154–56.
[5] *Ibid.*, p. 159.

dicated that she was ready to discuss the German question in its widest context. And it was at least possible that the Communist regime in the East might be sacrificed for the sake of a neutralized but united Germany.

Alert Western diplomacy would have called for a summit meeting on Germany right then and there. In fact this was the course of action urged by Churchill in a speech in May, but the Eisenhower administration did not want its image of a businesslike and stern policy vis-à-vis the Russians compromised by social amenities with those tricky people. Adenauer, visiting Washington soon after the President's inauguration, had established his considerable influence over American policy in Europe, which lasted until the end of the Eisenhower era, and needless to say he feared any discussion of the affairs of his country from which he would be excluded. He believed rather unrealistically that by keeping the Americans and Russians apart he would compel the latter to make concessions to him. The idea of a summit meeting had some rather unexpected partisans: General MacArthur had suggested that the President-elect should seek a meeting with Stalin. But Eisenhower and Dulles did not buy this: the President never liked international meetings or business visits, and the Secretary of State would have been hard-pressed at the moment to translate his tough talk into concrete demands at the conference table.

In the middle of June, the German situation underwent a new and tragic twist. Here enters an element of mystery. The East German government suddenly raised the work norms. Coming on top of the recent considerable concessions to and still more considerable expectations by the population, this step was bound to lead to trouble. Even a regime as clumsy as Ulbricht's must have realized that. Was it an intentional provocation, somebody in Moscow or Pankow sensing a possible accommodation to and sacrifice of the East German Communists, and counseling a step which would lead to disorders and require Soviet armed intervention? There was bound to be a considerable reluctance in the Kremlin to any response which might be interpreted as yielding in the face of riots, and equal reluctance to tokens of appeasement such as "sacrificing Ulbricht." False or real hopes in the eastern zone might lead to another flare-up that could spread to the other satellites.

The riots which erupted on June 16 and 17 in Berlin and other East German cities were proletarian uprisings not dissimilar to the one in Petrograd in March, 1917, which toppled the Romanovs and inaugurated the Russian Revolution. Widespread strikes led to manifestations directed against both the Ulbricht regime and the Russians; finally, Soviet tanks had to be brought in to put down the revolt.

The June events seemed a made-to-order opportunity for the United States to probe for diplomatic means leading to "rollback." A request by the West for an immediate four-power meeting would have put the Russians in an embarrassing situation. Or at least the United States could have adopted that technique of ominous and vague warnings which Khrushchev was to put to such good use in the years to come. Things were coming to a boil in the intraparty struggle in Russia, and the Soviets might well have felt on the defensive and forced to make concessions. But nothing was tried and nothing gained. President Eisenhower saluted the uprising as an "inspiring show of courage" but dismissed the possibility of even diplomatic steps. The Western commandants in Berlin condemned the repression and execution of alleged *agents provocateurs* from the Western zone as "acts of brutality which will shock the conscience of the world"—language that would be repeated in connection with the Hungarian revolution of 1956. Dulles' formula was now exposed for what it was: hollow campaign oratory, and the lesson was not lost on the Russians.

One must credit the Russians with having the good sense not to try to follow suppression of the revolt with reversal to the Stalinist pattern. The East German government acknowledged its mistakes once more. Some of its members were demoted and punished, and it was to be found conveniently enough that they were protégés of Beria, who for the next three years was blamed for all untoward developments in the U.S.S.R. or the satellites.

By August the Soviet regime had weathered the immediate post-Stalin hazards. The succession crisis was over. From the triumvirate the supreme authority devolved upon the duumvirate of Malenkov in the government and Khrushchev in the party. The expected troubles and disorders in the Soviet Union had not materialized. China was being bought off by the Korean armistice and extensive economic help, and nobody in the West suspected how serious and potentially dangerous already the gap was between the two countries.

Strategically, the Soviets were no longer in that position of helplessness vis-à-vis American nuclear and industrial power which had been obscured by Stalin's resourceful diplomacy. The recovery of Soviet industry was complete, and the heavy-industry segment of the Soviet economy was growing rapidly. (Agriculture was still in deplorable straits, and the Soviet consumer was only beginning to get relief.) In August the Soviets exploded a hydrogen bomb, and the U.S.S.R. now had a bomber force capable of reaching the United States. Soviet research on long-range missiles was proceeding apace, and soon the Russians would be able to achieve spectacular successes which with their talent for propaganda they converted into solid political assets. The Soviet armed forces, substantially increased following the outbreak of the Korean War, were apparently still further built up following Stalin's death, and now stood at about 5 million, as against 2.8 million in 1948.

To be sure, behind these impressive achievements there still lay grave political weaknesses as well as economic backwardness. But the Soviets had had always a simple, disingenuous but amazingly effective way of discounting rumors about their weakness: they denied and ridiculed them. It was thus predictable that when on August 8 Malenkov undertook to present to the Supreme Soviet a general review of the domestic and international scene, he took special pains to straighten out foreign observers and experts. Why, every sensible person had to be impressed with how strong the country was, how united its peoples, how harmoniously cooperative its leaders! An ignorant foreigner might well ask at this point: How about Beria? But precisely, Malenkov hastened to explain: "It is clear to everyone that the fact that a double-dyed agent of imperialism has been exposed and rendered harmless in good time cannot in any way be taken as evidence of weakness of the Soviet state." Only a heartless critic would question what Malenkov meant by "in good time," since the "double-dyed agent of imperialism" had headed Soviet security forces for fifteen years. With more sorrow than indignation, Malenkov felt it necessary to expatiate on the strange and sinful activities of the American government. Would the Comrade deputies believe that "Certain American circles have gone so far as to elevate subversive activity against the lawful governments of sovereign countries to the level of governmental policy"? [6] And was it not shameful that at a time when opportunities for international *détente* are so bright the United States should sponsor such agencies as the Psychological Warfare Committee, which has just published a report with all sorts of recommendations as to how to conduct the "cold war"?

It was true that beginning in the 1950s the United States government undertook belatedly, and somewhat ponderously and amateurishly,

[6] *Ibid.*, p. 28.

a major effort to counter Soviet propaganda. Russia, it was recognized, was scoring considerable gains through enterprises such as the Stockholm Peace Appeal. Communist efforts were especially successful in enlisting a number of intellectual and artistic luminaries in their cause or as fellow travelers. Hence discreet efforts were made to channel CIA funds into highbrow magazines and those conferences so beloved by the intellectual community, so that anti-Communism might become as respectable and profitable among the West European in-intelligentsia as anti-Americanism already was. The President's official family now included a dignitary whose title and functions would have startled the forefathers of the Republic: Special Assistant for Cold War Strategy.

Malenkov's eagerness that the West should get the point about the strength of the U.S.S.R. and the unshakable unity both of the Soviet people and of the Communist bloc had a special reason. He was, for a change, truthful when stating the melancholy fact that each time the Soviet Union spoke softly and declared its peaceful intentions it was seen in the West "as a manifestation of weakness." And the new leaders decided to break with Stalin's technique of threats and hints. This they knew was a calculated risk, but it had to be taken: the Soviets felt they had to defuse some of the dangers inherent in the world situation. Dulles' utterances were soon to give rise to a new term: brinkmanship—the art of coming close to precipitating a war and yet avoiding it by impressing the opponent with your determination. With all due regard to Dulles, it was Stalin who had practiced brinkmanship over the past years, notably in Berlin and Korea. Well, for the moment his successors had no wish to emulate him in this respect.

Malenkov's theme was, "We are not angry with anybody." The regime resumed diplomatic relations with Israel, which had been broken in December, 1952, at the time of the Doctors' Plot and the height of the anti-Zionist campaign. With royalist Greece and Tito's Yugoslavia, the U.S.S.R. now exchanged ambassadors. The Russians had abandoned their territorial claims on Turkey prior to Malenkov's speech. The Premier spoke warmly of India's peace-making role in the Korean conflict. He urged France to revert to a foreign policy of her own and recalled that the U.S.S.R. and France had a treaty of alliance. There were hopeful words about the United Nations, where the Soviets finally agreed to the election of a new Secretary-General to replace Trygve Lie, whom they disliked because of the U.N. role in the Korean conflict. All those shifts, though they did not represent tangible concessions, were still a clear repudiation of Stalin's policies.

Even about the United States Malenkov chose not to speak with that bristly hostility which had so often characterized Molotov's and Stalin's references to the main capitalist power. "We stand, as we have always stood, for the peaceful coexistence of the two systems."

Less ambitious and probably more fearful than it had been under Stalin, the new regime, however, did not have that freedom of action in foreign policy which Stalin had enjoyed. In Asia, and very soon elsewhere, the need to appease China put a severe limit on possibilities of a *détente* with the West. With foreign as well as domestic policy now emanating from a group of men rather than ultimately from a single man's will, there were additional reasons for hesitations and against bold initiatives. Thus the possibility of a fairly basic accommodation with the West, of a "solution" of the German problem, inevitably receded with Stalin's death. If the United States was precluded because of her alliance problems from having a clear-cut policy vis-à-vis Russia, then the same thing was true in reverse, though to a lesser extent. It was only after 1957 that the Soviet Union developed again a specific *American* policy. Moreover, the prospect of German rearmament in 1954 or 1955 was no longer so alarming as it was in 1949 or even 1952; a West German military intervention in the case of a revolt in a satellite country was unlikely in view of the Soviet Union's possession of nuclear weapons—and the events of June, 1953, had shown this. The danger now assumed a somewhat different form: a sovereign and armed West Germany might soon dominate any Western alliance or European community; in fact, in view of the Soviets' low opinion of the capacity of the American policy-makers, Bonn might well bend Washington to its designs.

But Soviet proposals held out little prospect of real concessions. At the Berlin meeting of the Big Four foreign ministers in January, 1954, Molotov proposed that the East and West German regimes set up a provisional central government or, barring that, that the existing regimes continue "for a certain period of time." The increased Soviet solicitude for its satellite was reflected in the demand that elections should be conducted by this "provisional" regime rather than by the four occupying powers, as under the 1952 Soviet draft. The East Germans would thus be able to interfere with the elections in the West, and in the unlikely eventuality that the Western Powers would agree to this bizarre scheme, there were conditions to be attached to the elections designed to open them to Communist chicanery or to subsequent Soviet questioning of their validity: they were to be held "under conditions of genuine freedom which would preclude pressure upon voters by big monopolies." Presumably under such monopolies the Soviets did not include the Socialist Unity party in the Eastern zone. The Russians also wanted the occupying powers to withdraw their forces prior to the elections "with the exception of limited contingents left to perform protective functions." It would have been interesting for the three Western states to probe this aspect of the Soviet draft: Were the Russians—with the events in East Berlin only a few months behind, with thousands of Germans still escaping to the West—ready to deprive their Communist friends of the reassuring presence of tanks and soldiers? There was an escape clause: in the event that "the security in either part of Germany is threatened," the occupying power could move right back.

At this point the Americans were less inclined than ever before to engage in diplomatic fencing over Germany. If the more amicable style of Soviet pronouncements strengthened Dulles' conviction that it paid to be tough with the Russians, then on British and French public opinion it had the intended and predictable effect of suggesting that the Russian danger was not so great, the need of arming West Germany not so urgent as before Stalin's death.

Concurrently, after long and protracted negotiations, the West was approaching the realization of a European Defense Community. The plan for the EDC was a laborious and somewhat awkward formula elaborated to reconcile the need for German soldiers with French fears and reservations. A multinational army with German units mixed in with those of other nationalities could not, it was hoped, arouse the memories of 1870, 1914, and 1940. Still, the mood of French politics was more hopeful about the Russian intentions and more depressed about the war in Indochina, and this tended to increase hostility to the idea of arming *"les boches."*

Dulles' precise legal mind chafed under the ambiguities and subtleties of the international situation. Again one is impressed by how the factors of timing and of the whimsicalities of domestic politics worked to the disadvantage of American foreign policy. The doctrine of massive retaliation, had it been pronounced in 1949, might conceivably have spared the world the Korean War. But in 1954, while it undoubtedly had a sobering effect on the Russians, it frightened America's allies much more. The speech in which it was first elucidated contained quotations from Lenin and Stalin of dubious authenticity and purported to show how Communism planned to conquer the world by inducing bankruptcy of free nations, but the gist of Dulles' argument was quite sensible: the United States cannot be expected to intervene with troops in the case of each and every Communist aggression; it cannot afford a military force to provide for and ward off every contingency. Nor could the United States go on expanding its defense expenditures "without grave budgetary, economic, and social consequences." Dulles went on to say that the way to deter aggression was "to be willing and able to respond vigorously at places and with means of its own choosing." A would-be aggressor ought to keep in mind that he would not always be able to fight under conditions of his own choosing: "Local defenses must be reinforced by the further deterrent of massive retaliatory power." Read with any care, Dulles' speech could *not* support the conclusion that he proposed to counter each and every aggression with nuclear weapons; he simply warned that in an emergency the United States would keep open all options, including massive retaliation.[7]

Reaction to the speech revealed once again a perennial handicap under which foreign policy must operate in any open democratic nation. Granted it is neither possible nor desirable for a democracy to operate without public discussion of foreign policy, yet there are times when excessive clarity is undesirable and a degree of ambiguity vital. But the "new" doctrine, new in the sense that now Dulles proclaimed that in the case of an aggression the United States would know what to do but was not telling, whereas before the United States did not know and could not tell, immediately provoked spirited protests in Western Europe. The more extreme of critics held that Dulles had unmasked the essentially aggressive and adventurist character of U.S. foreign policy. Take this possibility: a few junks begin landing Communist soldiers on Quemoy and Matsu to wrest them from Chiang and *bang!*, you have a nuclear war. Paris and London go up in smoke because the Americans are too stingy to finance a large land army *and* atomic

[7] In the late 1960s, the principle of flexible response was recognized as desirable in the case of student disorders, with professors and enlightened public opinion deploring it when a university administration stated clearly what it would do in the case of students seizing a dean or building. But the application of the same principle to American foreign policy was held as immoral and impermissible.

weapons! In the United States, Democratic politicians with some justification took Dulles' formula as a retrospective criticism of Truman's
action in Korea. It meant, said Acheson, naturally sensitive on the
last point, that any, even minor, Communist aggression would lead to a
third world war. No, said Adlai Stevenson, since even the most minute
Communist aggression would offer the United States the choice between
initiating a nuclear holocaust or doing absolutely nothing, the result
would most likely be that Moscow and Peking would "nibble" the
free world up piece by piece, since the United States would do nothing.

Both Dulles and his critics had some good points. But how, under
such conditions, one might ask, can one impress a potential enemy without frightening one's own nation and allies? How does one have *any*
foreign policy at all? The Republican administration executed a strategic
retreat to prepared positions: Dulles, it was pointed out, did not mean
the use of nuclear weapons on *every occasion* of Communist aggression.
Then it was remembered that it was possible to have small as well as
big nuclear bombs, and soon the theory of *limited nuclear war* sprouted
in some academic and military circles.

There was another, this time specifically American, trouble. All
parties to the debate became engrossed with the question of what the
United States could or should do, but they lost sight of the equally
important question of what were one's opponent's intentions, strengths,
and weaknesses. For Dulles, the problem either did not exist or seemed
so simple that it did not require discussion: the evil and all-encompassing
aim of Communism was world domination. Its strength lay in the vast
manpower at the disposal of the "Moscow-Peking axis," as the phrase now
went in the State Department. Its weakness lay in the field of nuclear
weapons and delivery systems for them, hence in the ability to withstand
a "brinkmanship" approach to foreign policy.

In the mid-fifties, it would have been difficult for any American
politician to question these assumptions without sounding as naïve as
Henry Wallace. It was as widely believed in 1954–55 that the Russians
were up to no good as it had been believed in 1945 that Stalin could
be reasoned with. This was fairly sound as a general principle, but
the next article of belief was less so: that there was a Moscow-Peking
axis with two Communist powers in firm agreement. Here again the
record of past illusions prevented a realistic appraisal of the present:
those who had believed in 1944–47 that the Chinese Communists were
"different" were being publicly pilloried, fired, or demoted if they

were in the State Department, or dragged from their academic havens to testify before Congressional committees. Nobody dared to point out the inconsistency in Dulles' position on the subject: If it is a good maxim not to believe what the Communists say, why should one put such trust in the continued and excessive declarations of mutual love between the Chinese and the Russians?

For Dulles, Communist China was "fanatically hostile to us and demonstrably aggressive and treacherous." His own background made him especially bitter about Peking's abusive language. His grandfather had negotiated the Sino-Japanese treaty of the 1890s; he himself had striven mightily on behalf of peace in the Pacific. The Secretary of State was a prominent Presbyterian layman; he had recalled before the United Nations that American missionaries performed a multitude of good works in China, that American philanthropy had been generous in its efforts to rescue the Chinese from their heathen ways. And now the unfeeling Mao and Chou En-lai had sold their souls and their people to the Russians. For General Eisenhower, Peking was "beyond the pale," as he put it, and this feeling was, as we shall see, to have consequences toward the end of his term.

Potential weaknesses and vulnerabilities within the Communist camp were thus neglected by American policy-makers. Yet there was Yugoslavia to show that Communism was not monolithic, that even a small nation could chip away at its unity, that in fact this was by now the most practical way of effecting that "rollback" of Soviet power which Dulles had promised in the campaign. Tito was in fact a valuable ally. Only a few years before eager to provoke the West, he was now bound by an alliance with Greece and Turkey. Churchill in the waning moments of his ministry must have felt that it had not been such a bad mistake after all to sponsor the mercurial Balkan leader during the war. The Russians were trying to undo their previous mistakes in regard to Yugoslavia, but as yet Tito remained wary. He longed for a trip to Washington, but Eisenhower and Dulles did not relish contacts even with repentant Communists. The Yugoslavs, however, cheerfully accepted American arms and economic aid, became reasonable over Trieste, discontinued their most costly social reforms such as collectivization. Yet this palpable lesson in how Communism could be transformed by nationalism, how a rebellious Communist country could become a more useful ally than a democratic one, was largely ignored in Washington. Khrushchev and Bulganin were in a most undignified and insistent manner to invite themselves to Belgrade, while Eisenhower and Dulles would have been shocked at the suggestion of even informal diplomatic connections with Peking.[8]

For all its new sense of direction, for all the undoubted respect Dulles inspired in the Russians, his policy was neither imaginative nor flexible. The Secretary of State expended much of his energy in building and strengthening various systems of alliance and treaty organizations, but these could not have the decisive importance in international affairs that they had before 1914, or between the wars. Now, alas, they only extended American commitments rather than adding substantially to American strength or "world security." Regional defense arrangements had been much desired by Churchill during the war and were vetoed by the Americans in their all-consuming passion for and hope in the United Nations. A decade or so later they could not decisively affect the greatly changed disposition of forces and dangers.

In Europe the situation was different. NATO was a factor of great importance, even though Soviet acquisition first of the atomic and then of the hydrogen bomb frustrated much of its original purpose and concept.[9] With the American intervention in Korea, and especially after Stalin's death, Soviet military effectives were substantially increased, and the Soviets by the mid-1950s had the capacity to move massively into the West.

To themselves, the Soviets undoubtedly considered this increase as being justified by *defensive* considerations. Be that as it may, the belief in Western capitals in the existence of huge Soviet land armies was now justified, and strengthening of NATO appeared imperative. If the Russians' friendlier tone inclined London and Paris to drag their feet, then Dulles' musings on massive retaliation imparted new alacrity to the efforts to build an effective Western defense system. Already the

[8] It must be added that Britain did not secure any advantages or even civil treatment from the Chinese by its early recognition of Peking. Also, during the Republican administration there began those periodic conferences, or more properly mutual monologues, held by the American and Chinese representatives in Warsaw. Certainly, at least during Eisenhower's first term, the Chinese would have responded frostily to any advances from Washington and used them to extract more from Russia. Still, such contacts and a more open mind on the whole issue would have been especially useful when Sino-Soviet relations took a decisive turn for the worse after 1958.

[9] This concept, in oversimplified form, was to enable the United States in the case of Soviet aggression to have other options in addition to the stark alternatives of letting the West be occupied by Soviet armies and/or using nuclear weapons on Russia. Let us repeat that since the Soviets knew (which the West did not) that they had no intention or power to occupy Western Europe in 1948 or 1949, they interpreted NATO and its prelude, the Marshall Plan, as aggressive steps.

West Europeans were becoming exasperated not only over the Soviet threat, but also over the Americans' overeagerness to defend them from it, and what was worse, the stern admonitions from Washington that if the United States was going to pour money and men into the effort, the West European states should not stint theirs.

These tangled analyses, feelings, and fears found their expression in the bizarre sequence of events concerning the key issue of Western defense: the rearmament of Germany. Only nine years after the utter devastation of the war, here was part of Germany already outpacing economically every other European state, bound to dominate any West European defense organization. Mounting fears of Germany, lessened fears of Russia, apprehension about Britain not coming in sufficiently to offset the German weight—all these elements contributed to the French National Assembly's rejection of the treaty for a European Defense Community on August 30, 1954.

Thereupon emerged another of Dulles' memorable formulas: America would have to undertake an "agonizing reappraisal" of its obligations and policies in Western Europe. The whole promising and salutary trend toward European unity had been endangered, the Secretary of State said. He was harsh toward France: "It is a tragedy that in one country nationalism, abetted by Communism, has asserted itself so as to endanger the whole of Europe." [10] He implied the threat of a separate American arrangement with Bonn. Thereupon France, having vetoed in August participation of German soldiers in a European army, in October agreed to West Germany's joining NATO and having an army of her own—a prudent and realistic concession.

The German army was reborn too late to influence decisively the course of Soviet policies in Europe. Still, the Russians did everything up to the last moment to prevent this outcome. But it is interesting to note how even in Europe their freedom of action was affected by the emergence of Communist China. In July at the Geneva Conference, France, Britain, Russia, and China agreed on the armistice in Indo-china—in fact on partition of Vietnam into Communist and non-Communist components. Communist China took a prominent part in the negotiations, a startling acknowledgment of its emergence as a great power, and the Chinese were obviously pleased by its outcome, more so than any other participant. The war for the time being was ended; the imminent threat of American intervention, soldiers, and bases in the area bordering on her was dissipated; since Ho Chi Minh's

[10] *Documents on International Affairs, 1954* (London, 1957), p. 21.

ambitions had been but partly satisfied, the new Communist state would be dependent on China in a way that a united Communist Vietnam would not have been. For the Russians, the end of the French struggle in Indochina meant the disappearance of a useful lever for pressuring Paris to maintain her opposition to German rearmament.

But their last-ditch efforts to prevent German rearmament continued with furious note-writing and vague threats. They were ready, they said, to hold another conference to discuss German reunification, and they might have some interesting new proposals. They would denounce the treaties of alliance which bound them to France and Great Britain if those nations joined with the German *revanchists*. (It must have come as a shock to many in London and Paris to realize that the treaties were still in existence.) Some of the Soviets' proposals were not without an element of humor: they offered to join NATO, which would thus, they argued, be transformed at one blow from an imperialistic aggression-oriented organization into one genuinely concerned with security and embodying the spirit of the United Nations Charter. It is interesting that the Soviets raised hardly any fuss at all over Italy's accession to NATO, which took place at the same time, not a great tribute to the martial traditions of the heirs of imperial Rome.

But all such protests were, as the Soviets probably knew, unavailing. West German rearmament was finally decided upon, more than six years after it had been first seriously considered. Its initial scope was to be modest: an army of approximately half a million; and the Germans pledged not to manufacture nuclear weapons, long-range missiles, or bombers. In retrospect, the failure to adopt EDC was regretted by many Europe-minded politicians including Adenauer: it would have, it was thought, given a greater thrust to West European integration and unity than the alternative solution. But the future was to vindicate neither excessive hopes nor the excessive fear generated by the idea of German rearmament.

By the late 1950s, the economic unity of Western Europe was to appear, briefly but enticingly, to be a prelude to political unity. Then came a series of events involving an island in the Caribbean, the rancor of an old man, and the American overcommitment in Asia. The vision of unity faded. The very economic prosperity of the West, now without a broader sense of purpose and design, became a factor in perpetuating its political disunity, and eventually a subsidiary reason for the decline of social cohesion and political stability within the individual countries.

How the wider perspectives and, to them, dangers of West European unity were seen by the Soviet leaders it is hard to tell. Certainly their most obvious concern was about German rearmament. But in the back of their mind, the Soviets must have borne the thought of the greater danger of a united Europe. All the great successes of Communism, including the November Revolution of 1917 itself, had after all been due to the great schism within the Western family of nations, to that civil war of the West which had lasted since 1914. Even in the interwar years, even before Hitler, political and commercial hostilities separated Western nations and thus protected the Soviet state not only from attack but from what would have been a crushing example of economic prosperity and unity combined with free democratic institutions. No wonder Soviet theorists and statesmen clung desperately to their beloved faith in the "inherent contradictions within the capitalist camp." Without them, where would the Soviet Union be, especially in view of the still-hidden but growing "inherent" contradictions within the socialist camp?

Moreover, as pointed out before, American preponderance in potential military strength and in economic power vis-à-vis the U.S.S.R. could never again be as great at it had been from 1945 to 1950. In sheer terms of power, the growth of NATO effectives and the American bases encircling the Soviet Union could hardly compensate for the progress of Soviet military technology and heavy industry. In *military* terms, it would have been difficult to say in 1954–55 how the position of the West might become substantially more favorable. But *politically* every step toward greater unity in the West was immeasurably strengthening its hand vis-à-vis the Russians, forcing them to make concessions.

On the surface the Russians, of course, admitted none of this. The expansion of NATO was greeted by those scowls and threats which seldom failed to impress the faint-hearted West and to elicit pleas for yet another attempt at compromise. Yet when the smoke dissolved, the substance of Soviet countermeasures could be seen fairly anemic.

With much fanfare the Soviets convened a conference on European security in November, 1954, to which came, though everybody was invited, only its obedient satellites of Eastern Europe, as well as a Chinese observer; in the context, this was a poignant hint of the millions of men the Russians could count on in any conflict. The conference once again pronounced an anathema on NATO and engaged in blood-curdling threats about what would happen if the West, even at this very late moment, did not desist from its evil designs.

What materialized from this next spring was the Warsaw Pact, a defensive alliance of European Communist states (including East Germany, which joined a bit later), a counter-NATO with similar arrangements, councils, and joint command. The armed forces of the satellites had been at the Soviet Union's disposal and under virtual Soviet command before, and it was hard to see how the situation was changed by making the arrangements formal and public. Any extensive arming and expansion of the satellite armies was from the Soviet point of view a double-edged weapon. If fear of German militarism was and remains today a factor of importance in countries like Poland and Czechoslovakia, and one which binds them closer to Russia, then by the same token their people were not likely to be enthusiastic over a closer association with an arming of East Germans. If this was the worst the U.S.S.R. could do to counter West German rearmament, then Westerners who had feared provoking Soviet power with a German army might have asked themselves why the step had not been taken before and why so much precious time had been frittered away.

Consider, on the other hand, the *concessions* that this phantom of European unity exacted from the Russians! Suddenly in 1955 they were ready to sign an Austrian peace treaty. In view of the previous false starts and wrangles, the Austrian treaty was signed and occupation forces departed with what must appear as dazzling speed. The preamble of the treaty, published on May 15, 1955, struck a deeply anachronistic note: the U.S.S.R., Great Britain, France, and the United States were "hereinafter referred to as 'the Allied and Associated Powers.' " The fortunate little country had to pledge to remain neutral and grant some minor economic concessions to the U.S.S.R. Still, it is a fair assumption that without the rearming of Germany, Austria would have continued to host Russian soldiers.

An even greater shock was forthcoming. In the summer of 1955, the Soviet government invited to Moscow none other than the chief *"revanchist,"* the man who, according to the Soviet press, was ceaselessly plotting aggression against the U.S.S.R.: Konrad Adenauer. Adenauer was given a rather cold reception in Moscow. The Russians were not going to be so unsubtle as to court him too obviously or spell out their fears. If he expected to be offered Ulbricht's head on a platter—or in more prosaic terms German unity in exchange for a less intimate relationship with Washington—then he met with a definite rebuff. Even when it came to returning the thousands of German prisoners of war who were still being retained in the U.S.S.R., Adenauer encountered at first a brutal refusal: they were not prisoners of war but war criminals, claimed the

Russians. (Eventually, however, they were constrained to make this concession to humanity.) The Russians then compounded the surprise by establishing diplomatic relations with the Bonn republic. This could not have been welcome in Warsaw and Prague, and was of course especially infuriating to the East Germans. Yet all these steps were taken with considerable finesse. Just as the Russians had been clever in concealing their fears, so they were adept at masking their concessions, or rather, at making them appear not as concessions but as either unilateral acts of good will or diplomatic successes. In the West, the Austrian peace treaty was taken as evidence of a new and peaceful spirit in Moscow, while the invitation to Adenauer and the diplomatic relations with Bonn were treated as a *coup* worthy of Talleyrand. It was only dimly perceived that the Soviet maneuvers were the product of grave fears rather than of a desire to be "nice." In the absence of a sober analysis of Soviet motivations, their blandishments to Adenauer were not without a certain effect: there was some unhappiness in West Germany over Adenauer being so close to the Americans and neglecting opportunities for bargaining with Moscow. There was renewed hesitation in Paris, London, and even Washington: Can one really trust the "old fox" Adenauer? These mutual suspicions were naturally encouraged by Soviet diplomacy; once again, by watching each other anxiously and concentrating on their own troubles, the Western Allies had failed to perceive the full extent of the Russians' troubles and the opportunities they opened to the West.

Indeed, Dulles could have reflected gloomily on the premium his religion placed on a repentant sinner as against a man who has always followed the path of virtue. There was visible and universal relief when on one occasion Premier Malenkov avowed that a nuclear conflict could be disastrous to both sides.[11] Some Westerners indeed hailed it as a momentous turning point in world affairs. Yet the same theme when stressed continuously by American spokesmen hardly aroused any interest, since the point was so obvious. The Soviets were feared when they scowled and threatened, trusted when they smiled and murmured about coexistence. The Americans, on the other hand, were only half believed when they threatened, while professions of good intentions were greeted with a "what else is new?" air.

These rather nimble Soviet responses to old dangers and new oppor-

---

11 Almost immediately Malenkov felt constrained to explain that of course what he meant was that an atomic war would be disastrous to capitalism. The socialist camp, needless to say, would survive and flourish.

tunities on the world scene reflected the personality of the man at the helm in the Kremlin. Here it is necessary to go back a bit.

By the end of 1953, it became clear that Malenkov could probably not preserve his primacy within what was now a collective leadership. A moralist must be hard-pressed to explain why at each crucial point in Soviet history there appeared a man endowed with precisely the qualities needed to hold together the bizarre structure. Lenin's pragmatism enabled him to create the Soviet state after the Revolution, something a more literal follower of Marx could not have achieved. With the Communist party threatening to split into hostile factions following Lenin's last illness and the struggle of the oligarchs, it took a man of Stalin's guile and cruelty to impose the kind of monolithic unity which was to enable the U.S.S.R. to survive collectivization and the war. And after Stalin's death, the crying need was for a man to provide a new image for Communism, in the parlance of Madison Avenue, to humanize it.

Nikita Khrushchev fitted the bill. A man of the people (unlike Lenin, who was by background and habits very much a product of the pre-revolutionary intelligentsia), a Russian (unlike Stalin), he more than any of his colleagues or the Presidium could bring the leadership closer to the people. For all his years as Stalin's satrap, there remained about him something of the 1918-vintage Communist (the year when he joined the Party), of the *élan* and conviction of the revolutionary, of the agitator addressing a crowd and carrying it along with him partly by bullying and partly by converting it to his point of view. These qualities could not in themselves have enabled Khrushchev to rise to the top, for the choice, needless to say, was not the people's. But he received strong support in the Central Committee, whose dominant element, the local party secretaries, remembered Malenkov as Stalin's favorite a shadowy figure of Stalin's personal entourage. Molotov and Kaganovich were also compromised by too close associations with the man everybody would but could not forget. Mikoyan was Armenian. Others on the Presidium were either too young or too old or too inconsequential. There remained Khrushchev.

In 1954 Khrushchev began to assume an increasingly dominant role in party and domestic affairs. He was a born improviser, and as yet his improvisations had not been exposed, as they were to be described unfeelingly ten years later, as "hare-brained schemes." He told the Party leaders what they all knew but what they were loath to acknowledge: that Soviet agriculture was in a mess and dragging down the national economy. He had a flair for public relations, for drastic and dramatic proposals which, at the time they were enacted, even though not a few years later, appeared to provide all the answers. If Stalin had impressed Secretary Hull as a man who would have gone far in American public life, then one could with much greater justification see Khrushchev as a man taking charge of a giant U.S. corporation which had been going downhill and convincing the press and for a while the shareholders that here was a dynamic and innovative leader who would do the trick.

Throughout that same year Malenkov continued to slip. That his star was waning even when it came to foreign policy was demonstrated when an extremely important Soviet mission to China in October was headed by Khrushchev, with the Prime Minister staying home.

The mission, whose purpose was to negotiate on the main issues of economic and political cooperation, could hardly be deemed a success from the Soviet viewpoint. The Soviets were forced to secure outward Chinese support and the appearance of that "unshakable unity of the socialist camp" so important to them by rather far-reaching concessions: the last Soviet soldier was to leave Chinese soil—Port Arthur was to be finally evacuated.[12] Sino-Soviet joint-stock companies, Stalin's favorite way of milking the satellites' resources, were to be turned over entirely to the Chinese, and with them evidently went the Russians' last hopes of clinging to a special position in Manchuria and Sinkiang. Further and considerable Soviet economic and technological help was to be extended. Mao was to reveal some years later that he also proposed that this would be a fine time for the Russians to return Outer Mongolia to Chinese sovereignty; but that far the Russians would not go. Apart from this bargaining, the two leaders evidently developed a strong and lasting mutual antipathy. But the harsh facts underlying declarations of solidarity between the two Communist powers, and their defiance of the imperialists, were not known in the West or, except to a very small circle, in the U.S.S.R.

Malenkov's demotion was probably speeded up by an attempt on his part to mount a counteroffensive. He allowed himself to be associated with the view that there should be a greater stress on the production of consumer goods. This brought ominous reminders of how the security of the country was bound up with the primacy of heavy industry. It is somewhat surprising that this struggle for power was resolved in what

---

12 The Russians clung tenaciously to this outpost so closely associated with their modern history, even in contravention of the clear stipulation of the Sino-Soviet treaty of 1950. And still now they evidently attempted to stay on. Would not the Chinese comrades appreciate having Soviet soldiers in Port Arthur in view of the American bases in Japan? But Mao would not.

was, bearing in mind the precedents, a fairly civilized way. In February, Malenkov was forced to resign as Premier, but he retained a seat in the Presidium and the government. Khrushchev was now clearly in the leading, but as yet far from dominant, position. The new Premier was Bulganin. His career had been mainly an administrative one; during and since the war he had been a political general reaching the rank of marshal. He had a most dignified bearing, something that could not be claimed for Khrushchev. His short beard was then in the U.S.S.R. affected mostly by scientists and veterans of the Revolution, and it endowed Bulganin with a similarity to a Czarist governor circa 1900. Bulganin's successor as Minister of War was Marshal Zhukov: for the first time since 1925, when Trotsky was dismissed from the post, the ministry was held by a man who could become a contender for supreme power.

Khrushchev clearly ranked Bulganin. His colleagues, while awarding him primacy, undoubtedly believed that he would observe the principle of collective leadership; that he would not be around them too long. They were in for some surprises.

Khrushchev's approach to politics was that of a gambler and enthusiastic dilettante. He would embark upon a most risky speculation, confident that when the time came to honor the bill he would have another line of credit available. Consider his attempt to resuscitate moribund Soviet agriculture. First there was a grandiose enterprise of opening to cultivation millions of acres of virgin land in southeastern Russia and Kazakhstan. Experts, though privately skeptical, were bullied into agreeing; climatic conditions were bound to render the whole venture disastrous. Huge expenditures of capital and manpower managed to secure a few spectacular crops, but the whole area was fated to turn into a dust bowl. By then, however, Khrushchev would be in the midst of another spectacular campaign to divert attention from the failure and to introduce another scheme to revive agriculture: corn! His advocacy of growing corn under all conceivable conditions and for all conceivable purposes was to earn him the sobriquet Nikita the Corn Grower, but again it proved something of a dud: the Russians, like most Europeans, consider corn as animal fodder not suitable for human consumption. But by then the ebullient leader was juggling other balls in the air: he wanted to expand acreage for beans; he extolled the nutritional value of horsemeat; the Soviet chemical industry was to increase production of artificial fertilizers; the party was going to be reorganized to assure better direction of agriculture. Throughout, experts sighed unhappily while forced to acclaim the leader's latest improvisation. Local party secretaries diligently falsified figures for crops and livestock in their districts, which when sucessful brought them promotions and decorations, when uncovered, public abuse and instant dismissal.

In politics Khrushchev employed the same technique. He used the old Stalinist guard to get rid of Malenkov, and then turned around and, having enlisted the army (Zhukov) and more liberal elements, settled accounts with the Molotovs and Kaganoviches, as well as finishing off Malenkov. Almost immediately it was Zhukov's turn to walk the plank. Toward the end Khruschev, as we shall see, developed some ingenious techniques for overcoming the growing resistance of his colleagues. But you cannot fool all the members of the Presidium all the time.

Foreign policy offered rich opportunities for the Khruschev approach. With one exception, Khrushchev felt that there was hardly a country whose leaders could not be outwitted, frightened, or smothered with cordiality so as to fall in with his designs. That exception was China.

It would be unfair to see in Khrushchev a cynic and operator. On the contrary, unlike the tyrant who preceded him and the colorless bureaucrats who followed, he obviously retained faith in Communism as a humane ideal and not merely a system of repression and social engineering. His attempt to combine totalitarianism with the "politics of joy" was not carried out in the manner of Stalin, whose slogan "Life has become better, life has become gayer" was proclaimed at the grimmest period of terror. For all his madcap improvisations, Khrushchev undeniably improved the lot of his subjects, raising both their material well-being and their morale. But in foreign relations his policies were overly subtle and overambitious.

In the immediate context of the mid-1950s, the Khrushchev approach was to make Soviet diplomatic language more threatening, while, somewhat incongruously, Soviet diplomatic wooing became more assiduous. Restraint was not a characteristic of Nikita Sergeievich. Seeing the effect of his blustering atomic threats, he laid them on very thick in the years to come. Did the British realize how few well-placed bombs it would take to finish them off? Why did they then let the Americans have bomber bases on their crowded island? How sad that the antiquities and orange groves of Italy might have to be burned because the Italians had joined NATO. Yet when the Chinese Communists picked up the same theme and embellished it (some *small* socialist countries might not survive a nuclear conflict, while China with her hundreds of millions dispersed throughout the vast country certainly would), the Russians became incensed and apprehensive.

But in 1955 this bluff was still restrained. Russia had the hydrogen bomb and a long-range bomber force, but Dulles' doctrine of massive retaliation was still quite recent, the American nuclear capacity had been considerably increased, and NATO air bases ringed the U.S.S.R. Those on both sides who had begun to "think about the unthinkable" had to conclude that an actual nuclear war, while gravely damaging to the West, would mean absolute devastation to the Soviet Union. But beyond such grim calculations, there were obvious psychologico-political ones which made it plain that a democracy could not initiate, or barring the most far-reaching provocation, could not respond by unleashing, a nuclear holocaust. More eloquent than the frightful statistics was the stony silence in which the United States Congress had listened to Syngman Rhee on his visit to Washington the preceding year. The South Korean leader had pleaded for force to reunite his country and to overthrow the Communist regime in China: were the U.S.S.R. to intervene it would be an "excellent thing," for America then would be able to destroy Russia before the latter could accumulate a sufficiency of nuclear weapons. But whatever the experts said and calculated, it was a simple truth that the mere fact of possession of nuclear bombs by a totalitarian system offset any, even the most devastating, superiority of the weapon in the hands of a democracy.

Soviet defense reflected an awareness of this truth. By 1955, Soviet armed forces had swollen close to 6 million men, a figure which reflected not only the Korean war but the leadership's nervousness over various contingencies following Stalin's death. The regime now proceeded to prune this number and to return as many men as possible to the factories and farms. The stress was on advanced military technology to compensate for reduction in manpower. The Soviets were eager to convince the West that they were in possession of the most up-to-date tools: long-range bombers, soon intercontinental ballistic missiles, and, a bit later, nuclear-powered undersea craft. They were to exhibit and discuss those weapons in terms implying not only their advanced quality but their existence in great quantities. It was only later that Western experts realized that they had been largely fooled, despite the famous U-2 overflights which began in 1956: the Soviet armament in heavy bombers and then in missiles between 1955 and 1962 was much smaller than was thought at the time. But it was sufficient for the Russians' purposes to make the West *believe* that it had the frightful weapons in great quantity and to record spectacular feats in the space program, rather than actually to divert huge sums from agriculture and industry to mass production of missiles and long-range bombers. One cannot eat missiles, Khrushchev said in one of his more coexistential moments.[13]

As against threats and impressive exhibitions of military hardware,[14] there were good-will trips and personal diplomacy, which were Khrushchev's distinctive contribution to Soviet techniques in foreign relations. Their significance, incidentally, transcended considerations of foreign policy. They were also meant to prove to the Soviet citizen that his country was a civilized and "normal" state: you leave the Kremlin confident that in your absence your colleagues will not brew any fatal intrigues.[15] It was a fitting symbol of the new era when more than a trickle of foreigners began to be admitted to the Soviet Union, and when the West in turn was opened to a handful of Soviet tourists, to be sure still carefully guided and selected by Soviet authorities.[16]

The Khrushchev-Bulganin team traveled in 1955–56 to mend diplomatic fences (Belgrade), initiate new political and economic ties (India, Burma, and Afghanistan), and simply convey the impression of international *détente* with the West (Geneva and Britain). These advances, even when most crudely fashioned, were seldom without a positive effect from the travelers' point of view. For the most part the weaknesses of their country's power position and the opportunities they afforded to the West

---

[13] There are some indications that Khrushchev's admission led to some unhappiness within the military leadership, since generals never feel that they have enough weapons, and drastic reduction of the land forces meant that many a career officer had to seek civilian employment. Khrushchev cited the case of a former colonel who volunteered and was performing brilliantly as supervisor of livestock on a collective farm, but few officers could have greeted such a change with enthusiasm.

[14] Allen Dulles was to decry Soviet deception: "on Aviation Day in July, 1955, in the presence of diplomatic and military representatives in Moscow there was a 'fly by' of a new Soviet bomber. The number far exceeded what was thought to be available. . . . Later it was surmised that the same squadron had been flying in circles, reappearing every few minutes." *The Craft of Intelligence* (New York, 1963), p. 149.

[15] In Khrushchev's case, alas, this confidence was to prove misplaced on at least two occasions, and fatal on one.

[16] The problem of defection has been with the Russians since the founding of the Grand Duchy of Muscovy. Although no society has been free from this phenomenon—and America since the Vietnam war has no reason to be complacent on the score—the Russian record is still impressive in terms of its length and number of cases. Czar Boris Godunov at the end of the sixteenth century made the first and abortive attempt to start what is now known as cultural exchange by sending a few young men to study in the West. None chose to come back. Political migration was common in the sixteenth and seventeenth centuries: the highest nobles often were required to deposit bonds to ensure that they would not flee to Poland or Sweden or even the Crimea.

could be only imperfectly guessed by even the most perspicacious observer of the Communist world. The Khrushchev-Bulganin tours were a key piece in the public-relations campaign to convince the outside world of the solidity and unity of the Communist camp and of the freer but still stable and confident mood of Soviet society. Stalin had tried to mask postwar Russia's desperately weak position vis-à-vis the United States through isolation and by giving the impression of ominous belligerency; the new leaders sought to conceal their still inferior poker hand by outgoing and cheerful ways, suggesting that the Russians were now less threatening not because they were fearful of NATO and Dulles or because they had troubles at home or with China, but simply because they had become more reasonable and civilized.

The trips served another, related purpose. The most dynamic element in the international situation in the mid-1950s was the impressive economic strength of the Western world. Almost forgotten were the postwar predictions of optimistic Soviet economists (and of gloomy ones in America) of an inevitable and major depression in the United States and the whole capitalist world. Little was heard of the frequent refrain of so many social scientists in the West before 1945 of the inherent superiority of a planned economy over one dependent on "the anarchy of the market" when it came to providing for the needs of the people and avoiding crises. Russia's rate of economic growth was impressive, though even there statistics concealed the basic weakness of the economy when it came to agriculture and consumer goods in general. But the spectacular recovery of Western Europe was even more impressive. Soviet calculations had envisaged the pleasant prospect of the western zones of Germany struggling helplessly with the ruinous consequences of an unbalanced economy, growing out of the loss of the agrarian territories, of millions of refugees from the East, etc. But the "German economic miracle" was now in full swing. Less spectacular but also remarkable were the recovery of France, for all her colonial wars, political instability, and labor strife; and that of Italy. Whatever happened to Lenin's old thesis that capitalism managed to survive in the advanced industrial countries because they exploited their colonies? Britain, having now shed most of her empire and in the process of liquidating the rest, had a general standard of living superior to that before the war. If the West continued its growth in prosperity and unity, the new pattern of relations between Europe and its former colonial possessions promised to be one of economic interdependence, at once healthier and more stable than the old one-sided political domination.

The Soviet offensive of international amicability was, then, designed to erode this sense of growing unity. In view of the friendly trips and declarations, who could believe that the Soviet danger was as real and pressing as it had seemed only a year or two before? Such ancient enmities as those which had traditionally separated the Turks, the Yugoslavs, and the Greeks had melted in the face of the common danger, but in the more relaxed atmosphere, Athens and Ankara could remember the clashing interests of the Greek and Turkish communities on Cyprus. Yugoslavia's signature on the Balkan Pact was becoming less meaningful: Tito was developing a certain cautious nostalgia for his old links with the Communist world.

In the Third World, the Russians' new tactics were also bearing some fruit. Unlike Dulles, the Soviets did not consider neutralism as immoral and did not want Asian powers to belong to regional defense pacts; on the contrary, they had discreet praise for neutralism and wanted their Asian friends simply to remember that *they* had never kept them in colonial subjugation, that *they* did not seek to cling to special rights, bases, and privileged positions. India and Indonesia were discovering that neutralism, apart from bearing witness to their moral superiority, could also be profitable: one received economic help from the East as well as the West. To others, like Nasser, the siren songs of Russia's diplomatic travelers were more dangerously tempting. The Americans, for all their anticolonialism, were allies of Britain and France and protectors of Israel; they expected recipients of their help to devote themselves to economic development and to arm against the nonexistent Communist danger. American public opinion, while broadminded enough to concede that the new nations, as opposed to say Spain, could not institute instant democracy, still tended to carp in its schoolmasterish way at the absence of elections and freedom of the press. As against such grumbling, the Russians' attitude resembled that of an indulgent uncle who expects the young to sow wild oats.

Soviet motivations were often quite transparent. The Khrushchev-Bulganin tours embodied no basic changes in post-Stalin foreign policies as laid down in Malenkov's general review of international relations of August, 1953, but the new style of Soviet diplomacy fitted in well with the spirit of the age: the era of communications, television, and growing universal awareness and concern over the cataclysmic possibilities of nuclear weapons. The old type of closet diplomacy, of international conferences, seemed out of date; even the old type of Soviet propaganda, as exemplified in the Stockholm Peace Appeal and those carefully contrived congresses of peace partisans, artists, and scientists friendly to the Soviet cause, was outmoded. What was important was the problem of communication, to use a cliché of the late 1960s. People wanted to become familiar with and reassured about personalities whose decisions could mean the difference between life and death for millions.

The challenge implied in the Russian approach was well appreciated in Washington. In his second term, General Eisenhower also began to make far-ranging trips. But for the moment, the soothing melody of coexistence played by the Soviet leaders threatened to and did in fact destroy much of the sense of urgency which had led to NATO and West German rearmament. The West Europeans showed signs of becoming unduly complacent about Soviet intentions. The impetus for unity, for laying aside quarrels which had poisoned relations between neighboring countries for generations, was still strong. Problems which had seemed intractable, such as that of Trieste, which separated Yugoslavia and Italy, and that even more cumbersome one of the Saar, which divided Germany and France, were resolved amicably. But further advances were bogging down.

In contrast, pressures were building up again for the kind of comprehensive negotiations with the Russians which had been dreaded by American statesmen ever since 1945. Even the Chinese Communists were getting in on the act. At Bandung, Chou En-lai announced that his regime, though not recognized by the United States, was ready to negotiate with her over Formosa. Though the Chinese offer implied that the main subject of negotiations would be the most efficacious way of Peking's extending its authority to the island, the State Department's brusque refusal was thought unfortunate both by the emerging nations and by some circles in the West.

Soviet proposals for negotiations could not, however, be rejected out of hand without alienating the West Europeans as well as a sizable segment of public opinion at home. The Soviets showed themselves infuriatingly open-minded. On May 10, 1955, the government of the U.S.S.R. announced a series of extensive proposals for ending international tensions. Of special interest were the proposed measures for disarmament. Conventional forces of the Big Four *and China* were to be reduced within two years to specified manpower levels (1.5 million troops for the U.S., the U.S.S.R., and China; 650,000 for Britain and France). Within the same time limit—i.e., by the end of 1957—nuclear weapons were to be removed and destroyed; production of fissionable material for war purposes and all atomic testing were to be ended. The Soviets contributed to American discomfiture by *apparently* agreeing to a far-reaching system of controls to prevent a surprise nuclear attack and stockpiling of atomic weapons. The U.N. General Assembly was to set up an international control organ with inspectors in all states capable of producing such weapons.

On the surface this was a dazzling concession. Reading the fine print and from the perspective of years one can see that there were sizable loopholes in this concession. Organs of control were to be established at "railway junctions, on the main motor highways and at aerodromes." [17] This was 1955, and the Soviets were presumably in the process of installing launching pads for their missiles, installations not mentioned among those to come under international control. One also notes that missing from the list of facilities to be inspected were plants and research institutions involved in the production of fissionable materials and actual weapons.

The most fundamental omission touched on the problem which has frustrated all efforts at nuclear controls since 1945: there was no guarantee of effective sanctions against a violator. The control organ could merely report violations to the Security Council, where the Great Powers could of course invoke the celebrated veto. If to a jaundiced State Department eye the plan envisaged but few sacrifices from the Russians, then it promised in effect to nullify the whole strategic concept behind American military policies. Already in the first year, preliminary measures were to be taken for the liquidation of all foreign military, naval, and air bases on the territories of other states; these measures were to be completed at the end of the second year. And it was precisely at this point that the United States was developing a great network of air bases ringing the U.S.S.R. to provide a countervailing force to the Communists' preponderance in land armies. To go along with the Soviet scheme would have meant virtual unilateral disarmament, compensated for by unverifiable Soviet promises and the presence of a few teams of inspectors on some Russian airfields and highways.

Hence in their own turn, the Americans reversed their previous position: technical measures of disarmament could not be discussed until the major political issues of the day were resolved. How about Germany? How about the captive nations of Eastern Europe? Here the Russians had a chance to express polite surprise as to how the country which had advanced the Baruch Plan could now deny the *urgency* of solving the problem of nuclear weapons. And when it came to political problems,

[17] *Documents on International Affairs, 1955* (London, 1958), p. 120.

rather than dealing with fictitious ones like the alleged enslavement of Eastern Europe, how about the very real and major problem of the People's Republic of China and the scandalous denial of its sovereign rights over Formosa and the equally scandalous nonrecognition of its rightful place in the United Nations, where the Chiang Kai-shek clique had usurped its place?

In this verbal sparring, the Americans were obviously being bested. The Soviet proposals were full of holes, but then, like any diplomatic initiative, they were to provide nothing more than a basis for discussion. Dulles on his part was not being nimble enough: if the Soviets were gently stirring up disagreements and divisions among the Western Allies, he might well have reciprocated by inquiring how far the Chinese Communists were ready to go along with the Russians. Were they ready to forsake *their* atomic ambitions and to admit foreign inspectors on *their* territory? But this was a vicious circle: any extensive dialogue with or about Communist China was held to contravene the official American position that China was "beyond the pale."

But there was another, more fruitful opportunity to probe the Russians' proposals as to limitation in conventional armaments. Here seemingly the United States could not lose. With barely a million and a half men in their army, the Soviets would feel positively naked: How could they police the satellites? Then it would be up to *them* to make embarrassed explanations that they did not mean to reduce land armies without at the same time tackling the problem of nuclear weapons, etc. The issue of foreign bases could also have been turned around: the United States could propose to make a beginning by drastically reducing its forces in West Germany. Would the Soviets reciprocate and in the case of East Germany submit their withdrawals to verification? But in Washington every Russian initiative was held to be a trap: if Moscow proposed a joint declaration in favor of motherhood, this would have called forth position papers from the State Department's Policy Planning Council, somber warnings from Senator Knowland, and eventually a declaration that while the United States welcomed this recognition of the sanctity of family life on the part of the Russians, it would require clear indication that the U.S.S.R. did not mean to derogate the status of fatherhood.

The predicament was, however, more tragic than humorous.

American inflexibility and diffidence about negotiating were all the more pathetic because the Soviet moves to a large degree reflected considerable respect for American power and leadership. In Eisenhower the country had a President who more than any other postwar leader

inspired national confidence and unity. With American help and prodding, West Europe was on the road to becoming united and a formidable
partner of America. Those already considerable assets could be translated into further and very substantial gains. All that was required was
a degree of flexibility: the Europeans could be made to see that the
United States prized them *not only* because of the Communist menace,
and that, while resolute in its opposition to Communism, the United
States would patiently negotiate with the Russians to prove to all but
the most inveterate of skeptics that obstacles to peaceful accommodation
lay in Moscow and not in some strange obsession in Washington.[18]

But patience and flexibility were precisely the missing elements.
Some time later, Dulles was to state his reason: How could one negoti-
ate with people whose favorite tactics were those of violence and guile?
"These teachings of Marx, Lenin and Stalin have never been disavowed
by the Soviet Communist Party of which Mr. Khrushchev is the First
Secretary. . . . Therefore I believe that at least that part of the Soviet
Communist creed be abandoned."[19] Even though written for public
consumption and addressed to an organ traditionally hostile to the
United States, this statement most likely corresponded to Dulles' inner-
most convictions. And, for all of his personal and family diplomatic
background, it reflected a rather limited concept of international negotiations.

The preoccupation with Communism weakened the American policy-
makers' perception of one very important factor. To the West Europeans, resistance to Communism was but one element in a search to
recapture at least some of the world-wide importance and prestige of
a bygone era. Professional diplomats are well aware what an important
role *amour propre* plays in politics, among nations as well as in personal relations. But as the events in 1956 were to show, there was
little awareness of this in the highest echelons of the American government, little patience with the political and psychological problems involved in Britain's dismantling of her empire, in the French position in

[18] American resistance was being fed by pleas from Bonn: then, as during the
next several years, Adenauer was fearful lest one incautious step by American
diplomacy undo his labors in raising Germany from ashes to the status of an
almost equal partner. He himself had barely prevailed over the socialists and
other circles in his own country who clung to the hope that the Russians would be
willing to allow Germany to reunite if only Bonn were "nice" to them. Now the
old warrior believed that both Western unity and the eventual reunification of his
country loomed on the horizon, and he did not want American inexperience,
British weakness, or French absorption in other matters to divert the West from
the right course.
[19] Letter to *The New Statesman and Nation* (London), February 8, 1958.

North Africa. Viewed from the perspective of Washington, the British and French were wasting time and resources. Why did they not give those troublesome nationalities what they wanted and concentrate on the important things: increasing their contingents in NATO and "standing up" to the Russians? This insensitivity had serious consequences in that it allowed Soviet diplomacy to recoup much of the ground it had lost as a consequence of the increasing power and unity of Western Europe.

The Geneva Conference of the Big Four in July, 1955, marked, though it was not realized at the time, the end of the most promising phase in the development of NATO and Western unity. The mere fact that it took place indicated a degree of success in the post-Stalin Soviet diplomatic offensive. This was not a summit meeting in the old style, such as had been urged ever since 1953 by Winston Churchill, who had just turned the reins over to Anthony Eden. The conference took place in the full glare of publicity, hence with little prospect of arriving at any meaningful agreements. The statesmen and their large staffs would not so much negotiate as read prepared speeches and issue declarations to be reproduced in the press and on the radio. It was thus even in its original concept an exercise in public relations, an occasion to display international amiability. As such, it was bound to dissolve some West European fears, but also to weaken the appreciation of the still basic and dangerous split between the East and the West.

Agreement to hold the conference had been wrenched from the administration by the British and the French. The shadow and the (misread) lesson of Yalta lay heavily on the American leaders' gingerly approach to the matter of talking with the Russians. There were stern warnings that there would be no Munichs or Yaltas. President Eisenhower hastened to assure the American people that no secret agreements would be reached—something which in view of the proposed format of the conference went without saying. Among the American officials there was some very private but serious nervousness about what the President actually *might* say were he buttonholed by some Soviet leader when Dulles was out of the room. Further official warnings pointed out that this assembly of the world's top potentates would indulge at most in "exploratory talks," something which is usually done by ambassadors or even lesser dignitaries.

The Geneva meeting, then, could not be, as Churchill had wished, a conference in the style of those of the nineteenth-century Concert of Europe, where the Great Powers stated their interests and ambitions and then, through a process of bargaining, adjusted their differences and established an international equilibrium to last until the next great crisis. Even the pattern of wartime "summitry" disintegrated because of the inherent American inability to conceive of *international* politics as bargaining. To be sure, the President of the United States was a man who, unlike his immediate predecessors or successors, enjoyed unusual discretion and freedom of action in dealing with foreign affairs, and especially concerning the Russians. The fires of McCarthyism were extinguished at home; not even the most right-wing elements, short of the lunatic fringe, could accuse the Eisenhower-Dulles team of being "soft on Communism." But the President approached the whole business of sitting down with the Russians with diffidence; his Secretary of State, with distaste.

General Eisenhower's intellectual stature has been unduly and unfairly disparaged by caustic academic and journalistic critics. To be sure, his oratory (when not fashioned by a speech writer) tended to be baroque rather than lucid. It certainly required shrewdness, as well as unusual tact and ability to get along with people, to manage the command of armed forces of an alliance over a long period of time and with a minimum of friction. The General's good sense was also much in evidence during his two terms of office. He vetoed a proposal, seriously considered in 1954, for armed intervention in Indochina, a prudent decision. His style of political leadership was often criticized as lackadaisical, and it undoubtedly reflected a certain indolence, but it also conformed to the sage advice of a French statesman: "Above all, not too much passion." (Privately, Mr. Eisenhower could be quite passionate when it came to politics, something that the unfortunate Eden was to realize during the Suez crisis.) In the America of the fifties, already burgeoning with problems and tensions which were to erupt so tragically in the sixties, it was the President's outward serenity and counsel of moderation which did much to contain the trouble and preserve national cohesion.[20]

However, Eisenhower's own account of the Geneva conference throws vivid light on his limitations when it came to foreign affairs, or more precisely, to dealing with and understanding Communist leaders. The root trouble lay in the traditional concept of the democratic leader as that of a politician relying on professional advice and the counsel

---

[20] An inevitable rejoinder would be that by being contained, the social problems were bound to become more troublesome and violent during the next decade. But it is unlikely that future historians would endorse such a fatalistic conclusion.

of experts when it came to the intricacies of international relations. In the postwar age, this concept was inadequate. Nor was it sufficient for a Secretary of State to be, as John Foster Dulles eminently was, a specialist in foreign relations in the sense of knowing their recent history, techniques of negotiations, international law, and precedents. The new era called for the policy-makers themselves to be something in the nature of experts. Negotiations as such were perhaps less important than the ability to assess your protagonist's needs, fears, and goals, and that in turn required some broad acquaintance with Russia's internal politics, with the problems besetting the Communist bloc.

Eisenhower's account of Geneva offers ample testimony as to how difficult it was for him to probe beneath appearances when it came to the Soviets—represented in this case by not only the now inseparable duo of Khrushchev and Bulganin, but also other notables: Molotov, his influence clearly on the wane, but still Foreign Minister; Zhukov, his star rising; and Gromyko, who played an important role because of his unique diplomatic experience with the Anglo-Saxons dating back to 1943, when, virtually unknown, he replaced Litvinov as Ambassador to Washington. It took the President some time to find out what any student of Soviet affairs could have told him immediately—that though Bulganin was the official head of the delegation, the First Secretary was the real boss. Zhukov's behavior struck Eisenhower as reflecting considerable nervousness. But then his account, written in the 1960s, must have been influenced by the Marshal's subsequent, abrupt fall. Gromyko's unsmiling ways were thought to indicate antipathy to the West, but most likely *he* was nervous, operating under the eye of his superiors, whom he had briefed as to the probable behavior of those incomprehensible Americans.

The other Russians smiled a great deal, and this rather ungraciously was attributed by the President to mere political calculation, as was Marshal Zhukov's statement that he had to miss his daughter's wedding in order to be there. This was unfair: when the circumstances allow it, the Russians are a most gregarious people. And apart from political reasons, there was every inducement for the delegation to be cheerful: Stalin was dead and they were alive, hobnobbing with the highest capitalist dignitaries. Who would have thought it possible? And what a relief to be in Switzerland rather than, say, in Peking. That they were under some constraint, however, is obvious from another circumstance which did not escape Eisenhower's eye: they drank only little.

There were smiles on the other side, too. In fact, Eisenhower's famous grin clearly outshone that of Bulganin, France's Faure, and Britain's Eden in the official photograph. Thus was born the "spirit of Geneva," which was to sustain hopes of peace during the severe crises of the next three years, and then sadly evaporate in the wake of the U-2 episode and the bitter and aborted summit meeting in 1960.

This subsequent failure and unpleasantness colored and distorted the main participants' recollections of the encounter in Switzerland. Eisenhower's estimate of Khrushchev was "He is not . . . a statesman, but rather a powerful, skillful, ruthless and highly ambitious politician." [21] And in 1960, Khrushchev remarked that he had noticed, at Geneva, that whenever a question of substance came up, Eisenhower had to seek information from an adviser, usually Dulles. In both cases subsequent experience distorted original impressions. The President saw Khrushchev, and in the main correctly, as a man who though devious and stubborn was nonetheless devoted to peace. And it is clear that Khrushchev believed Eisenhower to be one of those rare capitalist statesmen who do not have sinister ultimate designs against Communism. This estimate of the President played an important role in subsequent Soviet policies.

In substance, Geneva could offer but little. The vast staffs, the voluminous documents—the U.S. delegation had twenty "basic documents" and 150 "secondary papers"—brought by the conferees assured that the discussion of the most important problems would bog down in detail and amidst propaganda statements. The Soviet disarmament proposals viewed longingly, if not by the governments then by public opinion in Britain and France, met an expected American rebuff. To soften the negative impact of this refusal, the American psychological experts came up with Eisenhower's famous "open-skies" proposal: the United States and the U.S.S.R. were to exchange blueprints of their military establishments and enable each other to photograph them from the air. From the Soviet point of view, this would have been a very poor bargain, since the American system does not allow of much secrecy: any exchange of information concerning military capabilities, bases, etc., would reveal more to the United States than vice versa. And the events of the next few years serve as an illustration of the reason for their refusal: the U-2 planes notwithstanding, the legend of Soviet

[21] Dwight D. Eisenhower, *Mandate for Change: 1953–1956* (New York, 1963), p. 522.

superiority in guided missiles was not discounted until 1962. How different American policies could have been had more realistic estimates of Soviet power been available!

Apart from the open-skies proposal, the conference produced no surprises. The American attempt to discuss the East European satellites was put down firmly by Bulganin, and the United States spokesmen in turn refused to talk about Formosa and Communist China. The question of the unification of Germany was brought up, discussed, and abandoned. And in tried and true fashion, all unsolved and, under the current circumstances, insoluble questions were referred for further disagreement among the foreign ministers of the Big Four, who reassembled in Geneva in a few months with the usual results.

Today, Geneva is only a minor footnote in the chronicle of the Cold War. Yet at the time, for all the lack of concrete results, it was widely hailed as indicating a thaw in international relations, paralleling that which was taking place in Soviet domestic politics. Here were two sides that had quite recently completed elaborate defense organizations —NATO and the Warsaw Pact—directed at each other and dividing Europe into two fortified camps. Yet now they met amidst smiles and conviviality, generating universal and vast relief that all those defense arrangements would remain on paper, that the dreaded clash of arms would never take place.

As such, the score was clearly in the Russians' favor: Dulles' threats and fears seemed obsolete and out of place. France could concentrate on her very considerable troubles in North Africa and feel more indignant than ever about America's lack of understanding and sympathy. Britain's attention could return to the Commonwealth and domestic economic problems. At Geneva, Sir Anthony Eden invited the Khrushchev-Bulganin team to visit Britain next spring. The British tried to compensate for their lost imperial power and prestige by persuading themselves that it was their masterful diplomacy which was bridging the dangerous gap between East and West, that it was they who were restraining the Americans from foolhardy adventures. Already, the 1954 Geneva Conference, at which France conceded North Vietnam and at which a truce was arranged in Indochina was, with some exaggeration, hailed as a triumph of *British* diplomacy, and Eden, who, to be sure, had helped to devise the compromise, was given the Order of the Garter by the Queen. Now, after the second Geneva, there was an added impulse, and not only among the British, to feel somewhat condescending toward the Americans with their obsession with the Communist danger, with their constant proddings of the Europeans to rearm and unite. A great part of West European opinion was ready to be instructed by the American Left when it came to explaining the mainsprings of American policy: McCarthyism, always exaggerated as to its lasting impact on the American scene, was assumed to be a powerful force in U.S. foreign policy, long after the death of the Senator from Wisconsin; the interests of oil companies with their fears of offending the Arabs were held to be the key to State Department actions in the Near East (though, incongruously, the United States was also criticized for its excessive solicitude for Israel); the China Lobby was held to keep Dulles in bondage and thus to prevent any constructive moves toward Peking. There was *some* truth in each of those opinions, but together they added up to a gross distortion of the official aims and policies.

Viewed from Washington, various elements of the world picture in the mid-fifties added up to considerable frustration. The sense of urgency and dispatch imparted to the Europeans, largely through Dulles' threat of agonizing reappraisal, was now evaporating, and all on account of a few Soviet smiles and soothing words. France was sinking deeper into the Algerian mire. The Commonwealth, now hardly more than a debating society (even that perhaps an exaggeration, seeing that India and Pakistan were barely on speaking terms), was still deflecting the British from seeking closer ties with their Continental neighbors, and at the same time the fears and illusions of its Asian members pushed London into disagreement with American policies in the Far East. A cynic might liken the predicament of the European powers to that of an aging woman requiring constant reassurance and flattery to keep her peace of mind. But Dulles was hardly cast for the role of a tactful suitor: his was rather that of a stern family adviser, censuring the Europeans for their memories of past glory and pretensions, warning them to take stock of their reduced stature in the world and to act accordingly.

Frustrated over the behavior of their principal allies, the Americans tended to rely more on others. West Germany had no troublesome colonial or commonwealth ties. Chancellor Adenauer stood firm in the face of both Soviet threats and cajoleries (to be sure, the latter were not as far-reaching as he had expected), hence his stock rose even more than was justified by Germany's returning strength. But a more serious consequence of French fickleness and British foot-dragging, as it was seen through the eyes of Washington, lay elsewhere. Though there was no logical connection, nor is there any documentary proof for it, there is a strong presumption that the frustration over Europe and irritation with the Edens and Mendès-Frances was to lead to a greater involvement in Asia as well as stronger commitments to such potentates as Chiang, Rhee, and Diem than would have otherwise been the case.

Thus passed the immediate post-Stalin era, the time of unduly great relief in the West, of great hopes for a stable peace, of great opportunities opening up to democratic statesmanship, opportunities which for the most part were not exploited.

We said before that the great fault of American policy-makers in the immediate postwar era was *not knowing*: not knowing how strong America was in relation to the rest of the world, and how a firm stand taken on behalf of the principles for which the war had allegedly been fought would have been not only the right but also the safe course of action. In the era that began with Russia's acquisition of advanced nuclear weapons, Communist China's emergence as a great power, and Stalin's death, the situation was to be quite different, but the main fault of American policy-makers was still to lie in *not understanding*: in not understanding this time the internal weaknesses and tensions which gripped the Communist world and which still offered great opportunities for American diplomacy; in not realizing that the economic strength and great military potential of Western Europe still concealed a grave psychological weakness, but one which could perhaps be overcome by a more sympathetic rather than schoolmasterish attitude on the part of its powerful ally. America's record for this and all subsequent periods will not lack defenders: with all the good intentions underlying America's policy, with the generosity characterizing her actions, what more could have been done by any government in Washington, especially in view of the follies or lassitude of America's allies, and the brutality and deceit on the other side, in view of madcap ventures like Suez and acts of repression as in Hungary? But the first and most important answer must still be: to understand.

8

The Point of
No Return

The spirit of Geneva which hovered over both NATO and the Warsaw Pact organizations made them seem less like hostile alliances than bargaining counters in the inevitable diplomatic conflict that accompanied peaceful coexistence. Russia was going through a quiet and unostentatious de-Stalinization: the worst features of the past were being disbanded or curbed; a modest effort was being made to improve the lot of the people. Foreign experts as well as many within the Party could judge that this was a prudent and judicious way of dealing with the terrible legacy of the past: it seemed better than expatiating upon the evils of the past and ascribing them solely to the man who had dominated their lives for a generation. Ancient Slavs would not call the bear by his real name for fear the beast would come out of his lair and into their settlements. Khrushchev, a great connoisseur of folk sayings and customs, was following the same tradition.

The same cautious liberalization was the rule in the Soviet Union's satellite states, though the pattern varied from country to country. Not unexpectedly, *their* police chiefs were unmasked as "enemies of the people" and, if not sharing the full severity of the treatment meted out to their former model, Beria, were now guests in the same installations to which they had previously consigned the "enemies of the people." In Hungary and Czechoslovakia, party leaders were dragging their feet on liberalization, hoping (perhaps on the basis of inside information) that the present aberration in Moscow would pass. Some may have genuinely felt, and their misgivings were to be justified, that it was all right for the Russians with their forty-year-old regime and their strong nationalism to mobilize these energies of self-criticism and liberalization. *They* were dealing with people whose experience of being submissive was of only recent vintage, whose nationalism would urge them to oppose Communism rather than favor it. All in all, rather than being grateful, their people would likely demand more. But orders were orders. With a heavy heart the Rakosis, Bieruts, and Novotnys complied or pretended to.

Khrushchev and his allies in the Politburo were moved by several considerations in conferring such boons on the subject countries. One was an honorable one: to restore the good name of Communism and to dissociate it from the excesses of the past era. There were also motives of a personal political nature. But another powerful argument must have been the case of China. By evolving new relationships for the Communist commonwealth of nations, one would avoid, it was hoped, future and odious comparisons and squabbles; it was better to grant out of free will and enlightenment now what you would have to concede out of necessity later. The new pattern of relationship *within* each country propagated by the Kremlin would also have its uses in regard to China. If collective leadership was now the fashion, would not Mao, already viewed with secret apprehension in Moscow, be constrained to share his power? And would not the Chinese Communists follow another Soviet example: devote a large part of their effort to raising the standard of living of their vast population, and relent in their, in Russia's view, unreasonable haste to obtain heavy industry and nuclear power? Altogether, the new policy, which bore every imprint of Khrushchev's personal style, was considered a considerable gamble, but one which, if successful, promised manifold benefits. Indeed, the Russian expectations were in 1956 not entirely unfounded. The Chinese leaders were constrained to follow the current Communist fashion of liberalization. Though Mao's "Let a hundred flowers bloom" speech was not delivered for another six months, their policies, especially in the cultural sphere, became more moderate. It was only in late 1957 that Mao and his group decided that de-Stalinization was a trap and that they had to consolidate their personal power and expand their heavy industry before their covert conflict with Russia became public.

These far-reaching internal and intrabloc reforms, for such they were, lent special interest to the character of the continued Soviet peace offensive. In January, 1956, Prime Minister Bulganin addressed himself to

President Eisenhower with a rather unusual proposal: to have their two countries sign a twenty-year treaty of friendship and economic, cultural, and scientific cooperation. Bulganin's letter was Soviet diplomacy at its most seductive. The President was wooed personally with a handsome compliment as "one of the outstanding military leaders of the anti-Hitler coalition." It was recalled how the United States and Russia, except for those minor unpleasantnesses of intervention during the Civil War, had never clashed in war. They had no basically conflicting interests, no territorial claims against each other. On the contrary, life itself had shown that "cooperation between the U.S.S.R. and the United States was based not on chance or transient but on vital and long-term interests." [1] They had been comrades at arms during both world wars.[2] Altogether, the language of the Bulganin letter was as remarkable as the actual proposals were banal.

In Washington the letter created a minor panic. Where was the catch? To be sure, the actual provisions of the proposed treaty, a draft of which was enclosed, were commonplace and obligated both parties to nothing they were not doing or going to do anyway. In the opinion of experts it was pronounced a propaganda stunt, a further attempt to weaken the West's vigilance, to persuade the Europeans that America and the U.S.S.R. were about to strike a bargain behind their backs. Eisenhower's reply was polite but evasive. He pointed out that the treaty would not obligate the two parties to do anything they were not pledged to do under the U.N. Charter anyway. If the Russians were so eager for real friendship and cooperation, why did they not start by agreeing to his proposal for aerial inspection? And how about the reunification of Germany? Marshal Bulganin's reply was a good-natured rejoinder: the Russians were also eager for deeds rather than words, but they had already done so much—reduced their armed forces, signed the Austrian peace treaty, given Finland back the base they had held, etc. All those other problems General Eisenhower mentioned could be worked out once you had the treaty, so please, Mr. President!

The correspondence continued along the same lines until the fall, when the affairs of Suez and Hungary were to terminate it amidst some bitterness.

What *really* were the Russians after? With hindsight, we must accept

---

[1] *Documents on International Affairs, 1956* (London, 1959), p. 578.
[2] The reference to World War I was rather unusual, since the official Soviet view considers it an imperialist war and Russia's participation in it not a matter of pride or a fit subject of commemoration.

a strong presumption that the Soviets had more in mind than merely propaganda, though undoubtedly that was one of the side benefits they hoped to gather from their initiative. What is interesting is what was *not* in the original letter and only barely alluded to in the subsequent Soviet epistles—namely, any reference to Communist China. Previous Soviet references to the long-range improvement of relations with the United States, including Bulganin's recitation in Geneva, had always contained ritualistic references to recognizing the rights of the People's Republic of China over Formosa and to a seat in the U.N. The January letter, on the other hand, contained only a rather enigmatic acknowledgment that during the period of the "cold war" there arose "serious differences" between the two countries concerning disarmament, the German question, and "certain problems of the Far East."

Only the most suspicious Kremlinologist or . . . somebody in Peking could see in Bulganin's innocent initiative an invitation to an American-Soviet alliance against China. Yet, it is quite likely that Moscow was signaling, or to use plain English dropping hints about, its readiness to have far-reaching discussions with Washington about China, among other things. How, after all, had the Soviet-Nazi flirtation begun? In the midst of official Soviet vilification of Hitler, in the midst of negotiations with the British and French about an alliance against Germany, the Soviet ambassador dropped in on the German deputy foreign minister one spring morning (April 17) to tell him, in the latter's words: "There exists for Russia no reason why she should not live with us on a normal footing. And from normal the relations might become better and better." [3] And in two months the U.S.S.R. and Nazi Germany were secretly discussing an alliance and division of Eastern Europe among themselves. Now, one should not push parallels too far, but undoubtedly the Soviets were interested in exploring various possibilities and options, including one of the eruption of an open crisis in Soviet-Chinese relations. What then would be the attitude of the Americans? But how could one sound out the Americans without surrendering probably the most valuable asset Soviet foreign policy had—namely, the State Department's firm conviction that relations between Peking and Moscow were those of "eternal amity" and "unshakable unity"? This problem of communications was to perplex the Kremlin during the next few years and become an important factor in the great and dangerous crises which threatened the world between 1958 and 1962.

[3] R. J. Sontag and J. T. Beddie, *Nazi-Soviet Relations 1939–1941: Documents from the Archives of the German Foreign Office* (Washington, D.C., 1948), p. 2.

In view of the Russians' oversubtlety, Washington cannot wholly be blamed for failing to perceive in the Soviet initiative more than a routine propaganda move. Having cajoled the West Europeans into dropping their guard with hopes and illusions centered on the Geneva conference, the Soviets were trying to accomplish the same in regard to the United States by pushing this meaningless treaty. Oversubtle when it came to deep and devious designs in foreign policy, Khrushchev tended to be unsubtle when it came to the personal element in politics. The President, on his part, could not but be irritated by this all too obvious attempt to play on his vanity on the one hand and on the other by the possibility that a strenuous warding off of the Soviet embrace might injure his chances of re-election. Eisenhower's testiness was evident in a rejoinder later that summer. He appreciated, he wrote Bulganin, efforts made in Russia to eradicate "the evils of an earlier period"—a transparent and less than tactful reference to Khrushchev's recent denunciation of Stalin, seeing that the First Secretary's speech at the 20th Party Congress was supposed to be secret and certainly not read abroad, much less referred to by the President of the United States. But Eisenhower went even further and with what almost amounted to Khrushchevian indelicacy hoped that "you and your associates will not confine these efforts to those evils as manifested within your Party and nation. Those evils were also projected into the international field." [4]

Then came Khrushchev's turn—his hand is unmistakable though the signature is Bulganin's. The Russians, a letter of October 17 affirmed, were broadminded enough to understand that in a Presidential campaign many things are said for "polemical reasons." But even so, why do administration spokesmen, and especially Secretary Dulles, keep saying things about the U.S.S.R. which are false? Adlai Stevenson had just attempted to revive his faltering campaign by proposing an agreement to suspend the testing of nuclear weapons. Eisenhower had denounced the proposal on grounds that the Soviet Union would not abide by such an agreement: the Soviet letter dwelt with some surprise on the President's unwarranted distrust and his rejection of this far-seeing proposal by his Democratic opponent (delicately referred to as "some prominent official persons in the United States"). Eisenhower's official reply stressed the impermissible character of this interference in American domestic politics and the offensive tone in which the letter was couched.

The whole sequence is not uncharacteristic of Soviet diplomacy of the Khrushchev period: when frustrated in an elaborate diplomatic maneu-

[4] *Documents on International Affairs, 1956*, p. 595.

ver, the Soviet leader would become irritable, then, often in a puerile fashion, mischievous. His impatience at what he undoubtedly saw as American obduracy and insensitivity was matched on the other side by lack of imagination and equal impatience. There were humorous aspects to the Bulganin-Eisenhower exchange: not much time had elapsed since the Soviets had denounced their treaties of friendship with Britain and France on grounds that those countries had conspired with the United States to rearm West Germany. Yet here they were imploring the main instigator for a similar treaty! But it was not wholly funny: here were two countries whose *real* interests did not have to be antagonistic, but who were kept from a more meaningful *rapprochement* not so much by ideological differences as by a vast and seemingly unbridgeable gap in communications.

In their approaches to the United States, the Soviet statesmen were prompted by the belief that Eisenhower, because of his great moral authority and popularity, was one American statesman who could effect a basic *détente* with the U.S.S.R. But in 1956, American foreign policy, and not only in regard to Russia, was stymied and incapable of major initiatives or probes for a new approach. The most troublesome problems of the world had persisted and refused to yield to the Republicans' gruff incantations as little as they had been solved by the hopes of the postwar period. "Negotiating from a position of strength" seemed to be as incapable of making the great evils and dangers of the nuclear age disappear as had that other bracing slogan: "The United Nations is the best hope for peace." The Soviet Union was still there with a growing stock of nuclear weapons. China presumably would have them before too long. American foreign policy, as elaborated by the Republican administration and on the bases of the shattered hopes of the recent past, was well suited to counteract Soviet misbehavior, to isolate and contain a Russia of the Stalinist model. But it was ill suited to deal with *intermittent* Soviet misbehavior combined with appeals for friendship and eulogies of coexistence. The formulas and policies of 1952–53 had served their purpose, and they were useless in coping with the new opportunities. The President, as is not infrequently the case with generals acting in a political capacity (witness de Gaulle), was skeptical of military solutions for political problems.[5] Yet his eminently peaceful disposition was not accompanied by a temperament conducive to negotiation, i.e., to bargaining with the Soviets. Thus for the balance of the Eisenhower ad-

[5] One recalls also MacArthur's warnings against committing U.S. forces in a land war in Asia.

ministration, official policy remained one of waiting for events, of reactions rather than initiatives.

In contrast to a certain torpor in Washington, the Soviets were to exhibit hyperactivity. In February, Nikita Khrushchev dropped the other shoe with his famous speech at the 20th Party Congress giving Stalin as the reason for the evils which had beset Soviet society since the 1930s. What made Khrushchev disregard that wise injunction of an American philosopher and sports figure—"Don't look behind, something might be catching up with you"? [6] Again, taking account of a personality as complex as Khrushchev's, there must have been several reasons: the first, a genuine feeling that a clean break must be made with the evils of the past. There also were a politician's motives: he would steal the march on his fellow oligarchs, show himself the main proponent of liberal reforms while they dragged their feet because of complicity in Stalin's crimes. The First Secretary would gain additional popularity among the rank and file of the party. From being the first among equals he would become the boss.

For the next eight years, these calculations proved in the main correct. Khrushchev lived largely on the capital accumulated by his denunciation of Stalin. To be sure, his version of his late and terrible boss would vary somewhat, according to what he considered the needs of the hour. Stalin certainly knew how to deal with enemies of Communism, said the First Secretary approvingly at a reception in the Chinese Embassy, after trying experiences that fall with Poland and Hungary. At other times he would go beyond the rather restrained condemnation of 1956 and picture Stalin as a psychopath and sadist, his activities from the beginning stained by excessive cruelty. But all in all, Khrushchev's courageous if not disinterested act was a momentous one, and its effect can never be entirely undone. For all his considerable sins of omission and commission, despite the general apathy which greeted the news of his overthrow, one must conclude that Nikita Sergeievich gained through the speech a claim on the gratitude of his great and unfortunate people, and a firm and favorable place in their history.

Internally the speech was a calculated risk. With their long historical experience of tyrants and oppression, the Russian people were not likely to storm party and government offices in the wake of the fearful revelations. That to many Russians, especially the young brought up

[6] And indeed it did. It is clear in view of their careful but determined refurbishing of Stalin's image that the successful conspirators against Khrushchev in 1964 had all along considered his denunciation of Stalin as having gone too far.

in the Stalin cult, it was a shattering personal experience there can be no doubt. But to most people, after the initial shock, the speech appeared, as it was intended to, as a repudiation of the evil past and a pledge of better times to come. Only within the intellectual community were the revelations to lead to general questioning of the premises of the Soviet system and Communism, and there the tale is not yet ended.

In the satellites the shock was to contribute mightily to that turbulence which shook Eastern Europe in the fall and at one point threatened to destroy the Soviet empire there. The Chinese hastened to add their approval to the condemnation of the "cult of personality." There was little reason for Peking to feel sentimental about Stalin: in his speech Khrushchev had referred to demands of a "colonialist nature" the late despot had made upon Communist China (and how one wishes he had gone into details!). By destroying the aura of infallibility surrounding the Soviet leadership, by incurring political risks at home and abroad, Khrushchev and the Soviets were putting themselves in a position where they would need Chinese approval and support more than ever before, and where obviously they would have to pay for it.

Privately, as subsequent events were to show, Mao Tse-tung had very grave reservations. These bore on two main points. Was the attack on Stalin what it purported to be, or was it part of a scheme to establish ideological coexistence with capitalism, as the phrase later went, a retreat toward a more nationalist orientation for the Soviet Union and eventual abandonment of active propagation of Communism? If by striking at the cult of personality in general the Soviets were denouncing the idea of any leader standing above the party and claiming allegience and homage in his personal capacity, it implied covert criticism of the position Mao had claimed and gained within China.

In the West, the *immediate* reverberations of Khrushchev's denunciation of Stalin were strong. There the Communist parties were caught in a tragicomic dilemma. There was little in the revelations that the more cynical Communist leaders in the West had not known for years; some of them must have chafed under Stalin's iron hand and they probably relished his humiliation, even if posthumous. Others welcomed the opportunity to assert their greater autonomy from Moscow. But to the majority it was an infuriating and unnecessary act of indiscretion, for they stood revealed as dupes or worse: surviving Trotskyites, and the Voice of America had a field day repeating what in official parlance of but a few months before had been termed "infamous slanders of reactionaries and imperialists."

It then must remain a vivid illustration of some irrational aspects of twentieth-century politics that the revelations caused so little damage to the Communist parties in the West. There were to be no mass defections. The French and Italian parties retained their sway over a large part of the electorate and over organized labor. Among those who were disenchanted by the revelations were some who were hurt not so much by the truth as by the overturning of an infallible idol through whose worship they could satisfy their religious needs and focus personal and political frustrations. Some were to recapture their earlier zeal when, with the open clash between Russia and China, the latter could be seen as representing a more uncompromising and militant form of Communism, and Mao could replace Stalin as an object of personal worship. Others sought new idols among the Communist leaders who represented the romance of revolution and defiance of capitalist power—hence the successive cults of Castro and Guevara.

Such involved psychological and political repercussions could not be clearly seen in the wake of the 20th Party Congress. No one knowing Stalin's successors could suppose for a moment that they would spend an undue amount of time in morbid introspection and in beating their breasts over past crimes and errors. In fact, the mere ability to raise the curtain on the horrors of the past was held to be proof of the superiority of the Soviet system: [7] To reveal and curb the worst abuses of the past in the spirit of self-congratulation must appear to an outsider both revolting and ridiculous. And yet one cannot deny the Soviet leaders a certain psychological insight. Collective guilt feeling is a heavy and debilitating burden for any society to bear. A nation must learn to live with its past.

This insight led the ruling organs to react vigorously to any assertions or intimations that Stalinism was somehow inherent in the Soviet struc-

[7] In the years to come, many prominent victims of the purges were rehabilitated and commemorated, often in this one might say boastful spirit, as if the deceased and his family had a veritable honor conferred upon them. The head of Soviet economic planning, Politburo member Nicolai Voznesensky, was abruptly dismissed, then executed in 1949. Years later, his secretary reminisced about the last moments with his boss. Voznesensky was gathering his papers in preparation for an interview with Stalin. Whatever happened, Voznesensky told his secretary, he was confident that the Central Committee would defend his good name. And, added the secretary, Voznesensky's faith was vindicated, for ten years after his death a resolution of the Central Committee fully rehabilitated him. Talk about cultivating a cheerful outlook on things!

ture. A resolution of the Central Committee of June 30, 1956, indignantly attacked hints of some foreign Communist leaders (such as the Italian Togliatti) that perhaps Soviet society had reached a measure of degeneration. Once again it was stated that the revelations of the 20th Party Congress were "the best proof of the strength and viability of the Soviet socialist system." To refute such unworthy speculations, the resolution quoted approvingly another part of Togliatti's statement, where the nimble veteran asserted that "notwithstanding everything, this society [Russia's] has preserved its basic democratic nature."

Formulas, rebuttals, and even internal reforms were not enough to prove the point. One consequence of Khrushchev's daring leap was to make Soviet foreign policy more venturesome. The proof of the viability of the Communist system could be demonstrated in its competitive ability vis-à-vis the capitalist world. This competition was many-sided. Not only the old idea of the Soviet Union catching up and overcoming the West insofar as industrial growth was concerned. Soon, and rather incautiously, Khrushchev was to promise to pass America in the production of meat, butter, and milk per head of population. The Soviets burst upon the international sports scene with a massive effort and success which brought cries of anguish and prophecies of gloom from American coaches and sportswriters. Even more wounding were Soviet achievements in that other field where even the most internationally minded American assumed his country to be in a class on its own: technology. Here the Soviet Union's initial primacy in space exploration was to have far-reaching political and psychological results.

If the Soviet Union under Khrushchev had confined its competitive zeal to those fields, the course of world history in the 1950s and 1960s would have been quite different. But the Soviet statesman also expanded the already dangerous rivalry between the United States and the Soviet Union to areas hitherto little affected by it. The need to vindicate the Soviet system led Khrushchev to conceive of this rivalry on a global scale and to commit Soviet resources and prestige to parts of the world where until recently they were but little or not at all involved: the Middle East, Latin America, and Africa. The Soviets, for instance, had chosen not to interfere in the very acute conflict between Egypt and Britain between 1946 and 1954, when the British finally agreed to evacuate the Canal Zone. Even the original expansion of Soviet diplomatic activities which followed Stalin's death and was expressed by the Khrushchev-Bulganin Asian tour of 1954 was designed to propagate the idea of neutralism, rather than expand the Soviet sphere of interests. In 1956, this restraint began to disappear.

What was to impart a special character to Soviet policy between 1956 and 1962 was then its outwardly schizophrenic character: Khrushchev sought a more basic *détente* with the West than would have been thought possible or desirable by Stalin; yet incongruously, exploited every major trouble spot, every embarrassment, to damage Western influence and prestige. There appeared to be two Khrushchevs: one, a "coexistentialist" eager for enhanced intercourse between the U.S. and the U.S.S.R.; dropping hints (to be sure so obscure as to remain at the time undecipherable) about the necessity for a virtual alliance of the two powers; the other, a militant Communist and bully ready to cash in on each and every weakness and hesitation of the West, threatening nuclear obliteration if his opponent would not submit.

This double-edged policy not only diverted attention from internal tensions and difficulties, but also masked the increasing difficulties encountered by the Soviets in managing their East European real estate. The condemnation of Stalin had explicitly spelled out his errors in connection with Yugoslavia; now the socialist family of nations was to be transformed, with the U.S.S.R. no longer the absolute master but merely the leader, the people's democracies not satellites but junior partners following Moscow's injunctions in foreign policy, coordinating their defense under Russian guidance but having considerable internal autonomy. This new model would preserve harmonious collaboration of the Communist countries yet soothe the national pride of the dependent nations. New bonds of union would be forged by the gratitude and free assent of the Eastern Europeans.

To advertise the new scheme of things, Marshal Tito was invited to Russia in the summer. Once a humble official of the Comintern and only recently a vilified heretic, he was now feasted and eulogized as if he were head of a major world power. Not long before, the Cominform had been dissolved, and Molotov, personally involved in the beginning of the quarrel and reputed to be opposed to a *rapprochement* with Belgrade, was dismissed. But Tito was a wary and experienced politician who remembered how once before he had been flattered and feasted and then. . . . He would never again fall into the trap of complete dependence on Russia; Yugoslavia with fine impartiality between the East and the West would accept credits and compliments from both sides. That in turn was far from meeting the Russians' expectations, for they presumed that Yugoslavia would take its place in the socialist family of nations, eventually perhaps to join in the Warsaw Pact and other intrabloc organizations, and forgo close relations with the West. Official communiqués stressed that various countries may pursue different roads to socialism, and Tito was profuse with advice about the people's democracies.

It would have been unreasonable to expect this new policy to work smoothly. In many of the people's democracies, the great majority of the people were not Communists of any kind. Throughout that summer and fall, the revolution of rising expectations swept Eastern Europe. The old satraps cowered and appealed for help. Some were shunted aside, others propped up by Moscow. As the Catholic Church was to discover in a few years, it is easier to initiate the process of liberalization of an organization based upon absolute authority than to set safe limits to this process. There were obvious divisions within the Kremlin as to how far it was safe to go, and it does not take a great deal of insight to deduce that there were some in high positions who would be happy when this damn liberalization would blow up in Khrushchev's face.

If the Russians were trying to modify their imperialism as a matter of policy, the West was going through a much more excruciating process of retreat from colonialism—partly through choice, partly through disenchantment with the empires of old, but also through the pressure of rising nationalisms and, not an inconsiderable element in this situation, American disapproval. For all practical purposes, the process was completed in Asia, where there remained only a few enclaves of Western possessions. The British presence "east of Suez" was still substantial, but designed to protect the soon to be independent state of Malaysia rather than to stand guard over colonial possessions. In South Vietnam, the Americans replaced the discredited French and assumed, in a fateful moment, the burden of defending and subsidizing that new, struggling country. This was done in accordance with Dulles' policy of extending help to worthy anti-Communists on the periphery of the Communist world. In the case of Vietnam, it was the Catholic and celibate Ngo Dinh Diem, whose personal and political virtue shone exceedingly brightly in comparison with his predecessor and French creature, ex-emperor Bao Dai[8] The United States' all-too-

[8] Celibacy and virtue have played a curious role in Vietnamese history since World War II. The first postwar French High Commissioner, who may have contributed to the future tragedy by his high-handed policies, was Georges Thierry D'Argenlieu, who combined two most incongruous professions, those of admiral and Carmelite monk, and was on this count known in the French navy as the admiral "who never

hasty sponsorship of Diem reflected not so much his celibate virtue (at the time Washington looked rather kindly on Indonesia's Sukarno, who on this count presented a rather strong contrast to Diem) nor, as was maliciously alleged, Cardinal Spellman's intercessions on behalf of this devout Catholic, but the current belief that the best buffer against Communism was to be found in public figures who combined *a nationalist past* of strong opposition to colonial rule with personal incorruptibility. Diem, it was said, rated high marks on both counts.

The move into Indochina reflected an American attitude which already was and would become even more productive of trouble in other areas. Americans believed that they, unlike nations with an imperialist past, could count on a great fund of good will in the Third World. American know-how, obvious disinterestedness, the record of emancipating dependencies (such as the Philippines) or allowing them the status of free association (as Puerto Rico)—all that was assumed to secure for the United States popularity where other Western nations were disliked or distrusted. The misleading example of the American experience in Japan (it was disregarded how modernized Japan had already been by 1945 in many aspects of its economy and culture) led to the belief that with American technical assistance and through social reform, a recently feudal society could be transformed into a thriving and progressive democracy. In contrast, the British and the French were held to be not only selfish but inefficient when dealing with underdeveloped countries. Their clumsiness as well as their clinging to relics of an obsolete past threatened to turn those nations into a fertile field for Communist movements, rather than, were the enlightened American example or advice followed, willing associates of freedom.

Even in the relatively hopeful atmosphere of the 1950s it should have been clear that there were large areas of the world where those simple and bracing formulas would not work. The Near East was an obvious example. Age-long conflicts of interest—economic, national, and practically every other variety—crisscrossed along the southern reaches of the Mediterranean. It would take a very bold and per-haps foolish analyst to assert that there was, at any time after World War II, any master solution which would render equal justice to the conflicting claims of Arab nationalism vs. Israel, to Greek Cypriotes

has known love." (His sobriquet "*L'amiral qui n'avait jamais connu l'amour*" was coupled with that of another colonial governor, Admiral Robert, known as "*l'amiral qui n'avait jamais connu la mer*," "the admiral who has never been to sea.") A strange navy.

vs. their Turkish co-citizens, to fighters for Algerian independence as against both French and Algerian proponents of a continued connection with France, and that even with the best will in the world and the most consummate statesmanship, some of the dramas would not have to be played out. What was required of a bystander such as the United States was, first of all, awareness that there were no perfect solutions but at most only tolerable ones, and that there was no magic formula to dissolve passionate enmities but at best patched-up arrangements to gain time while passions subsided and ground could be prepared for a compromise.

In 1954, American pressure helped push the British to sign an agreement with Egypt under terms of which by 1956 the last British soldier was to leave Egyptian soil. Thus was removed what had been the dominant fact of Near Eastern politics since 1882: Britain's hold on the Suez waterway. British acquiescence, which did not come easily to the government in London, still headed by Winston Churchill, and the United States' not so gentle prodding had been based on recognition of the undeniable fact that in the nuclear age a British base in the area could hardly protect the Canal. It was firmly believed in Washington (and not so firmly in London) that the new regime in Egypt would be appeased by this gesture and less inclined to succumb to the wiles of neutralism (few as yet had the vision of something worse). Nasser and his young officers who ran Egypt had at first a good press in the United States. But the fault lay not so much in the British abandoning yet another outpost of their imperial past—something which probably could not have been delayed much longer—but in the absence of forethought as to the quite obvious consequences of the withdrawal. In view of the current fashions in international politics it was unthinkable that the proud and ambitious Egyptian colonel would put up for long with a foreign-owned company running the Canal and collecting profits. A much more serious contingency was that with the disappearance of the British soldiers, there would vanish the major psychological and mechanical barrier to a great intensification of the conflict between the Egyptians and the Israelis. Like many a young and ambitious politician, Nasser was not content with promoting internal reform and economic development. Arab nationalism was both an article of fervent belief and a vehicle for personal ambition. Hostility to Israel in turn was a great cementing element in that nationalism, one which would assure the country and the man who assumed the leading role in the anti-Israel movement—in this case Egypt and Nasser—the kind of popular following in other Arab countries which otherwise they could not obtain.

The tragedy inherent in the Near Eastern situation was, then, that the passionate nationalism which made France's and Britain's position difficult and threatened to overturn moderate Arab regimes militated at the same time against an acquiescence in the existence of Israel. American public opinion applauded Arab nationalism when it was directed against the vestiges of Western influence or against native "feudal" regimes but tended to oppose it when it was directed against Israel. There was little understanding of the inevitable link between those two tendencies, of the fact that if it was right for an Algerian to demand a complete end to French presence in his country, then it was quite natural for a Palestinian Arab to resent Israel, that if it was excusable for Egypt to assist the Algerian guerrillas against the French, then one had to understand the same activities in connection with the Arab refugees from Israel. In brief, one could not expect Arab politicians to be twentieth-century nationalists in one respect and broad-minded nineteenth-century-style liberals in another. Nasser could not be viewed as an Arab George Washington, insofar as his fight against Western influence in the Near East and efforts to subvert more conservative Arab regimes were concerned, if at the same time, vis-à-vis Israel, he appeared as a sort of Arab Hitler. There were obvious political and psychological reasons for this inconsistency—consistency in politics may not always be possible, or even desirable—but at least it should have been realized that every success by radical Arab nationalism, every retreat by Britain and France in the Near East, was making the position of Israel more precarious.[9]

Soviet Russia's policies, on the other hand, had a certain consistency and logic. The guiding principle was very simple: follow the course of action which is most likely to create difficulties for your antagonists. Before 1948, this meant support for the creation of an independent Israel. Once the new state was established—and who is there to remind them now that they were the first power to recognize Israel officially?— Soviet policies shifted predictably to support of the Arab position and denunciation of the new state as an outpost of Western imperialism. What was principally dictated by Machiavellian considerations was strengthened by some emotional undertones of Soviet policies in the last years of Stalin: Zionism was labeled an outgrowth of American

[9] Not in a military sense, but in the sense of having its right to peaceful existence recognized by its neighbors.

imperialism and a threat to the loyalty of Soviet Jews, and beyond this anti-Zionism, anti-Semitism also raised its ugly head. Stalin's death brought an amelioration of relations with Israel, but the general thrust of Soviet policy in the area remained the same.

Until 1955, the Soviets were content to observe the West's increasing discomfiture from a distance, supporting the Arabs through propaganda and by making sympathetic noises in the United Nations. But the activist turn of Khrushchev's foreign policy would not allow such a passive enjoyment of the Near East spectacle for long.

In 1955, Soviet diplomatic contacts with Cairo grew more frequent. Washington's hopes that Nasser would concentrate on internal reforms and become more friendly to the West and less hostile to Israel were jolted by the announcement that Egypt had contracted for deliveries of arms from Czechoslovakia, for which she was going to pay with her cotton crop. In 1956, Secretary Dulles sought to discourage Nasser from further flirtation with the Communist bloc by rather abruptly withdrawing the offer of American assistance toward the construction of Nasser's pet project, the Aswan Dam. This was the prelude to the Suez drama: the emotional Egyptian leader announced seizure of the Suez Company. The further sequence of events is well known. Between July, when the blow fell, and late October, the British and French planned their joint military intervention. It was an elaborate plan which underwent several modifications. The Israelis joined the intrigue: they believed that the Egyptian dictator was the main inspiration behind Arab guerrilla incursion into Israeli territory. The Israelis struck on October 29; the Anglo-British ultimatum demanding that the two powers come as "neutral" mediators and occupy the Canal Zone came next day. This transparent ruse was unlikely to fool anyone; rather, it aggravated the position of the two Western powers. On the expiration of the ultimatum, the British began bombing Egyptian airfields and dropping leaflets urging Egyptians to overthrow their government, another psychological blunder of major proportions. The Israelis trounced the Egyptians almost as expeditiously as they were to do eleven years later. And on November 5, the Anglo-French landings in the Canal Zone began. On the next day, harangued by the Americans and threatened by the Russians, Prime Minister Eden, with his own Cabinet divided and himself on the verge of a breakdown, called off the venture, his more cold-blooded French partners reluctantly following his lead.

All in all a frightful mess. What lay behind this display of political

imbecility—the expression is not too strong—exhibited in varying
degrees by London, Paris, and Washington?

In the first place, and most fundamentally, between July and November, 1956, the United States abandoned the role it had exercised ever
since World War II as leader and protector of the Western powers.
After the first shock of the nationalization of the Canal, the United
States could have insisted on and taken the lead in finding a compromise
solution, and/or warned the British and French of its determination
to oppose any use of force. In fact, after leading up to the first policy,
Dulles backed off from any solution implying pressure on Nasser.
Asked in a press conference on September 13 whether in view of his
declaration that the United States under no circumstances would use
force to keep the Canal open, America did not "leave all the trump
cards in Mr. Nasser's hands," the Secretary offered the pious insight
that for great powers with vital interests at stake and possessed of
great military and economic strength it was an act of great virtue to
exercise self-restraint (i.e., to be led by the nose by Nasser): "History
will judge it that the exercise of that self-restraint . . . in deference
to the obligations undertaken under the United Nations Charter adds
more from a moral point of view to the so-called nations . . . than if
they had used their force." [10]

This was bound to create the worst possible impression in London
and Paris, even on those who were opposed to the Suez venture. Here
was Nasser propagandizing against Britain and France in every area
of the Near East, not to mention the immediate issue of the dispute,
and the British and French were called upon to exercise charity and
self-restraint! Were the Americans exhibiting that virtue when they
plotted the downfall of the Guatemalan government in 1954? Would
they show the same degree of patience the two European powers had
already demonstrated in the face of Egyptian provocations if a parallel
situation arose over the Panama Canal? Dulles' tone was wounding
and harmful: not only were the two countries being chided for imperialist sins, but they were being openly treated as powers no longer
of the first rank.

If the American policy-makers felt that the contemplated military
action against Egypt was bound to have disastrous consequences,
which was probably correct, they should have made it explicit to the
governments concerned that the United States would take a resolute
stand against it. While expressing hope that the British and French

[10] *Documents on International Affairs, 1956,* p. 219.

would not resort to drastic steps, the Americans never issued any clear and unambiguous warnings. The British Conservative Cabinet was seriously divided on the wisdom of the plan, and it is unlikely that it would have embarked on the foolhardy venture had it been plainly (and confidentially) told of steps the United States would take: joining in a U.N. demand for an immediate cease-fire, financial and economic sanctions until the fighting ended, and promises to withdraw speedily from Egyptian soil.

The actual American actions reflected several factors. One, of course, was the Presidential election: the crisis came at the supremely inconvenient and, for the administration, dangerous moment of the concluding phase of the electoral campaign. Secondly, Dulles—whose attitude was, needless to say, decisive in determining policy for the President, despite Eisenhower's pro-British sympathies—bore traces of lingering resentment of the British and French, and of Eden personally, over what he considered as undue concessions made to the Communists in Indochina in 1954. There was, finally, one suspects, an undercurrent of grim satisfaction that the wicked were reaping their deserts.

Still, the United States' holier-than-thou attitude does not excuse, even though it help to explain, the imbecility of the whole stratagem and the clumsiness of its execution. It should have been obvious that the Suez Canal might be nationalized not much later than when the British soldiers left Egypt, yet no plans had been formulated for such a contingency when the Anglo-Egyptian treaty was concluded in 1954. The act of nationalization itself could hardly be challenged on grounds of international law. And whatever the other consequences of the military move against Egypt, it was clearly foreseeable that it would bring a run on the pound, blockage of the Canal, and a grave diminution of the flow of oil from the Near East.

To the French, the main objective was to overthrow Nasser. In their frustration over Algeria, they saw in Nasser one of the main reasons for their inability to finish off the rebels. The whole concept of the anti-Egyptian plot made it probable that no matter what the military outcome, Nasser's political position would be immeasurably strengthened not only in Egypt but throughout the Arab world. Here he was being attacked not only by Israel but by two Western giants; the ineptitude of his regime and the incompetence of his army were obscured in the aura of martyrdom and heroism of his defiance of the mighty. Conversely, to the still-sizable pro-British element among Arab politicians, British collusion with the French, and especially with Israel, spelled out political bankruptcy and was an augury of their eventual downfall, as in the case of Iraq in 1958. Politically, and probably militarily, it would have made more sense for any of the three interested countries to attack Egypt separately.

It is thus idle to indulge in the increasingly popular American parlor game of asking, when contemplating disastrous results of an ill-conceived venture, "Who was guilty?" Each of the three Western powers made every conceivable mistake, plus some inconceivable ones.

The consequences of the Suez episode are still with us. The U.N. peace-keeping force, which moved in to replace the Anglo-French expeditionary corps, helped for the next ten years to preserve an uneasy truce between Israel and Egypt. But essentially, in view of the progressive collapse of Western influence in the whole region, the overall situation there grew more precarious and the threat to Israel and of war more dangerous. America's support of Arab nationalism and acquiescence, indeed one might say assistance, in the destruction of British and French influence, was premised on the notion that it was the best way to keep the U.S.S.R. out of the region, yet in effect the policy had the opposite result.

For the Soviet government, the Suez crisis was in fact a veritable godsend. Nasser's seizure of the Canal had *not* been part of a Soviet plot to penetrate the Near East—that summer and fall the Russians had plenty of troubles of their own to keep them from embarking on new adventures—but once the crisis ripened and the confusion and divisions within Western ranks became apparent, they were delighted to jump into the situation with both feet. The crisis coincided with the Soviet armed intervention in Hungary and hence it was doubly welcome as a means of diverting attention from their own imperial troubles and of profiting from Western quarrels.

The day of the Anglo-French landings on November 4, Chairman Bulganin addressed letters to the heads of governments of the United States, Britain, France, and Israel. (Again the signature was Bulganin's but the epistolary style unmistakably Khrushchev's.) To the President of the United States, he magnanimously proposed that the forces of the two countries join in repelling aggression against Egypt: with what must be described as breathtaking gall—Soviet tanks were at the moment pouring into Budapest—the Soviet letter affirmed that such action would "greatly enhance the United States' prestige, and peace will be restored and strengthened." [11] In letters to the other three

---

[11] *Documents on International Affairs, 1956*, p. 293.

powers, there were most revealing and interesting variations in tone. The *least threatening* (though by no means can it be described as polite) is the letter to the Israeli Prime Minister, David Ben Gurion: Would Israel reconsider, cease being the tool of "outside imperialist forces," and pull its forces off Egyptian soil? For Guy Mollet, the tone is more ominous: "The Soviet government is fully determined to use force in order to smash the aggressors and restore peace in the East." [12] Yet the letter also contains a touching appeal to Mollet's conscience as a fellow Socialist. Poor Mollet, evidently still believing in the "Left talking to Left" gambit, had told the Soviets on his visit to Russia that socialism inspired him in all his work. But, said Bulganin severely: "What has socialism in common with the predatory attack on Egypt?" [13] In their communication to Eden, the Soviets were at their most brutal: "In what situation would Britain find herself if she were attacked by stronger states possessing all types of modern destructive weapons?" [14] There is an explicit threat to use rocket weapons. And would that be any less inhuman than what they, the British, were doing to the poor, defenseless Egyptians? An interesting gradation of threats, almost disingenuous in revealing the Soviets' estimate as to who among the recipients had strong and who weak nerves. At the same time, an enterprising Soviet consul in Port Said tried to persuade the Egyptian garrison and population there to keep on fighting the Anglo-French invaders, promising them that before long London and Paris would be laid waste by Soviet nuclear missiles.

With how much gusto Khrushchev and Bulganin were showing the world how atomic diplomacy can be practiced! There was none of that guilty feeling which inhibited American statesmen between 1945 and 1949, fearful even among themselves of discussing any possible *diplomatic* exploitation of their monopoly of nuclear weapons. From their prime minister on down to a lowly consul, the Soviets were cheerfully announcing that they were going to visit destruction on the United States' ally, when America still enjoyed a huge superiority over the U.S.S.R. both in nuclear weapons and in the means of delivery. On any rational count, the Soviet threats were ridiculous. But could one be *absolutely sure* that the regime, a small group of elderly men menaced by developments in their own country and in their East European domain, might not pull off something incalculable in consequences?

[12] *Ibid.*, p. 291.
[13] *Ibid.*, p. 290.
[14] *Ibid.*, p. 289.

The U.S. Strategic Air Command was put on alert. But this was not made public, while Soviet threats became immediately and widely known. It was, in fact, a grave error of American diplomacy not to spell out their strategic superiority most unmistakably and forcibly in their communications with the Soviet Union and other countries. For one outcome of the Suez crisis was to be a conviction on Khrushchev's part that one could freely and profitably indulge in this kind of atomic blackmail, and this conviction stayed with him until one fall day in 1962.

With the armistic in the Canal Zone a fact, the Soviet bluff took a different form. It is possible that there were people in the Kremlin who felt that Khrushchev was laying it on too thick. Anyway, the Russians now proclaimed their eagerness to send volunteers to help the brave Egyptian people. Thousands of veterans were allegedly seeking to enroll. How they were going to get there, and why they should go, since the fighting had stopped, and most of all why land troops were needed if Soviet nuclear rockets were targeted on Britain and France, were questions nobody thought of asking, much as it would have been worth the time of a State Department official to do so. American diplomatic utterances dwelt indignantly on the hypocritical inconsistency between the Soviet actions in Hungary and their sentiments over the Near East. But the world needed no lessons about Soviet inconsistency, nor about their readiness to employ brutal measures. What was needed was to call the Soviet bluff.

In view of this feeble reaction from Washington, it was not surprising that the Soviet diplomatic offensive continued. On November 17, another letter over Bulganin's signature went out to the heads of governments of the United States, Britain, France, Communist China, and India. It repeated Soviet disarmament proposals of some years standing, including a ban on the testing of nuclear weapons. But what it is more of interest than the proposals themselves was the tone of the memorandum.

Diplomatic notes in the Khrushchev period tended to be long-winded. Here too was the usual long advertisement for the Soviet system. Eisenhower, Nehru, Mollet, Eden, and Chou En-lai were once more acquainted with all the facts about "the unprovoked aggression against Egypt" and warned that the British and French were not through with their tricks.[15] *En passant* the note referred indignantly to unworthy rumors in connection with "the failure of the counterrevolutionary military plot against People's Hungary, which as has now become absolutely clear

15 The full text of the memorandum in *Ibid.*, pp. 605–12.

was an integral part of the general plot of the imperialists against peace and security" of peoples everywhere. Why are the imperialists indulging in such unworthy doings? International tension, explained Khrushchev the Marxist, is of benefit to the "monopolists of the United States, Britain, and France" since it enables them to rake up fabulous profits which they exact from the taxes paid by the "working people."

Apart from the solicitude for the working masses of the West, the note dwelt with sympathy on the problems created for NATO by the Anglo-French venture in the Near East. It was regrettable that the aggressors had to strip their forces in Europe to pursue their adventures elsewhere. How generous of the Soviet Union not to take advantage of this situation and, if you please, move into Western Europe: "It may be said outright that the strategic situation that has arisen in Western Europe at the present time is even more favourable for the armed forces of the Soviet Union than was the case at the end of the Second World War." (Then, had the Soviets so wished, they could have "been able to gain a firm foothold in the whole of Western Europe, if the Soviet Union had set itself such aims.")

The impudence of addressing this message to the man who had been Supreme Commander of Allied Forces is breathtaking. But it showed that the Soviets were paying close attention to Western misconceptions of recent history. Not even Stalin had claimed that the U.S.S.R. was in the position to occupy Western Europe in 1945; and one sees what a precious asset it had been for the Soviet Union that neither the U.S. government nor its public understood the true relationship of forces at the end of the war, and what an opportunity this misunderstanding provided for indulging in repeated bluffs, from the Berlin blockade to Suez.

There must be another digression. Khrushchev's epistolary style surpassed in brutality and invective anything found in the diplomatic notes of the Stalin era (the prize samples were to come in 1960 and 1961). It was a considerable psychological error for the American government, not to mention the British and French, to tolerate this style of diplomatic correspondence. It would have been out of character for Eisenhower or Dulles to match Soviet brazenness (say, by reminding the Kremlin that they should deem themselves fortunate that in 1945, with the Soviet Union devastated by the war and the Americans having the atom bomb, they had not been called upon to pull back to the Dnieper!), but there were sound reasons for refusing to accept the November 17 note and informing the Russians that the interesting tidbits of information contained in it were perhaps suitable for a political speech but inadmissable in a communication addressed to the President of the United States. Instead, Eisenhower answered on December 31, 1956, that he was in "basic disagreement with the analysis of your government as it relates to the sources of international tension." One cannot in this day and age expect the punctilio of nineteenth-century diplomacy, but it is a bad mistake, and was to prove also a costly one, to accept such unequal terms of diplomatic dialogue.

The last point leads to the most momentous result of the Suez crisis of 1956: that it brought the realization, first to the governments, then to public opinion, that they could no longer act in the manner of great powers, not so much because of the realities of the nuclear age or the Soviet challenge, but because of the American insistence that it was the only *Western* power entitled so to act.

The Suez crisis and its antecedents were to play, in relation to international politics of the late fifties and the sixties, a role somewhat similar to that which the evolution of the Polish problem between 1943 and 1945 had in determining the course of world politics after World War II. Neither Poland nor Suez were in themselves issues of transcendent importance. Yet the manner in which each was handled by the United States was to have most fateful consequences. The case of Poland demonstrated to Stalin that America was unsure about her policies and ignorant of the vast material and moral assets of which she disposed vis-à-vis the Soviet Union. Suez was the most convincing demonstration yet of the vulnerability of the Western alliance, indeed of the whole Western world, whenever any area outside of Europe was concerned. One word, "imperialism," was sufficient to throw the whole course of American foreign policy into disarray, would make Washington forsake and chastise her closest allies. And anti-Americanism, resentment against this strange people always critical and meddling in the affairs of their friends, ineffective against enemies despite their vast power, would often unite disparate forces.

Though this was not to become apparent for some years, the Suez crisis dealt a crippling blow to NATO. The alliance remained in effect, the joint command structure persisted, periodic meetings of allied political leaders continued to take place. But much of the underlying spirit of cooperation, of the Europeans' readiness to shoulder a proportionate part of the burden, was bound to evaporate. The "Geneva spirit" had already made the Soviet threat appear much less imminent; in view of Russia's advances in nuclear and missile technology, Soviet power was bound to be fearsome, and whatever Britain, France, and West Germany might do, it was obvious that U.S. nuclear power ultimately provided the only credible defense against it. At the same time, it had been demonstrated that the United States opposed the use of British or French power against Nasser, the Algerian rebels, etc. What logic could impel French, British, and West German citizens, not to speak of Italians, Belgians, etc., to sanction large defense expenditures and sizable armed forces which could be employed only in the case of an unimaginable holocaust? This very natural skepticism was bound to undermine the *political* significance of NATO, make it an adjunct, and not a very significant one at that, of American power.

The U.N.'s role in the Suez crisis marked its evolution into a tribunal sitting in perpetual judgment on sins past and present, real and fictitious, of the West European states. Nothing could be more eloquent than the contrast of the dispatch and effectiveness of the U.N. action in countering Anglo-French moves in the Near East with its hesitations and complete lack of success in curbing Soviet action in Hungary. When interests of the Third World and of the United States coincided, the U.N. could perform useful peace-keeping functions, and occasionally it would facilitate the task of defusing a dangerous situation. But ordinarily, the international organization would be most effective and censorious vis-à-vis the West European powers, this activity putting in more striking relief its impotence and reluctance even to discuss transgressions of the Communist powers or of countries of the Third World.

The vulnerabilities of the Western alliance bared by the Suez crisis were predominantly psychological. By the same token, the Communist camp in 1956 demonstrated grave organic weaknesses. For the time being they were mastered, but the problems and dangers were to remain.

The Soviets had meant to be more lenient in dealing with their East European satellites. Ideology and community of interests, and not mere repression and the Red Army, were to be the unifying bonds. But first in Poland and then in Hungary, the premises of this new policy were challenged and then exposed as unrealistic. Relief and rejoicing at the end of the worst abuses were followed not by gratitude to the fraternal Russian people for allowing their subjects a degree of internal autonomy, but by demands for an accounting of the sufferings of the very recent past. Soviet leaders in turn were deeply divided as to how far it was safe to let the situation evolve, whether or not to call off the whole experiment.

Though the most dramatic moment was to come with the repression of Hungary, the crucial and the most dangerous point for Soviet domination of Eastern Europe came with the split within the Polish Communist party in 1956. Had this rebellion *not* been localized and then contained within the Communist party, had it spread to the nation at large and led to Soviet armed intervention, it is safe to say that the drama and danger of Hungary would have been exceeded by far. As it was, the peaceful resolution of the Polish crisis was to have an important stabilizing influence on the population of the satellite countries: it nourished hopes that there could be a reasonable compromise between nationalism and Communism, between independence and association within the socialist bloc. Time was to stamp such hopes as illusory, but by then the moment of the greatest danger to the Soviet empire had passed.

Another and perhaps fundamental piece of luck from the Soviet point of view was that the Polish party contained a man who was a faithful Communist while at the same time enjoying the stature of a national hero. Because of his past sufferings at the hands of the satraps, because of the official propaganda which had painted him, not quite deservedly, as a "Titoist," Gomulka had become the symbol of defiant anti-Russian nationalism and of the Polish road to socialism. And with the elevation of this honest but narrow-minded and doctrinaire man to the leadership, most of the revolutionary potential in the atmosphere was dissipated.

Even so, Soviet acquiescence in the selection of the man who in years to come was to be one of the most valuable bulwarks of the Russian position in Eastern Europe did not come easily. Gomulka, a victim of that pathological witch-hunt for Titoists which had swept the satellites between 1949 and Stalin's death, did not enjoy a good reputation in the Kremlin. Since by good luck he happened to be alive in 1953, it was felt quite proper, in accordance with the current liberal fashions, that the Polish Communists should rehabilitate this victim of past errors and even provide him with a respectable and unimportant job. In October, however, when the Central Committee of the Polish United Workers Party proposed to elevate Gomulka to the position of First Secretary, and not, say, to the directorship of the National Library, and to bring into the Politburo some other victims of past persecutions, the Soviets were propelled to the brink of armed intervention. Khrushchev, Mikoyan, Molotov, and Kaganovich flew to Warsaw for one last try at a peaceful resolution of the dispute. There, after some tempestuous sessions with the Polish comrades, the Soviet leaders finally reached the decision which they were to bless repeatedly in the years to come: Gomulka could stay. As icing on the cake, the most pro-Russian of the Polish Communist notables were thrown to the wolves, or, in more prosaic language, demoted to inferior party positions, while the very symbol of Soviet domination, Marshal Rokossovsky, of whom Stalin had so generously made a gift to the Polish nation to command its armed forces, was courteously but firmly invited to rejoin the Red Army.

What had threatened in Poland came to pass in Hungary. Pent-up wrath and hopes broke through the confines of intraparty discussions and into the streets. There was no Hungarian Gomulka. Imre Nagy, whose public image was closest to that of the Polish leader insofar as he enjoyed a reputation for honesty and moderation, was not sufficiently strong and decisive; most important of all, under the impact of popular wrath, the Hungarian party virtually disintegrated. Its long-time and long-hated leaders Rakosi and Gero were forced to escape to the U.S.S.R. What took place then was a genuine popular revolt. Revolutionary committees and workers' councils mushroomed throughout the country. Secret-police headquarters were stormed, the most hated of petty oppressors of the past (the major ones, as is usual in such situations, had fled in good time) were lynched. Nagy, who had been called to head the government to stem the revolution, became its instrument: he was compelled to include in his government some prominent non-Communists. At first he called for Soviet military help to put down the excesses, but then he was constrained to request the withdrawal of Soviet troops. At the end of October, Nagy, whose entire past had been one of unblemished party loyalty,[16] now declared that Hungary would cease to be a one-party state and that she would leave the Warsaw Pact.

As they were to do again in 1968 in the case of Czechoslovakia, the Soviets continued issuing soothing and reassuring declarations until they were ready to strike a swift and decisive blow. Two days before troops began pouring into Hungary again, an official Soviet declaration

---

[16] The liberal reforms of his first and brief premiership in 1953 were in line with Soviet post-Stalin policies.

reaffirmed the policy of noninterference in the internal affairs of fellow-Communist states.

Then, on November 4, the Soviets' massive military force was brought into play, and the small and lightly armed Hungarian forces were unable to offer effective resistance. Nagy's government collapsed; he, with some leading figures of his regime, sought asylum in the Yugoslav embassy and then was lured out and kidnaped by the invaders. Janos Kadar, recently installed as First Secretary of the Hungarian party, became the Soviets' tool, and he now agreed, or was forced, to form a puppet government.[17] Though strikes and sporadic resistance continued throughout the winter, the main thrust of the Hungarian revolt was crushed in a few days.

From the beginning of the disturbances, the United States made it clear that it would support the cause of the Hungarian people *solely* through action in the United Nations and through appeals to world public opinion. At one level this was both humane and realistic: one ought not to arouse false hopes which could only lead more Hungarians to sacrifice their lives or freedom vainly. At yet another level, it was both impolitic and shameful. Against the background of the Soviet Union's resounding threats over Suez, the United States confessed *in advance* that it would not and could not do anything about this forcible intervention to repossess a part of the Communist empire. It was not open for the United States to use the kind of threats of which Khrushchev and Bulganin had availed themselves, yet at least more vigorous diplomatic action was in order: recall of the ambassador to Moscow, absolute refusal to acknowledge the Kadar government, proposals for its expulsion from the U.N. Most of all, the United States government need not have acquiesced passively in, not to say lent its hand to, the one-sided character of international morality as interpreted by the United Nations. It could have simply declared that it would not continue to censor actions of its friends and allies while transgressions by the other side remained unchecked after a resolution or two was hastily passed by the world organization. Such an attitude might not have altered the tragedy of Hungary, but it would have affected the future policies of countries like India and Indonesia who, while full of pious indignation about the Anglo-French enterprise against Egypt, abstained from or voted against the resolution demanding that the Soviet Union withdraw from Hungary.

17 Kadar himself had been imprisoned and allegedly tortured before Stalin's death.

The Polish and Hungarian events marked a definite defeat of the policy with which Khrushchev had been identified. Molotov, Kaganovich, et al., were not the people to deny themselves the satisfaction of saying "I told you so." Khrushchev had been a mere upstart when they already were principal counsellors of the leader whose reputation he had besmirched, thus precipitating all the recent unpleasantness and danger. And was it wise to court Tito so strenuously, thus putting ideas in the heads of the Poles, Hungarians, etc.? Suppose, just suppose, that the Americans had taken a leaf from Khrushchev's book and that upon entering Hungary the Soviets had found themselves recipients of a letter from Eisenhower reminding them that the United States had the Strategic Air Command and a stockpile of nuclear weapons, that just as the Soviet Union was gallantly ready to risk war to help the Egyptian people, the Americans could do no less for the Hungarians. What then? Fortunately, the worst had not come to pass, but could one go on with so irresponsible a leader? It was thought unwise, with the emergency not quite over, to advertise internal dissensions and splits. The First Secretary's authority would simply be curtailed, leaving his actual dismissal for quieter times. At the December, 1956, Plenum of the Central Committe, Khrushchev did not deliver the main speech, a sign to those in the know that his job was in jeopardy. The First Secretary was, however, a fighter. It was unwise to give him so much warning about his impending fate and to expect him to await the impending demotion philosophically in the manner of Malenkov in 1954–55. [18] In February, 1957, Khrushchev was ready with another improvisation. This one played a crucial part in saving his political life and in assuring color and interest in Soviet and international politics during the next seven years, but how many tense and nerve-wracking moments! His plan was for a thoroughgoing reorganization of economic administration through a system of regional economic councils, which in turn would bestow enhanced authority on local party secretaries at the expense of the central economic ministries. Party secretaries constituted the dominant element in the Central Committee, and most of them could be expected to appreciate this increase in their power and prestige as well as the man who was instrumental in securing it for them. In May, the proposals were put into effect; the anti-Khrushchev majority in the Presidium was outmaneuvered.

They decided to hurry up. Upon returning from a state visit, Khru-

18 His enemies would not make the same mistake in 1964.

shchev and Bulganin were, on June 19, invited to a meeting at which the First Secretary was informed that he had been dismissed. The anti-Khrushchev majority included Stalin's old guard—Molotov, Voroshilov, Malenkov, and Kaganovich—but also the younger economic administrators—Pervukhin and Saburov—as well as (this must have been a particular surprise, not that one learns to put special trust in personal loyalty and gratitude in Soviet politics) his inseparable traveling companion Premier Bulganin.

But in a flagrant violation of all the traditional rules and proprieties, Khrushchev refused to be sacked. He had been selected by the whole Central Committee; let the same body decide his fate. A group of Central Committee members tried to break in upon the deliberations of their elders but were barred by Bulganin's bodyguards. The venerable Voroshilov was delegated to appease them. In the meantime, Marshal Zhukov dispatched army planes to bring pro-Khrushchev party notables to Moscow. A full session of the Central Committee reversed the verdict of the Presidium. Molotov, Malenkov, and Kaganovich were ejected: with them into disgrace and obscurity went an alternate member of the highest body, Dmitri Shepilov. A protégé of Khrushchev, who had advanced him first to the post of foreign minister and then party secretary, he evidently became, with the help of his personal dossier which recorded various misdeeds and indiscretions of party notables, a key figure in the plot against his benefactor. Other participants in the plot were identified and fired in the course of the next three years: it was held unwise to advertise how widespread the intrigue had been and considered judicious to present Stalin's former minions as the main villains.

Collective leadership then seemingly gave way to the undisputed primacy of Khrushchev. Within a few months, he got rid of Zhukov, who, rewarded by a full membership in the Presidium for helping in the June crisis, was dismissed from that post and from the Ministry of Armed Forces in October. For a while, Khrushchev would still travel with Bulganin, but in 1958 his fickle companion was dismissed and Nikita Sergeievich added the chairmanship of the Council of Ministers to his other duties and inaugurated a modest "cult of personality" of his own.

From today's perspective, Khrushchev's maneuvers seem a throwback to the type of politics which existed in the Soviet Union between Lenin's death and the consolidation of power by Stalin in the 1920s. Unlike his successors, Khrushchev appealed to the people at large, for this was the sense of his denunciation of Stalinism in 1956, and of even more far-reaching revelations about and attacks on the evils of the past in the early sixties. But in the main he was constrained to work through the system: he won in 1957 by appealing from a narrow elite—the Presidium—to a larger one—the Central Committee. And when, damaged by the failures of his most ambitious foreign and domestic schemes, he tried to emancipate himself from the latter group he was overthrown.

It was Mao who emerged as the main beneficiary of the troubles and turmoil within the Soviet leadership. The Chinese had cashed in on Soviet disarray in the wake of Stalin's death. Moscow needed friends, or more precisely it could ill afford any revelation of additional troubles within the Communist world. The year 1957 was clearly China's year.

At the height of their troubles and hopes in 1956, the East Europeans expected that the Chinese would show at least an understanding of their need to loosen the Soviet yoke. This was based on more than wishful thinking, as had been the case with similar expectations by the Yugoslavs in 1949–50. We have some evidence that a Polish Communist leader visiting Peking that summer received discreet encouragement to stand up to the Russians. But in the wake of Budapest, the Chinese hastened to demonstrate their support of the Soviets. In January, 1957, Chou En-lai visited Moscow, Warsaw, and Budapest. Everywhere he praised the firm and timely steps taken by the U.S.S.R. to save Communism from an imperialist plot. Some Russians must have ruefully reflected that this was the first intervention by East Asians in the affairs of Europe since the Middle Ages, when the Mongols suddenly descended upon the very same countries whose capitals the suave Chinese foreign minister was now visiting. It could not have been a pleasant thought. . . .

In the fall, the modern equivalent of the Great Khan deigned to grace Moscow with a visit for the fortieth anniversary of the Great October Revolution. This time Mao was greeted with full honors. He lent his authority and signature to a document, subscribed also by the representatives of other parties in Moscow for the occasion, which condemned revisionism. This term was used to lump together such undesirable phenomena as opposition to the Russians, indulgence in unduly liberal measures, failure to display proper vigilance about baneful influences from the West, etc. (The Yugoslavs refused to sign it, thus revealing themselves as . . . revisionists.) Others did sign, but because of spirited objections by some parties, notably the Poles, the declaration was not so categorical as the Chinese would have wished. It acknowledged that "dogmatism and left-wing sectarianism" (i.e., Stalinist practices) were also harmful. No new international organization was set up to replace the defunct Cominform. The declaration stressed the leading role of the Soviet Union. But the obvious reason behind Chinese insistence on this assertion of Soviet primacy was to place upon the Soviet Union the onerous charge of protecting other Communist states and of assuming the risks and burdens of advancing the cause throughout the world. Apparently this formulation aroused some qualms within the Soviet leadership. This untypical modesty was related to Khrushchev's intention to expand the *détente* with the United States, something of which the Chinese were not unmindful.

It was on this occasion, as the Russians were to tell us in 1963, when the correspondence between the two central committees was published, that Mao shocked them and their foreign comrades by professing considerable nonchalance about prospects of a major nuclear war. China was a vast and populous country and she would survive, he intimated. It was unfortunate that a *small* Communist country like Czechoslovakia might be obliterated, but Communism would still go on, and that was the important thing! Mao's attitude shook the Russians; it was one thing to profess such confidence vis-à-vis the capitalists, but another to frighten fellow Communists. Could the Chinese really mean it?

But Mao required payment for his moral and political help not only in formulas but in fresh technological and economic help. A special agreement promised very extensive Soviet assistance for China's development of nuclear technology. (According to a later Chinese version, which Moscow never denied, it included a Soviet promise to furnish Peking with a sample atom bomb.) The Peking regime was in an understandable hurry to capitalize on their current assets: with things stabilized in the U.S.S.R. and in Eastern Europe, Khrushchev might soon be up to some new tricks.

The outside world remained mostly unaware of the maneuvers and calculations which took place while the main stage was occupied by festivities and resounded to ringing declarations. It was little realized by foreign diplomats that the Kremlin's ambitious plans were being thwarted or made to suffer delays. Without such special knowledge it was reasonable to assume that the Soviet Union had triumphantly overcome all its main difficulties, internal and external.

9

The Third World

Stalin and Budapest were now replaced on the front pages by the Sputnik. This artificial satellite circling the earth and carrying the emblem of the U.S.S.R. offered a preview of the great space feats to come, but to paraphrase a future American astronaut, even if it was but a small step forward in space technology, it was a giant step forward for Soviet propaganda and a major blow to American prestige and self-confidence. It hit where it hurt most. Where was the renowned American "know-how," that assumption of America's God-given technological superiority bred into every child in the United States and taken for granted for so long by most foreigners? Was the Soviet economy perhaps also catching up with America's?

More concretely and ominously, the Sputnik testified as to Soviet advances in missile technology. Even after the Soviets exploded their atom and hydrogen bombs, American leaders and public opinion had remained if not complacent then confident of over-all American superiority in nuclear armament. Now this confidence was shattered. Some were quick to proclaim that Russia had forged ahead. If the Soviets had been hard to live with before their spectacular achievement, what would they do now? Of what use now were NATO and the whole rambling structure of the Western alliance?

For the next ten years or so, the Soviets were relentlessly to exploit one space effort after another and in the process torture those vain and presumptuous Yankees. In Washington there were at first some half-hearted attempts to pooh-pooh the whole business: interesting from the engineering point of view, but hardly significant scientifically or militarily. But to a people whose imagination and dollars are captured by mechanical gadgetry, this was cold comfort. There was also an attempt, haughtily ignored by the Soviet press, to ascribe the feat to German scientists captured by the Russians, to whom they had conveyed German—i.e., "Western"—technological secrets. But then one ran up against the uncomfortable fact that some German scientists who had been working on missiles for Hitler were now employed in the Pentagon. Eisenhower went on television to reassure the anxious nation. Some years and many billions of dollars later, the Americans scored in their turn: they landed on the moon. The Russians were politely appreciative but hardly carried away: interesting from the engineering point of view, but hardly significant scientifically or militarily. And after the initial elation, the Americans, true to form, had twinges of doubt and guilt: Was it right to spend so much money on space spectaculars when there were such pressing domestic needs?

At one time it was assumed that the Americans, because of the vast superiority of their technology, could *both* stop Communist expansion and retain their free, open, and increasingly prosperous society. By the time the Soviets narrowed the gap, Western Europe would be restored, united, and capable of relieving the United States of much of its oppressive overseas burden. Yet America's advantages vis-à-vis Russia seemed by now to have disappeared. Europe had recovered, to be sure, and beyond the rosiest expectations of 1945 or even 1947, but it was very far from being united. As for sharing America's burdens in policing the world, to use the by now anachronistic-sounding phrase of Roosevelt's, Britain and France were currently proceeding in exactly the opposite direction.

In the case of Britain this was to be a conscious and hurried policy. Harold Macmillan, who succeeded the ill and broken Eden as Prime Minister in January, 1957, drew a straightforward moral from the Suez venture. Britain could not afford, politically or economically, extensive responsibilities outside of Europe. Before Suez, Britain's colonial retreat had been measured and gradual; now it became a veritable scramble to get out of any territory and situation where trouble might arise if she stayed. Before the Conservative government left office in 1964, practically every colony, no matter how small, had been either endowed with or was set on an irreversible path toward independence. The emancipated countries remained within the Commonwealth, but this fact no longer had any practical, and soon no symbolical, significance. What indeed could be the meaning of an organization which contained two states in an acute conflict with each other and on the verge of open warfare (India and Pakistan), a dictatorship seeking links with the Communist world (Ghana), and a state in which there was virtually perpetual civil war between its two national communities (Cyprus)? Nor did the Commonwealth provide Britain with political and psychological compensation for the loss of the empire. It was already becoming a source of embarrassments and troubles, a kind of purgatory in which the former masters were expected to atone consistently for their past sins. More important, it prevented her from becoming a European state. She had been deprived of power without being allowed to shed completely her overseas responsibilities. Grown-up children in this Freudian age are encouraged to blame their troubles on the past sufferings they endured at the hands of their parents. Something of the same phenomenon could be observed in the psychology of relations between emancipated colonies and former colonial powers.

French colonialism had not encompassed the idea of eventual, even if distant, self-government of the dependent peoples. This more cynical attitude meant that there was more resistance to the abandonment of the imperial role, but by the same token, there was less disillusionment and sense of failure in the wake of the discovery that an independent Chad or Malawi did not follow constitutional and democratic paths. But in the period under discussion, the tragedy of Algeria overshadowed problems of the rest of the French colonial empire.

Here was the rub: from the legal point of view—therefore even for those who believed in its eventual independence—Algeria was not a colony but a part of France. Thus even the humiliation of the French defeat in and loss of Indochina paled in comparison with the shock of the Algerian rebellion of 1954. Seemingly the issue of Algeria was resolved in 1962, when that country became independent, but repercussions of the long ordeal weighed heavily on French politics and foreign policies for many years to come. And it is especially in connection with French policy toward the United States that the Algerian war left a definite and unfortunate imprint.

The Algerian rebellion was obviously the work of a handful of conspirators sheltered and supported from abroad and directing a numerically not very imposing guerrilla and terrorist movement within the country. Yet it was equally incontestable that the great mass of Moslem inhabitants were living under conditions of abject poverty and had been subject to all kinds of discrimination within their own country. Could any present and future reform retrieve France's sins of the past and justify Algeria's future association with France? Militarily the rebellion might never prevail. Even the guerrilla operations could not be indefinitely sustained without help and sanctuary rendered by the neighboring Arab countries. The main weapon at the disposal of the rebels was indiscriminate terrorism which, exercised against the Moslems, intimidated them and inhibited any cooperation with the French authorities, and used against the French settlers drove them, as was intended, into excesses against innocent Arabs, thus widening the breach between the two communities and rendering their reconciliation even more improbable. A democratic country in the twentieth century could not be expected to cope with such revolutionary tactics, even if employed by a small minority. Revolutionary terror can never be an effective challenge to a totalitarian regime; the latter answers it with mass terror that leaves the population terrified and unwilling to render even passive support to the rebels. But sporadic terror as practiced by the French in Algeria could only be demoralizing to themselves and self-defeating. In theory, then, the only way for a democracy to cope with such a situation was with firmness and restraint: a resolve not to yield while abjuring those means of repression inconsistent with humanity. This in turn would imply the ability of a democratic electorate to tolerate a long and costly conflict. The whole story of Algeria offers an eloquent commentary on how unreasonable it is to expect such restraint, readiness for sacrifice, and, hardest of all, patience from a democratic community.

Apart from any scoreboard of rights and wrongs, the case of Algeria struck at the major premises and strategies developed by U.S. policymakers between 1947 (the Marshall Plan) and 1955 (accession by West Germany to NATO). It was not a case of Communist aggression pouring over a border (Korea), nor was it a case of internal Communist subversion fed by outside support. Yet it did not take an official French propagandist to argue that the loss of Algeria would harm not only France but the West as a whole. Not for nothing did Khrushchev make support for wars of national liberation one of the cardinal points of his foreign policy. The Algerian war evidenced many features which would reappear in the tragic story of Vietnam in the next decade, and which could already be observed in the case of a handful of Cuban revolutionaries and guerrillas holed up in the mountainous part of the island and slated in 1959 to achieve a brilliant success. In fact, the Western predicament was somewhat parallel to the discomfiture of the British defenders of Singapore during World War II. Then the guns of the fortress were pointed in the wrong direction: the aggressor had been expected to come from the sea; instead, he attacked from behind, moving through the jungle. Now America's nuclear power stood on guard over Europe and over Japan, yet it was incapable of keeping the West from being outflanked not only in the geographic but in a psychological sense.

For the Soviet Union, the wars of national liberation [1] presented an opportunity to weaken the opposition and to expand Russian influence without the risks and inconveniences involved in outright Communist expansion. An attempt to seize West Berlin would carry with it the risk of a world war. Even when it came to such a backwater of world politics as South Korea, the Communist move there had posed incalculable consequences. Yet here was the war in Algeria tying down most of the French military effectives, undermining French political and social stability, causing dissonance within the Western alliance—and it was costing the Soviet Union nothing apart from some anticolonial rhetoric in the United Nations and a few shipments of arms. Most of all, the Soviet Union could not lose no matter what the outcome. In the unlikely eventuality of the rebellion being suppressed, this could in no sense be considered a blow to Soviet prestige. And in the event of their victory, the Algerian rebels were unlikely to draw close to the United States.

Indeed, by purely rational calculations Moscow had to prefer a non-Communist Algeria, whether in the torment of rebellion or independent and ruled by nationalist revolutionaries, to a Communist one. Communist regimes were increasing liabilities rather than sources of solid benefit to the Fatherland of Socialism. For one thing, the former pattern of outright economic exploitation of other Communist states was giving way to the Soviets' expanding, as yet modestly and reluctantly, their economic foreign aid. Here again, independent Algeria was to be supported by French, and for a while considerable American, aid rather than becoming a major charge upon the Soviet taxpayer. In brief, the relationship of the Soviet Union with the Algerian rebels

---

[1] The Soviets arrogated to themselves the right to proclaim, to license so to speak, what was and was not a war of national liberation. A tribal revolt, a street riot would, if it fitted the purposes of Soviet policy, be elevated into such a war; a major and genuine popular revolt if it did not meet that criterion would be relegated to the category of "imperialist plot." Few in the West had the energy and persistence to match every Soviet accusation with a countercharge, the boldness to stop apologizing for their imperialist past and to dwell on the Soviet Union's current imperialist practices, the alertness to point out that if the term "national liberation" had any meaning at all, it should be applied to the struggle of the Hungarian people in 1956.

before and after independence seemed to offer all the advantages of concubinage and none of the confining and dangerous burdens of a lawful marriage. No wonder that this would become the pattern the Soviets would seek in their future diplomatic ventures in Africa and Latin America.

In view of these Soviet considerations, then, and from a purely rational point of view, there are ample reasons for the Americans being irritated with the French irritation with *them*. It was yet another case of the tendency to blame the United States for so many major and minor troubles of the world. The United States had not invented Algerian nationalism, did not train the rebels, gave no ultimatums.

It was not, likewise, within the power of the U.S. government to curb those American public figures, journalists, or professors who expressed sympathy and support for the Algerian people. Neither Eisenhower nor Dulles had authorized a speech on July 2, 1957, by a U.S. senator in which he denounced the French policy of repression and called on the United Nations and the United States to take a hand in facilitating a solution which would satisfy the just aspirations of a people fighting for its freedom. (Western governments were insensitive to those urgent aspirations of oppressed nations which sought merely what the Americans themselves had claimed in 1776. The State Department, out of an excessive concern for outworn rules and amenities, was forfeiting that fund of good will which America had accumulated throughout the Third World because she had stood against colonialism.) John F. Kennedy was expressing a widespread and sincere opinion. He was also displaying that well-informed interest in foreign affairs which was to be expected in a man with Presidential ambitions. It was not so many years later that *President* Kennedy had to cope with de Gaulle's offended feelings, while immediately upon Algeria's independence its new regime professed brotherly feelings toward Castro's Cuba and announced that much as it was amenable to accepting American help, it would seek intimate links with the Soviet Union and Communist China.

Seemingly the tragic Algerian dilemma was resolved in 1962. General de Gaulle's courageous decision was based on considerations adduced above: a democracy could not afford to tolerate indefinitely the festering sore of a colonial war. Algeria became "independent" and "free." One might object, and not merely out of pedantry, that neither of those terms was precise. French financial aid kept the new republic from economic collapse, and, while foreign domination ended, the new regime quickly turned into a dictatorship, political repression striking harshly and widely, not the least at those who had led and fought in the struggle for independence.

The story, then, does not have the happy ending required by the American mythology of decolonization. The Algerian people have not lived happily and democratically ever after, with their rulers eschewing expansionist plans of their own and turning their energies to promoting economic development and social welfare. Nor has the Algerian problem been "solved" in relation to French and world politics.

As for its influence on U.S. policies of containment, the premises of those policies were now exposed as inadequate. Anarchy was increasing in international relations; the West's weakness in coping with it was not military or economic in its nature but mainly psychological. This anarchy in turn was abetted and exploited by the Soviet Union (Communist China played as yet a minor role in this respect), but its sources could in no wise be traced to Soviet policies.

Colonial emancipation had been a necessary item on the agenda of the West following World War II. It was as absurdly unrealistic and nostalgic to cling to the shreds of the imperial past, de Gaulle endeavored to tell his countrymen in one of his most incisive statements on the subject, as to reject electricity and the automobile out of longing for the charm of oil lamps and horse carriages. The moralistic thrust of the American political mind, however, imparted to this urgent and inevitable task of decolonialization an element of religious obsession. Every demand of local nationalism vis-à-vis the colonial power, no matter how unrepresentative of the population at large, was held as a priori justified; every plea for delay, for time to impart the skills necessary for self-government, held a priori as an evasion and deception. This attitude in many cases vitiated the meaning and purpose of granting self-government. Political or social reforms can seldom be productive of good unless they are a rational response to changed conditions and needs. A guilt-stricken and remorseful posture before the Third World could not enhance the prestige of such Western institutions as civil liberties, parliamentarianism, etc. To reduce a process as long and involved as Western expansion to the dimensions of a morality play, to judge actions and motivations of the past according to political criteria which acquired wide currency only in this century, meant not only a distortion of history but a crippling of the power and attraction of those very ideas of democracy and liberalism in the name of which freedom of the colonies was being vindicated. It is a debilitating ailment for a society just as for an individual to engage in an overlong inquest and excessive apology for its past. For the West as a whole, the prevalent American attitude on colonialism became both a symptom and a cause of that deepening crisis of self-confidence, and the growth of doubt and guilt about its traditional values which has been such a prominent feature of today's scene.

While the West's self-confidence was being eroded, that of the Communist bloc was restored, in view of what was to the Kremlin's way of thinking a successful resolution of the East European crisis through a combination of timely concessions (Poland) and exemplary severity (Hungary). The American self-image was shaken severely by the excessive importance attributed to Soviet technological and economic advances. In China, the ruling group took realistic stock of the likelihood of continued and considerable aid from the Russians and embarked on an accelerated economic and technological development. Such were the underlying realities of international politics.

In trying to cope with them, American policy failed once again to make allowance for changed and changing conditions, for new opportunities and dangers. Some of the main lines of America's approach to world problems, set between 1947 and 1955—such as the idea of the monolithic unity of the Communist bloc, the efficacy of economic aid to counter appeals of Communism—obviously called for re-examination. It was finally recognized that a country like China could not be a mere satellite of the Soviet Union, but what exactly was the nature of the Sino-Soviet relations and what could the United States do about them? Since 1955, there had been only a mere whisper of a diplomatic dialogue between the United States and China: the intermittent conversations held between the American and Chinese representatives in Warsaw, the only tangible result of which was the release of some imprisoned Americans in China, in return for which those Chinese who so desired were allowed to leave America.[2]

It was recognized more clearly—how could one miss it?—that in Eastern Europe nationalism clashed with Communism. But again, what could the United States do about it? Could Eisenhower invite himself in Khrushchev's manner to East European capitals? Should the United States expand its trade with or offer credits to a country like Poland, which was still exhibiting a certain independence from Russia in the style if not in the substance of its foreign policy? This might be called

---

[2] These included some scientists and engineers who were instrumental in China's later nuclear development program.

aiding a Communist power, albeit a somewhat independent one. Tito's renewed flirtation with the Soviets after he had received so much help from the West was not encouraging, even though the Russians and Yugoslavs had now fallen out again and in 1958 exchanged unpleasant charges reminiscent of their mutual abuse of the old days.

The administration attempted to use old formulas to deal with new problems. In January, 1957, the Eisenhower Doctrine was proclaimed with much fanfare. This was an administration-sponsored Congressional resolution authorizing the United States to render military and economic aid to those countries in the Middle East which required and requested it. This aid was "to protect the territorial integrity and political independence of such nations requesting such aid, against overt armed aggression from any nation controlled by International Communism."[3] This was a clear extension of the principle of containment inherent in the Truman Doctrine of 1947. However, in 1947, "International Communism" was not merely a figure of speech but described fairly realistically the danger faced by the two countries covered by the Truman Doctrine: Turkey was being directly threatened by the U.S.S.R. over some territories; Greece by a Communist uprising indisputably helped and made possible by neighboring Communist countries, equally indisputably encouraged in doing so by Moscow. But in 1957, what dangers there were in the Arab countries came from other sources, primarily from their internal social and political instability. That instability in turn was being exploited by "Nasserism," as that version of Pan-Arabism, or more properly speaking Egyptian imperialism, was being called, or by other forms of revolutionary movements. "The hand of Moscow" could hardly be seen in those revolutionary strivings. Russia was standing by, ready with propaganda support, perhaps with a discreet shipment of arms or two, but she could hardly be blamed for *creating* the Near Eastern mess. She was merely exploiting it.

Western, i.e., primarily British, influence had once kept the precarious balance of power and equally precarious peace in the Middle East. The Suez affair had dealt a fatal blow to that influence. The United States, short of introducing a massive military presence, could not fill the power vacuum. The United States was viewed by even the most conservative Arabs as Israel's protector, and hence dependence on the United States served to compromise moderate Arab regimes in the eyes of the volatile nationalist and radical elements found among the Arab intelligentsia and young army officers. The Eisenhower Doctrine was designed to "warn

[3] *Documents on International Affairs, 1957* (London, 1960), p. 238.

off" Russia, in the traditional Cold War parlance, from the Middle East. But Russia did not have to do anything but wait. Sooner or later there was bound to be another Arab revolution, a pro-Western regime would bite the dust, and *then* the Soviet Union could issue warnings against the Western imperialists and their intrigues against Arab independence.

Thus in 1957, a pro-Soviet tendency asserted itself in the Syrian government. The ponderous American diplomatic machinery sprang into action: an American diplomat was dispatched on a "fact-finding" mission to the Middle East, though the facts of the situation were obvious and painful even from a distance. Efforts to counteract Soviet influence in Damascus were ineffective. Turkey, America's only steadfast ally in the region, concentrated troops on the Syrian border. This was an excellent opportunity for Khrushchev to come out with his threats. The Soviet Army was allegedly mobilized on the Turkish border, and Moscow warned Turkey against being the cat's-paw of American monopolies against Syria. Did the Turks know that the Russians had missiles . . . bombs . . .? The crisis passed, but Soviet influence in Syria remained and grew stronger. Colonel Nasser's star, however, was not to be dimmed. In fact, it is a measure of how strange our world, and especially the Middle East, that every successive defeat and discomfiture of the ambitious Egyptian leader has seemed to increase his hold on his country and his standing in the turbulent Arab world.

In 1958 came the crucial first (and as it turned out, last) test of the Eisenhower Doctrine. One of those young officers' plots, plus an uprising by city mobs, overthrew the royal Iraqi government, the last major preserve of British influence in the area. The man who in or out of office had dominated Iraqi politics for decades, Nuri Es-Said Pasha—a link with another era, one of Lawrence of Arabia's companions—as well as members of the royal family met death from the mob, and a new regime under General Kassim was installed. This government at first promised to be so pro-Soviet that it aroused public objections from none other than Colonel Nasser. Stung by such ingratitude from a man to whose country the Soviets had just pledged vast economic help for the Aswan Dam, Khrushchev called his Egyptian protégé a "hot-headed young man." (The tempestuous colonel was now over forty, and Khrushchev was hardly the man to give lessons in restrained and decorous deportment.) They still approved of the Egyptians, said the Soviet leader, but the new Iraqi regime was more progressive. Soon, however, things fell into their place. Kassim, it turned out, was not more "progressive" than Nasser, only more irresponsible. In a few years he met the same grisly fate his followers had dealt out to his predecessors. Khrushchev and Nasser made up, and throughout his subsequent and usually misbegotten political ventures, Nasser received Soviet support.

There was considerable fear in Washington and London that the Baghdad horrors would be repeated in two of the rapidly diminishing group of pro-Western Arab states: Lebanon and Jordan. The Americans sent Marines to the tiny Mediterranean republic, the British airlifted troops to Jordan to save its king from the fate of his cousin in Iraq. There followed, as we shall see later, a typical choleric and blustering reaction from the Soviet Union, but soon the Western troops were withdrawn. Then things returned to normal, i.e., from an acute crisis they lapsed into a lingering and less acute one. But the application of the doctrine pointed out its relative futility; the barn was half locked after the most valuable horse (Iraq) was lost, and again not to "International Communism." Internal anarchy, abetted by the Arab-Israeli conflict, had created opportunities for Soviet influence to move into the vacuum created by the British withdrawal. Western influence could not be recouped through Congressional resolutions. Revolutionary upheavals throughout the area were bound to continue. Were the Marines and paratroopers to be rushed in on every occasion a king or a government was overthrown or threatened? This was hardly practical, and anyway, was it not the kind of evil imperialist practice the United States had condemned in the case of the British and the French? As against such perplexing dilemmas for Washington, Moscow's task was simple: if the Marines materialized, this was imperialism; if they did not, the Russians assumed credit for warding off neocolonialist tricks.

In the Middle East more than in any other area, there was a huge gap between what the American people expected their foreign policy to be and what it could humanly accomplish in view of the harsh realities of the actual situation. The United States, most Americans have believed, should favor the cause of the people vs. kings, camarillas, and oligarchies. It should support the right to independence of colonial areas vs. the imperial powers. It should not selfishly base its policies on considerations of economic self-interest; perish the ignoble thought that its policies should be attuned to the protection of American oil-holdings in the area. This extensive list of virtues would have required this country to be in the state of continuous conflict if not indeed of actual warfare with each and every state and regime in the area: with Britain and France over their remaining colonial possessions, with Egypt over its expansionist aims, with Israel over its occupation of territory which had been Arab for centuries, with Saudi Arabia over its feudal political structure; with every other state because in one way or another they failed to measure up to the democratic ideal. Common sense, indeed, kept the American passion for self-destructive virtue from going that far, but there was enough political force in that relentless moralism to frustrate the purpose of securing peace, stability, and progress in the region.

The Eisenhower Doctrine, then, was a desperate attempt to formulate American policies in the Middle East in the only terms which at the time could secure widespread popular support, i.e., anti-Communist rhetoric. But the threat of International Communism, if it existed at all, had largely resulted from previous American policies; the Soviet Union was not so much moving into the area as being sucked in.

Since World War II, the Americans have consistently confused rhetoric with policy and have failed to distinguish between those ultimate goals which a democratic society must profess and strive for and those practical adjustments and compromises (both with the ideal solution and with one's protagonists) which are the stuff of international politics. There has been a curious inability to recognize that most great problems are composed of a multitude of small ones. Much of the success of American and British domestic politics has been due to their pragmatic spirit. As against preachers, philosophers, and ideologues, practical men of affairs have recognized for a long time that it seldom pays to ask questions of vast cosmic dimensions, such as what are the rights of Labor vs. Capital in the eyes of God and history; that the settlement of any contention between the two must vary according to circumstances and be reached through bargaining, not according to some abstract table of rights and wrongs. But this pragmatism has been submerged when it comes to international politics.

In reading the enormous volume of American literature on international affairs, one is struck, on the contrary, by how much of it is devoted to the search for *one* master formula, a philosopher's stone, which when applied to American foreign policies would solve all the problems, set at rest all the perplexing doubts, indicate the one true and sure course to follow. A former chairman of the Atomic Energy Commission wrote in the introduction to a very influential book on American strategy, "Abhorrent of war but unwilling to accept gradual Russian enslavement of other peoples around the world, which we know will eventually lead to our own enslavement, we are forced to adopt a posture that, despite Russian military capabilities and despite their long-range intentions, freedom shall be preserved to us." The writer goes on to spell out this excruciating dilemma as he sees it. Virtual parity has been reached in nuclear capabilities of both sides (this in 1957!) and "so long as this condition is coupled with a fear that any strong action on the part of the United States anywhere in the world may ignite a full-scale nuclear war, we find ourselves more and more reluctant to frame a strong foreign policy or implement it so as to preserve the vital interests of the free world. We fear force as never before, and we even fear economic and political measures which might lead to the use of it." [4]

At the time these words were written, the United States was facing the problems of restoring the strength and morale of its European allies bruised by their misfortune in the Middle East, of formulating its own attitude to the evolution of colonial peoples. The U.S.S.R. was struggling to preserve its domination in Eastern Europe, and it could already be clearly seen that its relationship with China was certainly not one of enslavement of the latter; perhaps not so clearly seen that, granting the nature of Communism and the world, China was bound to become a number-one problem for the Soviet Union. The immediate and also fairly long-range concerns of the two superpowers could then in no sense be described as "preserving the freedom of all people," on the one hand, and "enslavement of other peoples around the world" on the other. One could not formulate a realistic picture of the world in 1957 if one began with such assumptions; one could not begin to see clearly the choices and dangers facing the United States and the Western world. Yet the panel members whose discussion formed the setting of Henry Kissinger's book consisted, in Mr. Dean's words, of "framers of our military and foreign policy, experts knowledgeable in the effects of modern weapons, persons in responsible positions in government, persons . . . who brought to us the benefit which comes from reflective thinking within the confines of our universities, persons who had been hardened by the realities of the business world." [5]

The belief that the question of nuclear weapons encompassed all the problems of preserving peace, all the problems of U.S.–U.S.S.R. relations, was both understandable and incorrect, understandable because one cannot disregard the numbing knowledge of what a nuclear conflict would be like. Democratic leaders cannot, like Khrushchev, let alone

[4] Gordon Dean, in the Foreword to Henry A. Kissinger, *Nuclear Weapons and Foreign Policy* (New York, 1957), pp. vii–viii.
[5] *Ibid.*, p. viii. One cannot help observing that today it is the academician who is more likely to be hardened by the realities of *his* world, while it is the businessman who is freer to pursue reflective thinking.

Mao, adopt a nonchalant attitude to the threat of atomic war; their public, regaled by fictionalized as well as factual depictions of what the hideous weapons could and would accomplish, cannot preserve the attitude of people in a totalitarian country where these unpleasant subjects are confined to technical journals.

Yet for all those understandable and very human reactions, the frightful problem ought not to have preoccupied makers of American foreign policy and the public to the point where it obscured other dangers and opportunities inherent in the world situation. Moreover, if one analyzes the form this preoccupation actually took in the public mind, if not in the memoranda of the Joint Chiefs of Staff or the Atomic Energy Commission, one runs into another curious phenomenon: there was little inclination to analyze soberly Soviet claims, to consider whether the Soviets *then* had really the means to wreak such destruction upon the United States, whether those men in the Kremlin were really as nonchalant about the dangers of an atomic war as they pretended.

Kissinger's book nevertheless tried to cut across the moralistic miasma surrounding the nuclear-weapons problem. Without the usual undertones of hysteria, the author attempted to analyze rationally the various options open to a democracy in the nuclear age. His conclusion was that, granted the development of a rational and appropriate doctrine of foreign policy by the United States, a future war between the two superpowers was not unavoidable; furthermore, that even if it were to come, it need not be all-destructive, that in fact a *limited* nuclear conflict was possible. Kissinger's notion of the possibility of a *limited nuclear* war preceded by a careful delimitation of its extent by the prospective enemies never really caught on. It would appear extravagant to expect such eighteenth-century amenities in this day. Anyway, the Russians were quick to scotch the idea that one could have a nuclear war which would not be an all-out affair. Moscow had little incentive to relieve the Americans of their most acute anxiety. In retrospect, it is easy to see this approach as an attempt to take the curse off Dulles' doctrine of massive retaliation. Indeed, the book coincided with the development and exploration of possible uses for tactical nuclear weapons, and with a reconsideration of the whole thesis that Western interests could be adequately protected by America's concentration on weapons of mass destruction.

Yet Kissinger's book of necessity neglected those problems of international life which, while separately dwarfed by the nuclear threat, constituted, when taken together, the most pressing dilemma of American policy in the coming decade. The United States could, through a proper position on nuclear weapons, discourage the U.S.S.R. from initiating a course of action leading to a holocaust. But as we have seen, much of the anarchy in international relations since 1945 came not through the actions or ambitions of the Soviet Union but, to put it most simply, through what the West did to itself. If the Soviets had both frankness and the kind of insight into their own actions which is seldom given even to the most cynical of politicians, they could have pleaded that it was not their fault that they were better at exploiting the difficulties created for itself by the Western world than the West was at exploiting theirs.

The last point brings into relief another great danger of an exclusive preoccupation with the nuclear problem. It was supremely important for the United States, as Kissinger argued, to develop a doctrine of foreign policy that would encompass the realities of a world in which weapons existed that could put an end to civilized existence, if not indeed human life. But not even the most astute doctrine of this kind could be a substitute for knowledge, i.e., for an understanding of the Soviet Union and its policies. Kissinger indeed argued that "we should be as ready to profit from opportunities in the Soviet orbit as the Soviet bloc feels free to exploit all the difficulties of the non-Soviet world." [6] But as we have seen from the foreword to his book, Soviet ambitions were assumed to be limitless, Soviet ability to cause mischief well nigh inexhaustible. Soviet vulnerabilities were seen mainly as being technologico-military—i.e., the U.S.S.R. was still behind the United States in some ranges of weapons, but if so, this was hardly a consolation, for the U.S.S.R. would soon catch up. The record of negotiations with the Russians ever since the war's end led even Kissinger to the edge of despair: "almost everything conspires against the subtle negotiation, the artful compromise, of classical diplomacy." [7] Yet for all the exasperating quality of Soviet diplomacy, one could hardly credit that of the United States with displaying the art of "subtle negotiation." In due time our clumsiness would be confused with wickedness.

Our criticism of American foreign policy in the late fifties must be balanced by the consideration that at no other time did the Soviets make it so difficult for an outsider to perceive or even guess what they were after. Indeed, Khrushchev's moves and public pronouncements could leave a foreign observer breathless, shivering with terror at the imminence of a nuclear conflict at one time, astounded by the extent of Rus-

6 *Ibid.,* p. 431.
7 *Ibid.,* p. 203.

sian amiability and willingness to resolve all contentious issues between the East and West at another. Governments for their part could not improve much on the casual observer, though there was among them, especially in Washington, more inclination to treat Soviet threats as humbug and Soviet advances as propaganda. But one could never tell; hence the resolve to batten down the hatches on the one hand, and on the other to go ahead with the dreary business of notes, counterproposals, and conferences, hoping that the worst would not come, uncertain that much good could be accomplished through another summit.

It is only now that we can perceive, though still only dimly, a design apparent through Khrushchev's madcap moves and pronouncements. But at the time only in one place was there anything like a realization that Russia's seemingly discordant moves in four corners of the world added up to a plan or, as it was very likely seen by the Chinese, a plot.

Chairman Khrushchev [8] looked toward the solution of what to the Soviets were the most perplexing dilemmas of international life. They centered, as they had to, on the problem of nuclear weapons. His occasional nonchalance notwithstanding, Khrushchev's policies were to be directed to the imperative need of minimizing chances for an atomic war between the two superpowers, and to preventing other countries from acquiring the fearsome weapon. This goal was more important than any other, including that of preserving Communist unity.

Here the reader might be forgiven a degree of skepticism. If Khrushchev sought a thoroughgoing accommodation with the West, if he wanted to banish the specter of an atomic war for a long, long time, he certainly chose a strange way to pursue these objectives. The world between 1958 and 1962 resounded to his bellicose declarations and threats. Russia challenged and vexed the West in a number of new areas: it compounded troubles in Africa, and for the first time dared to intervene in Cuba.

One might liken this exceedingly strange approach to an accommodation with the United States to that adopted by a man who seeks to have a friendly chat with a man next door and a settlement of their differences: our peace seeker, instead of knocking politely on the door of the apartment, climbs on the window ledge outside, makes ferocious faces through

---

[8] In March, 1958, a decent interval having elapsed from the events of the last spring, Bulganin was dismissed as Prime Minister and began his descent down the Soviet administrative ladder to oblivion. Khrushchev's assumption of the office marked his definite ascendance, and from then on the signature on the most important diplomatic documents as well as the style was to be his.

his neighbor's window or loudly bangs at the door, threatening to break it open. In the interval, he explains that all he wants is friendship and neighborly comity.

To understand the reasons for this behavior, one must ponder the dilemma inherent in dealing with the *Americans*. President Kennedy was to enunciate a noble principle when he said that America must never negotiate from fear. Like many other noble principles, this one was hardly a practical one. True, there are areas of negotiations where the element of fear does not enter: postal conventions, matters pertaining to fisheries, perhaps—a vast array of subjects where an agreement is reached because of mutual convenience. Yet when it comes to vital interests, fear, alas, must play a role. It is strange that the nation in which the game of poker was invented should be so reluctant to acknowledge this truism, or for that matter that it should allow itself to be so often bluffed and outplayed in the game of international politics.

It has been a cardinal point of Soviet diplomacy that it could not reveal its weaknesses and anxieties. Like Stalin, Khrushchev was unwilling to throw away this great asset. What was likely to happen were Khrushchev to reveal the full extent of his apprehensions about China? About Russia's still pronounced inferiority in nuclear armament? About Russia's fear of an atomic war? Would the Americans negotiate in a businesslike, give-and-take manner, or would they demand that the U.S.S.R. behave in that ultramoral fashion which the United States expected from and often enforced upon its allies? The Soviet Union was blamed by an American writer for the disappearance of classical diplomacy, of the "subtle negotiation" and the "artful compromise." Yet the setting of American politics made confidential diplomatic negotiations well-nigh impossible. Any "subtle negotiation" was likely to be denounced by a chorus of clergymen, columnists, professors, etc., as "power politics" or "secret diplomacy." "Artful compromise"? In the American vernacular this read a "dishonest deal."

There was another and huge difficulty the Soviets faced in any approach to the West. Ever since at least 1953, the U.S.S.R. had not had an absolutely free hand in ordaining priorities for its foreign policy. Peking watched closely and suspiciously to detect anything which might imply a sacrifice of the interest of world Communism, as seen from the Chinese perspective, to Soviet Russia's national interest. There were ample reasons, grounded both in the ideology and in self-interest, which made it imperative for Peking to insist on the continuation of the East-West conflict.

We can now see the true proportions and difficulties of the task Khrushchev set himself. He was to seek an accommodation with the West, yet in a way which would not communicate to the Americans how eager he was for it. The usual task of skillful diplomacy is to make your opponent believe that he is concluding a mutually advantageous agreement while in fact he is giving in to you on most points. But what Khrushchev proposed to accomplish was more difficult: the Americans were to be *frightened* into something they really wanted all along. A more traditional form of trickery was to be reserved for the Chinese: Peking was to believe that the Soviet Union was protecting its interests as well as advancing those of Communism, while in fact the Soviet moves were to keep China indefinitely from achieving the technological and military appurtenances of a great power and thus secure her continued dependence.

It will be objected that a design of such oversubtlety could have hardly been conceived by real-life politicians. But it will not appear improbable to any student of Soviet internal politics who followed Khrushchev's maneuvering between 1953 and 1957: his alliance with the Stalinist old guard to dispatch Beria and then to remove Malenkov; his warding off of the counterattack by Molotov, Malenkov, et al., with the help of Zhukov, only to dismiss the latter when he no longer was needed and might become dangerous. As for the actual design, we shall let the evidence speak for itself.

In 1958, various strands of the Grand Design were already barely perceptible. But what can be seen most clearly are the concerns which would motivate it. These concerns were China and Germany.

In China, 1958 was the year of the Great Leap Forward, a fantastically ambitious plan for a massive economic and especially industrial advance. Ideologically, the Communist rulers attempted to perform a momentous shortcut through history as seen in Marxist terms: China, still a rural society, was to leap over the stage of socialism and land right smack in Communism, a stage which even the Soviet Union did not claim to have reached. In more prosaic terms, this was a frantic effort to achieve instant industrialization, defying laws of economics and common sense alike, through sheer will power and the stupendous manpower at the regime's disposal. Collective farms were merged and transformed into communes, a myriad of tiny industrial plants were to compensate for the lack of heavy industry. The economic campaign was accompanied by an ideologico-political one: the brief period of liberalization was abrogated: only one flower, that of Maoism and rapid industrialization, was to bloom. In foreign policy the voice of Peking was severely doctrinaire: Yugoslavia was denounced in much harsher terms than any other power in the Communist camp; "revisionism" was attacked in terms implying that even Russia was not free from its baneful influence.

To the Soviets, the Great Leap Forward carried an unmistakable warning: China was in a hurry to emancipate herself from her economic and technological dependence on the U.S.S.R. The implications that the Chinese considered themselves purer ideologically than the Russians and that they could outrace the Soviet Union to the goal of achieving a Communist society were met by the Kremlin with a mixture of ill-disguised secret irritation and sarcasm. As usual, Khrushchev could not hold his tongue: whether in his foreign trips or in general pronouncements, or even in talks with visitors like Senator Humphrey, he criticized China's rulers for their presumption. Did they really think they could improve upon Lenin and even Marx? They foolishly believed that the task of building a socialist society did not require material incentives, that people could build heavy industry with their bare hands and rest content to defer any improvement of their standard of living to the distant future. As for himself, Khrushchev was to avow while, appropriately, visiting Hungary, that he believed in "goulash Communism," a Communism where social and industrial advance did not mean asceticism and false egalitarianism but a better life for the masses.

But it was not ideological scruples or solicitude for the Chinese masses that was the main reason for Khrushchev's irritation. If the Soviet leaders were worried before about China and her presumptuous boss, then they must have consoled themselves with the reflection that it would be generations before heavy industry and an up-to-date military technology would be joined with the vast population to constitute a real threat. The Great Leap Forward was very likely to end in an economic disaster, but it was indicative of Peking's determination to achieve the sinews of power and not just rest content with the protection afforded by the "unshakeable friendship" with the Soviets. *Something* had to be done before the Chinese achieved a nuclear capacity and started talking again about Outer Mongolia being returned to them, about how their country could afford to lose three hundred million casualties in an atomic war.

The other pole of Soviet fears was, of course, West Germany. The West German army in the NATO force could hardly be a cause for alarm. For all the outcries about Bonn's *"revanchist"* pretensions and

"Hitleristic generals" taking their place in the NATO command structure, it was clear that the military spirit in West Germany was for the moment dead and that considerable difficulties were being experienced in recruiting even a modest armed force. Russia's earlier fear of a West German army lending a helping hand to a revolt in a satellite had been effectively dispelled. The NATO force was in fact what it was designed to be: a "trip wire" to balk a Soviet advance, and certainly nobody could see in it an offensive threat to the Communist bloc. But another danger lurked behind the over-all German problem.

The Western powers had "bought" the Soviet boast about the Soviet monopoly for the moment and superiority for the foreseeable future in intercontinental ballistic missiles. The SAC force seemed a clumsy and ineffective answer to those hundreds of missiles that allegedly stood ready to rain destruction upon American cities and bases within half an hour or so of the initiation of hostilities. Suddenly the atomic umbrella over Europe had been blown away by the explosion which launched the first Sputnik. It had thus been natural for American strategists to install American intermediate-range missiles first in Britain, then on the Continent, to offset, at least partially, the Soviet advantage. The communiqué of the North Atlantic Council of December 19, 1957, had spelled out this consequence of Soviet boasts and taunts: "NATO has decided to establish stocks of nuclear warheads . . . intermediate-range ballistic missiles will have to be put at the disposal of the Supreme Allied Commander in Europe." [9] Eventually the U.S.S.R. was ringed by American missiles, at the same time that Khrushchev knew that the vast number of ICBM's targeted on the U.S. existed mainly in his oratory.

Nuclear weapons in the hands of Americans were accepted by the Russians with some equanimity. With NATO's possession of such weapons, the problem became somewhat complicated: For all the elaborate control mechanisms and the authority to employ them resting in the American Supreme Commander, could one be absolutely sure that following a frontier altercation, let us say, a subordinate French or German commander might not trigger an atomic war? More fundamentally, there were already voices in France and Germany calling for an independent nuclear deterrent. The Russians had no fear of the Americans suddenly precipitating a nuclear war, but at the same time they had a rather low estimate of American political acumen. It was entirely conceivable that "Bonn *revanchists*" would bend both U.S.

9 *Documents on International Affairs, 1957,* p. 408.

foreign policy and NATO to their purposes. Already, Dr. Adenauer seemed to exercise a veto on many American policies and initiatives. If West Germany had even a small stock of nuclear weapons, she could engage in a rather far-reaching blackmail, if not of the Soviet Union, then of East Europe.

It thus seemed absolutely imperative for the Soviets to remove the most remote possibility of a German "finger on the trigger," of West Germany in any way being allowed to produce, possess, or control as much as a single atomic device. But how? Were the Soviets to state their objectives in those terms, they would be revealing their real fears; Adenauer and Dulles, realizing how desperately the Soviets wanted a denuclearized Germany, might have some interesting ideas of what the Russians should give in exchange for such iron-clad guarantees.

Toward the end of 1957, Adam Rapacki, Foreign Minister of Poland, offered a plan (subsequently to bear his name) which looked toward a nuclear-free zone in Central Europe. Specifically, the zone would include four countries: Poland, Czechoslovakia, and the *two Germanys,* in which atomic, hydrogen, and rocket weapons would be neither *manufactured nor deployed.* It would be surprising if so much as a single sentence of this Plan was composed in Warsaw. Having "carefully studied" the Rapacki (i.e., its own) proposals, the Soviet government hurried to accept it in a note of March 3, 1958. "The problem of the establishment in Central Europe of a zone free from the production and stationing of atomic, hydrogen and rocket weapons is one of the most pressing international problems, calling for immediate solution," [10] the note said.

Predictably, the Western chancelleries began searching for the catch. Did the Soviet Union want the United States to remove its nuclear weapons from NATO, thus to be able to blackmail the West more effectively with its long-range missiles and superiority in conventional forces? How could the Russians be trusted to abide by any agreement? Predictably, the proposals were rejected, since the Rapacki Plan provided "no method for balanced and equitable limitations of military capabilities and would perpetuate the basic cause of tension in Europe by accepting the continuation of the division of Germany," [11] said the United States.

It can be unhesitatingly stated that the rejection of the Rapacki Plan was one of the most fundamental errors of Western policy in the

[10] *Documents on International Affairs, 1958* (London, 1962), p. 134.
[11] *Ibid.,* p. 135.

postwar period. Rejection would have made sense *only* if the West planned to use the threat of nuclear armament for Bonn as a bargaining card with the Russians. Since at the time it did not (*later* this possibility was lamely raised and abandoned) the United States and its allies had nothing to lose by accepting the Plan. In fact, they had a great deal to gain: the rebuilding of German conventional forces was seriously hampered by the realization that in the case of an actual conflict, West Germany would be pulverized by atomic weapons, whether "tactical" or otherwise. Psychologically, acceptance of the Rapacki Plan would lift much of that apprehension from the Germans, would make them more willing to build a sizable Bundeswehr (which even then would have constituted a considerable political asset for the West). The idea that the Russians wanted a nuclear disarmament of NATO in Central Europe only to "steal" Germany with conventional forces was simply not realistic. In fact, if the West had been able to shake off its by now pathological feeling of diplomatic inferiority vis-à-vis Moscow, its feeling that in every agreement it was likely to be taken in, it would have seen what considerable advantages and opportunities the Rapacki Plan opened: it would have meant the installation of some form of international control in the territories of East Germany, Czechoslovakia, and Poland.[12]

The Soviet offer reflected—and this was not even well concealed—how much they were willing to give and risk so that the Germans should not have access in any form to nuclear weapons. The West should have noted another interesting sidelight of the Rapacki proposals: the Soviets were *not,* even for propaganda purposes, suggesting that they might equip *their* allies with atomic weapons. More than that, they were willing to dispense with nuclear weapons and launching sites on the territories of their alleged friends. It is unnecessary to elaborate this point, and we shall come back to it when discussing what the world knows as the Cuban missile crisis.

The West, in brief, could not read Soviet fears and hopes correctly, and this was nothing new. Its statesmen and analysts were so engrossed in the technology of nuclear weapons that they did not pay enough attention to the politics of this awesome problem. In human terms there was ample excuse for the Western statesmen's inability to decipher Soviet actions. Soviet proposals, even when containing concessions,

---

[12] The Soviets could not have hoped to evade the inspection of and hence information about their military facilities and capabilities in these areas if they wanted reciprocal rights in West Germany. Psychologically at least it would have meant less fear of and hence dependence on the U.S.S.R. in those countries.

were clothed in the language of threats, bombast, and propaganda. Correspondence about the Rapacki Plan had barely subsided when the Middle Eastern crisis of 1958 brought the Soviets back to their most threatening and abusive posture.

The Near Eastern crisis brought out a gambit of Khrushchev's which may or may not have been connected with his broader schemes. This was his proposal in July for a meeting of the heads of governments of the Big Four *plus* India. He was willing to hold this meeting within the context of the Security Council in Geneva or even New York. Now whatever the Soviets' real intentions, this proposal was bound to set off alarm in Peking. Khrushchev was apparently attempting to elevate *another* Asian country to the status of a Great Power. What did they mean by agreeing to have a conference within the Security Council, i.e., with the at least formal participation of Chiang's ambassador? On July 31, Khrushchev flew to Peking for a four-day visit, an extremely odd time to go paying visits to a friendly country if, as his frantic messages implied, the world was on the verge of a nuclear holocaust.

On his return on August 5, the Soviet leader was constrained to withdraw his proposal. The Soviet Union could not go to the Security Council, the majority of whose members supported aggression in the Middle East and in which the great Chinese People's Republic was not represented. It was the first clear-cut case of a Soviet political move being reversed at the behest of China. August 5, 1958, marks the beginning of a new phase in Sino-Soviet relations.

There is no doubt that the celebrated Matsu-Quemoy crisis of the fall of 1958 was related to Peking's deepening suspicions of its Russian allies. The bombardment of these offshore islands—where Chiang had placed a large part of his army, though they were probably both undefensible before a determined Communist assault (China's soldiers could fairly swim over, which would have been in line with Chairman Mao's favorite sport) and not essential to the defense of Formosa—was designed by the Chinese to test both the Americans' determination and the Soviets' support. American pledges to Chiang were reiterated, though there was more than an undercurrent of irritation. Soviet support for Peking came in the form of two repetitively threatening letters from Khrushchev to Eisenhower: "To touch off a war against People's China means to doom sons of America to certain death and to spark off the conflagration of a world war." But as the Chinese were to say some years later, Khrushchev's promises and guarantees were extended only after it had become clear that the United States was contemplating no attack on China and the threat of a war had largely passed. The crisis was allowed to simmer down in November. For all its secret resentments and future recriminations, Peking scored a diplomatic victory: the world had been told that an attack on Communist China meant nuclear war; if Khrushchev's recent ruminations had led anybody to doubt the "unshakable unity of the socialist camp," then his forthright public declaration was bound to dissipate such unworthy conjectures. And if Chiang had had any ideas of exploiting the tensions and disruptions on the mainland (already taking place as the consequence of the Great Leap Forward), then the Americans had read him a severe lesson.

To the Kremlin, the meaning was unmistakable: the Soviet Union was increasingly being used by China to further her own aims; the most cherished Soviet foreign-policy designs were being balked and frustrated by Peking's moves. It was one thing to be exploited economically and technologically by fellow Communists; it was another to be compelled to share the gravest decisions about peace and war, about the general policy of the Communist bloc, with another Communist power. The Russians tried to reason with their increasingly burdensome ally: If the U.S.S.R. and China were to be linked in readiness to meet an aggression, should there not be a joint command, perhaps on the Warsaw Pact order, i.e., under over-all Soviet leadership? The Chinese would not buy.[13] The Soviets had for long lived with the wonderful feeling that unlike other powers they were masters of their destiny. Now they were brought out of this complacency: a foreign power could send armed junks across a few miles of water, and as a consequence the Soviet Union might find itself in a war. And the man in whose hand lay this decision was the same man who had stated that Communist China could survive a nuclear war and 300 million casualties!

To the urgency of forestalling China's nuclear development was thus joined that of squeezing the maximum possible benefit from the Chinese alliance before its fragility became apparent to the West. The Chinese problem then made a resolution of the German question all the more urgent. And with the latter settled, the Soviets hoped to put their

[13] This is the only possible interpretation of an official Peking statement in 1963: "In 1958 the leadership of the C.P.S.U. put forward reasonable demands designed to put China under Soviet military control. These unreasonable demands were rightly and firmly rejected by the Chinese government." Quoted in William E. Griffith, *The Sino-Soviet Rift* (Cambridge, Mass., 1964), p. 399.

détente with the West to use in curbing Chinese ambitions and pretensions.

The first phase of this involved design had unfolded with the Rapacki
Plan. On March 31, 1958, the Supreme Soviet passed a resolution
unilaterally suspending atomic and hydrogen weapon tests and calling
upon other powers to do likewise.[14] And on November 27, a Soviet note
to the Western powers marked the opening of a new Berlin crisis. The
U.S.S.R. was not going to wait indefinitely for a German peace treaty.
If, within six months, such a treaty was not agreed upon by the Allied
powers of World War II, then Russia would sign a unilateral agreement
with East Germany, turn over to her the Eastern sector of Berlin. It
would be up to the three Western Powers to negotiate an agreement
with East Germany concerning their rights of access to West Berlin
and the mechanism of transforming West Berlin into a "demilitarized
free city." For the East Germans to agree to such a status for West
Berlin would be a great sacrifice, for after all it lay inside their territory, but Russia in the interests of peace was willing to counsel its
German friends to make this concession. If, however, the West should
refuse to negotiate with the East Germans and continue its illegal
occupation of West Berlin, the German Democratic Republic would
have every right to regulate traffic to and from the enclave any way it
should see fit, and if the West tried to breach any prospective blockade,
it would be an act of aggression not only against East Germany but
against the U.S.S.R. and other signatories of the Warsaw Pact.

There you had it: the West had to read the Soviet note as the most
definite and frightening challenge to its rights in Berlin yet thrown down.
On December 21, the Communist Chinese regime issued a declaration
supporting the Soviet proposals. It was an unusual step for Peking to
take official notice of a purely European dispute, and doubtless it was
done at the Kremlin's request to add weight to the pressure. But for
Peking, the language was unusually mild: no suggestion that should the
mad imperialist dogs unleash a war over Berlin, 600 million Chinese
would stand as one man by the side of their Soviet brothers. Such untypical restraint could not be appreciated in the Kremlin. The Russians
had pretended that they had been ready to go to war over two miserable
offshore islands. Why could the Chinese not do the same over Berlin?

The remaining cardinal point of the Soviet grand strategy was announced at the 21st Party Congress held in January, 1959. With

---

[14] The suspension, of course, could have been ordained by a simple government
announcement, but it was given this more solemn character.

special emphasis Khrushchev said that an atom-free zone must be
constructed in the Far East and the whole Pacific Ocean.[15]

Here, then, was the ambitious plan designed to remove the most
pressing anxieties of the Soviet leadership for the immediate future.
By threatening Berlin, the Russians would exact a German peace treaty
which would make it impossible for West Germany to possess or produce atomic weapons. Then a version of the Rapacki Plan would be
applied in the Pacific, i.e., Communist China and Japan would be
prohibited from producing or possessing nuclear weapons. The U.S.
and the U.S.S.R. for their part would pledge that they would not place
nuclear weapons in the area nor furnish them to their allies; the latter
could protest tearfully when the moment came but would still make
this sacrifice to "world peace."

Were this involved maneuver to succeed, the U.S. and the U.S.S.R.
would share the world's domination as the only two "real" nuclear
powers, but for a devoted Communist this did not mean an abandonment of his creed or of the task of its propagation. In one of his franker
moments Khrushchev described his idea of peaceful coexistence as
similar to that underlying marriages which he understood often
took place in the decadent West between young men and rich old
women. The young and vigorous Soviet Union would grow in strength
and vigor; wars of national liberation would continue to shrink the
sphere of influence of the West and undermine its internal cohesion.
No one begrudges a young man in such a situation a discreet affair or
two on the side, and by the same token, the U.S.S.R. would have its
opportunities in the Middle East, Africa, and Latin America. The
United States would grow more and more debilitated and, as they
say, would stop caring. It was a revealing simile. But to pursue it further,
the old lady was to prove suspicious and obdurate to both blandishments and threats. And in his worldly wisdom, Nikita Sergeievich
should have realized that in the situation he described there was usually
a third party—a mistress alert to the threat of betrayal, and vengeful.

---

[15] The relevant passage of his speech was italicized in the official record of the
Congress.

III

Lost
Opportunities

10

Khrushchev's Gamble: What the Russians Sought in Cuba

The road toward the achievement of Russia's master plan had to lead through a summit. One had to alarm the Americans sufficiently to make them agree to one, and yet not so much that they might do something rash. There were some voices in the West saying that it would be foolish to go to war over the question of who was going to stamp your entry permit to West Berlin, the East Germans or the Russians. And what was so wrong, some senators were saying, with having West Berlin a demilitarized free city policed by the United Nations? Since Berlin was the means rather than the objective of Soviet maneuvers, and Khrushchev had to be sure that his proposals were not in fact too reasonable, he explained that when he spoke of Berlin being a free city he meant of course only West Berlin; furthermore, an international force patrolling West Berlin would have, naturally, to include a *Soviet* contingent. He was sorry he had not made himself clear on that point.

Soviet diplomatic moves throughout 1959 presented a crazy quilt of threats, bluster, and cajolery. At the 21st Party Congress, Khrushchev was somber in his warning: the world faced a serious threat of nuclear conflict over Berlin if the six-month time limit passed without something being done—i.e., by May 27. In the same speech he extended a cordial invitation to Eisenhower to visit the Soviet Union. Asked at a press conference to explain his ultimatum, the Soviet Premier exploded: What ultimatum? It was a slander of the capitalist press that he had presented the West with an ultimatum. All he had said was that the U.S.S.R. was going to sign a peace treaty with East Germany within six months. Was that an ultimatum? And perhaps six months should not be taken too literally. But the West had better hurry!

The most efficacious way of securing agreement on a summit conference appeared, at one time, to persuade the British to persuade the Americans. The British Prime Minister hurried to Moscow (to the dismay of Chancellor Adenauer and those Americans who feared a breach in Western solidarity), but having arrived he refused to cave in. Khrushchev wanted a summit meeting; Macmillan wanted, as he had been briefed by Washington, a foreign ministers' conference of the Big Four. The Soviet leader exploded. Foreign ministers' meetings, he said with considerable justification, never settled anything. Who could imagine that Gromyko could make any far-reaching policy decisions on his own? Khrushchev's behavior toward poor Macmillan became deliberately rude. Instead of accompanying the Prime Minister on one of those little tours of the Soviet Union which he usually fancied, he let Macmillan go by himself, after giving him the kind of a personal rebuff which in nineteenth-century days would have led Her Britannic Majesty's government to break off diplomatic relations. Then on second thought he relented and flew to join the Englishman on his rather forlorn tour of the provinces. He was again cordial: all right, let it be a foreign ministers' conference; while it lasted the six-month limit would be suspended. But a summit meeting had to come.

American policy at the time was in a state of disarray, largely because of first the intermittent indispositions, then the fatal disease which struck Secretary Dulles. Strangely enough, the Soviets saw his illness and his subsequent death as complicating their task. He had grown more flexible lately, and the Soviets had always respected him. And Eisenhower was reluctant to repeat his Geneva experience of four years before, especially without the presence of Dulles.

America's allies, except for Great Britain, now were increasingly cool to any Soviet-American *rapprochement*. General de Gaulle, to put it bluntly, trusted neither America's intelligence nor determination to protect Europe's interests vis-à-vis Russia. He was eager for France to assume a more independent Great Power posture, partly to compensate for the loss of imperial grandeur, partly to keep the world from being divided between the "Anglo-Saxons" and the Russians. Chancellor Adenauer, though more discreet, was even more on guard against any possibility of a Soviet-American "deal," and he strongly opposed anything which smacked of even *de facto* recognition of the East German regime, a concession on Berlin, or derogation of the rights, status, and claims of the Bonn republic. Though eighty-three years of age, the German statesman postponed his previously announced retirement from active politics. Privately, he explained that this was necessitated by Dulles' absence and hence the added need for firm opposition to the Soviet diplomatic offensive. In fact, Adenauer would have stayed on even had his American friend been alive and well: even under Dulles, American foreign policy had shown some dangerous tendency to favor an accommodation with Russia.

As it was, U.S. policy-makers were in a state of confusion. Among them there was no perception of the Soviet Union's wider aims: it was a *Berlin* crisis both in the press and in public statements from the State Department and White House, though a careful study of the Soviet notes should have made it clear that it was a German peace-treaty crisis. But was it yet another of those tests of the West's determination and unity, or were the Russians really in earnest? The President and his closest advisers had sound reasons to believe that Khrushchev was bluffing when he implied readiness to risk war. But they could not let the public in on the main reasons for their confidence: that their intelligence sources, and especially the evidence gathered through U-2 flights, indicated that the Soviets were not nearly so strong in nuclear bombs and rockets as they pretended. Anyway, with somebody like Khrushchev one could never be sure what the Russians were really after.

Even if Talleyrand rather than Christian Herter had been in charge of the State Department at that time, American diplomacy still would have been hard put to decipher the meaning of the Soviet moves. The outward pattern suggested the old German saying: "You will either be my brother or I'll crack your skull open." On the one hand, there were those frequent threats of nuclear obliteration of American cities should it come to a war; on the other, there was cordial talk of commercial and cultural exchanges between the two countries, a great volume of mutual visiting. High-ranking Soviet officials would invite themselves to the United States, where they kept dropping hints that an even more important person would like to be invited. Thus Anastas Mikoyan suddenly felt the urge to visit his old friend Menshikov, who was currently Ambassador to the United States, and incidentally of course had to chat with Eisenhower. Then the No. 2 man in the Soviet Union, Frol Kozlov, came to open a Soviet exhibition in New York and also talked with Eisenhower. In return, Vice-President Nixon appeared in Moscow to open an American exhibition. He arrived to find Khrushchev furious over Captive Nations Week in the United States, which President Eisenhower had just proclaimed with characteristically bad timing. Khrushchev followed Nixon through the exhibition, making pointed remarks about how the United States was trying to deceive simple Soviet people by pretending that all those luxury products were mass-produced and could be enjoyed by the average American. Thus the famous "kitchen debate," in which Nixon tried to defend the reality of the American way of life against the sneers and taunts of his host. Then, as he had with Macmillan, Khrushchev simmered down and reverted to the famous traditions of Slavic hospitality. One would give much to have similarly well-documented accounts of Khrushchev's encounters with Mao.

All in all, Eisenhower was virtually forced to invite Khrushchev to the United States. To fortify himself for this strenuous experience, the President first went to Europe to reassure Adenauer, soothe de Gaulle, and to see Macmillan and the Queen and play golf in Britain. In the meantime, the Soviet time limit on the peace treaty with Germany came and went without the world being plunged into war. The foreign ministers who met during the summer in Geneva predictably accomplished nothing. There were some minor Soviet chicaneries over American communication with West Berlin, but obviously there could be no major confrontation while the head of the Soviet government was preparing to pay his respects to the President of the United States.

Theatrics could not, however, affect the very serious setback to the Soviet designs which was occurring at the same time. It must be strongly presumed that the key Soviet gambit at the eventual summit was a pledge that China would not become a nuclear power. How exactly this could be given—whether in return for a U.S. pledge not to place nuclear weapons in Japan and Formosa or through a more complicated arrangement—we cannot be sure. But the extent of American apprehensions about China's getting hold of the deadly weapons was well realized. At the same time *nobody* in the United States except an air force general or two presumed to know what to do to prevent this dismal prospect: the eventual status of China as a nuclear power was accepted as inevitable as death and taxes.

The Russians thought that they could obtain a Chinese agreement for such, at least temporary, forebearance. In 1958, Mao had declared publicly that an elaborate nuclear and rocket technology was too expensive for China. Khrushchev's emphatic declaration about the imperative need for a nuclear-free zone in the Far East and the Pacific was approved in January, 1959, by Chou En-lai. In February, the Soviets agreed on the most extensive plan yet for economic and technological aid to Peking: 5 billion rubles' worth of Soviet service and goods within the next seven years; more training of Chinese technicians. This clearly was a bribe to secure Chinese compliance.

But then something went wrong: the Chinese continued to assert that they favored an atom-free zone in the Pacific, but they rather whimsically implied that they meant it should comprise all the countries bordering on the ocean, i.e., the United States and the Soviet Union as well as China. Soviet patience was running out; the Chinese were told, we learn from the correspondence, to be serious. How could the Russians press the Americans not to give nuclear weapons to West Germany and Japan (nobody had even raised the possibility of Japanese accession to the nuclear club) while sanctioning China's nuclear ambitions?

It is not clear whether the Chinese ever seriously considered giving up or postponing their own nuclear ambitions, or whether they just pretended to in order to squeeze the last drop of aid out of Russia before the inevitable break. At the 21st Party Congress, in January, Khrushchev was eager to dispel rumors about a forthcoming rupture: people who like the Yugoslavs (still in the bad graces of Moscow) talked wildly of a quarrel between China and Russia were talking nonsense; they would never see a quarrel between the two fraternal countries any more than they could see their own ears!

But the Chinese did not go along. No doubt the Soviet Union's erratic behavior was being read differently in Peking than in the West. There, Soviet threats were taken seriously and Soviet overtures seen as a veneer of deception, but in China, the Soviets were believed to be working toward a design by which they could share world rule with the United States.

In June, 1959, the Soviets stopped their help to China's nuclear development. Such at least was the bald statement made by the Chinese in the bitter public exchange they engaged in with Moscow in 1963. What it actually meant it is difficult to gauge. Presumably the Soviets withdrew their advisers, or stopped providing China with fissionable material. As yet the break was not complete, nor was it made public. In July and August, the Chinese Central Committee held lengthy meetings in Lushan. It was there that the Mao faction struck at Marshal Peng Teh-huai, who was dismissed from his post as Minister of Defense, and his alleged followers, who were similarly disgraced. Subsequent Chinese documents identified him as the man connected with Soviet attempts to overthrow Mao; the Marshal, who had been the Chinese commander in the Korean War, was sent to a forced-labor camp, according to a later Soviet version of the incident.

When Khrushchev boarded his plane for the trip to the United States on September 15, 1959, he knew that his visit was bound to be what it had been announced as, a largely social one. He would not be able to dangle before the Americans the prospect of a China foreswearing atomic armaments. In fact it is likely that the Chinese did not publicly denounce his trip only by reason of his promise to go there on his return from the United States. As if things were not bad enough, the visit coincided with a frontier clash between China and India. The Soviet press adopted a position of virtual neutrality on this issue: it was regrettable for two friendly countries bound by the famous Bandung principles of coexistence to quarrel and fight over some mountain wastes. The Chinese in their current mood saw another evidence of black treason: as if scheming with the Americans were not enough, Khrushchev was evidently engaged in some intrigue with India. How could one be impartial in a dispute between a fellow Communist country and the Indians, who for all their neutralist posturings were encroaching on territory which had always been rightfully China's and who criticized Chinese actions in Tibet?

In the United States, there was no inkling of the great strain under which the Chairman was operating. It was hoped to assuage the Russian by showing him the peaceful and friendly attitude of American society, its healthy preoccupation with material and cultural progress. It was hoped, at least by General Eisenhower, that any involved business negotiations could be avoided.[1]

If the visit could not settle any outstanding international issues then Khrushchev took good care that it should be scored as a great promotional success for himself. We know now, of course, that his personal position in the U.S.S.R. was not as strong as it seemed then. It was therefore important that to his colleagues in the Presidium he should appear as one Soviet statesman who was well known and liked in America, and who if things ever got out of hand could always retrieve a miscalculation or overcommitment. He was also genuinely interested in making a good impression and appraising the political climate and lead-

---

[1] There were difficulties about protocol, minor in themselves, yet characteristic of American insensitivity to the nuances of Soviet politics. Khrushchev wanted to be treated as head of state, which he of course was not, and it took the Americans some time to agree to this. The Soviet ambassador wanted to be the first to greet the chairman when his plane landed, but General Eisenhower vetoed it: protocol required that he, as host, meet the Chairman at the foot of the ramp. Obviously poor Menshikov, knowing his boss' terrible temper, was eager to make sure that the visit not begin with some terrible *faux-pas*.

ing personalities of this puzzling country. His retinue included not only officials and newspapermen but members of his family, doctors, physicists, and the closest thing Soviet Russia had to a poet-laureate, Mikhail Sholokhov, Stalin's and Khrushchev's favorite author. This traveling party in a somewhat clumsy way was meant as a gesture of friendship: those distinguished representatives of Soviet culture were expected to be entertained and honored by their opposite numbers in American life. Politics and ideologies apart, the two great nations should get to know and respect each other.

Soviet clumsiness was matched by American insensitivity. It was only Khrushchev who was "newsworthy," and other members of the party, except for his wife, as restrained and dignified as her husband was boisterous and earthy, were virtually ignored. As to the treatment accorded to Khrushchev personally, it was difficult for the Americans, for all their hospitable instincts, to devise one that fitted in with his image of himself as both a man of the people who could plunge into any group and establish immediate rapport and mutual sympathy and the head of a great state and political movement to be treated with respect, if not awe. To the Americans, he appeared mainly as an object of curiosity to be feared—could not one word from him launch a war?—and at the same time as a somewhat comical figure, with his rages and his boasts about Russia. In those it now must seem distant days, dignitaries could travel the length of America without being molested or subjected to vulgar abuse. But Khrushchev was not infrequently baited by newspapermen: How about Stalin, how about the purges? At other times he was subjected to excessively anxious affability: See how friendly we are. Why do you want to destroy us or make us all Communists? Khrushchev employed a formula that he probably thought would reassure his listeners, reaffirming his faith while leaving to his successors the pleasant prospect of dealing with an American Mao: "Your grandchildren will live under Communism." It was felt to be in poor taste. But President Eisenhower had also sinned in this respect, by his well-meant but unfortunate hints about American affluence; it was not simply a lack of free enterprise but two devastating wars and other tragic vicissitudes in the history of the Russian people that accounted for the difference.

The substantive discussions that took place after Khrushchev's return to Washington and at Camp David could not achieve much. One attempt to steer conversations into wider dimensions was Khrushchev's mention of Communist China. He had been asked, he said (he did not specify by whom), to discuss American attitudes toward Peking. Eisenhower refused emphatically to pursue the subject. Thereupon Khrushchev begged the President not to believe any rumors of quarrels between the two Communist countries: the U.S.S.R. and China would always stand together in any international dispute; he and Mao were great friends. It is tantalizing to speculate what Khrushchev would have said had the President pursued the subject. (Perhaps Dulles would have been more alert.) But for the American officials who had briefed Eisenhower, all hopes and aspirations of Soviet foreign policy were assumed to center on Berlin. The subject was sprung suddenly and the President was wary to discuss something on which he had not been thoroughly briefed. And thus passed a moment which might have changed the course of history.

An official Soviet release before the visit had stated, "One can hardly overestimate the significance of the forthcoming meetings of the leaders of the U.S.S.R. and the United States." Yet in fact the visit produced nothing beyond the predictable agreement to hold a summit meeting of the Big Four as soon as possible. Also predictably, the Russians abandoned the idea of a time limit on the German question, or as the Americans would have phrased it, of an ultimatum on Berlin. Eisenhower felt this to have been a great success achieved through his firmness. (He himself at Camp David had admitted that the situation in Berlin was "abnormal." His entourage felt this had been an incautious slip, yet what better description of the situation of the unfortunate city could there have been?)

Khrushchev pressed for a return visit by the President to Russia as soon as possible. Again there was caution among Eisenhower's staff and at the State Department. The visit would take place in 1960, after the summit. Having explained to his Soviet visitor that pressure of business would not let him visit Russia in the fall, the President soon set out on an extensive tour that carried him to places as distant as India and Morocco.

Upon his return to Russia, Khrushchev was given a triumphant reception, as if in fact he was returning from a conference that had resolved most of the world's pressing problems rather than from what had turned out to be mainly a ceremonial visit. Again there was more than mere personal promotion in this extravagant welcome: the Soviet people, just as the Americans, stood in need of reassurance that the world crisis would not lead to a nuclear holocaust. Some of the Chairman's colleagues must have been skeptical of Khrushchev's intricate plan: Was there enough political intelligence and peaceful resolution in

Washington? Was American foreign policy perhaps too much under the baneful influence of Adenauer to meet the Russians in an over-all settlement of the German problem? It was for their benefit that Khrushchev publicly praised Eisenhower as a man of peace, a wise and resolute statesman.

This praise of the American President was repeated in October in Peking, which Khrushchev visited almost immediately after his return. This time the praise was more restrained, but it was most unusual for a Soviet statesman in China to refer to an American President in favorable terms.

If the Americans did not understand what the Soviets were after, the Chinese understood only too well. "What is in it for us?" was the most restrained question asked of Khrushchev in Peking. Russia, they were told, was going to get a German peace treaty and a ban on nuclear weapons in Bonn. But what were the Chinese going to get for forswearing nuclear weapons? Khrushchev had not even brought a promise that the United States would change its policy on Formosa. He pleaded for patience: the U.S.S.R. was not going to leave them in the lurch. As to Formosa, he said, could they not wait? After World War I, the Soviets had not hurried to reoccupy their Far Eastern territories: they had set up a bogus independent republic and then, after a few years, when everybody was looking the other way, they quietly annexed it. Couldn't the Chinese comrades emulate the patience of the great Lenin?[2] No, this was not intended to imply that there should be two Chinas. With the Americans it paid to be patient and crafty rather than belligerent.

We do not know what other arguments or threats Khrushchev used. When the Chinese chose, in 1963, to be indiscreet, they naturally published only those bits of information that presented the Soviet leader in the worst possible light. But he clearly succeeded somewhat in mollifying Mao, for an open break between the two regimes was for the time avoided. Indeed, the Chinese government issued a statement supporting the Soviet Union's disarmament proposals.

On the Western side there was no perception of how strained the relations between the two Communist giants were becoming, no idea even to probe for cracks and fissures in the alliance. True, intelligent

---

2 Not a very good analogy, as Khrushchev was probably told: the Far Eastern Republic was from the beginning a Soviet satellite, while Formosa was held by *enemies* of Communist China.

people had to recognize the divergent views and interests of the two nations; the Yugoslavs gossiped about them; General de Gaulle, with his sense of history, talked of long-range incompatibility between the two Communist empires. But in the absence of palpable evidence of a split, the State Department went on talking about a "Sino-Soviet bloc." The exigencies of American politics made probing moves vis-à-vis China well-nigh impossible. It was only Eisenhower's and Dulles' irrefutable anti-Communist virtue which had made such tenuous means of dialogue with China as the Warsaw conversations possible without creating a wild outcry. Nobody suspected that there was or could be a link between problems of nuclear disarmament, Soviet pressure on Berlin, and relations between Peking and Moscow. The ingenuities of American and British diplomacy were addressed to the means of solving what was assumed to be a *Berlin* crisis in a way which would preserve the Allies' rights in the city, save "face" for Khrushchev, and yet not irritate Adenauer. Nuclear disarmament was considered in a light mostly unrelated to the German question. Here again there was much tedious discussion of whether the Russians could be trusted.

The summit, somewhat to the relief of the weary State Department officials charged with writing countless position papers, was adjourned to the spring of 1960. This was mainly because of de Gaulle. After his triumphant tour of the Far East, Eisenhower stopped in Paris, where he was faced not with garlands, festive processions, and acclamatory mobs, but with de Gaulle's and Adenauer's reservations and demands that the West stand firm on Berlin. De Gaulle, who had said earlier that he did not believe that trips such as Khrushchev's to America served any useful purpose, now exacted that the Soviet leader should visit France, only after which would the summit be held—and of course in Paris. De Gaulle was insistent that France should have an equal place in the Concert of Powers. (If the British were content to play second fiddle to America that was their business.) His intransigence was, one feels, not unconnected with his by now obvious determination to conclude the Algerian war, albeit at the price of Algerian independence, in which event the French needed a psychological compensation for this blow to their pride. De Gaulle quite sensibly urged that the three Western powers should coordinate their policies concerning the Third World. Eisenhower's refusal even to discuss this proposal was due to the old American fear that the United States might be tarnished by associating with two "imperialist" powers. De Gaulle eventually had the satisfaction of observing how many of the Third World countries professed friendship for France while brand-ing the virtuous United States as imperialist.[3]

De Gaulle's imperiousness and Adenauer's obstinacy thus carried the day against American hesitations and British eagerness: the sum-mit was postponed and the gist of the Western pronouncements in-dicated that the Western powers would go to it with little beyond a resolution to hold firm on Berlin and to examine what the Russians had to offer. Apart perhaps from the British, nobody credited the Soviets with any other motivations except to push as hard and get as much as they could without a war. The Americans looked half hopefully, half skeptically for any evidence that the Russians had *really* changed, that the "spirit of Camp David," or the "dialogue," as we would say today, would continue and expand. *Then* one could begin to talk business with the U.S.S.R. about disarmament, Germany, etc. Chancellor Adenauer was still not entirely disabused of the notion that if only he could induce the United States to hold firm and not fall prey to foolish illusions about Khrushchev, the Russians would come to *him* bearing Ul-bricht's head, so to speak, as a peace offering. As for de Gaulle, since the Americans had rejected his hints about the three Western powers closely coordinating all their defense and foreign policies, he played his own hand. And eventually, perhaps, the Russians would compre-hend that France, the leader of a united Western Europe, was a fit partner for a policy that would secure peace and lift Europe as a whole to its old position in the world. There was no basic discord between the four Western powers—presented with a real threat they would stand together—but there was a multitude of mutual recrimination and suspicion that in the absence of any clear leadership, and in view of the lack of perception of what the Russians were really after, barred any strategy except one of strong resistance to their demands.

Nineteen-sixty—a bad year all around. Reality caught up with the Russians' schemes and the Americans' illusions. The U.S.S.R. was not strong enough to frighten the United States into an agreement on the

[3] Eisenhower's itinerary was not arranged to take count of de Gaulle's enormous sensitivity: before going to Paris, he touched down in Tunisia, after which he stopped in Morocco, both until recently French protectorates and both serving as sanctuaries for the Algerian rebels. Eisenhower's insensitivity to such personal elements in diplomacy was in line with some of the observations he made about the potentates he had encountered: he found no signs of extravagance in the style of living of the King of Morocco; General Franco's simple and engaging personal-ity made him wonder why the Spanish dictator was afraid to risk free elections; in Pakistan he was touched by President Ayub Khan's eloquent denunciation of countries which took American money and then affected neutralism without recognizing it as a subtle reference to his next stop, India.

German question or China into giving up her nuclear ambitions. To the United States, the year offered abundant proof that the Russians "had not changed." They would not "behave," would not negotiate "in good faith." More fundamental and long-lasting was the disillusionment on another score: the problems of the Third World had not been solved by wholesale grants of independence ("freedom," as American politicians and newspapers phrased it) to colonial states, nor did independence confer immunity to Communism. Economic development did not look so enticing to many of the new rulers as did the allurements of personal power and international intrigue. But the most shocking disillusionment for the American people was to be in a discovery that the whole complex of issues—imperialism—underdevelopment—Communism—was right at America's doorstep, 90 miles off the Florida coast.

The collapse of Khrushchev's plans had been ordained long before that day in May when an American U-2 plane was downed in the heart of Russia. For as the summit approached, the Chinese stiffened their position. At the meeting of the Warsaw Treaty powers in Moscow in February, the Chinese delegate stated emphatically that Communist China would not recognize as binding any international disarmament agreement or any other agreement reached without the *formal* participation of his government. In April, Peking's *Red Flag* published an article (later identified as having come from Mao's pen) in which a barely veiled attack was launched at the Soviet leadership: China was not afraid of nuclear war; should it come, it would destroy imperialism and upon its ruins the victorious peoples would build a new and more beautiful civilization. Khrushchev thus could not go to the summit and in effect guarantee that China would not produce or obtain nuclear weapons. He evidently had hoped at least to have a test-ban treaty to offer as an inducement to a political settlement.[4] Now that hope was gone. China would not be bound. Moreover, his bargaining power was weakening: there were people in the West who could read Chinese.

Western moves at the same time spelled out that the Russians would not even get the European half of the loaf. The West Germans were talking about equipping their armies with intermediate-range rockets; the Americans hinted they might give their allies access to nuclear

[4] The Soviets had let disarmament talks in Geneva drag, specifying that any binding agreement would be reached only at the summit conference.

information, perhaps even nuclear weapons. At first the Russians thought of countering this by threatening to give nuclear weapons to "their" Germans, but this threat was rather abruptly dropped. The possibility of a satellite state in the possession of nuclear weapons was undoubtedly felt to be as dangerous as having those weapons in Bonn or Peking.

It was difficult to see what the summit conference could accomplish, and indeed the tenor of speeches made by Secretary of State Herter and Under-Secretary Dillon implied that the United States would, at least for bargaining purposes, raise such issues as the status of the satellites, the Korean question, etc. Did the Americans really think that this conference would constitute just another exchange of views and bring no concrete results on disarmament and Germany? If so, declared Khrushchev, increasingly out of sorts, they were going to be chased out of Berlin. But he voiced the hope that those officials did not speak for the President.

Gary Powers' unintended and uninvited arrival on Russian soil on May 1 paradoxically enough enabled Khrushchev to get out of his box: there would be no summit. Yet it is unlikely that his deeply insulting behavior and great wrath toward the President of the United States was *entirely* simulated. Given the kind of man he was, Khrushchev probably had felt for some time mounting irritation with Eisenhower: here was a unique chance to be a co-author of a historic international agreement, which among other things was almost bound to bring a victory to the Republican party in the Presidential elections, and yet Eisenhower let first Adenauer and de Gaulle, and then some subordinates ruin the prospects for a summit. To top it all, and here we must grant Khrushchev reason, the President showed both naïveté and insensitivity by assuming personal responsibility for the U-2 flights and blithely adding that, yes, he still expected to visit the Soviet Union!

Certainly there was no reason for Khrushchev to go to Paris unless he savored exposing Eisenhower to the kind of insults the President of the United States had never had to listen to before. He continued his personal vendetta with remarks reflecting on the President's alertness and grasp of international affairs. And the vengeful Russian not only insisted on coming to the United States but encouraged a horde of Communist and neutralist leaders to do likewise. This was bound to embarrass and disturb the President, whose career as an international peacemaker was thus given a finale more appropriate to a musical comedy. Years later, Nikita Khrushchev, then a powerless and obscure pensioner, claimed with some relish in an interview that he had helped elect Kennedy.

He was probably right. Traditionally it has been argued by the experts that foreign-policy issues play an insignificant role in the American electorate's decision.[5] Yet in view of the extremely narrow margin by which John F. Kennedy was elected, a spectacular success in foreign affairs by the Republican administration in its waning months, or even an absence of that exacerbated tension which Khrushchev's antics had brought about in May, undoubtedly would have made a difference. The atmosphere of 1960 was one of severe crisis which strained the nerves not only of the American leaders but also of that not inconsiderable number of American people who read and listen to foreign news. At one time the tension was great enough (following the Paris fiasco, when Khrushchev visited East Germany) for the Secretary of Defense to order a world-wide alert of the U.S. armed forces.

The first open break between the Soviet Union and Communist China—i.e., before other Communist parties and leaders—took place in Bucharest in June, 1960. It is too bad that Eisenhower could not have been present at this Communist conclave. He could have witnessed Khrushchev outdoing himself in his ravings and rantings behavior—this time against a man he had described as his good friend, Mao. The Chinese Communists, he screamed, were madmen and "left adventurists" who wanted to unleash a war. The Chinese answered him in kind. In the fall, a hastily arranged conference of eighty-one Communist parties in Moscow patched up some sort of joint declaration, but behind the closed doors another violent confrontation took place between Khrushchev and the head of the Chinese delegation. (China, the most populous Communist country, was joined in her defiance of the Soviet Union by the smallest one: Albania. The Albanian party had long suspected that Khrushchev, in one of his tender moments with Tito, might make a present of their country to the Yugoslavs. Now they found an ally and protector and attacked Khrushchev with the kind of abusive relish which even their Chinese friends and instigators had not yet used.) In the meantime the Soviets pulled out their experts from China.

A dispute of such proportions and of such reverberations, before

[5] This truism was certainly overturned in 1968. Will it ever again be applicable?

so large an audience, could not be kept secret any more than Khrushchev's "secret speech of 1956. But in the United States attention was riveted on other things: on the Congo, the generally chaotic situation in Africa, and the elections. And, finally, Khrushchev had decided to grace America with his presence again by appearing before the U.N. Assembly. (Perhaps in the belief that sea voyages soothe the nerves, he set out by ship, sandwiching his trip between two bouts with the Chinese.) This was to be a great boon for the American news media: Khrushchev embracing Castro in a Harlem hotel, interrupting a decorous Macmillan speech by shouting loudly and then banging his shoe on the table at an Assembly session.[6] But if there was a purpose to all this madness, it was not the rather feeble bombshell Khrushchev exploded before the Assembly, a proposal that the Secretary General's office be transformed into a commission of three, one neutralist, one Communist, and one "capitalist." [7] The new African and Asian states were going to hold the balance in the General Assembly; in addition, some interesting political changes were taking place in Latin America. It was therefore to appraise these promising new opportunities at first hand that the chief of the Soviet government traveled to New York by slow boat, as well as to search for needed rest and entertainment, not to mention the additional incentive of causing irritation and embarrassment to the President.

But it was not only in terms of the United Nations that the Soviets were induced to turn their attention to Africa, Southeast Asia, and Latin America. There were possibilities for pressure, for outflanking, so to speak, the West in the Third World. Pressure in Berlin was turning out to be a rather dangerous and ineffective way to force anything out of the Americans. The *inconvenience* for the West of Berlin as a place at which to stand firm, and the real impossibility of its defense, was matched by a clear-cut moral case *for* its defense. Apart from out-and-out Communists, not even those Westerners who saw sinister motivations and implications in every American move and posture could discover in West Berlin any sinister colonels (as in the

[6] For all the psychological sophistication of the American press and academic milieu, for all the propensity of distinguished analysts to volunteer in-depth studies of such political figures as Goldwater and Johnson, and indeed Woodrow Wilson, Khrushchev's actions were interpreted as menacing rather than as reflecting deep insecurity. No one suggested tranquilizers.

[7] This proposal, which saddened and alarmed U.N.-lovers in the United States, was rejected by most representatives of the newly emergent countries. The Afro-Asian group recognized Secretary General Hammarskjöld as a staunch supporter of their general position.

pre-1945 Polish government), embarrassing cardinals (Hungary), rapacious landlords (Kuomintang China), or bellicose dictators (South Korea).

Thus, to the Russians' undoubted puzzlement, the Americans, who had accepted the fact that one-fourth of the human race found itself under a hostile regime in Peking as one of "those things," *seemed* to be ready to risk atomic war for the sake of 2 million Germans.

Without giving up on Berlin as the means of pressuring the United States, the Soviets had to look for alternative weak spots. It was thus natural that Khrushchev should seek an opportunity to size up Fidel Castro personally. Perhaps the road to barring nuclear weapons in Germany and China might lead through Havana.

The spectacular rise of Fidel Castro from a hunted guerrilla to the dictator of the Caribbean island had taken place in the face of considerable bewilderment in official Washington. He did not fit any of the categories which in the past had helped the State Department and CIA to determine whether a given revolutionary movement was a good or a bad thing. He was not an "agent of international Communism." [8] Nor did he fall clearly into that other category—i.e., "fighter for freedom." Some of his stunts, such as seizing American hostages and destroying the property of American companies, had aroused apprehension. But it was undeniable that the regime this courageous man had been fighting was a dictatorial and increasingly repressive one. State Department officials scratched their heads and sought advice from knowledgeable businessmen and newspapermen. The first tended to be against Castro but were somewhat embarrassed to plead for the disreputable Batista. Newspapermen were more sympathetic: Castro and his handful of followers holed up in the mountains made good copy, and he had a flair for publicity. That a small group of revolutionaries should, while fighting the local tyrant, be somewhat impudent toward the great North American giant made them at least intriguing and was testimony to their fervent independence. Thus when Batista—universally loathed and abandoned even by his army—fled on New Year's day, 1959, Castro reaped the benefits of publicity and a romantic image. Democratic and liberal Cuban politicians, distrustful of each other and confused by Washington's confusion, turned to this man, not yet thirty, and asked him to install democracy and parliamentar-

---

[8] Later on there was much understandable but incorrect speculation that Fidel must have been a Communist, and rather fanciful accounts making him such practically from his high-school days. Yet all available evidence clearly disproves such *post facto* reconstruction.

ianism in Cuba. He did not *seize* power, for at the time of Batista's fall he was still in the mountains with fewer than two thousand armed followers. Power was *offered* to him by diverse social and political groupings.

Castro's subsequent career offers eloquent evidence for his considerable political acumen. It was perhaps not too difficult to fool the well-meaning liberals who expected a liberator and then found themselves saddled with a dictator. But the young leader performed a considerably more difficult task: he used old-line Communists to fasten his rule on the island and liquidate the opposition. But if the Cuban Communists thought that they could have things their own way, they were in for a surprise. Too late did some of the duped veterans run with tearful tales to the Russians. By then Castro's value to the Soviet Union was too great, and old-liners who could not get reconciled to working for him had to go abroad or to jail.

In fact, Castro was an embodiment of what was to become known as the New Left. This Left is in fact hardly new—in some ways it is as old as the tale of Robin Hood, to whom Castro was at first more closely related than to Lenin—but on the international scene it appeared as new. Here was an adventurous brand of radicalism, impatient of elaborate theories and rules, devoted to revolution for the sake of revolution, rather than as a beginning to those stages of social and economic development so tediously prescribed by Marx and Lenin. This existentialist yearning for struggle as giving sense and meaning to life is temperamentally more akin to old-fashioned anarchism and even fascism than to Communism. It was an ex-anarchist and one-time radical socialist, Benito Mussolini, who made the hymn to youth the official anthem of fascism. But in the fifties, fascism was not fashionable or current. Its last extension on the American continent, Perónism, had collapsed the year before Castro raised the banner of revolt in the Sierra Maestra mountains.

Until the late 1950s, the Soviet Union had resolutely rejected the temptation of active involvement in Latin American politics, of exploiting that considerable fund of anti-American feeling which had always existed within Latin America. But Khrushchev was a gambler who, if stakes were high enough, threw prudence to the wind. And Castro needed outside support if the Cuban Revolution was to be a prelude to a greater South American one.

The Soviet-Cuban flirtation, in which Castro was the pursuer as much as if not more than the Russians, gained in momentum during the last months of the Eisenhower administration. With the summit wrecked, the Soviets had no reason to remain coy about this relationship; a few days after the U-2 incident, they opened formal diplomatic relations with Castro. Then Khrushchev, in one of his outbursts, threatened the United States with his famous missiles should the Pentagon dare to attack the brave Cuban people. This threat had to be watered down; there were officials in Moscow still not convinced that the U.S.S.R. should commit itself on behalf of the Cuban adventurer. The threat was explained as being "symbolic" rather than literal. But missiles/Cuba . . . it was an interesting association of ideas.

The historic embrace at the Hotel Theresa in Harlem between the *Lider Maximo* of the Cuban Revolution and the First Secretary of the Communist Party of the U.S.S.R. sealed what each hoped to be a profitable bargain. Castro hoped for Soviet protection against a now very probable American move against him and the still-possible move by Cuban Communists to make him into the Kerensky rather than the Lenin of the Cuban Revolution. Khrushchev believed he was acquiring another counter in that game he was playing for such high stakes.

The United States' attitude toward Castro in power developed ponderously and slowly. With the death of John Foster Dulles, the Eisenhower administration lost the one man who probably would have urged a quick "Guatemalan" solution for Cuba—rather than the warnings, then threats, then suspension of the sugar quota, etc. By 1960, when it was realized that Castro would not hold democratic elections and that he was first discreetly, then openly flirting with the Russians and even Peking, other preoccupations weighed on American minds: the abortive summit, fears over Berlin, worries over Africa, and finally the electoral campaign. It was during the latter that Senator Kennedy taxed the Republicans with doing nothing about the Caribbean dictator, whose regime was a source of subversion threatening the whole hemisphere.

Not long afterward, President-elect Kennedy was told that the departing administration *was* doing *something:* that the CIA had secretly been training in Guatemala a group of Cuban refugees for armed operations against Castro. It was a *secret American style,* i.e., any assiduous reader of the American press could have discovered the fact by the time Eisenhower left office and Kennedy entered upon it.

The new administration began in an air of considerable self-congratulation and somewhat pitying disrespect for the departing Republican businessmen and politicians. It thought of itself and was very much regarded by the mass media, on whom the homely virtue of the

Eisenhower administration had palled, as embodying Youth, Brains, and Elegance. Years later, with so many hopes dashed and the nation so beset by a crisis of faith, a moralist could look back at this self-congratulation and discern in it that Pride which seldom remains unpunished by history. Yet discarding such retrospective moralizing, one can recognize in the initial Kennedy attitude toward international affairs some of the seeds of the troubles still with us today.

There was first of all the New Frontiersmen's assumption that the outside world would view them as they viewed themselves. The Eisenhower-Dulles team had been stodgy, unimaginative, and illiberal; now the world and especially the Russians would be bound to recognize that they were dealing with people who on the one hand did not want to "make the world safe for capitalism" and did not object on principle to revolution, yet who on the other hand were tough and alert to tricks and even capable of trickery themselves. The Soviets, however, felt exactly the opposite. They have always preferred to deal with capitalists who run true to the type, which, if one reflects on the *real* character of the Soviet rulers, should not be surprising. Khrushchev, it is clear, resented this young, debonair millionaire; a man of his background and age was bound to feel more comfortable with men who had been boys when he had been a boy and who had come up the hard way. In the drama of the next few years, when Khrushchev would take risks and indulge in insults surpassing even his previous standards, this personal factor would be of some importance.

That the Russians respect strength in international relations is one of the more correct clichés. But more important than that, they appreciate steady nerves and determination, as against spasmodically brilliant but anxiety-ridden policies. Even the circumstances of the setting up of the Kennedy administration must have suggested that at least for awhile there would be no single firm hand directing American foreign relations, no one man whom the young President would rely for advice and coordination, in the way that Truman had leaned on Acheson and Eisenhower on Dulles. In fact, Kennedy named an Under-Secretary and Assistant Secretary of State prior to designating Dean Rusk to head the State Department. The position, or more properly speaking the person who assumed the position of Special Assistant to the President for National Security Affairs now took on a much greater importance. It is not too much to say that the leadership of American foreign policy was put in commission with the Secretary of State as only one, at times far from the most important one, of the advisers to the

President. Napoleon had said that in war it is often *man* rather than *men* who is of decisive importance; the same probably holds true of foreign policies in this age. The President, despite his great intelligence and grasp of the complexities of the world situation, lacked that element of self-assurance and outward confidence which had enabled F.D.R. to be his own secretary of state. His readiness on any crucial issue to defer to the opinions of a number of brilliant and argumentative men was only too human, but the impression the outside world might often get would be one of indecisiveness, a dangerous impression to give the Russians at the time and in view of the character of the man directing their policies.

The great concern of the Americans that the world should think of them as they liked to think of themselves—liberal, friendly to progress, not opposed to revolutions, in fact approving them in view of their background—was probably felt more strongly by the men who surrounded the new President than by any previous administration. For all the advice forthcoming from the Russian experts of the State Department, many of the liberal intellectuals and politicians of the New Frontier felt that if the Russians would only realize that they were no longer dealing with capitalist ogres but with forward-looking men not averse to change, things would go much easier. The President was bound to be popular in the Third World, where his youth and charm and the record of anticolonial utterances assured him of warm feelings. But his advisers were too ready to translate this personal popularity into political assets. Eisenhower convinced himself that the great popular acclaim he received on his foreign travels was of great political significance, and indeed that one reason for Khrushchev's wrecking the summit was his fear that a visit by the President of the United States to Russia might have incalculable consequences for the *Soviet regime*. So now the new administration tended to exaggerate the effects of the personal rapport the President could establish with such potentates as Ben Bella or Sukarno, of foreign guests being treated to Mozart musicales rather than Fred Waring and his Pennsylvanians, of a better cuisine and more scintillating conversation. All such touches were not without a certain effect, but were in themselves incapable of arresting Algeria's growing drift toward the Communist bloc, or the Indonesian President's conviction that Moscow and then Peking could offer him more.

As against the great, some might say excessive, concern to make a good impression on new states, old friends were being taken somewhat for granted by Washington. It was characteristic that the President requested and obtained that a personal friend be appointed British Ambassador to the United States. British subservience in turn did not improve the disposition of General de Gaulle, and Adenauer's regime was viewed by the new team with some private irritation because of its inflexibility about Russia; the new administration planned to be firm about Berlin, etc., but perhaps not that firm.

Khrushchev had generously promised not to do anything terrible while the Americans went about electing their President. But by February 22, Ambassador Llewellyn Thompson was instructed to return to his post. Once in Russia, he set off in pursuit of Khrushchev, who was on a tour of Siberia.[9] On March 9, the Ambassador cornered his quarry in Novosibirsk and handed him an invitation to meet the President in late spring in Vienna or Stockholm. Khrushchev was not to reply and accept until May 12. By then, the Soviet Union had put the first man in outer space, and the Kennedy administration had had its disheartening experience with the Bay of Pigs.

The April 17, 1961, invasion of Cuba by about one thousand five hundred CIA-trained (not very well, at that) Cuban refugees was exceedingly amateurish in conception and preparation. But the important thing is not to distribute blame for this but to assess what it revealed about American policies and Soviet conclusions about them. Concerning the former, we have Arthur Schlesinger's informative and brilliant account.[10] It makes clear that in sponsoring and then, after much hesitation, in giving the go-ahead sign to the venture, the administration was laboring under two contradictory impulses. One was the temptation to show Khrushchev that "we are just as tough as they are"; the other was the fear of failure, of revealing the new administration to be at once ineffective and illiberal: "We are just as bad as they are, only we cannot do those naughty things as well." Hence the impulse was to be both virtuous and sneaky, and to get the whole distasteful business over with as soon as possible, before the crisscrossing memoranda, position papers, and verbal pro and con arguments could drive the President to distraction.

The great psychological handicaps were, then, excessive fear of failure and secrecy. Concerning the first, a realistic view of inter-

[9] What he saw on the domestic trip was unlikely to put him in a better mood than his previous trips to China and the U.S.: he could contemplate the failure of his virgin lands scheme and the continuing mess of Soviet agriculture.
[10] In his *A Thousand Days: John F. Kennedy in the White House* (New York, 1967).

national affairs and of life in general should have argued against this growing sense of inferiority vis-à-vis the Russians. As to secrecy, granted the facts of American political life—i.e., that secrecy of such a venture was impossible anyway—the best course would have been one of openness. There were ample reasons for the United States to recognize a Cuban government-in-exile, acknowledge that it might be planning an overthrow of Castro (just as he was planning the overthrow of, say, the government of Venezuela), and wish it best luck when and if the venture should materialize. Such a course would have still brought upon the President the anathemas of assorted intellectual luminaries, plus *vague* Soviet threats, but it would have been an understandable course, and it would have subjected the Cuban dictatorship to greater stress (even if no invasion took place) than this "let's get it over with" plunge.

For Castro, the Bay of Pigs venture was exactly what the doctor, i.e., Khrushchev, would have ordered. In their discomfiture and guilt feelings, the Americans were less likely to repeat the attempt, which in turn could be and was seized upon by Castro to export to the United States a considerable portion of the population of Cuba. What regime, indeed, would *not* succeed in perpetuating itself in power by executing or imprisoning a relatively few of the malcontents, while permitting upwards of 10 per cent of its population to leave? By any rational standard, this was of course a prodigious waste of manpower and skills. But what remained was the kind of "silent majority" which Castro's vocal, and armed, minority would have little trouble in controlling.

To the Soviets, the Bay of Pigs surely confirmed their initial feelings about the Kennedy administration and offered the temptation to turn the screws tighter. Khrushchev's messages to the President were startlingly insulting, though (as over the Suez affair) he had recourse to the most terrifying threats only after the business had been definitely given up. And then—while recriminations, "inside" revelations, and explanations were tantalizing the American and foreign public— Khrushchev replied that he would be pleased to meet the President whose administration indulged in "aggressive bandit acts." That Kennedy accepted this at such an awkward time was perhaps understandable: even the most steel-nerved democratic leader still would have felt the need of doing something for peace. But his remarks on departing for Vienna indicated a misconception as to what kind of arguments carried weight with the Russians: "I go to see Mr. Khrushchev in Vienna.

I go as the leader of the greatest revolutionary country on earth." [11]

The President's reaction to Khrushchev's behavior in Vienna reminds one of that of the man in a zoo who, after gazing for a long time at a giraffe, finally said, "It's impossible." Khrushchev was at his bullying worst. It is embarrassing to see the degree to which the President let himself be put on the defensive. Kennedy's well-meant efforts to be polite and reasonable only drove the Russian to more violent threats. If Eisenhower had been insensitive in extolling the American way of life to his Soviet guest, then Kennedy erred in the opposite direction by his attempt to placate Khrushchev after being subjected to an ideological tirade (the United States did not object to Marxist governments in Guinea or Mali; if governments ruled in the interests of wealthy minorities, of course they were doomed) and by apparently giving up an all-important bargaining asset ("the United States opposed any military build-up in West Germany which might threaten the Soviet Union").[12] For Khrushchev, of course, the governments of Mali and Guinea were not Marxist, and as for nations ruled "in the interests of wealthy minorities," one must credit Nikita Sergeievich with *some* delicacy in not pointing out to the President that he had just referred to his own country!

Khrushchev's behavior probably surpassed his original plan insofar as bullying Kennedy went. Once again, if there was to be no German peace treaty, the West's rights in Berlin would *have* to go within six months; the Secretary General's office of the U.N. would *have* to be turned over to a *troika*. On the nuclear test ban, the United States would *have* to accept Soviet conditions. And so on. In a speech given on his return to Russia, he was fairly restrained and emphasized that Vienna witnessed both sides conducting what now would be described as a rational dialogue. But one cannot endorse Schlesinger's verdict that "each man came away from Vienna with greater respect for the mind and nerve of his adversary." [13]

Khrushchev must have wondered what had really been gained at Vienna. The Soviet purpose was not to scare the Americans out of their wits, or even out of Berlin, but into a general agreement. And how could one savor this humiliation of the President of the United States if one found oneself at the receiving end of similar treatment, not only from the Chinese but also, of all people, the Albanians?

[11] *Ibid.*, p. 325.
[12] *Ibid.*, pp. 338 and 346.
[13] *Ibid.*, p. 352.

In Washington it was indeed a long, hot summer, as Russian threats continued, while position papers flowed to the President's desk, some "soft," some "hard," but all trying to answer the question which appeared as difficult as squaring the circle: How could the United States hold firm and not provoke a nuclear showdown? Marshal Konev of World War II fame took over command of Soviet forces in Germany. On August 13, the infamous Berlin Wall was erected: the flow of refugees from East Germany, which had cost the puppet regime 3 million of prime manpower and threatened literally to depopulate the country, slowed to a trickle. The West was helpless in the face of this step, which, amazingly, no pundit or position paper had foreseen. Vice-President Johnson and General Clay were dispatched to cheer up the West Berliners, but they could not dispel the Germans' fear and bitterness.

Then came ominous blackmail. Khrushchev had assured the President that the U.S.S.R. would not be the first to resume atmospheric nuclear tests, but he had lied, for the greatest test series yet was now begun at the end of August. Continuing for two months, it culminated in the detonation of the most powerful hydrogen device as yet tested by either power. There was understandable alarm and outrage in Washington, but at the same time, impassioned appeals came from the neutrals and from Prime Minister Macmillan not to resume American nuclear tests. The President, and rightly, decided otherwise. Other decisions were made in response to the crisis: an increase in defense estimates, calling up some American reservists. These steps were met by Soviet reminders that any war in Europe was bound to be a nuclear one. The President, weighing his agonizing alternatives, preserved outward composure, but, his chroniclers tell us, vented his frustration on the State Department. There were people who could have told Kennedy how to deal with Khrushchev and what to make of his threats, but, alas, Washington was not on speaking terms with Peking or Tirana.

One may speculate that one step undertaken by the administration did have a significant effect. This was the widespread effort to encourage the construction of fall-out shelters. It turned out to be a flop: a few individuals became so impressed by the danger that they took off for the antipodes; some divines and lawyers addressed themselves to such questions as to whether a fortunate owner of the shelter had the right to deny strangers access to it, if need be with a gun; while John Kenneth Galbraith lent the weight of his authority to the view that private shelters were undemocratic, the Congress rather sensibly refused to sanction a great outlay for public ones. But in Moscow, the furore probably led to sobering reflections: Were the Americans really thinking that it might come to that . . . ? Ambassador Menshikov, who had been following Khrushchevian tactics in Washington, assuring his American acquaintances that in fact the treaty with East Germany had already been signed and that of course the United States would not fight over Berlin, was soon recalled.

The 22nd Congress of the Communist Party of the U.S.S.R., which assembled on October 17, 1961, had been awaited by many in the West with dread. But instead of announcing the signing of a treaty with the East Germans, Khrushchev gave the world another reprieve: no need really to have the peace treaty by December 31, now that we have the Berlin Wall, he said. But after that! The Soviet Union would not wait indefinitely for a final regulation of the German question. He dwelt, but without the previous emphasis, on the need of atom-free zones in Central Europe and the Far East. But the U.S.S.R. did not want to frighten anybody: people should not draw wrong conclusions from the recent nuclear tests at which the Soviets had just exploded a huge bomb. They could have, said the leader, popped off one of a hundred megatons, but then it might have rattled windows in Moscow.

To compare this Congress to a three-ring circus would be to understate its effect. For once this usually incredibly dull conclave with endless speeches, all on the same pattern, interspersed with masses of statistics, with humorless and ritualistic self-congratulatory phrases—breathed with animation and drama. The main official theme was announced in the document proclaiming that by 1980 the U.S.S.R. would enter the phase of communism. Apart from production statistics, there were few concrete details of what this blissful state would mean, beyond the promise that public transportation would be free and that sports would no longer be run by the state committee but by the spontaneous initiative of the masses. Pardonably no one at home or abroad could concentrate on such rather distant perspectives, reassuring though they might be, against the implication of the recent nuclear tests. For the world was treated to a tantalizing revelation of the Sino-Soviet split. Khrushchev, violently attacking the Albanian party leadership, accused it of Stalinism and of inhuman atrocities against the pro-Soviet faction. This in turn was condemned by Chou En-lai as an unheard-of deviation from the norms of Marxist-Leninist behavior. Having delivered this reprimand, the Chinese Premier then ostentatiously deposited a wreath on Stalin's tomb and departed for Peking before the Congress ended.

The delegates were subsequently treated to a renewed and even more violent denunciation of Albania.

The Russian party's attack on Stalin and Stalinism, and upon Stalin's old cronies defeated in 1957, surpassed in violence and detail anything previously heard in public. The dead despot was no longer pictured as a man who had erred during his last years, but as a veritable criminal from the very beginning of his leadership of the state and party. His closest collaborators, Molotov and Kaganovich, were not mere intriguers but men with countless victims' blood on their hands. While the Congress sat, Stalin's mummy was removed from the Mausoleum and reburied in the Kremlin Wall. The political history of the Soviet Union before Stalin's death was retold, in much more detail and more vividly than in Khrushchev's secret speech of 1956, as a somber and frightful chronicle of crime. The destinies of a great nation, it was revealed, had been decided by intrigue and deception within a small elite.

In a way, this drama was intended to strengthen Khrushchev's hold on the Party, which we can now recognize was not so firm as the outside world had been led to believe; and, again we can see it now but could not clearly do so in 1961, the effort was not entirely successful. But to a large extent the Congress reflected the terrible frustrations under which Soviet policy was then laboring. The split with China was widening and was now public knowledge. Albania, prompted by Peking, tossed the Soviet diplomatic mission out of the capital and forced the U.S.S.R. to evacuate her naval base in the Adriatic. The attempt to frighten the West into a German peace treaty had stalled. A Western Europe united economically, and equipped with nuclear weapons, hence not easily blackmailed, would exercise an almost irresistible pull on the Communist states of Eastern Europe. The U.S.S.R., with its mounting economic problems, would be caught between a Europe on the move and a hostile China.

Virtually overlooked in the drama and hubbub was the speech of Gromyko, which contained, to be sure among less complimentary remarks, the most cordial references to the United States to be uttered by a high Soviet official almost since World War II. One was led to believe that the Vienna meeting had been a feast of amity surpassing any encounter since the Stalin-Roosevelt conference. He was happy, said the usually deadpan Foreign Minister,[14] to have been at that historical meeting. Everybody, including the American man in the

[14] During one of his more relaxed moments in Vienna, Khrushchev asked Kennedy if Gromyko did not remind him of Nixon.

street, would tell you, perorated Gromyko, that peace would be inviolable if only those two great leaders reached an agreement.

To the weary analysts of the State Department, Gromyko's honeyed words could bring little comfort, contrasted as they were with the threats lurking in Khrushchev's speech and quite explicitly stated by Marshal Malinovsky, who boasted of the quality of Soviet *long-range* missiles. To the Western experts, Gromyko's speech was yet another of those Soviet performances which would, upon American requests for elucidation, turn to ashes. Was there, then, no more in that virtual plea for alliance with the United States? One wonders. Was it dismissed readily in Peking? Unlikely.

In 1962, the Soviet government decided to bring to fruition the plan which had been with Khrushchev and his advisors ever since the original Berlin ultimatum of November, 1958, if not before, of seeking to force the United States to sign a German peace treaty renouncing for West Germany the right to own or manufacture nuclear weapons and to prevail upon China to forgo her own nuclear ambitions. The general outline of the plan must be gathered from circumstantial but very strong evidence; its exact details may never become known until and unless Moscow and/or Peking choose to tell the story,[15] which the Chinese *almost* did in 1963, when they released their part of the correspondence between the Russian and Chinese Central Committees.

Between 1958 and 1960, Khrushchev attempted to reach an understanding with the United States on Germany, hopeful that with a successful German peace treaty achieved through playing the Berlin card, he could then pressure China into joining a general agreement on nuclear nonproliferation (atom-free zones in the Pacific and Central Europe) and on a test-ban treaty. By 1960, this two-phase plan lay in apparent ruins. But in 1962, Moscow saw new opportunities on the horizon. It now appeared that what had been planned as a two-phase plan could be settled through one bold operation.

The conflict with China was now in the open and, as witnessed above, quite acute. Yet at the same time there were some signs that faced by

[15] The version presented here follows in general the theory presented in my *Expansion and Coexistence: The History of Soviet Foreign Policy 1917–67* (New York, 1968), particularly pp. 661–77. Most of the reviewers, while favorable to the general thesis of the book, expressed reservations as to my interpretation of the Cuban missile crisis. Yet as of today no alternative theory has been presented explaining Soviet motives in initiating the Cuban gamble, the apparently sudden and bizarre character of Soviet moves on Cuba, and the vehemence of the Chinese reactions.

a *fait accompli* and offered some inducement, the Chinese might be forced into an accommodation. In 1961, the Russians were to tell us in 1968, and Chinese accounts seem to corroborate this view, strong opposition to Mao's policies developed in the highest party circles, and the Liu Shao-chi faction, while not in any sense pro-Soviet, challenged and for a while succeeded in curbing Mao's power and in arresting the drift toward a complete break with Moscow. This was not unconnected with the great economic distress China was undergoing in 1960–62 as the fatal consequences of the Great Leap Forward made themselves felt.[16] There was a modest *détente* in Sino-Soviet relations, signaled by a commercial treaty and a less acrimonious tone in the press polemics. Thus there was some ground for hope that the Chinese might yet be persuaded to defer their costly atomic ambitions.

The Berlin issue was stalled, but the Soviets were pursuing in a more amicable spirit two other lines of negotiations with the West. One was over Laos, where the Americans and Russians had agreed to something in the nature of neutralization, with a triumvirate of princes—one neutral, one pro-Communist, one representing the "forces of freedom" —sharing in the government and a figurehead king presiding over the bizarre structure. And the disarmament discussions were evolving, as the West believed, in a fairly hopeful fashion. The Russians on occasion appeared close to an agreement on a test-ban treaty, but then discord over technical details would lead to delays.

In retrospect it is clear that the Soviets were waiting for a *political* breakthrough, so that any disarmament agreement was to be part of a package deal with the West, or with the United States. But from Washington's or London's perspective, each issue—disarmament, Berlin, Laos—was separate and unto itself. It was perceived that the Soviets were unhappy about the possibility of the West Germans disposing of nuclear weapons, suspected that they would not be overjoyed about the Chinese getting them, but somehow this was not being related to other aspects and moves of Soviet foreign policy. At times the American view of Soviet goals had been hugely oversimplified: viz., Dulles' belief that the Soviets were out, by force or deceit, to seize and communize

[16] The year 1962 brought new alarms about a possible invasion from Taiwan. Refugees poured over into Hong Kong. The extent of the actual distress was only faintly realized in the West, but it would not be surprising if it had been on the scale of the troubles the Soviet Union had suffered on account of collectivization in the early 1930s. This might be decried as exaggerated, but how many in the West were aware of the cruel trials the U.S.S.R. underwent then? And Russia in the 1930s was considerably less isolated from the outside world than the China of the 1960s.

anything they could get their hands on. But this oversimplification was preferable as a working hypothesis to the apparent conclusion of the Kennedy administration that there was little connection between various strands of Soviet foreign policy.

As 1962 progressed, it became clear that another crisis was forthcoming over Berlin. Khrushchev was reverting to threats of a separate peace treaty; the winter of 1961–62 had witnessed petty annoyances and interference with American access rights. Had the Russians been out for a prestige victory over Berlin, it is possible they could have gotten *something* in the way of an agreement diluting the Western rights. The Kennedy administration was amenable, to Bonn's dismay, to negotiations along this line, even some concessions on recognition of East Germany. But the Soviets were not out for prestige victories; they had no patience or time for long-range solutions, and they were not after Berlin in itself. And to try to get something big out of the West through Berlin still risked a nuclear showdown. While the Kennedy administration was still apprehensive, still had not recovered its balance after the Cuban fiasco and Vienna, it looked unlikely that it could be pressured to fall in with a Soviet master plan on Berlin. Better intelligence, drawn from such sources as the soon-to-be-unmasked spy Penkovsky, finally convinced the American government that the United States was incomparably stronger in nuclear weapons and means of delivery than the Russians. Deputy Secretary of Defense Roswell Gilpatric had made this public and explicit in a speech of October 21, 1961, in which he expressed confidence in the American power to withstand Communist blackmail and deter attack, for "we have a second-strike capability which is at least as extensive as what the Soviets can deliver by striking first." [17] It is clear that Kennedy and others did not feel all *that* confident—Khrushchev had impressed them, possibly as he had intended, as a man who would not be deterred by sheer arithmetic—but to the Soviets, Gilpatric's speech was probably one indication of many that they needed something more than Berlin. Careful weighing of the evidence leads to the conclusion that by keeping up the harassment of Berlin, the Soviet Union in 1962 could have gotten from Washington a pledge against nuclear arms for West Germany and some sort of international authority for control of access to Berlin from the West, which in due time would have enabled them to interfere with Western presence in the city even more effectively. In 1959 or 1960, Khrushchev would have considered such concessions a

[17] Elie Abel, *The Missile Crisis* (New York, 1966), p. 39.

significant step forward in his over-all plan. But in 1962 he was in a much greater hurry, and the Americans, he estimated, could be more intimidated. And it was high time Castro started earning his keep.

Khrushchev's new plan began to unfold in July, 1962, when Raul Castro visited Moscow. The evidence seems to suggest that it was at this time that the Cuban Minister of Defense was told that the Soviet Union would like to establish missile installations in Cuba, under Soviet control and with the Cuban population removed from the vicinity of the bases. That the Cubans *requested* these missiles, as Khrushchev asserted later on, is obviously a clumsy lie.[18] In fact, it is almost certain that Castro's government was not even told what kind of missiles were being installed, and completely certain that they were not told why. The very fact that the Cubans throughout the summer talked about the missiles, that Che Guevara went to Moscow at the end of August, just when the Russians were desperately trying to draw attention away from Cuba, is strong presumptive evidence that they were entirely in the dark as to the Soviet game. For *themselves,* the Cubans got some obsolete Ilyushin bombers, probably the original reason for Raul Castro's trip.

The time sequence now becomes of great importance. Common sense dictated that before long-range missile sites were established, the Soviets should construct a network of anti-aircraft missiles (surface-to-air, or SAM) to discourage prying American planes and establish a camouflage. This is what the Soviets did until the first days in September when, forsaking caution, they began with feverish haste to erect the actual long-range missile sites and emplace missiles. When completed, by a normal schedule sometime in November, there would have been twenty-four launching pads for medium-range missiles (500–1,000 miles) and sixteen for intermediate ones (1,000–2,000 miles), enabling the emplacement of sixty-four nuclear missiles able to reach a large part of the United States.

What accounts for this incautious hurry? Here the Chinese help to provide the answer. Their indiscreet revelations of 1963 tell us that on August 25, 1962, the Soviet government notified Peking that at the initiative of Secretary of State Rusk the Soviets had agreed with the United States on a nuclear nonproliferation agreement that would not only prohibit nuclear powers from transferring atomic weapons and information to third states, but that would also require that "the coun-

---

[18] Castro was later on to vary the story as to who initiated the missile business, stating at one time it was the Russians, then the Cubans, then the two jointly.

tries not in possession of nuclear weapons should undertake to refrain from manufacturing them" or seeking them from the nuclear
powers.[19] This would have meant in effect that the membership in
the atomic club would be closed and that China and West Germany
would never be allowed to join it. The Chinese (again in their own
version) replied to the Soviet Union on September 3 and October
20, stating that they would never let the Soviet government pledge nuclear "abstinence" on behalf of China and should the Soviets persevere
in their bargain with the United States, Peking would publicly denounce them and repudiate any Soviet infringement of China's sovereign
rights.

Here then is the clue. The Soviets wanted to force not only the
United States to agree on a German peace treaty with absolute prohibition of nuclear weapons for Bonn, but also China. Now how would
Soviet nuclear weapons trained on the United States force Peking?
Here we can only speculate. It is possible that Khrushchev intended
to demand as a condition for removing the nuclear missiles in Cuba
that the United States remove its protection of Formosa. He might
have been planning to repudiate the Chinese if they did not go along
with a nuclear treaty—he possibly had grounds to believe that for
all their protestations the Chinese would be forced to agree when
confronted by the dazzling Cuban operation, by a U.N. resolution
endorsing the alleged U.S.–U.S.S.R. agreement about nonproliferation,
by a threat of joint American and Soviet action against any violator
of this momentous undertaking.

In any case, the Chinese protest of September 3 did not affect
Soviet confidence about carrying out the coup. Khrushchev intimated
in early September that he would personally appear at the United
Nations General Assembly session in late fall, when disarmament was
going to be a main topic. The Soviets must have made another secret
remonstration with Peking, since the Chinese reiterated their stand on
October 20.

That there had been a Rusk proposal as described by the Russians
to the Chinese was, of course, to put it mildly, a lie. Secretary Rusk
and Gromyko were, it is true, in Geneva in July to initial the final
agreement on Laos, and they also talked about disarmament. Yet, as
of early September, the Soviets and the West were still far apart on
the subject of a test-ban agreement. If there had been a nonproliferation
agreement in the offing, the administration in Washington would not

19 William E. Griffith, *The Sino-Soviet Rift* (Cambridge, Mass., 1964), p. 351.

330 : LOST OPPORTUNITIES

have behaved as it did. It was one of those "What are they going to do about Berlin?" summers, with the President obtaining Congressional authorization to call up reservists in the hope of impressing the Russians with American determination. It was impossible to imagine that the United States and U.S.S.R. had just concluded a virtual alliance to keep China from becoming a nuclear power.

Another worry supplemented the concern over Berlin: the Russians were up to something in Cuba. In July and August, American intelligence sources detected the Soviet ships bringing in "transportation, electronic and construction equipment." [20] In the face of now widespread rumors and further intelligence reports, the President on September 4 acknowledged that the Russians were setting up anti-aircraft missiles and radar equipment on the island and that a few thousand Soviet military technicians were in Cuba. But, he stressed, no offensive missiles had been installed nor were there indications that they would be. Any Soviet attempt to introduce ground-to-ground missiles would carry the gravest consequences, he emphasized.

In trying to deceive the Americans, the Soviets were direct, crude, and frantic. The very day of the President's statement, Attorney General Robert Kennedy received personal reassurances from Soviet Ambassador Dobrynin. Dobrynin also told Robert Kennedy that Khrushchev was personally fond of the President and would not try to embarrass him in any way before the Congressional elections. Two days later, the same reassurances were carried by the Ambassador to Theodore Sorensen, the President's assistant. After the elections, however, the message continued, the question of a German peace treaty and Berlin must be finally solved. The Chairman proposed to come to the United States in November to appear at the U.N.

This approach was, one should think, rather unsubtle. So was the less formal way of communicating to the Americans Khrushchev's touching solicitude that the President should devote himself to the Congressional campaign with a calm mind: a Soviet official who made friends with people in the President's entourage kept repeating that he had it from Khrushchev and Mikoyan themselves that they did not have the remotest intention of placing offensive missiles in Cuba. The Americans were taken in. Various charges by Republicans—and it has never been established how much they reflected campaign oratory and how much genuine information—that Cuba was being turned into a missile base were indignantly denied by administration

[20] Abel, *op. cit.,* p. 17.

spokesmen as late as October 14. Only one high official, the CIA director John McCone, remained suspicious: If the Russians had nothing to hide, why were they installing SAMs to discourage American snooping?

The expert opinion which fortified the President and most of his administration in their denials had clear logic behind it. The Russians had *never* entrusted any of their satellites with nuclear weapons. More than that, they had never placed such weapons and means of delivery in any other country. If they would not take any chances with a docile satellite like Bulgaria, let alone Poland or Hungary, would they place them at the disposal or within the reach of Castro? No Soviet expert, no intelligence officer could have given an affirmative answer to this question. And to affirm that they were putting them into Cuba only to pull them out after they had worked their blackmailing purpose seemed absurdly improbable. Less reasonable was the conviction that the Soviets could not possibly believe they could "get away" with it. There was finally the all-too-human wish to believe in what one prayed for: that the Soviets would not present America with that frightful choice between a nuclear war or acquiescence in having nuclear weapons in Cuba targeted on the United States.

On the Soviet side, the gamble was stupendous. It is no exaggeration to say that international politics had never seen anything like it. In the minds of Khrushchev and his associates (it is unlikely that more than a handful of the Presidium and a few of the highest military officials were in on the plan as a whole) everything depended on speed and secrecy. Sometime in late November, Khrushchev would step up to the rostrum of the U.N. and confront the startled world with the news. The shock of the news would be almost immediately followed by relief, for the Soviet Union would propose a far-reaching settlement of the outstanding world problems, a vast diminution of the danger of a nuclear conflict which had hung over the world since 1949. The U.S.S.R. would pull out the deadly weapons in exchange for the United States agreeing on a peace treaty with Germany and on atom-free zones in Central Europe and the Pacific; other countries would pledge nuclear abstinence. The Americans' bitterness at having been deceived would be assuaged by the knowledge that the Chinese acquisition of nuclear weapons could be postponed indefinitely. The Chinese rancor could be overcome by demonstrating that it was not through secret collusion with the United States but by a boldly aggressive policy that Russia was exacting this settlement.

Such probably is the scenario planned in the Kremlin. As against this admittedly conjectural reconstruction, what other theory can account for the vast risk involved in the Soviet actions? Writing in 1969, former Prime Minister Macmillan still could ask: "Why did the Russians risk so much? What was their ultimate purpose?" [21] The standard answer has been that the Russians were motivated by the wish at least partly to redress their inferiority in nuclear delivery means vis-à-vis the United States. But one does not risk an immediate nuclear war just to ensure that your opponent will be only twice as strong rather than four times. To protect Cuba? This is laughable. Even the Chinese Communists, not known for their charitable explanations of U.S. intentions, were to tell Khrushchev in 1963 that there had been absolutely no danger of a U.S. invasion of Cuba until he put in his missiles. That the missiles were to be used for bargaining was the view urged after their discovery by Ambassador Llewellyn Thompson, who participated in the "Executive Committee" devising America's counter-strategy: the Soviets would pull them out in exchange for West Berlin. But the magnitude of the risk involved clearly indicates that much, much more must have been at stake. If the objective of the blackmail had been just Berlin, and if the Soviets had succeeded, what next? Common sense would argue that the most probable consequence would be a vast increase in American armaments of all kinds, and the Kennedy administration, utterly discredited before its own people, would be unable to negotiate with the U.S.S.R. again. Chances for a nuclear war would have been vastly increased.

Even by Soviet standards the secrecy surrounding the Cuban gambit was extraordinary. Of course, the Chinese were told nothing; they would hardly have launched military operations against India in October if they had known that a crisis of such vast proportions and incalculable consequences was in the offing. But it is significant that even those on whom the Soviet Union usually counts to keep their mouths shut, the governments of the East European Communist states, had not been told that there soon would be some momentous developments. It was an embarassing sequel to the crisis as it actually developed when they descended on Moscow, eschewing any secrecy about their coming, obviously to demand an explanation from Khrushchev himself of what he had been up to and why they had not been told. As for the Cubans, they kept talking about some new weapons *they* now had (President

---

[21] In his Introduction to Robert F. Kennedy's *Thirteen Days* (New York, 1969), p. 19.

Dorticos at the U.N. in early October), about a fishing port the Soviets
would build for them (Castro)—the best proof that they all were in the
dark. But their boasts led Khrushchev to lie in person. On October 16
he told Ambassador Foy Kohler that he was furious at Castro for his
indiscretions, that President Kennedy could concentrate on the elections
and forget about Cuba, for "Soviet purposes in Cuba," he said, "were
wholly defensive." [22] By his own lights, Khrushchev was telling the
truth. But also true was the subsequent statement from Peking that
without consulting anybody, the Soviet leadership had embarked on a
reckless course which risked the lives of millions upon millions of
people.

The risk, of course, was there, for the tangled web woven by
Khrushchev completely disregarded one possible contingency: that upon
a premature discovery of the missile sites, the United States would
forthwith bomb Cuba or the U.S.S.R. Here was a striking contrast
with what Soviet propaganda had shouted for years—about how "madmen" ruled the U.S., waiting for the slightest pretext to unleash a
nuclear holocaust. The Soviets could even have had an inkling that the
Americans had spotted the missiles, when the President lectured Gromyko on October 18 on the impermissibility of nuclear weapons in
Cuba. The visiting Soviet Foreign Minister raised obliquely the threat
of war: after the elections, the German-Berlin question had to be
resolved; nothing could change Soviet determination to have it resolved;
this was 1962—in view of modern weapons, who would be impressed
by 150,000 additional men under arms?

The anatomy of American decision-making, of the deliberations that
led to the President's announcement on October 22 which revealed the
Soviet deception and announced the blockade-"quarantine" of Cuba—
all this has been exhaustively discussed in several books, including one
by a man who played a crucial part in the final decision, Robert F.
Kennedy. To the Soviet leaders, who have undoubtedly read these
accounts, they must have suggested something they evidently had forgotten since 1950 and Korea: the incalculable nature of the American
response to an outright provocation. While in the small group advising
the President there were at first some voices advocating simple diplomatic steps—Secretary McNamara professing to see no difference between Soviet missiles in Cuba and those in the U.S.S.R.—the group
soon realized the inevitability of a forceful action on the part of the
United States. As in the case of Korea, one is struck by a certain almost

[22] Roger Hilsman, *To Move a Nation* (New York, 1967), p. 166.

mechanical nature in this kind of response: To previous unwillingness and hesitation to incur *small* risks succeeds a partly fatalistic, partly rational determination to risk *all* because the limits of endurance have been reached and transgressed. Thus, an earlier disposition to do nothing (or to protest to the U.N., which would have amounted pretty much to the same thing) gave way to a fairly general feeling in favor of drastic action: an air strike against the missile sites, probably followed by an invasion. It was Robert Kennedy's intervention which swung the opinion in favor of blockade. It is not ungracious to suggest that his deeply and genuinely felt revulsion against an action reminiscent of the Japanese attack on Pearl Harbor gave the others an easy way of supporting his position: the U.S. would not take *the* most drastic steps, not because they were afraid of consequences but because it was not in accordance with the American way of doing things.

The Soviets' first reactions to the President's announcement of the blockade indicate that they still had some hope they could brazen it out. Khrushchev's first message was moderately defiant: there was a *public* announcement of an alert for Soviet rocket, air, and submarine forces, thus advertising to the Americans that the U.S.S.R. would not bow to a bluff. In the meantime, while feverish efforts continued in Cuba to make the missile sites operational, Khrushchev and his colleagues ostentatiously went to the opera and congratulated the singers on their performances. The Americans could not frighten them with the blockade: if need be, the ships could be turned around, but the rockets would be set up; then we will talk!

What shook the Russians from their composure was evidently the receipt of news, one assumes through their intelligence sources, that, not content with a blockade, the Americans were readying an air strike, to be followed by an invasion. This, *unlike the blockade,* changed the situation drastically. The Soviet preoccupation was now to save face, for they *had* to give in: there was no time to drag the thing out, to interfere, perhaps, with access to Berlin, to arrange for a meeting between Kennedy and Khrushchev. Hence the two messages by Khrushchev on the twenty-sixth, the first in effect proposing removal of the offensive weapons in return for the President's pledge not to invade Cuba. Then somebody must have brought to Moscow's attention Walter Lippmann's somber column arguing that in order to avoid an unspeakable holocaust, American Jupiter missiles sited in Cuba be bartered for the Soviet ones in Cuba. The second message created considerable depression in Washington as indicating the hardening of the

Soviet line, but this merely was Khrushchev trying to pick up another dime, so to speak.[23] Far from indicating that the Russians were stiffening up or that somebody had overruled Khrushchev, the second message was further evidence that they were ready to cave in. Anyway, Khrushchev accepted the bargain sketched out in his letter of the twenty-sixth. The Soviet missiles came out, the United States did not invade Cuba. And after some theatrics by Castro, even those obsolete bombers which were to be his own were evacuated.

American accounts of the crisis omit—perhaps rightly so, for too much has already been revealed—any discussion of two tantalizing questions. The first: What would the U.S. have done, had the Soviet Union, as almost everybody expected, chosen to blockade Berlin? One suspects that a graduated response was planned: an attempt to run a convoy through and, if this met with force, then the use of conventional and ultimately nuclear weapons. And the other: Though admittedly there were guided missiles in Cuba (aerial photography identified sheds for nuclear warheads for them), did the Russians at any time actually have nuclear warheads on the island? One suspects the answer is "no."

Yet for all this added touch of irony, one cannot maintain that the danger of an atom war was negligible. In a situation of this kind there is no absolute guarantee against things getting out of hand: a U-2 plane was shot down over Cuba and another spy plane had wandered over Soviet territory on one of those nerve-wracking days. Another accident, say of one of the Soviet submarines prowling in the Caribbean, might have set in motion an incalculable train of events.

With the crisis over, the administration, it is fair to say, collapsed in relief. This is very understandable, and it was prudent for Kennedy to order that there be no public gloating over the Russians' discomfiture. But one feels that Washington went too far in this chivalrous regard for Soviet feelings. Not that the President should have sought to "get even" for Khrushchev's intolerable bullying and boasting over the Bay of Pigs, over Suez, and over many other occasions, or for his obvious assumption that Americans were at once less intelligent and more prone to intimidation than Yugoslavs or Albanians. But this touching regard for Khrushchev's sensitivity overlooked the possibility that this was the time to wrest some solid concessions from the Russians.

[23] If the Russians were really seriously worried about the missiles in Turkey, then it is at the least remarkable that they had not been mentioned in any previous Soviet message to the President during the crisis. This detail is in fact an eloquent testimony as to how little the Soviets were worried about the possibility of an unprovoked nuclear attack by the United States.

Khrushchev had condescended to meet Kennedy after *his* Cuban fiasco. Was this not a good time for the President to propose a meeting? Khrushchev would not have been able to decline. There was some fear that if the United States pressed too hard, the Chairman might be overthrown and a belligerent or pro-Peking faction take over. But there is no evidence that such factions existed except in the imagination of some Kremlinologists. The Soviets seldom change their leaders in the midst of a foreign crisis, and any shift would have put them at a greater disadvantage vis-à-vis the United States.

Khrushchev cornered probably could not have offered as much as Khrushchev springing a triumphant surprise on the world—another irony of this topsy-turvy world. Certainly the Chinese part of the design was out. The discovery of the missiles and the blockade was merely a second blow to his plan; the first must have been the Chinese note of October 20 reiterating their refusal to let the Soviets speak for them in any discussion of nuclear nonproliferation. If the Soviets had through their Cuban maneuver made the United States abandon its protection of Formosa, then it was barely conceivable that they could have extracted something of Peking. But as of October 28, the Chinese Communists would have more likely followed advice from Chiang Kai-shek than from Moscow, and the Soviet statesman was proclaimed to be an adventurist and a coward. On November 7, the anniversary of the Bolshevik Revolution, not a single prominent Chinese leader attended the reception at the Soviet Embassy.

Still, an immediate summit conference could have produced beneficial bargaining over a wide variety of subjects. If it was excessive to be unduly solicitous of Soviet feelings, then it might have been wise to be understanding and responsive to their real fears, precisely at the moment when the element of blackmail had disappeared. If, in the first flush, the Soviets had to assume the pose of defending Castro, then it is quite likely that in over-all bargaining continued Soviet support for Cuba would become a negotiable item. Has not the aim of American policy for a long time been to negotiate from a position of strength? Here was just such a possibility.

As it turned out, the dividends of the confrontation, while real enough, were meager when measured against the danger that had been incurred. The Soviets let up their pressure for Berlin and a German peace treaty. A test-ban treaty was signed in 1963, but it was only a shred of Khrushchev's original grand design. Formal agreement on nonproliferation was not to come for several years.

One cannot endorse the view that the Cuban crisis marked the end of the Cold War. It signified the end of that acute phase of Soviet pressure and attempted blackmail which began with the November, 1958, note about the German peace treaty and Berlin, but while the subsequent period of rivalry between the United States and the Soviet Union has been easier on our nerves, it has in certain ways been less hopeful of a basic resolution and *détente*. It is certainly not a firm foundation for international stability for the two superpowers to agree to avoid just those situations which might lead to an all-out nuclear war but otherwise to be opposed on practically every issue, to have their policies in sharp conflict all over the globe.

This disappointing sequel to the high hopes raised by the fortunate resolution of the Cuban missile crisis can be traced to several causes. With the most pressing danger over, the governments of both countries were again constrained to concentrate on the management of their alliances rather than on the fundamental problem of reaching at least a partial accommodation between themselves. Theoretically, the bond between the two should have been forged by America's antagonism toward, and the Soviet fear of, China. But—and here is another of those ironic paradoxes—the United States could not exploit the Sino-Soviet conflict largely because of her *own* conflict with China. Thus there was no economic, military, or even diplomatic handle on the Chinese problem which the United States could use to unlock the door to an agreement with Russia, nor was the United States in a position to be of service to Russia in her conflict with China. Unwittingly, however—and this has been the strangest and most ironic paradox of all—the mere fact of America's existence and her nuclear power has protected China against the Soviet Union, at least as much as the U.S.S.R. has protected her against America. But somehow the Chinese are grateful neither to us nor to the Russians.

There were signs that a chastened Khrushchev would have liked a further dialogue with the United States. But we can now see (though at the time one could only speculate) that following the Cuban fiasco considerable restraints were put upon his power. Internal troubles kept piling up: food shortages, the slackening tempo of Soviet economic growth. As after 1956, his power was shaky and his enemies were biding their time; he had recourse to administrative improvisations and reorganizations, oscillating between repressive measures against dissent (rather timid pleas for more freedom in the arts and literature) and measures of tolerance. Favorable references to Stalin alternated with

338 : LOST OPPORTUNITIES

further revelations about and attacks against him. Under these developing conditions, a far-reaching approach to the United States and a definite break with China would mean a double danger: a threat to the ideological cohesion and discipline of the party and society at large and further ammunition for his enemies. Thus *détente* with the United States became less and less likely as time went by. The test-ban agreement and other moves (such as the installation of the famous "hot line" between the Kremlin and the White House) alternated with warnings about the impermissibility of *ideological* coexistence with the West, with typically hostile responses to the American position in crises in the Congo, Cyprus, etc. Cold-war "normalcy" was returning, replacing the intimacy of a shared and overcome danger of nuclear confrontation.

The crescendo of the Sino-Soviet dispute in 1963 further tied Khrushchev's hands. The impudence of the Chinese leaders must have been inspired partly by knowledge of the internal divisions and problems within the Soviet Union. In any case, with some relish the Chinese went into such embarrassing revelations as how the Soviets in 1956 *did* plan to move with their army against Gomulka and nationalist-minded Polish Communists (an impermissible intrusion in the affairs of a fraternal party!), and how they *did* hesitate before sending their troops to subdue Hungary (cowardly faintheartedness in discharging international proletarian obligations!). The Soviets, on their part, while giving back with some spirit could not help imploring the Chinese to cease their indiscretions. This comradely exchange of compliments had barely subsided when, in August, 1964, Mao in a public interview characterized the U.S.S.R. as an imperialist state and claimed for China vast areas of the Asian U.S.S.R. wrested in past centuries from China.

President Kennedy's hopes of a momentous improvement in Soviet-American relations remained unfulfilled. His heartfelt conviction was, as he expressed in a moving speech at the American University on June 10, 1963, that both countries had "a mutually deep interest in a just and genuine peace." [24] It was undoubtedly true of both countries, but was it equally true of both governments? No doubt the Soviet leaders craved peace, but did they want "genuine peace," i.e., peace without tension? How with such peace could they justify their ban on ideological coexistence, how could they hold on to the full rigor of one-party rule? A peace could be the product of a circuitous round of accommodations, of hard bargaining, but not of the Kremlin's sudden conversion to a philosophy utterly different than that which has guided it for more than

[24] Schlesinger, *op. cit.*, p. 823.

forty years. In the *long run,* the logic of both the nuclear weapons and of China's demonstration that the spread of Communism was no longer consistent with the national interest of the Soviet people could be expected to effect a basic reorientation. But there was no warrant for believing that the Cuban missile crisis had been a sort of road to Damascus on which they had found illumination about the folly of the old ways and the necessity for a new creed. The crisis undoubtedly inspired them with respect for the President of the United States. And it is only within the context of respect that the President's great gifts of intelligence, of personal appeal and earnestness, could serve as important assets in continued *détente* with the Soviet Union. All of which compounds the tragedy of November, 1963.

Khrushchev's disappearance from the scene was preceded by what from external evidence looked like some very vigorous sparring within the highest party councils. Every totalitarian leader has at one time or another to fight restraints put upon him by the party hierarchy which surrounds him or resign himself to being overthrown or to being a figurehead. Hitler had his "Night of the Long Knives" in 1934. Stalin had his savage purges. Mao was to employ, during the Cultural Revolution, frenzied youngsters and the army to shatter the party hierarchy, which evidently had come close to walling him in and turning him into a figurehead. Khrushchev in 1956–57 played the card of anti-Stalinism, which mobilized support of the intermediate party bureaucracy against the top oligarchs. In his struggle in 1962–64 he sought recourse to a rather strange device, reminiscent of the early days of the Revolution and of certain predilections for "participatory democracy." The Central Committee (and toward the end even the Presidium and the Council of Ministers), he ordained, was to hold its deliberations not in decorous secrecy but in the presence of hundreds, sometimes thousands, of just plain folks. The latter were supposedly party activists and officials concerned with the issues under discussion, but of course their main function was to inhibit any criticism of the policies sponsored by the First Secretary. The scandalously democratic procedure threatened to undermine the authority and power of the highest party organs as against the First Secretary and his closest collaborators.

The Chinese, with their nose for Soviet intraparty troubles, professed to see sinister implications in Khrushchev's formula of the "state of the whole people," proclaimed some time before. It was, they suggested, a subtle stab at the dictatorship of the proletariat, an unambiguous promise to undermine the authority of the party and to substitute one-man populistic dictatorship.[25] But for all his penchant for improvisations, it is unlikely that Khrushchev at the age of seventy contemplated what his Peking critic was soon to put into effect in *his* seventies: a virtual demolition of the party apparatus and central bodies. The "state of the whole people" was simply one of those cryptic propaganda or public-relations formulas with which politicians in all cultures feel constrained to beguile the people in this age of slogans.

The coup which toppled Khrushchev on October 14, 1964, was, even by Soviet standards, extremely conspiratorial. What evidently decided the issue was the fact that all the members of the Presidium supported the ouster and the Central Committee offered no resistance. The successors were seasoned bureaucrats who had reached their political maturity and received important advancement in the period of Stalin's purges. The problem before them was no longer that which had faced Stalin's heirs more than ten years before. Then, the new leaders had real fears whether the whole bizarre system of repression and bureaucracy could survive with its head and symbol gone. Now, the oligarchy could feel reassured in view of the ease with which Khrushchev, who had tried to curtail their powers and privileges, had been overthrown, and in view of lack of any public reaction to the removal of the man who had after all been *the* national leader for a decade. They set out to undo, cautiously, and step by step, most of the dangerous innovations and reforms of his reign, to repress those modest forms of dissent which had sprung up during Khrushchev's fits of liberalism, and finally to restore Stalin to respectability.

It was outside the Soviet Union that the Brezhnev-Kosygin team faced seemingly insurmountable difficulties. China became a nuclear power and persisted in her hostility, even though the fall of Khrushchev was received with glee in Peking. The challenge to Soviet domination of Communism was growing; even within the usually docile group of East European states, Rumania now asserted her claim to independence in economic matters and in certain aspects of her foreign policy. Prospects for a united Europe, though set back by de Gaulle's feud with Britain, still presented a long-range challenge to the Soviet position on the Continent. In view of the mounting difficulties faced by the U.S.S.R., the United States—its economy thriving, its government's self-assurance in foreign affairs restored after the Cuban crisis—disposed of dazzling diplomatic opportunities.

[25] Of course Mao was to use somewhat similar tactics to get rid of his rivals in the late 1960s.

11

American
Overcommitment
and Its Consequences

The year 1964 was one of portents which might well have suggested to the superstitious that the United States was entering a new and troublesome era. It was the year of the first major urban riot and the first major campus revolt. Less serious but still significant signs of the coming age of turbulence and change could be discovered in such phenomena as the apparent end of the domination of professional baseball by the Yankees and the intrusion of the Beatles on the American scene. All these were diverse portents of the shattering of habits, traditions, and complacencies to which the Americans had grown used for a generation. Yet this still might not have led to, to borrow the term from the Chinese, the cultural revolution we are witnessing today; except for a baffling and frustrating foreign war in which the government of the United States allowed itself to become involved.

Here it is necessary to have some perspective. In retrospect, it is amazing how well American institutions had withstood twenty years of "neither war nor peace," punctuated by one real medium-sized war and one crisis in which a nuclear conflict appeared imminent. But can democratic institutions survive for long in an atmosphere of constant anxiety over foreign dangers, of constant watchfulness over events taking place at far distance but directly bearing on what the American citizen pays in his taxes, on whether he may be required to lay down his life? How does democracy work in deciding what is the desirable level of nuclear armament, whether the interests of the United States are vitally affected by what is happening in Lebanon or the Congo? In all these respects, how can a democratic system compete with one which lives in and thrives upon constant emergency, where decisions on foreign policy and defense are reached without public debate, criticism, or explanation? Merely to ask such questions is to appreciate the achievement as well as the good luck of American democracy in having avoided the tragedy of a Vietnam situation for twenty years. Few in 1945 would have credited a democracy, especially the impatient, untried American democracy, with the ability to adjust to this constant din of international tension with the resilience necessary to avoid the extremes of turning either against the foreign enemy or upon itself. Much has been said in these pages of errors of omission and commission by American policy-makers, of oversimplified notions about world politics which have dominated American public opinion. Yet when all has been said, the over-all record of United States foreign policy during those years is one of prudence, restraint, and generosity. And domestically, the reverberations of the world crisis had not, for all the strains resulting from the Korean war and McCarthyism, obliterated that good-humored tolerance of different views and that non-passionate approach to public affairs which are the real prerequisites of a well-functioning democracy.

What, then, went wrong beginning with 1964? The stresses and strains of the past twenty years were bound to affect the tenor of American life *sometime,* but precisely at this point came a critical turn in the American intervention in Vietnam. The intense phase of American involvement, which may be dated from February, 1965, has been marked by neither a military disaster, which could have become a rallying point for national unity, nor a definite success which could have silenced critics. The Vietnam war has been neither a crusade which engages a nation's emotions nor a police action which involves but a negligible proportion of the country's resources and manpower. Korea had already offered an ample warning of the strain such an in-between war places on the institutions and morale of a democracy.

Much of the literature on Vietnam has been addressed to the problem, "Who was guilty?" Who took the first fatal step? Was it Truman's administration, when it first extended help to the French, then fighting the Indochinese war? Eisenhower and Dulles, who threw American protection around Diem and his regime? Or Kennedy, who significantly increased the number of American military personnel in Vietnam and in whose administration the American commitment to and interference in the affairs of Vietnam became explicit? Or another dimension of the same question: Is the guilt to be attributed to the United States, which through "arrogance of power" has presumed to dictate the way a distant country should be ruled, or is the responsibility to be borne by Hanoi, as the instigator of aggression designed to conquer South Vietnam and beyond it Southeast Asia?

Questions of that character are important for a moralist, sometimes for a historian, and they provide inevitable debating points for a politician. But preoccupation with the question "Who is guilty?" at the expense of "What is to be done?" is not a healthy sign. The logic of democratic institutions requires that political problems, whether domestic or foreign, be addressed in a rational and pragmatic rather than in a moralistic, essentially theological, manner. There are general moral criteria which set the rules of what a democratic state can and must do. But it is also obvious that democratic institutions cannot withstand having every important public issue scrutinized in terms of righteousness and wickedness. The main significance of Vietnam has been that it has exposed the hollowness of the moralistic rhetoric in which American foreign policy has been clothed for more than a generation, the tragedy that instead of importing the necessity of realism it merely turned that rhetoric around.

American interest in the affairs of South Vietnam was based initially not upon any original sin of abuse or arrogance of power but upon the assumption that it was in the interest both of the United States and of the people concerned to help to strengthen those forces which opposed Communism. Much recent discussion about the first phase of America's direct intervention in the affairs of Vietnam has turned on the alleged injustice done to Ho Chi Minh's regime by not holding the elections that, according to the Geneva agreement which ended the Indochinese war, were to be held in 1956 in both halves of the partitioned country. Such elections, the argument goes on, which would have resulted in a victory for Ho, denied him a legitimate way of unifying his country, so that no recourse was left to Hanoi and its sympathizers in the South but a civil war. But how does one run free elections in a Communist-ruled country? Without attributing democratic virtue to Diem and his regime in the South, one may still question the thesis of the vast popularity of the Communists throughout the whole country *at that time*. The partition of Vietnam was followed by a migration of nearly one million people south, while only about one-tenth of that number went in the opposite direction. Social and economic reforms in the North, we know, led to widespread peasant revolts which were ruthlessly suppressed, with the estimated loss of life ranging from between fifty thousand to one hundred thousand people. It is a testimony not so much to his undemocratic propensities as to his political clumsiness, one should think, that Diem did not *insist* on having elections.

Within the context of world politics between 1956 and 1960, Vietnam was a backwater. This reflected two factors: the need of the Communist regime to solidify its grip on the North, and the interest on both China's and the Soviet Union's part in avoiding turbulence in Southeast Asia. Any undue distraction from the intricate design then being woven in Soviet policies was not in Moscow's interest, while the Chinese, as usual violent in speech and prudent in action, were bent upon clarifying their relation with the Soviet Union, or, more precisely, in establishing the full extent of the latter's villainy before encouraging any moves which might bring a renewed confrontation with the United States.

On the American side there was a great temptation to consider it a blessing to have as a protégé in South Vietnam a man who *then* appeared as the embodiment of all the desirable virtues in a leader of a "developing" country. Unlike his predecessor Bao Dai, Diem was a misogynist. Whereas the former had been identified with French rule,[1] Diem had a long-standing record of nationalist and anti-Communist opposition. (He was a staunch Catholic.) No one could question the sincerity of his resolve to stamp out corruption and to eradicate those part-political, part-religious, and part-criminal organizations which had been such a prominent feature of Vietnamese politics. Like many others, Diem had a family and this was to lead to trouble, but at the time this failing was not widely advertised in the American press.[2]

Diem's regime was authoritarian, but again this was predictable in a country with absolutely no experience of representative institutions

[1] This fact had not prevented Ho Chi Minh, evidently less fastidious on this point than some American critics, from seeking at one time Bao Dai's support.
[2] Lest one think that a widespread family entanglement in politics is peculiar to right-wing regimes, one must point out that family ties have evidently played an important role in Communist China. Mme. Mao took a leading part in events surrounding the Cultural Revolution. Also prominent on the political scene have been Mmes. Lin-Piao and Chou En-lai, while the wife of the fallen Liu Shiao-chi has been vigorously denounced. The Soviet press was to discuss those sidelights of Chinese Communist politics with gusto and (especially when it concerned Mao's wife) lack of restraint and chivalry far surpassing the American press's fixation in 1962–63 on Diem's beautiful and ill-fated sister-in-law, Madame Nhu.

confronting another and much more rigorously authoritarian state. He himself was devoid of the kind of popular appeal which would have made him less vulnerable to intrigues of disgruntled subordinates. But in contemplating the careers of such potentates as U-Nu and Sukarno, one must consider how far, in a society which lacks democratic institutions, this gift reflects genuine rapport between the leader and his people and how much skill in public relations (or, if we take the Communist personalities such as Mao or Ho, the strength and all-pervasiveness of party propaganda).

The Vietnam crisis heated up in 1960. Even before, preparations had been laid for a renewal of guerrilla activity in the South and terroristic activities began, mostly in the countryside, directed against the government agents and village officials. In December, the National Liberation Front of South Vietnam was founded. Again, this stepping up of Communist and Communist-inspired activity (the NLF, though far from being entirely Communist in its leadership, evidently contained a core of pro-Hanoi elements) reflected several factors. The North Vietnamese regime felt itself sufficiently firmly established to encourage a challenge to Diem. While Hanoi had undoubtedly the decisive voice in initiating such policies, it is unlikely it would have ventured upon this risky course *against* resolute advice to the contrary by *both* Peking and Moscow. But after May, 1960 (the U-2 episode), the Soviets were not seeking accommodation with the United States and felt that measured pressure upon America and her protégés would better serve their designs. Though they were apt to counsel restraint, the Chinese were probably urging none in initiating an all-out war of national liberation in an area where American protégés were particularly vulnerable.

Soviet policy in the area was, then, nicely balanced between the desire to harass the United States and the desire to avoid a sharp conflict which would jeopardize the scheme Khrushchev hoped to bring off in connection with Germany and Cuba. Thus on Laos, the Soviet Union put in a lot of effort and supplies to frustrate the CIA intrigue to establish an all-out anti-Communist regime, but at the same time did not push the advantage to the point where the United States would intervene massively. What emerged finally was a fragile neutralist regime with pro-Communist forces still occupying part of the area, thus enabling North Vietnam to send men and supplies for guerrilla activities in the South. The Chinese and North Vietnamese might well have

346 : LOST OPPORTUNITIES

wished for a more favorable resolution of the Laotian question, but at that time, the Soviets still had an upper hand in resolving Communist strategies even in Southeast Asia.

The Kennedy administration, having by a very small margin avoided a major and probably unfortunate involvement in Laos, was becoming entangled more and more in the affairs of South Vietnam.

American involvement in Vietnam, as against the kind of economic and technical aid extended until 1960, should have been preceded by a thorough canvassing of the obvious question: Why? What were the American aims in that country? What would justify commitment of American wealth, manpower, and prestige to the defense of South Vietnam rather than to some other country in the area, or somewhere else in the world? Yet, as the reader of Roger Hilsman's excellent discussion of American decision-making is made to realize, these questions were never seriously and thoroughly considered.[3] Various agencies within the government, various policy-makers and officials, were impelled by different motivations, hopes, and fears in advocating a wide range of policies, the sum of which became the tragedy of the Vietnam war. It is only when a bitter national debate began to rage around the nature, morality, and prospects of success of the American involvement that the idea arose that perhaps at one time or another a decision had been made from which flowed the policies of continuous and increasing involvement from 1961 to 1968. The Cuban missile crisis offers one of the few examples in which a democracy reached a foreign-policy decision in such a clear-cut fashion. On Vietnam, an honest answer by an American official as to why the United States did become involved in the manner and to the extent it has would have been that given by a famous British mountain climber when asked why he persisted in trying to reach the summit of Mount Everest: "Because it's there."

Among the various rationalizations and impulses which contributed to the drift of America into the Vietnam war of the mid-sixties, a prominent and perhaps most unfortunate place has been occupied by the moralistic rhetoric which presents America's role in South Vietnam as that of defending democracy—well, freedom, anyway—against the encroachments of an authoritarian system. Thus in the very beginning of his testimony before the Senate Foreign Relations Committee in January, 1966, Secretary Rusk felt constrained to quite President Truman's words of 1947: "I believe it must be the policy of the United States to support free peoples who are resisting attempted subjugation

[3] Roger Hilsman, *To Move a Nation* (New York, 1967), especially pp. 413–537.

by armed minorities or by outside pressures." [4] This was then meant to apply to South Vietnam in 1966 as it had to Greece in 1947. Yet though most of his listeners on the Senate committee were skeptical of the democratic character of the then South Vietnam regime, it is fair to say that they would have been shocked had the Secretary of State chosen to offer a different justification for the American intervention. Had Rusk propounded the view that the United States was supporting one authoritarian regime against another because (1) it was in the interest of the United States to do so, and (2) authoritarian though the South Vietnamese government was, it was still less oppressive than the Communist alternative to it, such a public acknowledgment would have been decried as the height of cynicism. Yet it is lack of realism which begets cynicism, which in turn feeds masochistic disillusionment and defeatism. It is strange logic indeed to argue that if it cannot be clearly demonstrated that American policies *everywhere* are engaged on behalf of democracy, then it must follow that U.S. foreign policies have been consistently imperialistic and most of the regimes helped or sponsored by the United States have been reactionary dictatorships or oligarchies.

The moralistic rhetoric would alone have made the United States' position in South Vietnam virtually untenable once the regime there found itself under considerable internal and external pressure. Had the situation there remained quiescent and American help confined to economic and technical assistance, it is unlikely that the public interest in this country in the alleged merits and failings of the Saigon regime would have exceeded that shown in the character say of the governments of Philippines or South Korea. But with Vietnam becoming in 1960 a battleground and a focus of world-wide attention, the incongruity of the U.S. presence there was bound to be painfully revealed.

The United States was obviously not a master of South Vietnam in the sense of a colonial power controlling a dependent country and being responsible for its internal institutions. Indeed, a suggestion to this effect would have shocked both the American administration and the public. Was the United States then an *ally* of South Vietnam? But an alliance, and this would come as a surprise to many Americans, implies a certain equality in status of the allies, notwithstanding any possible disparity in their military or over-all power. Such a disparity entitles the predominant partner to the major, perhaps the decisive, share in

[4] *The Vietnam Hearings,* with an Introduction by J. William Fulbright (New York, 1966), p. 3.

348 : LOST OPPORTUNITIES

determining the over-all strategy of the alliance, but if the alliance is to endure, it must not grant one partner the right to interfere in the internal affairs of the other.

This commonplace perception has not always been lacking in the United States. During World War II, while various public figures and even some government officials undertook to lecture the Russians on how to institute democratic freedoms or the British about their colonial policies, it still would not have occurred to any responsible segment of American public opinion to demand that American help be conditioned on this or that internal reform in Britain or Russia. To be sure, that was a "real" war, and Britain and the U.S.S.R. were major allies. But in the postwar period, the United States virtually guaranteed Turkey against external and internal aggression, and the Turkish regime of 1947 was very far from being a model democracy. And beginning with 1950, very considerable help was extended to Communist Yugoslavia, again with no *visible* strings attached, even though the Catholic hierarchy in this country, then held in considerable respect by politicians, was obviously unhappy over this policy. This self-restraint on the part of Washington proved wise and not only in the interest of the United States but also of the Yugoslav people. Tito did not institute a democracy, but in view of the logic of his situation, he liberalized his regime and reduced discrimination against the Catholic Church, something he would not have done under pressure.

In any case, the basic trouble with the U.S. position was that South Vietnam was neither an *ally* nor a *protectorate* of the United States. In extending his offer of help to Diem in 1954, President Eisenhower stipulated that American assistance was provided on the condition "that your government is prepared to give assurances as to the standards of performance it would be able to maintain in the event such aid were supplied." And he went on to express his hope that an *independent* Vietnam would have a *strong* government. "Such a government would, I hope, be so responsive to the nationalist aspirations of its people, so enlightened in purpose and effective in performance, that it will be respected both at home and abroad and discourage any who might wish to impose a foreign ideology on your free people." [5] Here was a list of categories and stipulations entirely inconsistent with one another. How can you have an independent state, or a strong government, if a foreign power keeps looking over your shoulder to see whether

[5] George McTurnan Kahin and John W. Lewis, *The United States in Vietnam* (New York, 1967), pp. 382–83.

your domestic politics meet some vague "standards of performance" on which its aid depends? And if the Communists of North Vietnam represented a "foreign" ideology, so did many aspects of democratic and representative government which the United States tried haphazardly to introduce.

It was then almost inevitable that both sides would become victimized by this relationship. The United States could not ordain liberal and democratic institutions in South Vietnam; it could interfere with the authoritarian ways of the successive Saigon governments, making them not more democratic but merely less efficient and above all ensuring that they would *not* "be respected both at home and abroad." (It was a relationship in many ways more destructive than that which prevails in a Soviet satellite, where the Soviets are usually solicitous not to disparage *publicly* the authority of the government until and unless they are ready to install an alternative set of rulers.) It would not have been so bad had there been a single American authority laying down those "standards of performance" that Diem or his successors were to meet. But South Vietnam soon become a "showcase" of American assistance and counterinsurgency in Asia. This meant that a great variety of American agencies, official and private, presumed to tell the "independent and free" Vietnam how to run its affairs. There was the State Department—the American Embassy which might be desirous of political stability and inclined to overlook repressive features of the regime; there was the CIA and the American military mission, with their own and often divergent ideas on how the guerrilla war might best be fought; there were American professors and administrators bent upon testing their theories about "nation-building," land reform, etc.; and American newspapermen who through the reverberations in the United States exerted indirect but important influence on the policies both of Washington and Saigon. In other words, the beneficial effect of American aid and of many social and economic reforms undertaken at the instigation of the Americans was bound to be countered psychologically and politically through resentment, felt at several levels of Vietnamese government and society, of interference by foreigners. It was imperialism without even the redeeming feature of the straightforward source of authority and responsibility which a colonial relationship implies. It was an entangling alliance limiting the freedom of action of both partners in it without that necessary ingredient of successful partnership: mutual trust and understanding.

Without a renewed civil war, this bizarre relationship might have endured and led to an effective, if not an exemplary, democratic regime, on the order of, say, the one in South Korea which emerged after Syngman Rhee. But the increased tempo of terroristic and guerrilla activities beginning with 1960 confronted the United States with a need to re-examine its policies. There began the series of high-level missions to Vietnam which helped dramatize the American involvement, and largely through the sheer volume of travel and memoranda, newspaper and television accounts helped create the fateful illusion which then became reality that here was the central problem for United States foreign policy.

To the moralistic impulse was added another incentive for increased involvement in the affairs of this seemingly intractable area. This was the American penchant for gadgetry; the belief that every situation including the sociopolitical crisis which was engulfing South Vietnam could be handled and *promptly* solved if only the right technique of dealing with it could be found and applied. Vietnam seemed to offer an important opportunity for testing various theories of counterinsurgency, of coping with wars of national liberation, the problem which fascinated many officials of the new administration, including the President. Especially after 1962 it was assumed that Communist expansion through atomic blackmail was no longer practical. But there remained the threat of a guerrilla movement eroding the authority of the legitimate government and enveloping the whole country in a kind of war in which neither regular armies nor nuclear weapons could be successfully employed. The classical example of this technique was assumed to be the Chinese Communists' conquest of power between 1945 and 1949.

In view of the academic flavor of Kennedy's administration, it was natural for many of its leading officials to attribute great, sometimes exaggerated, importance to theories, official pronouncements, and treatises emanating from the Communist side on this new and menacing art. The somewhat platitudinous writings of Mao and North Vietnam's General Giap were scanned eagerly for clues on how to combat this peril on the political and the military level.[6] Yet one could hardly find in them the secret of the success of the Chinese and Vietminh Communists, any more than one can get any hint of Stalin's great if malevolent political gifts by reading his wooden theoretical writings. Guerrilla

[6] During the Cultural Revolution in China, a high Communist official met a dire fate for publicly and injudiciously questioning the profundity of one of Mao's principal tenets, that when the enemy attacks, the guerrilla forces should retreat, and when he retreats, they should advance.

warfare had, of course, set the stage for the Chinese and North Vietnamese victories, but it did not procure those victories. Mao's forces won after a series of pitched battles with the Nationalist Chinese and through the disintegration of Chiang's army. The French gave up the Indochinese war out of weariness climaxed by the psychological blow of the defeat at Dien Bien Phu. In the background were also the economic collapse of Communist China and the refusal of the French electorate to keep expending French lives for an obscure cause in a distant land. These then contributed to the Communists' successes at least as much as their own endurance and skill at guerrilla warfare.

The secret of successful counterinsurgency lies therefore not in some esoteric points to be gleaned from the works of Mao and Giap, but in the realization that it depends on endurance, stability, and psychological preparation of the country setting out to combat it or to lending support to another country already debilitated by guerrilla warfare. For a democracy it is the most difficult kind of war to fight, for it must be conducted so to speak with one hand tied behind the back. A totalitarian regime, especially a Communist one, seldom has much difficulty in repressing a budding guerrilla movement. It responds with mass terror which intimidates the most discontented segments of the population and discourages them from lending even passive support to the rebels. And the Communists, in view of their enormous experience in this field, have evolved special skills in infiltrating, appeasing, and buying off segments of a revolutionary leadership. In fact, a totalitarian regime is always in a state of emergency and mobilization. Hence a rebellion such as evidently broke out in North Vietnam in 1956 can seldom endure for long. Few regimes in history, it is fair to say, have ever been hated so passionately by the bulk of population as those in Poland and Hungary between 1948 and 1956, yet until the oppressive leadership became weakened and confused, there was no chance of popular revolt. An authoritarian non-Communist regime can sometimes deal with an incipient revolt with the same massive retaliation technique. The Indonesian Communist Party had been the largest and best organized in Asia, outside of China. In 1965, the Indonesian army shattered an attempted Communist coup with repression which, according to varying accounts, claimed between one hundred thousand and three hundred thousand lives. A democratic country simply cannot have recourse to such methods. Isolated incidents such as the use of torture by the French in Algeria, or the tales which horrified the American public in 1970 about American units massacring Vietnamese villagers, are as demoralizing to the army which perpetrates them as they are helpful to the cause of the guerrillas. The same must be said about the use of what might be called technological terror inherent in saturation bombings of guerrilla-held areas. All other criticisms of American policies in Vietnam have been to a lesser or greater extent the product of hindsight, but the one basic error, and one which ran contrary to common sense and all relevant experience, was the assumption that the injection of massive American power could suppress the rebellion speedily, that at any point a time limit could be set when guerilla activities could be suppressed.

The desire to master the allegedly esoteric art of guerrilla warfare had another aspect. It was commonplace and sensible to believe that successful counterinsurgency required popular support. What was not equally sensible was the deduction that lack of widespread support for the successive Saigon regimes indicated, especially in the countryside, the great popularity of the Vietcong. This deduction in turn led to the search for a South Vietnam regime which in the ritualistic phrase could win the "hearts and minds of the people." To this search was joined another one for some magical socioeconomic formula which if found and applied in the country could accomplish the same aim.[7] That a well-organized movement could secure acquiescence and often complicity of the large part of the population, not because of the attractiveness of its program or revulsion felt against the government but through a superior technique of intimidation, is something that the proverbial American follower of world events finds hard to believe. To a student of modern sociology and political science, such a view is unsophisticated; it smacks of the primitivism of some slogans of the earlier years of the Cold War. Of what use indeed are the elaborate techniques of social science, the labors of thousands of its licensed practitioners, if things are that simple? And yet, many Americans, social scientsts included, seem to have absorbed through countless Western films the idea that a group of armed and determined men can terrorize a sizable community.

Once the guerrilla movement grew in the face of numerically superior government forces amply helped and expertly advised by the United States, there was the natural tendency to blame its successes on the Saigon regime. The trick seemed, then, to find the kind of leadership

[7] Writes a British observer: "Saigon was inundated with teams of American political and social scientists and every form of expert researching and analyzing from preconceived Western ideas every facet of Vietnamese life and motivation." Robert Thompson, *No Exit From Vietnam* (London, 1969), p. 128.

which, again to use a ritualistic phrase, could win the support of the Vietnamese people. Most Americans in Saigon, whether there in an official or unofficial capacity, constituted themselves into a jury on the merits and failures of the Vietnamese regime. The unattractive American habit of blaming an ally for a situation which, for all shortcomings of the given regime, was primarily the product of armed assault upon it, asserted itself with a vengeance in South Vietnam between 1961 and 1963. Again, as in China between 1944 and 1949, there were ample grounds for criticism: President Diem lacked the ability to generate popular enthusiasm; his brother Nhu was a sinister political boss; Madame Nhu *was* overbearing. (The fact that unfortunately she spoke English made her lack of tact plus her dislike of the Americans all too obvious to the American public.) But a *public* debate and exposure of the shortcomings of the regime the United States had undertaken to protect and strengthen was bound to maximize these very faults and undercut its ability to reform itself.

The main point in foreign relations, and this is constantly obscured by American rhetoric, just as it is never forgotten by the Soviets, is that you deal with foreign *governments,* not "nations" or "countries." The United States could not help the South Vietnamese without helping the South Vietnamese government of the moment.[8] There is probably no area in the world where America and American institutions are as genuinely popular as in the countries of Eastern Europe. But the United States government does not deal with the peoples of Hungary or Poland but with their governments, not with the Russians but with Brezhnev, Kosygin, and Co. If Diem's government was thought beyond redemption, then the United States should have stopped its aid to it; if South Vietnam was thought to be of transcending importance to the United States and its government was incompetent, then the United States should have intervened overtly. The open criticism, the encouragement of a coup against Diem in a way that could not remain secret, and then washing one's hands of an intrigue that was crowned by the murder of officials who had entrusted themselves to U.S. protection—all this was to imitate the Communists at their most repellent and most inept. The United States reaped the worst of all possible worlds: a weak Saigon regime was succeeded by

[8] Failure to appreciate this rather self-evident point has been responsible for such bitter disillusionments as the realization that the Peace Corps, for all the devotion and idealism of most of its members, has been unable to improve significantly U.S. relations with the countries in which it has operated.

a succession of more unstable ones; the manner of the resolution of the Vietnam crisis of 1963 was inconsistent with U.S. honor and interests.

There is some evidence that before his downfall Diem, exasperated by the Americans and bedeviled by the rising strength of the Vietcong, was contemplating some sort of a deal with Ho Chi Minh. It is regrettable that some such arrangment could not have been reached. But rumors of the contacts between Saigon and Hanoi probably served to hasten Washington's resolution that a coup against Diem would not be unwelcome. The United States wanted to "conquer Communist subversion" in South Vietnam rather than reach a negotiated settlement that might lead to the eventual peaceful absorption of the South by the Communists. This again was a reasonable premise, but was the objective worth the massive investment of American resources and manpower decided upon and undertaken between 1963 and 1965?

Here, in addition to moralistic rhetoric and a passion for gadgetry, American policy-makers were strongly influenced by another factor: China. In fact, for much of the 1960s it was not the Vietcong or North Vietnam that the U.S. government thought it was fighting but the shadow of Communist China. The memory of the Chinese debacle of 1944–49 weighed heavily, whether consciously or unconsciouly, on policies and decisions of American strategists and diplomats. In China the United States *had* fallen for the Communists' ruse of negotiations for a coalition government; the Americans *had* supported Chiang's ineffective government of Chiang too long instead of stepping in and replacing it by one which could prosecute the civil war successfully; they had *not* intervened with their air power and soldiers to defeat the Communists. Studying American policies in Vietnam between 1963 and 1968, one realizes with fascination this inherent if perhaps not conscious premise—i.e., that one must take the course exactly opposite to the one the United States had pursued in China. Yet the American stake in the two cases is hardly comparable. The Communist victory in China was one of the master events of modern history. It is at least arguable that a U.S. commitment on the scale of that incurred in Vietnam, or even surpassing it, might have been justified to keep China non-Communist. What initiated the course of events which culminated in the Japanese attack on Pearl Harbor except U.S. resolve to keep China out of unfriendly hands? But with all due respect to several variants of the famous dominoes simile, the stakes in Vietnam were incomparably smaller. Every historical situation is in a sense unique; it is certainly a delusion to assume there is some truth writ in heaven, or to be discovered through games theory, which would enable us to deal with each and every case of Communist aggression or subversion.[9]

But Vietnam was not merely a strange form of expiation for previous mistakes and delusions over China. China influenced the commitment of American men, resources, and prestige in Vietnam in yet another and perhaps decisive way. In 1963 it was all too readily believed that the problem of a major nuclear confrontation with Russia had been solved. With that American propensity for veering from one extreme to another, the unbending belief in the existence of a Soviet-inspired, world-wide pattern of Communist aggression and subversion was replaced by a touching faith in Soviet Russia as a "responsible" power, interested in preserving a peaceful world. But there remained China, which now, from being mere cat's-paw of the U.S.S.R., as she had been viewed just a few years earlier, became the main threat. What would keep Peking from employing its virtually limitless manpower to conquer other Asian lands? China had to be taught a lesson.

The Chinese rationale of the Vietnam venture was buttressed when, in 1965, Marshal Lin Piao obliged U.S. policy-makers with an article expounding the thesis that in the revolutionary scheme of things, the Third World was comparable to what in classical doctrine was the countryside, the advanced industrialized nations to the cities. If revolutionary Marxism conquered this countryside, the cities—both the capitalist West and the revisionist U.S.S.R.—would soon have to succumb. This pronouncement was a veritable godsend for official apologists of U.S. Vietnam policy; here, out of the enemy's own mouth, was an admission that the Vietnam war was the right war in the right place against the right enemy—i.e., the Chinese.

There is no question that there was *some* validity in the dominoes simile. But life, politics, and history do not follow such neatly worked-out theories and analogies. In view of the over-all picture of world politics in 1963–65, was it wise to assume, even more to proclaim, that the crucial battle between the two worlds was taking place in South Vietnam? Was South Vietnam of greater importance than Indonesia, which at that time showed every sign of falling under Peking's

[9] This holds for the celebrated Munich analogy often paraded by the defenders of the American actions in Vietnam. It is far from certain that had the Western powers gone to war in 1938 they would have fared better vis-à-vis Germany than was to be the case in 1940. The main folly of Chamberlain's policy was to believe that by sacrificing Czechoslovakia one bought anything else but time.

influence? Yet about Indonesia the United States proposed to do nothing because in fact there was nothing it *could* do. The United States *was* in Vietnam, hence it was pronounced to be very important. Washington meant to increase the American commitment there, hence it had to be proclaimed an important commitment. How different from the Soviet practice. The Russians never proclaim a country of vital importance until it has been firmly secured by them; by definition, then, they never suffer defeats but only trivial and temporary setbacks (Yugoslavia in 1948, the Sino-Soviet split, little Albania).

Finally, it was the Sino-Soviet conflict that ostensibly emboldened the American administration, that in addition to all the other impulses pushed the United States into an unreasonable and all-out commitment which became explicit with the bombing of North Vietnam in February, 1965, and the massive infusion of the American soldiers some months later. Yet it is *precisely* the Sino-Soviet conflict which should have urged the opposite course of action. The *main* fact of world politics between 1963 and 1965 was open and intense conflict between the two Communist powers. It was clearly in the interests of the United States that nothing should obscure the significance of this momentous crisis. The conflict was dividing Communist forces, powers, and parties throughout the world, undoing many of the gains scored by them since World War II, fatally damaging the illusion that Communism was the wave of the future or the road to an international community free from war. And in both principal Communist countries, the enmity and mutual fear were obviously creating serious internal problems. In Russia especially, even the most ideologically motivated citizen was bound to ask himself of what use was the propagation of the creed abroad or sacrifices on its behalf if further advances of Communism might bring not greater strength and prestige for the Soviet Union but possibly new dangers and more enemies. Apart from such psychological effects, the Sino-Soviet rivalry meant that the U.S.S.R. would make an effort to arrest or counter the spread of Chinese influence in Asia and elsewhere. Even the most naïve practitioner of the diplomatic profession should have appreciated that, much as it was in nobody's interest in the nuclear age to initiate a war between major powers, the Sino-Soviet conflict enhanced Washington's bargaining powers with both Peking and Moscow.

With the United States opening aerial attacks upon a Communist state, however, the psychological effect of the Sino-Soviet conflict became blunted, and the superior diplomatic assets held by the United States were inevitably depleted. The American dilemma in Vietnam was the big news, and the ability of a small Communist state and guerrilla movement to withstand the attacks by the world's greatest power was brought into high relief. Logically there should have been considerable reason to fear that the two Communist powers would use Vietnam as a pretext for papering over their disagreements and mounting at least a temporary joint front against the United States. This has not happened, but by the same token, the United States involvement in Vietnam has undercut both the abilities and the incentives of Russia or China to seek a *rapprochement* with her. The reason, especially when it concerns the Russians, does not lie in any excessive sentimentality over the fate of their fellow Communists. Rather, it is that Vietnam has offered to both sides a welcome opportunity to claim that is still the imperialists who are the main danger. Conceivably, a Stalin determined to resolve the China problem would not be inhibited by Vietnam in reaching an agreement with the United States. But the post-Khrushchev leaders are divided and unsure of themselves. Fearful of China and yet uncertain as to what to do about her, Vietnam powerfully reinforces their tendency to go on doing things as before, to pretend to their own people and perhaps to themselves that the Sino-Soviet dilemma is temporary but the conflict with the capitalist world still fundamental. In the long run, the problem of China is for Russia fearsome and untractable. But middle-aged politicians in all systems try, when confronted with basic difficulties, to buttress their self-confidence by persuading themselves and their peoples how much better off they are than their competitors. At the price of material support to North Vietnam, which has probably run at several hundred million dollars in the last few years, the Russians made the United States incur expenditures of over $30 billion a year. And there have been enormous indirect benefits to the Russians in the disarray of American society, the loss in American prestige throughout the world, and enhanced credit which the Soviet Union has gained in the Communist world through its "flexible response" to the American challenge.

Soviet policy over Vietnam went through several phases. Until the summer of 1964, the Russians showed some signs, as the Chinese later commented bitterly, of wanting to disengage from any direct connection with this thorny and dangerous problem. The North Vietnamese, while trying to maneuver between the two Communist superpowers, were leaning toward Peking. In 1963, they had refused to sign the nuclear test-ban treaty; at that time this was a litmus-paper test indicating whether a given regime lined up with Moscow or Peking. In July, 1964, the Soviets indicated their desire to resign as one of the two conveners of the conference on the Geneva agreement of 1964. This meant that if the North Vietnamese, with Chinese encouragement, were stepping up the civil war in the South, the Soviets wanted to retain freedom of action as to the probable American massive involvement, which obviously carried the possibility of a U.S.–China confrontation.

Then the situation changed substantially. In August, the Gulf of Tonkin incident led to American bombing of North Vietnamese torpedo-boat bases, then to the almost unanimous passage of a Congressional resolution empowering the President to employ armed forces to protect U.S. interests in the area. A Presidential campaign was then in progress. President Johnson was emphatic that American boys would not be sent to do the job the "Asian boys," as he rather quaintly put it, should be doing. His opponent, Senator Barry Goldwater, advocated strong measures, including bombing, against the North. Whatever the disclaimers by Johnson and clear indications that Goldwater would lose, Ho Chi Minh's regime had to contemplate seriously the possibility of strong American measures in the South and North; bombing raids and perhaps an invasion. If these things occurred, the North Vietnamese were going to need more than just moral encouragement from Peking. But the Chinese for their part had an added incentive to be prudent. In October they exploded their first atom bomb. This was no time to pledge unconditional support to Hanoi, to offer the slightest provocation which might make the Americans yield to the temptation of a pre-emptive strike against the Chinese nuclear installation. North Vietnam, in need at least of material help, would have to seek closer ties with Russia, as well as to explore (undoubtedly with Soviet encouragement) political means of defusing the dangerous situation: in August, the Secretary General of the Communist Party of North Vietnam went to Moscow (Khrushchev, then on the wane, was, according to subsequent Peking releases, propagating the story that the Gulf of Tonkin incident was a "Chinese provocation"); and in September, North Vietnam transmitted through Secretary-General Thant hints of its readiness to negotiate with the United States over the entire situation.

From the American point of view, this was an excellent time to negotiate. Nobody can blame Washington for not knowing that there was a serious crisis within the leadership of the Communist Party of the Soviet Union, but it was public knowledge that relations between Russia and China were at their worst yet. Mao had just given his famous interview branding Russia as an imperialist power and asserting that she had stolen vast territories from China. Hanoi was obviously frightened: What would North Vietnam do if the Americans attacked while Russia and China were at each other's throats? If there was ever a moment to negotiate with the Communists, this was it. The United States refused.

Subsequent justifications of this refusal have dwelt on the undeniable fact that the mere fact of holding negotiations would have had a profoundly demoralizing effect on the South Vietnamese government and people. But negotiations would not have obligated either the United States or South Vietnam to *do* anything. The real reasons must be found in the Presidential campaign then going on and in the eagerness of some of the President's advisers to try out various counterinsurgency recipes once the elections were over. The election outcome was hardly in doubt, but Johnson was eager to create the impression of just the right balance between toughness and prudence in order to be elected by a huge popular margin—and in this he succeeded.

By the time Johnson had his popular mandate and could return to the perplexing problems of Southeast Asia, there was a new leadership in Moscow. After any dramatic shift at the top, the Russians are usually extra prudent in foreign affairs. In this case, the Brezhnev-Kosygin team was up to a point eager to propitiate the Chinese, but at the same time it desired further strengthening of a *détente* with the United States. The principal Soviet worry vis-à-vis the West was still the possibility of West Germany obtaining any form of access to nuclear weapons. The Soviets professed to see such possibilities in the then extant proposal for a multilateral nuclear force for NATO—the MLF —and had been denouncing it in their usual half-plaintive half-threatening way as the indirect means for delivering the deadly weapon to the "Bonn revanchists." [10] The United States had devised the plan as the means of satisfying its allies' desire for a share in the control of the

---

[10] The MLF was to consist of nuclear-missile-carrying surface (or submarine) ships manned by crews of mixed nationality, jointly owned and operated by the NATO powers, each one of which could exercise a veto over use of the weapons.

nuclear deterrent, but in view of the Soviets' rather excessive worry over the MLF, it was also a bargaining asset in any negotiations with the U.S.S.R. Eventually the plan was abandoned because of doubts and dissensions within the Western alliance, and it was never used as a bargaining counter with Russia.

On Vietnam, the new Soviet leaders elaborated a fresh policy which, they hoped, would achieve the Soviet Union's diverse aims. The Soviet Union would increase substantially its aid to Hanoi, thus disproving any Chinese charge that it was selling out the interests of Asian Communism. At the same time it was proposed to alleviate the Vietnam crisis through diplomatic means; here, of course, by providing extensive aid the Soviet Union was acquiring additional leverage to influence North Vietnam to move to the conference table. With Khrushchev gone, the possibility of a dramatic confrontation between Russia and China in a reconvened Geneva conference momentarily disappeared. Negotiations, which continued to be urged by the Soviets in the early part of 1965, would not have "solved" the Vietnam problem any more than it had been solved in 1954, but the United States had enough assets, one should think, to secure a makeshift arrangement that might have preserved independence of South Vietnam for some years.

The American intentions to expand its role in Vietnam and to punish Hanoi through air attacks and conceivably an invasion were well known in Russia, as any reader of the Soviet press for January, 1965, can testify. On February 1, a *Pravda* column warned in the characteristic manner, at once vague and ominous, against such a policy: "The Soviet Union would not remain unconcerned about the fate of a fraternal socialist state; she will be ready to render it all needed help." The only solution was a return to the Geneva agreements, continued the columnist. And the announcement in late January of a forthcoming visit to Hanoi by a Soviet delegation headed by Kosygin had an eloquence of its own: he was to be accompanied by a minister of civil aviation, a commander in chief of the Soviet air force, the secretary of the Central Committee in charge of intra-Communist relations. The announcement spelled out a plain warning that the Soviets would send supplies and possibly, in the case of air attacks, planes and pilots. At the same time, the Soviets evidently were still encouraging the North Vietnamese to be ready to negotiate with the United States.

When the United States began the bombing of North Vietnam in February, the challenge was only superficially to Hanoi; in fact, the United States struck at the "credibility" of the Soviet government as protector of other Communist countries. An increase, even a considerable one, in American troops in Vietnam would not have constituted such a challenge, but the bombing did—just at the point when the new leadership was trying out its first steps in foreign affairs, when it had to refute the Chinese charge of Soviet indifference to the fate of Communism in the outside world. Provided the danger to the U.S.S.R. was not too great, Kosygin's and Brezhnev's response had to be to make sure the United States would not be able to get away with it. Systematic bombing of North Vietnam, therefore, would (not too unpredictably) make it more difficult to force Hanoi to discontinue its efforts in the South. In the absence of the bombing, North Vietnam conceivably might have discontinued or reduced its operations supporting the National Liberation Front, but it was almost unbearable for the U.S.S.R. to allow the precedent of aerial bombardment by the United States forcing a Communist regime to its knees. There was considerable watchfulness and reserve to the Soviet reactions during the initial phase of the American bombing: horrendous but vague hints of what would happen unless the Americans ceased and desisted; some impressionable American visitors to the U.S.S.R. were given to understand that if the Americans continued, something absolutely indescribable might happen before too long. But the nature of official Soviet utterances, and of their interpretation of the conflict to their own people, suggested caution and wariness.

The nature of the American bombing was exactly that which, while strengthening the Soviets' determination that it should not succeed in its objective, did not appear to present *them* with a danger drastic enough to warrant excessive worry. The United States expanded the area and intensity of the air attacks gradually; North Vietnam was given the opportunity to adjust to it from both the defense and psychological point of view; the U.S.S.R., by providing Hanoi with sophisticated anti-aircraft systems, thereby making the attacks costly for the Americans, was able to escape most if not all of the blame for the lack of direct reprisals. As in Korea, Americans and non-Russian Communists were dying, and the U.S.S.R. was providing weapons and munitions; but with this difference—the North Vietnamese, unlike the Chinese between 1951 and 1953, *were not being charged* for them, at least not in cash, although the Soviet Union exacted a closer adherence to the main lines of Soviet foreign policy. The joint declaration signed by Kosygin and the North Vietnamese Prime Minister in February, 1965, registered Hanoi's support for the objectives of the

U.S.S.R., including the "normalization" of the status of "Western Germany." [11]

With the danger thus not judged imminent, the Soviets set about exploiting American policy for their own purposes. Kosygin extended his Asian trip. He paid an unscheduled visit to North Korea. And on the way there was a lengthy stopover in Peking, where Mao and Liu Shao-chi (still not unmasked as "China's Khrushchev" and Mao's enemy) deigned to receive him. There was a brief flurry of Sino-Soviet cordiality.

It was to last but three weeks. In that time it became abundantly clear to the Chinese that, under the pretext of helping a fraternal Communist state, the Soviets' real aim was, as the *Peking Review* obligingly informed the world on November 12, 1965, "to keep the situation in Vietnam under their control, to gain a say on the North Vietnam question and to strike a bargain with U.S. imperialism on it." Perhaps Soviet aims were not that clear-cut, but the policy was bound to raise Mao's worst suspicions. Specifically, the Soviets wanted China to allow them to establish bases on Chinese soil to expedite transport of war matériel and allow the passage of Red Army troops to North Vietnam. It took little imagination for Peking to recollect how once before, to recoup its own mistake in ordering the invasion of South Korea, Stalin had pushed the Chinese Communists into a confrontation with the United States. Were the Russians up to the same tricks? And if Hanoi became dependent on Soviet equipment and help, would not North Vietnam be compelled to negotiate, if and whenever it should suit the Russians' convenience, say, in exchange for some concessions the United States might grant in some other part of the world? For China, the proper way that Russia could assist North Vietnam would have been to press the United States elsewhere, say in Germany.

Within a month of the Kosygin mission, relations between China and the Soviet Union grew more acrimonious than ever before. In their passage through China, Soviet shipments of arms to Hanoi were interfered with and at times delayed. The Americans might well have feared, as a result of their bombing, a closing of ranks between the two great Communist powers, at least temporarily; however, it did not take place. This was a great piece of luck for the United States,

[11] This presumably referred to West Berlin, about which the Russians since 1962 preferred not to speak more explicitly. Also, the two countries solemnly reaffirmed their support for the five demands formulated by Castro after the missile crisis, something everybody (including the Cubans!) has almost forgotten about since then.

a chance to retrieve its mistakes, exploit the dissonances in the Communist camp, and work for some sort of alleviation of the Vietnam crisis through political means.

The good luck was compounded even further when in September the Indonesian army balked an attempted Communist coup and in effect deposed Sukarno, who had had "an understanding" with the Communists and was about to shift from an implicit following of their line to an explicit Communist position. From the Western point of view this was a fantastically fortunate occurrence. Indonesia had been virtually conceded to the Peking wing of the Communist camp. Her threat to Malaysia, the consequence of Sukarno's imperialist ambitions nourished by the Communists, was serious; and Malaysia's protector, Great Britain, might soon find herself in a Vietnam-like situation.

From every point of view—actual and potential wealth, population, strategy—Indonesia was vastly more important than South Vietnam. The defeat of Communism in Indonesia was then a much more important blow to Communism, especially to China, than even the most complete shattering of Communist insurgency in South Vietnam would ever be. By the same token, Moscow, while shedding some crocodile tears over the massacre of the Indonesian Communists, was not displeased. The loss in prestige to the Soviet Union was considerable: Sukarno had been the Russians' protégé; they had spent billions in the support of his ill-fated ventures. Yet the Soviets did not even go through the motions of a diplomatic protest to Djakarta.

The lesson for the United States should have been clear. Time was *not* working for the Communists in Asia. There was every reason for the United States to gauge its commitments carefully. Even a makeshift, unstable arrangement in Vietnam was preferable to a commitment of U.S. manpower and resources which could obscure and detract from the division between the two Communist powers. And the same moral shone clearly from the military conflict between Pakistan and India. The U.S.S.R. warned China not to repeat her 1962 attack against India and then, to Peking's obvious rage, mediated between the two contestants.

Thus America's deepening involvement in Vietnam had the ludicrous effect of unwittingly and in different ways aiding both China's and Russia's diplomatic position. The Chinese might trumpet loudly about Russia selling out North Vietnam, about revisionists and imperialists joining to attack China, but they could recognize that, for the time being at least, Vietnam was a barrier to an understanding between

Washington and Moscow, and in the absence of such an understanding the Soviet Union was not likely to attack China. When Mao and his supporters in mid-1966 launched the Cultural Revolution, which was to split the Party and state apparatus and bring parts of China to the verge of civil war, they could do so with some confidence that the indirect Soviet-American confrontation over North Vietnam would keep the Soviets, who were obviously itching to do so, from interfering.

For the Soviet Union, U.S. policy was helpful in a different way. During the first phase of the American bombardment of the North and the build-up of American forces in the South, Russia's prestige was clearly somewhat tarnished. At the 23rd Party Congress in March, 1966, some foreign Communists (notably representatives of North Vietnam and Cuba) implied strong criticism of the U.S.S.R. for not assuming greater risks in bringing this dangerous precedent to an end. But when it became clear that American bombs were not bringing Hanoi to its knees, when the domestic and foreign consequences of America's inconclusive war became apparent, Soviet actions vis-à-vis Vietnam were bound to impress most Communist leaders as just the right blend of firmness and moderation. What at first looked like faintheartedness then appeared as prudence, and when cultural revolutions shook both China and the United States, the restraint of the Soviet leaders began indeed to take on the appearance of a policy of masterful inactivity.

The decision to bomb North Vietnam thus transformed the conflict and made an alleviation of the Southeastern Asia crisis infinitely more complicated. Meanwhile, the Vietnamese war was having a tragic impact on American society. Here future historians will undoubtedly acknowledge that the initial and most violent shock to the public, and one which essentially precipitated the protest against the entire venture, was the news of the bombing. Vietnam was very far from being in the forefront of attention of the average American that day of February, 1965. To bomb Vietnam had been one of the more extravagant ideas put forward by Barry Goldwater during the campaign, but he had been overwhelmingly defeated, and the idea had been decisively repudiated by Johnson. The first shock was one of fear. One could conjure up visions of hundreds of thousands of Chinese soldiers pouring into the war and of the Soviets initiating some violent counteraction of their own, perhaps a nuclear war. The apparent suddenness of the action contributed to the initial shock. Previous periods of international tension had built up over a long period; here out of the blue the United States government was instigating a violent action which threatened all sorts of ominous consequences. There was just enough tergiversation (which perhaps reflected real hesitation on the part of the President and his advisers) about the purpose of the initial bombings—reprisal for random attacks by the Vietcong on American servicemen or part of a new strategy?—to undermine trust in the candor and responsibility of the President and his advisers. The "he took us into the war" charge against Roosevelt had been silenced by the knowledge that whatever moves on behalf of Britain and China he had made before December 7, 1941, it was the Japanese attack and then the German declaration of war that were responsible for millions of Americans finding themselves in uniform and abroad. The Korean conflict had strained the fabric of the American body politic, but then again the fact of an enemy aggression had been undeniable and the conflict lasted only three years. The Vietnam war, insofar as the great bulk of Americans was concerned, began more or less inexplicably in February, 1965.

The shock of the first news about the bombing was followed by a growing irritation that it was obviously not bringing the expected results. American forces in South Vietnam expanded to more than 500,000 by mid-1968. Soon the United States was spending $30 billion per year—a prodigious expense of manpower and wealth. Why was it not bringing results? And who was the enemy? North Vietnam? For all the help it was receiving, it was a primitive country with virtually no industry, no air force to speak of—a ludicrous enemy for the most powerful nation on earth. The Vietnamese people? Or perhaps the Communist bloc as a whole? Or, to pursue a different tack, was the United States fighting the forces of history?

Within a year of the fatal decision to bomb, the main lines of a critique of administration policy became as irrational as the administration's justification of the war and the way it was being conducted. As to the latter, Johnson held to two main points: (1) that the war was being won, which was true only in the sense that the enemy was not winning; (2) that any settlement short of Hanoi's calling off its instigation and support of the insurrection in the South would mean the eventual Communist takeover of Southeast Asia and an unprecedented defeat for the United States.

The opponents of the war categorically rejected the second thesis as entirely unfounded. But it was arguable that a coalition government in the South in a few years quite possibly might give way to an outright Communist regime, and this would undoubtedly be a blow to neighboring non-Communist countries. And such a settlement *would* have represented a setback for the United States; it would be, to use this by now somewhat fatuous-sounding phrase, a calculated risk in regard to the whole area. But the emotional phrase about not losing the war—and as time went on this became virtually the only argument for continuing with the grisly business—was not only inaccurate but misleading insofar as the course of modern history is concerned. Did we win World War II? An absurd question, on the face of it. But the United States went to war not just for the exhilaration of trouncing the Germans and the Japanese but to make sure that no single power should dominate the European continent and that China should not be controlled by a force or regime hostile to America; by 1949 it was obvious that the objectives had not been achieved.

What was being fought in Vietnam was not, by any rational standard, a war, but merely one battle in a continuing conflict the United States has been waging since 1945 to stem the advance of Communism by both political and military means. A setback in any one battle would be serious but by no means fatal. The United States has lost more important ones before—notably that of China, and in Eastern Europe. It was not only the vastly greater material resources of the West, but the stability and the essential unity of democratic society as against the already apparent inability of the Communist world to preserve cohesion which in 1965 provided grounds for measured optimism as to the outcome of the Vietnamese struggle.

But by setting up a Great Test of the Free World v. Communist Aggression, and inviting the whole world to the ringside, President Johnson was committing a monumental folly against which it had been warned even by such uncompromising advocates of "having it out" with the Communists in Asia as General MacArthur. As difficulties piled up and the optimistic forecasts were refuted, the United States government was thrown into a veritable catatonic posture, repeating that this was the great conflict of the century. American folk wisdom has some excellent precepts as to what is required in any competitive situation, political or athletic, such as, "Stay loose" or, as the immortal Satchel Paige put it, "Don't look behind—something might be catching up with you." Johnson and his advisers refused to heed those wise precepts. They grew more and more tense, allowing all the bitternesses and irrational impulses that had accumulated during twenty frustrating years of America trying to fashion the world in its own image to magnify and catch up with American politics. The seeming intractability of the Vietnamese problem led not to a questioning of goals and methods but to rather weird and guilt-ridden reflections on why these primitive people refused to be defeated by the outpour-ing of American men and resources. One administration official later wrote with superstitious awe: "Ours is a plausible strategy—for those who are rich, who love life and fear pain. But happiness, wealth, and power are expectations that constitute a dimension far beyond the experience, and probably beyond the emotional comprehension, of the Asian poor. For them there may be little difference between the condition of death and the condition of unrelieved suffering in life." [12] Yet this is sheer obscurantism: modern history offers abundant proof that men under certain conditions can fight bravely and fanatically against great odds regardless of their race, the material level of their society, or the justice of the cause they defend. The intrepidity of the Japanese soldier was not due to the fact that he was Asian or that the society he was defending was a model of social justice; the courage of the Russian fighting "for the country, for Stalin" did not testify that he was enchanted with a system that had killed or imprisoned or sent into exile members of his family. And the German soldier fought courageously and resourcefully in a long and hopeless rearguard action from the banks of the Volga to the suburbs of Berlin.

The Vietnamese war has thus *not* been a test of the virility, tough-ness, or social justice of American society, as both its opponents and defenders soon agreed. Like any war, especially a limited one, it has challenged primarily the political intelligence, the sense of proportion, and the psychological endurance of both the rulers and the society. And these qualities had been found wanting in the America of the sixties. Common sense should have urged that a really massive intro-duction of American manpower would not help but, on the contrary, harm the effort. Half a million American soldiers in a country of 18 million were bound to destroy the fabric of South Vietnamese society, quite apart from the ravages of war. Saturation bombings were to have the same effect. In China, Chiang's Nationalists had been defeated as much by inflation as by Mao's armies, and the same story was being enacted in Indochina. It is entirely conceivable that a much smaller force, partly instructional in character, would have been more effective

12 Townsend Hoopes, *The Limits of Intervention* (New York, 1969), p. 129.

than a huge army of which only a small part could be employed in actual combat. But Americans are an impatient people.[13]

The manner in which the war has been presented to the American people can be criticized as predictably disastrous. It was fatuous to proclaim the Vietnam conflict as the great historical test of the post–World War II period, to send half a million Americans there, and at the same time to expect that the people would *not* have to make sacrifices, *not* have to suffer inconveniences. There were no proclamations of national emergency, at first no increased taxes, no price and wage controls of even the feeble kind which had existed during the Korean war. And what is political wisdom in normal or near-normal times becomes suicidal naïveté in a crisis. Young Americans who thanks to their economic status or their abilities went to college found themselves exempt from military service. Now blanket exemptions in wartime have always been the source of trouble even in societies where the relative small handful of students had to be husbanded as an irreplaceable national asset.[14] The sense of guilt over not sharing burdens assumed by those less fortunate becomes mixed with the fear of losing one's privileged status and being exposed to danger. These incongruous feelings then blend in a current of resentment against the society which imposes such a burden of guilt and fear, against the government which cannot convincingly explain why some are called upon to serve and die while others may engage in peaceful pursuits. Many of the young men and women who in the last few years sought the release of their anxieties in acts of senseless violence would under different circumstances, one dares say, make good soldiers in a better cause.

Almost simultaneously with the intensification of its intervention in Vietnam, Johnson's administration launched an ambitious program of social and economic reform. In its conception and in much of its application, this program was an admirable attempt to eradicate some very obvious social evils and defects. It must have occurred to some politicians, being like most of us sinful men, that the not so popular war would be offset in the public mind by this grandiose enterprise of the "war on poverty,' of the pursuit of the "great society." But both the excellent intentions and the apparently clever politics behind the am-

---

[13] One of those dicta which pass for strategic-political sophistication and which has caught on in Washington is the precept that the counterguerrilla forces must have a 10 or 15 to 1 superiority to be assured of success.
[14] Nationalist China during World War II exempted university students from military service. They became one of the most vociferous opposition groups to Chiang's regime.

bitious social schemes were soon confounded by the impossibility of combining a foreign conflict of the dimensions of Vietnam with the task of reforming society at home. The main difficulty was again psychological rather than economic or military. Foreign commentators have never tired of pointing out that the U.S. outlay in Vietnam while enormous could still be afforded by the world's richest economy, that the American casualties while lamentable were yet only a relatively small percentage of those exacted at home by the automobile. Yet such calculations, while perhaps mechanically correct, neglect the psychological truth that both a large-scale war and a very extensive program of social reform require single-minded concentration by the government and the country at large. A revolutionary and totalitarian regime can and often does combine a drastic program of reform at home with a foreign conflict; indeed, real or alleged foreign danger is often used to stir up the emotions needed as the catalyst for the domestic upheaval. But for a democratic society a foreign war requires too much concentration by the government to be combined with a potentially divisive or disruptive program of internal reform. Franklin Roosevelt recognized this imperative when he said during World War II that "Dr. Win the War" replaced "Dr. New Deal." How indeed could that war have been conducted, still less won, if public attention had been distracted by a *government-sponsored* campaign to draw attention to and eradicate the undoubted social and economic evils which plagued America? With the war over, there followed a period of rapid social change and economic growth, the progress and growth far surpassing the rosiest expectations of even the most energetic reformers.

The internal reforms pursued by Johnson's administration did not, then, dull the edge of opposition to the war: on the contrary, they served to magnify it, to turn it from a critique of the way the war was being conducted to one of war itself, of American foreign policy as a whole, and finally of what used to be called proudly the American way of life. If America had to conduct "war" against "poverty," was this not palpable proof that the U.S. government had more urgent tasks at home than abroad? If American society was so diseased, what right did the United States have to try to impose its own ideas of government on other nations?

The evangelical fervor aroused by the "war on poverty" was to serve the cause of domestic reform no better than the moralistic rhetoric behind foreign policy helped toward a sober appraisal of the war in Vietnam. In both one could issue encouraging statistics, those hideous "body counts" of the dead enemy, in themselves enough to feed the growing revulsion against the war,[15] paralleled by more coldly repellent data on how many people had advanced above the "poverty line." Neither set of statistics could of course appease those in whom the emotionally colored appeal to either war had aroused expectations of a speedy victory. As generals and Pentagon officials kept asking for more and more men and money and deploring the restrictions on bombing which allegedly kept postponing victory, so another set of bureaucrats and officials, joined by a chorus of real and alleged experts, kept calling for more funds, more social improvisations, predicting dire consequences if their requests were not heeded and their bypassing of the traditional political channels not authorized or acquiesced in. The average citizen, confronted with this barrage of propaganda, threats, and claims, grew increasingly exasperated and confused and at times despondent over the efficacy of rationality and democracy prevailing in this suddenly unfamiliar and turbulent world.

The American crisis found both its symbol and its focal point in the universities (more broadly, in the intellectual community or stratum of our society).[16] Very early after the "real" beginning of the Vietnam war, American universities became scenes of "teach-ins," of debates about the issues and implications first of the war itself, then American foreign policy, and eventually the quality and moral foundations of American life as a whole. What was alarming was of course not the mere fact that these important questions were debated, but that the term "teach-in"

[15] Could the morale of the people have withstood a similar insensitive practice during World War II, estimates of how many thousands burned or suffocated during the massive air raids on Tokyo, Hamburg, and Dresden?

[16] "Community" is used here for the sake of convenience, but with some embarrassment, for here again is a term which when improperly and emotionally used has contributed to our troubles. Its proper application is to that kind of organization where what its members have in common is the most important thing about the organization to which they belong. Thus a religious order is a community; a university is not. The intellectual "community" refers to a large body of people who earn their living by intellectual pursuits, rather than manual, clerical, or business activity, but who otherwise can in no sense be assumed to have any rights, obligations, or ideology in common. The word "intellectual" *should* not then convey any sense parallel to that expressed by terms like "Methodist," "Jesuit," or "citizen." In the heated atmosphere of America in the late sixties, as in prerevolutionary Russia, this distinction became obscured. The intellectual community has become, we are told, "alienated," has taken a stand on this or that issue. What is meant by it is that a number of professors, writers, and others have seen fit to express their opinions on a number of social and political issues, assuming, whether explicitly or not, that their opinions (1) are representative of the whole mass of people earning their livelihood by similar pursuits and (2) should carry greater weight in affecting the decisions of the government or of the electorate than those of an equivalent number of, say, miners or shopkeepers.

took on implications transcending those of a rational debate intended to affect policy. It became a ritual, partaking at once of characteristics of a revival meeting and an endurance contest. What began as a well-intentioned fad soon became a national addiction. An increasing number of young people of college age found themselves in the grip of a strong emotion. Prosperity and government aid to education had freed many young men and women from the material concerns and inhibitions which in the past had acted as a check on the natural turbulence of youth. The loosening of many forms of traditional authority contributed to the seeming purposelessness and spiritual aridity of a society whose fantastic ability to create wealth did not apparently result in the improvement of the human condition.[17]

Disaffection became the reigning mood of only a minority of college-age Americans, and within that minority only a small proportion sought recourse in militancy or active "New Left" politics. But a social upheaval or even a revolution need not be certified in the polls. The Vietnam war made a significant breach in that wall of rationality and custom against which the waves of philosophies and impulses hostile to democratic institutions have always beaten. In the 1950s, few people were inclined to attribute much social significance to dissident minorities, to theories of existentialism, to the literature extolling the mood of the "angry young men." The lingering echoes of Communist rhetoric were a subject for curiosity and derision, discredited as the Communist critique of democracy had become not only in view of the West's prosperity but also through the Russians' own revelations about their grim past. Now all those esoteric theories and intellectual curiosities leaped as it were from the pages of specialized journals and from seminar rooms into real life. Young men who a few years before would have greeted with laughter, if they had listened at all to, tirades about the iniquity of the "system," "the Establishment," about American imperialism oppressing the Third World, now listened with attention and some with conviction. Their elders no longer dismissed their discontent as a normal, passing phase, and their impatience as eventually yielding to experience. Those commonplace and fairly universal phenomena now acquired more fashionable names and a more sophisticated rationale. "Our young are alienated," the middle-class parent in the America of the 1960s would say with an air of uttering something at once original, daring, and profound. "We have a generation gap," he would continue, triumphantly defying the competing cliché about "our

[17] There is a Russian proverb: "Excessive fat (wealth) may lead to madness."

372 : LOST OPPORTUNITIES

permissive society." [18] Thus a circular and mutually reinforcing flow of clichés: the anxieties and discontents of an originally small group were analyzed and theoretically elaborated by a small group of intellectuals, who would return to propagandize a wider sphere of the public. The news media, preachers, and finally politicians found it increasingly tempting and profitable to use the new idiom. Through a confluence of pressures and fads, American society found itself in a remarkable condition of being belabored about its essential corruption and about the inefficacy of democratic processes to deal with its multiform evils.

What makes this auto-indoctrination or dissent so disturbing is its diffused and basically nonpolitical character. A protest, even a revolutionary movement, can be channeled into constructive directions if for concrete social evils it prescribes concrete remedies. But many aspects of the current dissent seem religious rather than political in character. They protest the human condition rather than this or that institution. Struggle is prescribed, it seems, for the mere exhilaration of smiting the unrighteous rather than as a way of conquering political power. Economic inequality is protested by the very same people who in the next sentence decry materialism altogether and proclaim some vague longing for asceticism. One grows nostalgic for those psychologically uncomplicated forms of old radicalism, for socialism, which proclaimed that the key need was to nationalize the means of production, for Communism, which had the straightforward if objectionable aim of monopoly of political power for the Party. The Old Left, in brief, operated within the rational tradition, even if some of its postulates were unreasonable and its methods and goals incompatible with democratic ideas. The New Left, on the contrary, was more of a mood than a political movement.

Future historians will spend much time in an inconclusive debate as to the causes of the great American crisis. Yet whatever the "underlying causes" so beloved by historians, Vietnam was the catalyst, and the unhappy state of the world at large a powerful contributing factor. We must turn to the wider setting within and because of which America's drama has been taking place.

[18] The term "alienation" has, of course, a fairly technical meaning in Hegelian and Marxist philosophy from which it is borrowed, in contrast to whatever it means to those who use it as an elegant way of saying that the young do not like what they see around them. "Generation gap" carries the absurd implication that at other times and in other societies a man of twenty looked at things in the same light as one of forty.

Vietnam contributed to the deepening crisis in Franco-American relations which reached its climax in 1966 when France withdrew from the NATO organization. It is difficult to determine whether the dramatic "escalation" of American intervention in Southeast Asia had merely confirmed General de Gaulle's doubts about the "Anglo-Saxons'" capacity to lead the non-Communist world, or whether it provoked his ire at the Americans' presumption that they could succeed where France had failed. Britain's Labour government continued, at a quickened pace, the liquidation of Britain's overseas commitments, but verbally at least it supported the aims of U.S. policy in Southeast Asia. This chagrined the left wing of the Labour party but it solaced Johnson, for whom any diplomatic support, albeit a restrained one, became of importance amidst the rising chorus of foreign and domestic criticism. As time went on, the U.S. position on Vietnam put an increasing strain on the always fragile ties of understanding and cooperation linking the non-Communist world. Military help was forthcoming from a handful of countries with a direct interest in the containment of Communism in Southeast Asia: the Pacific dominions, South Korea, Thailand. But many governments which belonged in the same category and which *privately* may have wished for an American success, found it politically advisable to dissociate themselves publicly from the American intervention. The United States was reaping the harvest of its well-meant but infuriating, schoolmasterish attitude of superiority toward its Western allies, which went back to World War II, when American officials found it so easy to tell the British what they should do about India and to excoriate France for her imperialist sins in North Africa and Indochina. American policies found no greater understanding, not to mention support, among those countries whose independence had been hastened by American actions and whose first steps in statehood had been supported by American economic aid.

Within a year of the fatal decision to bomb North Vietnam, the negative by-products of the American policy also became evident in regard to the Communist world. The position of political advantage and considerable opportunity which the United States had enjoyed before February, 1965, vis-à-vis both China and Russia gave way to relative helplessness. In mid-1966, Mao launched the Cultural Revolution, destroying much of the government and Party apparatus and bringing parts of China to conditions of virtual anarchy. Though much of the motivation behind and mechanics of the Cultural Revolution still baffles the outsider, it is fair to say that Mao would not have risked it without a reasonable expectation that in view of America's involvement in Vietnam and the consequent tension between the United States and Russia they had little to fear from either of the two superpowers. For psychological reasons, official propaganda trumpeted the danger of an imminent attack by either or both on People's China. But any foreign observer of the American scene could well conclude that while Washington would escalate the war on North Vietnam, it would be careful not to risk an outright clash with China, and that because of the war, any understanding with Moscow was out of the question. China's terrible old man and his entourage could be confident that for all the itching fingers of some air force generals in the Pentagon and of their own ideological brethren in the Kremlin, the international situation prevented the Americans and the Russians from getting together. And as of today this certainty has been vindicated.

For the Soviets, the American overcommitment in Vietnam was also useful, as we have seen, obscuring as it has the great internal and external difficulties of the Soviet system. For the run-of-the-mill bureaucrats who took over from Khrushchev, their plans to undo Khrushchev's sporadic and quite modest concessions to liberalism and to reimpose some of the controls and spirit of Stalin's times gained both an impetus and a rationale from what was happening elsewhere. It would be fatuous to argue that without Vietnam, without the current disarray of American society, Russia would be moving toward a democratic system, but without those unfortunate developments, it would be harder for the rulers to justify to themselves and their people these measures of repression which have for the foreseeable future extinguished the hope for a more humane type of Communism such as appeared on the horizon in 1956 in Russia and in 1968 in Czechoslovakia.

But the over-all image of a peaceful and moderate Russia gained adherents in the most unexpected place: in Washington. Exasperated by the unending predicament, Johnson's administration clung rather pathetically to its original premise that in Vietnam it was combating *Chinese* Communism, hence that it was incumbent upon the Russians to understand the American actions, indeed to help the United States out of the mess. The Soviets were naturally not above encouraging this touching belief by an occasionally more restrained tone, by showing interest in American peace initiatives. There was an element of common sense underlying the American illusions—the Soviets have had a vital interest in the Vietnam situation not overheating—but why should the U.S.S.R. become unduly perturbed about a situation which threatens it with no immediate danger, and offers large ancillary benefits? At times Johnson indicated that it was a positive duty of the Kremlin to help bring the war to a negotiated settlement, but this, alas, was a pathetic misreading of the character and motivations of the men who govern the Soviet Union.

The Israeli-Arab war of 1967 demonstrated at once the strength and hollowness of these illusions underlying American attitudes. The Soviet Union did not instigate the war, but Soviet intelligence reports and advice were undoubtedly instrumental in Nasser's blockade of the Gulf of Aqaba, which in turn made inevitable the Israeli attack. The Soviets wanted not war but trouble, a prolonged crisis eventually resulting in America's humiliation, Israel's discomfiture, and the strengthened grip on their Arab clients. Still, the Arab defeat, embarrassing in view of its rapidity and completeness, was preferable to an Arab success which would threaten a head-on collision between the two superpowers.

It is the U.S. reaction to the Six-Day War which must lead to some somber reflections. There was every reason to be thankful that the war had been brief and remained localized. There was ample justification to admire bravery and resourcefulness of a small nation facing overwhelming numerical odds. But in the general America elation at the outcome there was also an irrational element of glee that for a change "we" got the better of "them"; that the Russians had suffered a grave blow to their prestige through the defeat of their protégés. Yet within a few weeks it became obvious that for all their embarrassment, the Soviets were planted in the Mediterranean more firmly than before.

More harmful than the elation, in itself foolish but understandable (few recent major developments in international affairs had been productive of anything but gloom), was the failure to realize that Israel's victory purchased nothing but time. Here, as after the Cuban missile crisis, was an opportunity for U.S. diplomatic initiatives, for discreet probing to determine whether the Arabs, perhaps temporarily disenchanted with their Soviet protector and with their own flamboyant oratory, might not enter upon the path of eventual accommodation with Israel, and whether the latter in the first flush of victory and relief might not be willing to trade the conquered territory for the right to a normal existence and security. There was little activity in that direction. The positions of the Near Eastern antagonists were allowed to harden, and the conflict resumed its festering and ever more ominous character. In America, the mood of self-congratulation soon passed; public attention turned back to the drama of Vietnam.

Partly to cover up their discomfiture, the Soviets in the wake of the Near Eastern imbroglio mounted frantic diplomatic activity: there was a summit meeting of the leaders of the Communist states in Europe, visits by Soviet potentates to soothe their Arab allies, and an imposing delegation to the United Nations headed by Kosygin himself. Since that institution happens to be situated in the United States, the Soviet Premier could hardly avoid meeting the chief executive of the government which, according to the Soviet press, had instigated the recent troubles in the Near East and was pursuing aggression in Vietnam.[19]

If one read the Soviet press, one was informed that the Glassboro meeting had been requested by Johnson and that Kosygin read him a stern lesson on American misdeeds in Israel, Vietnam, etc. But the Chinese Communists just *knew* that the chief imperialist and the chief revisionist had struck a deal to synchronize Soviet and American policies throughout the world. Alas, such a hopeful interpretation was belied by the facts. There was no "Spirit of Glassboro" resembling the ephemeral one of Geneva and Camp David.

The Soviets were little inclined to help Johnson with his problems, largely because he was already helping them with theirs free of charge. Like all sensible people, the Soviet leaders had to be interested in the long-range prospects for mankind, but as sexagenerian politicians, in a system where political and at one time physical survival had been in itself an art, they undoubtedly felt, to paraphrase Lord Keynes, that in the long run we would all be dead, and that as long as there was no considerable danger of that happening in the short run, they might as well settle down and enjoy the sight of America getting deeper and deeper into the mess.

In 1968, Johnson fell, victim of both the Vietnam war and of his craving for popularity. The humiliation of the seizure of the *U.S.S. Pueblo* by the North Koreans in January, the shock of the Tet offensive against South Vietnamese cities and American posts seemingly belied all the previous assertions and estimates of progress in the war; the war

[19] Soviet diplomatic activity bore an uncanny resemblance, both in the amount of sheer fuss and travel and in essential purposelessness, to President Johnson's celebrated "peace offensive" of the winter of 1965–66, when American government officials were dispatched to the four corners of the globe to proclaim that the United States wanted a peaceful settlement of the Vietnam crisis.

became hateful to a sizable and vocal element of the population. The always fragile national consensus which had enabled America to endure the tensions inherent in its role as a world power was broken. What had been the result of grievous errors of judgment seemed to many to be evidence of moral depravity of the "military-industrial complex," of the government, of the "system." Voices of dissent became universal—from bureaucrats high and low as they scurried from the government into the shelter of law firms, foundations, and universities; from ministers and professors. To the stale rhetoric seeking to justify the character of American involvement in Vietnam was opposed an increasingly frenzied protest. President Johnson's retirement and the opening of negotiations on Vietnam did not assuage the crisis, for it transcended both the question of political leadership and of the wretched war itself.

To one thinking in the Communist categories of the 1920s or '30s, these convulsions of American society would have seemed to be a prelude to the achievement of one's fondest hopes: the most advanced capitalist society was on the verge of internal collapse and anarchy. True, the crisis was hardly of the orthodox variety prescribed by Marx: it was not an economic depression but a complex social and cultural, in some respects indeed a religious, crisis. Nor was the Communist party in the vanguard of the revolutionary masses. In fact, there were no revolutionary masses. As for the orthodox Communists, it was only somebody as much behind the times as the ancient head of the FBI who could see them as even a serious influence behind the troubles. But then, neither the Russian Revolution nor the Chinese one had followed the script. The moment would come, ran the argument, when anarchist and radical movements would exhaust themselves in their separate and futile endeavors and protests, and their more serious participants would turn to the *one* revolutionary movement which history has designed as heir of capitalism. The future belonged not to the long-haired young men but to the American Brezhnevs and Kosygins, who would make short shrift of not only Wall Street (without damaging the precious managerial talent needed for the running of socialist economy) but also and especially those petty-bourgeois anarchists and exhibitionists who had no place in an orderly Communist society.

This vision, which at one time would have gladdened the heart of a Lenin disciple (and which may have a certain perverse appeal to a "square" proponent of law and order), cannot be reassuring today to a Russian Communist. There is a point, in the nuclear age, beyond which your enemy's troubles become a source of apprehension. One does not have to spell out the reasons. Authoritarianism is the heir of anarchy. And if today's America, with its faltering foreign policy, divided both by natural pluralism and all the conflicts which have ensued in the last five years, is a threat, what about an America with its vast resources and power at the disposal of a single will or a small group of men?

For the Soviet leadership, then, the American crisis has posed some very somber questions.

But being the kind of politicians they are, the leaders of the Soviet Union are not likely to go beyond this approach—advising North Vietnam to negotiate, showing eagerness to hold talks on strategic arms limitations, to reveal an attitude of *measured* hostility and of *restrained* satisfaction over America's troubles—toward a more fundamental solution of the world's problems. If war undermines the fabric of democratic society, prolonged international tranquillity eats at the foundations and rationale of any authoritarian system. The history of Czechoslovakia offers the most recent and instructive demonstration of this truth.

Two main reasons brought about the dramatic events in Czechoslovakia. One was the virtual collapse of the economy in this country which, of all the satellites, had hewn longest to Stalinist ways. The other was the relative tranquility and lack of tension in Central Europe when the Soviets relaxed their pressure on Berlin in the wake of the Cuban missile crisis. With no external enemy, with the Soviets engrossed in the China problem, the more progressive elements in the Czechoslovak party could turn their attention to pressing domestic problems. The enemy became the unenlightened leadership of the party, discredited by its economic incompetence, compromised by its participation in repression under Stalin, and regarded with ill-concealed scorn and impatience by the Russians themselves. It was easy to topple it in January, 1968, and replace it by a new team headed by Alexander Dubĉek—a Communist of impeccable credentials, who in fact had had a spectacular rise under the old regime. Economic reform and cautious liberalization were on the agenda, and those were accepted by the Kremlin as long overdue. But the new leaders found themselves propelled at a much faster pace of reform than they had originally intended. The people's aspirations had been too long repressed. The Czechs and Slovaks had not had the terrible lesson of the Hungarians in 1956, or the emotional release of the Polish October of the same year, followed by a gradual disenchantment. In May, the regime took the step which determined its eventual fate: censorship of the press was virtually abolished. There ensued the amazing phenomenon of a Communist country with free communication media and no police repression.

From the Kremlin's vantage point, the challenge was unambiguous. The Russians could tolerate, though with great distaste and ill humor, Rumania's somewhat independent behavior in foreign policy, for in their domestic policies, the Rumanian leaders ran a tidy totalitarian state. Finland could be allowed a democratic system because she had *never been* a Communist state. But Czechoslovakia might start an epidemic. And, then, how long before the demoralizing examples would have their effect in the Fatherland of Socialism itself? In the case of Eastern Europe, the domino theory was a most reasonable conjecture.

The remarkable thing about the Soviet intervention in Czechoslovakia was that it had not come earlier and that it followed considerable hesitation and divided counsels within the Kremlin. In June and July there were probably those who felt that even Dubček's regime would be unable to satisfy fully the people's aroused thirst for freedom. There were Czechoslovaks demanding a genuine multiparty system. Presumably then, the less "activist" members of the Politburo could argue, the Prague leaders themselves would eventually summon help from "fraternal socialist states." Against these arguments for delay there were undoubted pleadings (also from East Berlin and Warsaw) that it might be too late then.

It was to resolve such doubts that the Politburo of the CPSU held lengthy joint meetings in July with the corresponding body of the Czechoslovak party. For all the subsequent repression of Czechoslovakia, here was a significant portent of the times. Even in Khrushchev's era, no such elaborate consultation involving practically all of the real rulers of the U.S.S.R. took place with the Poles or Hungarians. The Soviet leaders probably had little hope that the Dubček team could or would moderate its liberal ways. They were more interested to find out whether there was any real chance of armed resistance if they invaded, if they could undermine the unity of the Czechoslovaks' leadership. Reassured on both counts, the Soviets struck not long afterward: an estimated half million Warsaw Pact soldiers invaded the country.[20] The second part of the Soviet premise proved at first incorrect: no replacement could be found for Dubček, and the imprisoned Czech

---

[20] Other Communist states' contingents were rather symbolic in character; the Rumanians did not participate.

leaders had to be restored to their offices, if not their previous power. But resolution and national unity could not withstand the passage of time and the apparent hopelessness of resistance against overwhelming odds. Within a few weeks a purge began which would soon encompass Dubček and his closest collaborators. It would be unfair to view their successors as mere time-servers and Soviet puppets; some of them might honestly have felt they could save at least part of the achievements of the past and prevent the worst of repression.

For all their dignity and defiance in the face of the superior force, the Czechs and Slovaks had to submit. As after Hungary in 1956, the chorus of disapproval subsided very quickly. Even at its most intense, the protest over Czechoslovakia was like a whisper compared to that over Vietnam. In any event, even without Vietnam and the appalling domestic situation, the U.S. government could and would have done nothing to stop the Soviet move. After all, it had done nothing about the Communist coup in Prague in 1948 or about the Soviet move into Hungary in 1956, when forceful diplomatic action *might* have made a difference. Yet there can be no doubt that the deplorable situation of this country both at home and abroad furthered the Russians' belief that they could move with impunity. The official Soviet explanation was found in a tale of anti-socialist plots encouraged by Western imperialists and Bonn *revanchists,* which impelled the "healthy elements" of the Czechoslovak party and working class to summon fraternal help. Yet even the Soviet press had to acknowledge the hostility of the vast majority of Czechs toward their "savior," ranging from sullen silence to tragic acts of defiance and suicidal attacks upon Russian tanks.[21]

In some intellectual circles in the Soviet Union this rape of a small country led to feelings of humiliation and some individual protests. Those less heroically inclined but more thoughtful must have reflected how illogical it was to attack little Czechoslovakia, which did not present any threat to Russia's *national interest,* while the regime stood confused and apparently helpless before China's threats and territorial claims on the Soviet Union. But it would be unduly romantic to

[21] The Soviet reader was treated to tearful accounts of how the Czechs simply would not understand: a typical Soviet soldier (for some reason usually blond or red-haired, *always* from the provinces rather than Moscow, *always* a Slav rather than from Asiatic Russia) would patiently try to explain to a sullen crowd gathered around his tank how the Soviets could not leave unanswered the cry for help of the Czech workers and would in return reap verbal abuse. Or there were those suspicious-sounding tales of Soviet tank commanders steering their vehicles into the ditch rather than driving through the hostile crowd blocking their path, thus displaying that humanity, international solidarity, and coolness in the face of provocation so typical of the Soviet soldier.

imagine that the majority of Russians were greatly perturbed by this gross exercise of force. Czechoslovakia had a higher standard of living than Russia; her citizens had been allowed much more freedom than granted in their own country. So what more did those Czechs and Slovaks want? A small country should respect the wishes of its big neighbor and protector. Such, alas, was the reaction of the Soviet man-in-the-street.

As this is being written, Soviet troops stand on guard in Czechoslovakia, "protecting" it from an invasion by West German and/or NATO forces, a threat as real today as that of Canada seizing Michigan. At the same time, American armed forces are deployed in Vietnam and Cambodia, their presumed objective being the "protection" of Southeast Asia from China, something which, thanks to the Sino-Soviet conflict, would be impossible anyway without the massive American intervention. Yet in both cases the presence of the soldiers is a testimony to the inability of the respective society to cope with one of the basic problems of post–World War II international relations. The Soviet soldiers bivouacked in Czechoslovakia are obviously not there to repulse Western tanks and infantry. They stand guard against a reinvasion of Czechoslovakia by *ideas*—ideas of a more rational, less dogmatic, and less bureaucratic organization of economic life, in fact of life in general. They bar the spread of influence of a more relaxed society offering scope for the individual's rights, interests, and whims. In this sense, those soldiers *are* guarding the socialist camp, for it and the U.S.S.R. especially have demonstrated up to now, for all their dazzling technological and economic progress, their inability to compete freely with the West when it comes to amenities of life, the willingness to accept the individual's autonomy within society, and many other achievements of Western civilization within the last three hundred years—achievements which do not have to be called by the grandiloquent terms "freedom" or "democracy," but can be more adequately summarized by one word, "tolerance."

The sheer inertia of the past policies pushes the Soviet Union on the road to expansion, though by now there is neither rhyme nor reason to this expansion. A large country which becomes Communist is thereby and inevitably a rival, perhaps an enemy, of Russia, and a small one is a source of headaches, risks, and, most obviously, expense.[22]

22 By invading Czechoslovakia and depriving her of the possibility of receiving foreign credits, the U.S.S.R. undertook the not inconsiderable burden of underwriting the Czech economy to save it from complete collapse. And recently the Soviets had similarly to bail out the Polish Communists. As some East Euro-

American foreign policy has also become the slave of a past and by now obsolete rhetoric. American soldiers are in Vietnam because the United States has failed to employ the weapons of diplomacy and political organization. Realistic and pragmatic in their domestic politics, the Americans have persisted in being doctrinaire in viewing the world at large, and it is no wonder that eventually this unrealistic vision of world politics impaired the rational fabric of her domestic political processes. If the world has refused to become one large America, then there must be something basically wrong with America.

For some time now, the United States and Russia have been struggling not so much against each other as against phantoms, their own fears of what each might become unless it scored points over the other or barred success to the other side. Fresh victories of Communism abroad may avail the Soviet Union nothing, but to Brezhnev and Kosygin (and one must suppose to a large number of the party following) they provide welcome evidence that history is *not* working against Communism, that the Soviet system is *not* the product of fortuitous accidents, held together by repression and indoctrination, but in fact the fulfillment of age-long dreams. Similar reassurance from the gods of history is sought by the Americans, both by the rulers and those who call themselves dissenters. In May, 1970, President Nixon sought to justify the entrance of U.S. troops into Cambodia, something which may or may not have been advisable on political and military grounds, as a test of the will for survival of American society, as proof of whether or not this country was to become a "helpless giant." And many dissenters seek reassurance in their demand that United States foreign policy be a constant demonstration of selflessness, that this country abandon and chastise those friends who depart from the path of democratic virtue, and that in contrast it grant every benefit of doubt and wholesale dispensation from such virtue to governments which are hostile to the West. It is not the rivalry between the United States and Russia which offers the main threat to peace. It is the irrational premises and impulses that underlie the policies of both which threaten the world with incalculable dangers.

---

pean economists have argued with the author, the old Stalinist pattern of outright Soviet exploitation of the satellites has been almost reversed. For political reasons the Soviet Union does not allow its protégés to do what she herself is strenuously pursuing, i.e., extensive commercial ties and credits from the West. Consequently the U.S.S.R. provides a guaranteed market for its satellites' goods. The Soviets then often get shoddy goods, while the Polish, Czech, etc. industries, especially those producing consumer goods, have no incentive to become efficient or competitive.

Conclusion

The Immorality
of Unrealism

As this book was being written, in June, 1970, it was commencement time on America's campuses. Formerly this occasion was solemn in its outward appurtenances, gay and even frivolous in spirit. Now irreverence has replaced solemnity; gaiety has given way to that self-conscious seriousness so unattractive in young men and women. In previous years orators chosen from the rich and successful gravely admonished the young that challenges awaited them in the world beyond the university (how easy it is to speak of challenges when they seem not too pressing). Now a prudent university administration would seek out speakers from the Establishment of Dissent, and they would dwell on the iniquities of this society, compliment the young on their moral fervor, which if persevered in and carried into the world at large offered great hope for changing this sinful world.

The rhetoric has been turned around, but the gist of the message is pretty much the same: idealism and moral passion can and must move mountains; to accept the world as it is, to acknowledge that it can be improved, but slowly rather than dramatically transformed, is considered for a young man unbecoming if not downright sordid.[1]

As with the commencement speeches so with American foreign policy. The ritual and rhetoric have persisted though their content has

---

[1] A truly startling commencement address in 1970 as in 1950 would have been one urging that an informed and dispassionate mind is the first and perhaps the most fundamental condition of the individual's contribution to social improvement.

greatly changed. It is easy to see how discussion of foreign policy has been riveted to famous "challenges": there was first the "challenge of the world community," epitomized in those extravagant hopes in the U.N.; then in a different and much more real sense there was a "challenge of Communism." But even here a common-sense notion became warped through rhetoric: instead of considering the rival to be the U.S.S.R. with its problems, its strengths, and its weaknesses, we persisted in seeing "godless Communism" or "international Communism." There was little disposition between 1945 and 1950 toward a realistic picture of the Soviet Union, to see through the Soviet bluff to what should have been the obvious truth: that Soviet vulnerabilities *then* made her a "paper tiger" if there ever was one, instead of that ominous dragon ready to uncoil and seize Western Europe. In the fifties, the preponderance of force on the American side was no longer so great, but a realization of its own vast assets and of the already perceptible splits and growing conflicts within the Communist would have enabled the United States to engage in a profitable give and take with Russia instead of those illusory exercises of Geneva and Camp David. The problem of making the Russians achieve what they *half* wanted—a comprehensive agreement with America on several areas of international tension—became more and more difficult. But again even after the Cuban missile crisis, an event which should have been a lesson as to how easy it was for the two countries to come close to agreement as well as to nuclear war, American diplomacy wanted not to strike a bargain with the Soviets but to force them to acknowledge what in American eyes were self-evident moral truths. And, finally, in their frustration over Vietnam, many Americans have turned their moralistic fervor against themselves, or rather their government and society. The same emotional intensity which before had gone into the speeches denouncing "Godless Communism" or "Communist aggression" rings now through the speeches not only of those on the left of the political spectrum, but of U.S. senators and former high administration officials as they denounce America's alleged moral derelictions, her arrogant presumption to defend freedom throughout the world while it is a very defective freedom that we have here at home.

In fact, the pendulum has swung to the other side: the American government and public used to demand that "they," the Communists, demonstrate their good faith, that "they" show signs of moral worthiness before the United States could or would negotiate with them. Now the argument has been reversed: it is the United States which must show that its intentions and aims are pure, that it does not or has stopped propagating capitalism and "neo-imperialism." Dulles once demanded in a public statement that the Russians repudiate or, as they would have put it, recant their previous ill deeds and give convincing promises and guarantees of their future good behavior. Now sober-minded politicians of both parties, not to mention preachers and professors, make the same demands on the United States, seek national penitence for sins and transgressions which even the most uninhibited Soviet or Chinese Communist propagandist has not thought to attribute to the United States. The mania of guilt and political masochism has assumed proportions which, except for their dangerous implications, would be truly comical. The demands for a pragmatic and less moralistic and emotion-charged approach toward foreign policy have never been popular in this country.

In January, 1966, testifying before the Senate Foreign Relations Committee, Secretary Rusk sought to defend American policies in Vietnam by defending the premises of the American policies in 1945: "It seems to me when we were thinking long and hard about these questions at the end of World War II, we did in fact come up with the wisest answer, and that is, small and large nations have a right to live without being molested by their neighbors, and that a small nation has a right to live in peace and without domination by somebody else. I am very much concerned about substituting the idea of spheres of influence among a few great powers for the structure of international life laid out in the United Nations Charter." [2] As a debating point this was a shrewd thrust. Pushed against the wall by Senate critics who argued the impracticality and dangers of American policy in Southeast Asia, the Secretary appealed to American "idealism"; would you have American policies determined just by what is prudent and practical rather than by the immutable principles of right and wrong? he seems to be saying to his tormentors.

Rusk's statement is a classical illustration of the confusion attending American foreign policy. It did not have to take much hard or long thinking to decide that small as well as large states have a right to be left alone, and not only by their neighbors (and *small* states have been molesting large ones as well as vice versa). But what does this irreproachable maxim have to do with the reality of international relations since 1945? Did the United States *in fact* proscribe spheres of influence in the wake of World War II? Certainly the practical effect

[2] *The Vietnam Hearings* (New York, 1966), p. 270.

of the Yalta and Potsdam agreements was to authorize the Soviet Union to consider Eastern Europe and Manchuria as its sphere of influence. From its allies, notably France and Britain, the United States demanded a strict adherence to international morality, but from its rival, the U.S.S.R., she did not, because she could not. Did the Monroe Doctrine mean that Latin America is within the U.S. sphere of influence? In 1945, such a question would have been thought in bad taste. But today, when even some *right-wing* Latin American governments confiscate the property of U.S. companies, the triumph of our policy of masochistic virtue is well-nigh complete.

It is often asserted that the United States has inherited the imperial role of Western Europe. This is at best a most imprecise manner of speaking: the U.S. has inherited and vastly expanded the Western powers' overseas *obligations*. What nineteenth-century apologist of imperialism would have classified as such the sacrifice of ten thousand dead and of 30 billion dollars per year in the defense not of a colony or of investments but of a hazy geopolitical concept? The "white man's burden" was by comparison very light: a handful of professional soldiers and administrators, and the rewards so substantial in economic gains and power. Many critics of American policy who once criticized it on the sensible grounds that it was unwise and dangerous felt constrained as the war went on to shift their attack to the same ground on which Secretary Rusk tried to defend it: a higher morality transcending the national interest. For Rusk, the moral transgressor has been North Vietnam, for his critics the United States who barred the legitimate aspirations of the Vietnamese people. This higher morality assumes the aspect of an exacting and vengeful god; from the dogmatic defenders of the official Vietnam policy, it demands a virtual destruction of a whole country, a continuing, heavy sacrifice of lives; from its dogmatic opponents, it exacts the sacrifice of 18 million people to a harsh totalitarian rule. The Vietnam story thus brings into full relief the immorality of unrealism in international politics. But this fatal flaw, as this book has attempted to show, has been with U.S. policies ever since World War II and since the active assumption by America of a leading role in international affairs. Much could have been saved in human lives, in human freedom and contentment throughout the world, if only U.S. policies had been guided by less elevated and more practical goals, had they been instructed less by a moralistic rhetoric and more by a realistic calculation of what assets this country disposed to help its friends and frustrate the designs of its adversaries.

Yet this view, commonplace as it might appear, has never found favor among either the defenders or the critics of America's foreign policy. The moralists, as we might call them, have usually a second line of defense to fall back on after their first one of proclaiming realism as ignoble and immoral. This is a strange form of fatalism, masquerading as historical or sociological wisdom. Nothing, say the defenders, could have avoided the melancholy turn of events since World War II: Communist expansion, the collapse of Western influence in Africa and Asia, the problem of all those explosive spots throughout the world which can at any moment ignite into vast conflicts. The United States has done all it could do; it must go on struggling on any periphery of the free world which the Communists choose to attack, hoping that sometime, somehow, the enemies of this world would be forced or inclined to undergo a dramatic conversion and mend their ways.

To assailants of America's record also the present mess has been preordained—but by the character of American government and society. The most extreme see this nation as trying to repress the historically inevitable movement against capitalism and imperialism. Hence it is America which has to undergo a conversion. But even those who reject this doctrinaire view see the world crises as caused primarily by the United States, in specific by the establishment which has a vested interest in piling up armaments, in preserving right-wing regimes throughout the world, in refusing to come to terms with global, historically inevitable changes. It is the United States which through its resistance to and failure to comprehend the inevitability of this change has forced the Communists to continue in their repressive and warlike ways. Here the moderate critic will echo the radical's refrain: it is the United States, the West, which has to change if the ultimate catastrophe is to be avoided. No, not through a revolution at home, but through understanding and assisting revolution in the world at large, through continuous concessions and proofs of good will toward the Third World and even the Communists.

Both the critic and the defender share a strange unwillingness to credit human intelligence with a major role in deciding the course of international affairs, in seeing our predicaments as resulting from right or wrong decisions, from acting on the basis of correct or incorrect information. For both the statesman's task is mainly to perceive those huge moral and historical verities which indicate the only right course of action for the republic. In brief, foreign policy may not be adjudged as wise or unwise. For its defenders, no matter what its failures or shortcomings, it has been a clear fulfillment of our moral and historical obligations; for its critics, it has been the unfolding of our moral depravity or our refusal to read correctly the ineluctable laws of history. And thus the Vietnam debate has not really been about U.S. policies in or concerning Vietnam; it has been about ourselves, about the character and moral worth of American society.

The moralist-fatalists have some obvious debating points against one who sees the present troubles as largely compounded of past errors and miscalculations. It is impossible to *prove* that if Roosevelt and his advisers had been better informed about Stalin's Russia, East European states might now enjoy internal freedom and democratic regimes; that greater realism about China and Communism could have led to at least a part of mainland China being saved from Mao's dictatorship; that a less rapid pace of decolonialization in Africa would have secured more stable foundation for political independence on that continent. But common sense certainly argues that those goals and cautions, if observed by a country with the vast powers and resources of the United States, were eminently practical. How suggestive in this respect has been the lesson of the economy. The prodigious performance of American industry and agriculture during the war stilled the doctrinaire debate about the relative virtues of pure "capitalism" and a strict "planned economy," discredited the fatalism which ever since the Great Depression had proclaimed that any nonsocialist system must mean huge unemployment and stagnation, or, contrariwise, that social-welfare measures were the "road to serfdom." The result has been the prodigious recovery and economic growth of Western Europe and an unparalleled period of prosperity for the United States. It has been the recent *political* troubles which have enabled the moralist to re-enter the lists with a proclamation that poverty and pollution are inherent evils of this materialistic and competitive society.

Tempting though it is to accept the thesis that the end of the Vietnam war would in itself work a miraculous transformation at home and abroad, that with American soldiers out of Indochina, or at least no longer in combat, this country could reorder its priorities, as the phrase goes, and devote its energies to domestic problems, it is hard to believe. *Any* solution of the Vietnam problem will have to be followed by a more rather than less intense concentration on problems of foreign policy.

For one, there will be the task of making up for the years during which American foreign policy has been virtually in abeyance while the main efforts of the government and attention of the country were riveted on Southeast Asia. Even granting the most favorable resolution of Vietnam, such as is not now on the horizon, the position of the United States will still be less influential, and the possibilities for an accommodation with the Communist world, the chances of alleviating tension in areas like the Middle East, much fewer than in 1965. The problems and dangers will not go away. It is a most dangerous delusion that other nations will allow America a breathing spell, will "behave," while this country devotes itself to internal problems. In fact, the more the United States tries to ignore foreign dangers and problems, the more they will intrude on the domestic scene, the less they will allow American society to recover its balance and employ rational ways of dealing with its problems.

It must appear disheartening to put the problem in this way. This country has grown weary of its foreign commitments and disenchanted with the task it had welcomed so eagerly after the war of teaching virtue and democracy to the world. And it has been shown abundantly how Vietnam has not been productive of greater realism in world affairs, how one form of unrealism has replaced another, how the naïve and uncritical assumption of America's superiority and mission has for many Americans been replaced by the brooding feeling of guilt about this country's role in the world. If the latter mood continues and gains ascendance, it would be hard to remain optimistic about chances of avoiding a major disaster, let alone of reversing the trend toward growing international anarchy. Our increasing incapacity to formulate a foreign policy might offer an irresistible temptation even for the usually prudent Soviet leadership to indulge in adventurism, to initiate or exacerbate small and local crises, one of which might sooner or later ignite a major and world-wide conflict. We can now appreciate that what had kept the Berlin and Cuban crises of the past from erupting into wars had not been so much American policies as Soviet prudence. And that prudence in turn derived not only from the undoubted fact of the overwhelming American power but from a strange mixture of trust and fear of this country by the Soviets: trust that this power would not be exercised wantonly, without an extreme provocation; fear that in the face of such a provocation American society was cohesive and determined enough to react. It has been then the cohesion and stability of American society even more than the nuclear arsenal which have provided a barrier against a new world war. And this consideration apart from any other makes internal anarchy or revolution an impermissible luxury in this age. There is a strain in current American radical thought which seems to echo a nineteenth-century Russian radical who wrote that everything which can be destroyed must be destroyed. But today the implications of "restructuring" society on this principle would be rather far-reaching.

Yet the present turn in the Americans' thinking about world affairs is not irreversible. The current breast beating may be a hopeful sign. Our rebellious young have grown up, after all, amidst a chorus of praise for the American Way of Life, amidst unquestioning acceptance of America's mission to save the world. And so the present debilitating clichés will lose their power to impress, will grow stale and boring. Perhaps the legacy of the crisis will be a more realistic and widespread appreciation of America's role in the world, of her opportunities and limitations.

Realism will also demand a sober appreciation of what is happening and is likely to happen in the Communist world. In the recent past there has been a strong temptation for both the government and the public to exaggerate the extent of the Soviet Union's "moderation," to assume that Russia *already* has become aware that she shares with the United States the responsibility for world peace. But as we have seen, this exaggerates both her rulers' inclination to see an *entirely* peaceful world and their ability to work for this goal even if they were inclined to do so. The events of the last twenty years have created a gap, ever widening and too large to be ignored even by the Soviet leaders, not to mention their subjects, between the interests of Communism as a world-wide movement and the national interests of Russia. But the *self*-interest of the Soviet ruling class compels it to preserve the myth, even if not always to act according to its implications, that the security of their country and the expansion of Communism are indissolubly bound together.

It is unlikely that anything in the near future will affect this picture. We have been exposed to a variety of enticing theories postulating that the chasm between the democratic world and the Communist one has been narrowing and might soon disappear. Industrialization has been indeed responsible for a degree of convergence of two *societies;* a Soviet engineer does indeed think in terms not too dissimilar from his opposite number in the United States. But a harassed Cabinet member in Washington has aims, fears, and hopes of quite a different order from a member of the Politburo, and indeed were this not so, the Soviets would be much more fearful of us than they are. Nor can the danger of a nuclear war in itself secure a peaceful world. In view of the situation in the Near East and in Southeast Asia, it is hardly necessary to expand on this theme.

What is then prudent to hope for from the U.S.S.R. in the near future is that her rulers will become more aware of the risks of their policy of *pretending* to try to win the world for Communism, of aggravating international tension in various areas not because it promises to bring them solid benefits but because it causes discomfiture and trouble to the United States.

The dangers of the nuclear age then impose a peculiar consideration of prudence and conservatism upon both superpowers. Neither can afford a violent internal conflict nor wish such troubles upon the other. This is a somber reflection, for it prevents us from wishing that for their own sake as well as that of the world the Soviet people could *drastically* alter the system under which they live. Requirements of peace, more particularly of saving the world from a nuclear holocaust which a tottering totalitarian regime might unleash, take precedence over those of democracy. We should not expect that the regime we will deal with in Russia for many years to come will be other than an authoritarian one, that any basis for accommodation with the U.S.S.R. will be other than one of mutual interest. And should the present situation in China endure for some years, the same uncomfortable truth may come to apply to her.

The growth of opposition in Russia, especially among certain intellectual and artistic circles and among the young, has of course attracted a great deal of attention and sympathy in the West, as well as a rather disproportionate amount of concern in the Kremlin. But it would be mistaken to assume that the dissent is widespread, that the enlightened ideas of a Sakharov, the passion for telling the truth about the Soviet past and present of a Solzhenitsyn, can now or in the near future be *openly* supported by a sizable segment even of the educated class. The limit of the regime's ability at self-reform is something on the order of Yugoslavia's: an authoritarian state but without the morbid elements of suspicion and persecution of all unorthodox ideas which the Soviets have retained even after Stalin. That it might evolve in this direction would still depend in a way on what was happening in the West. A conservative Soviet bureaucrat could have a ready-made answer to his more liberal colleague. Would he want the Soviet arts and intellectual world, and public attitude toward morals, to resemble those current in the West? Perhaps the United States can afford this license, but can the U.S.S.R.? Russian history has not seen many periods when the fall or even relaxation of traditional authority did not bring about the threat of *complete* anarchy. The present condition of American society could hardly be an inducement to totalitarian regimes to embark upon internal liberalization.

But the logic of the situation would dictate a different evolution for Soviet society. The regime may grow explicitly, as it already has implicitly, more nationalistic. Communism, already a bore in the eyes of Soviet citizens, may be recognized by the next generation of the Soviet rulers as a source of expense, of foreign entanglements and dangers. A bureaucratic socialist society might become disinclined to devote resources and expend energies in advancing the cause of foreign adventurers and fanatics. Here, of course, the crucial consideration is the future of the Soviet-Chinese conflict. Should the U.S.S.R. resume unchallenged leadership of world Communism, there would be less reason for some future leaders to break with or attenuate their connection with the international revolutionary movement. But it is difficult to see how such an eventuality would come about. Until the early 1960s there was some hope that China might be prevented from becoming a nuclear power and that it could be restored to the status of junior partner. Since then the Soviet Union has watched China acquiring nuclear technology and continuing and expanding its challenge and provocation of the country which made it possible for Mao and his partisans to become masters of the largest nation in the world. Up to now the Chinese have won their wager: even when infinitely weaker, they baited the Soviet Union with impunity just as the weak and backward Russia between 1945 and 1950 challenged the enormously more powerful United States. And just as the United States cannot shape the world to its liking as it could have up to 1950, so the U.S.S.R. will never recover its unchallenged domination of world Communism. The Soviets have not reconciled themselves to this situation. The possibility of a war between the two Communist giants cannot be excluded though its implications grow every day more catastrophic, for both countries and for the world.

What other hope for the Kremlin of "solving" the Chinese problem? Evidently it lies in the possibility of a crippling internal conflict in China, a civil war in which one faction would seek Soviet support, or at least Soviet good will.[3]

---

[3] One detects this longing in many Soviet commentaries on China, in their constant refrain that the country is ruled by a small family clique around Mao and that

Whether such a momentous development, a new Chinese revolution, is on the horizon, whether the Soviets could or would instigate it, are questions about which we can only speculate. Some time ago, the Soviet regime authorized the publication of a poem by Voznesensky in which this outstanding poet evoked the past threats and depredations of old Russia by the Mongols and drew not too veiled allusions to the present. The awareness of the danger from the East is deeply ensconced in the Russian national consciousness; it transcends considerations of ideology and the temporizing maneuvers of the leaders. What, compared to this threat, are the alleged intrigues of the American imperialists and the Bonn *"revanchists,"* the economic reforms in Czechoslovakia, the affairs of Cuba and North Vietnam, and all those other supposed dangers and problems with which the Kremlin has tried to distract the attention of its subjects from *the* problem which faces the Soviet state and peoples? This is one question which, if it is ever openly asked in the Soviet Union, could shake the foundations of the system.

For its own part, Peking, confident that it represents the wave of the future, is also unable to envisage any other ultimate solution of *the* problem except in terms catastrophic for its antagonist. The Chinese Communists want the Soviets to abandon their "revisionism," which in plain English would mean to acknowledge Chinese hegemony in world Communism and to subordinate their foreign policy to that of China. Without such a capitulation by Moscow, the Chinese are as eager and hopeful for severe internal conflicts within the Soviet Union as their Russian comrades are of similar developments in their country. And in their rancor against the Soviets, Mao and his colleagues appear unmindful of how dangerous to the whole world could be internal anarchy in a country with a full nuclear arsenal.

The vast danger inherent in the world situation, the apparent intractability of such outstanding problems as the Near East and Southeast Asia, ought not blind us to the vast opportunities and assets enjoyed by the Western world. The key among them is the ability of liberal democracy to endure peace. In contrast, the Communist states have

---

the army has virtually supplanted the Communist party. Yet Mao emerged supreme from the turbulence of the Cultural Revolution, just as Stalin's power remained unscathed after the vast disruption of the collectivization and the Great Purge of the 1930s. There is something at once pathetic and unconsciously ironic in the Soviets' pious indignation at the outrages perpetrated by the Mao clique. How can Mao get away with such crimes and oppression? How can the Chinese tolerate a regime at once so tyrannical and so preposterous? Is there not some Marxist god to punish such transgressions? ask the virtuous and peace-loving men of the Kremlin.

shown how difficult it is for them to exist, except in a virtual state of siege or in a world in which there is a constant and high degree of international tension. Peace brings with it the almost inevitable pressure on a Communist regime to liberalize itself: witness Czechoslovakia in 1967–68, where, with the threat of a conflict in Central Europe remote, the Communist leaders though trained in Stalin's school had to turn to reform. Peace brings with it an almost inevitable challenge to the cohesion and unity of the Communist camp. It is no wonder that the leaders of Russia see a degree of international tension as a safeguard of their rule, and those of China desire even more intense conflicts in all corners of the globe. History has neatly reversed Lenin's thesis that capitalism requires wars and foreign conquests in order to live and prosper. And in contrast it is the Communist world which has shown that its most advanced stage is that of rival imperialisms: whatever its other virtues and defects, Communism has amply demonstrated that it cannot secure peace, the main problem of this age. It cannot inherit the world, although it may destroy it.

The Communists have always spoken about the internal contradictions of capitalism. But here again the evidence of the last twenty-five years has neatly reversed this analysis: it is Communism which suffers from insuperable internal contradictions; it cannot improve the well-being of its people without bringing about the demands for a freer as well as more affluent life. The very internal mechanics of a Communist society are bound to maximize dissatisfaction. Its vaunted advantage of planned economy has turned out to be illusory: it has shown itself extremely efficient only in those areas of the economy which are connected with the sinews of power—hence the rapid development of Soviet and Chinese nuclear technology, and hence those amazing statistics of the growth of Russian heavy industry. The lessons of the last twenty-five years expose both the claim and the potential of Communism to become a new world civilization. Its apparent successes have in fact been the failures of will and intelligence on the other side.

In itself this inability of Communism to produce an alternative civilization can be of but little comfort to the West. For the latter has yet to prove that it can endure that condition of "neither peace nor war" which its own mistakes as well as the policies of the Communist states have imposed upon the world since 1945. Both American society in its present turmoil and Western Europe, for all its marvelous recovery and growth and the burying of its ancient national hostilities, are disenchanted about playing and unwilling to assume the world role warranted by their vast power, resources, and traditions: those are the uncomfortable facts of 1970. But the weaknesses of the West, unlike those of the Communist bloc, are psychological rather than organic. The "West," more precisely that complex of institutions and ideas which have passed their original boundaries and are now ensconced in societies like Japan and (to be sure somewhat shakily) India, has exhibited an amazing toughness and vitality. This is a way of life which after all has survived two major attempts at suicide, so to speak: World War I, and the complacent toleration of the rise of Hitlerism and fascism in the thirties. It is not too extravagant to expect that it can also withstand the current assaults.

If so, a balanced view of the recent past and present will enable the West and primarily the United States to deal with world problems in terms of neither moral self-righteousness nor guilt and contrition; foreign policy will be understood neither as the search for an instant millennium of a world community nor as a penance for past real or alleged sins of the West. It will be seen as the hard and often frustrating search for enlarging the area of accommodation with the Communist states, which in the foreseeable future means primarily the Soviet Union, an effort premised on their leaders' growing not more democratic or humane but more ready to follow their national interest rather than obsolete ideological delusions, on their becoming convinced not so much of the benevolent intentions but of the strength, the endurance, and the political intelligence of the West. It is only realism which can enable American foreign policy to work successfully for a more peaceful world, and it is only in such a world that democracy and social justice may resume their advance.

Index

Acheson, Dean, 130, 157–58; China, Communist victory in, 159–67; definition of defense perimeter, 165; Dulles, 212; foreign policy of, 186–88, 201; Korean War, 184–85; MacArthur, 177, 181–82; Philippines, 165–66

Adenauer, Konrad, 216, 231n., 319; Eisenhower, 202, 205, 300–303, 308–309; U.S. attitude toward, 237, 290, 307; U.S.S.R., 218–19. *See also* West Germany

Africa: decolonialization of, 388; Soviet interest in, 275, 285, 295, 313

agriculture in U.S.S.R., 6, 129–30, 207; Khrushchev, 223–24, 319n.

Akhmatova, Anna, 111

Albania, 131n., 139; Communist China, 312; Khrushchev, 321, 323–24; U.S.S.R., 356

Aleutian Islands, 85, 165

Alexander, Harold, 60, 61, 66

Alexander I, Czar, 11, 180

Algeria, 195; Egypt, 253, 256; France, 237, 252, 272–76, 308, 351; U.S.S.R., 274–75

Aliluyeva, Svetlana, 10n., 23, 111

Allied Control Commission, 73, 117

Allied powers in World War II, 3–4, 7–8, 25

American Communists, 142, 377. *See also* McCarthyism

American Legion, 142

anti-Americanism in U.S.S.R., 109–113

anti-Semitism in U.S.S.R., 111, 254

Arab nationalism, 251, 253, 257

Argentina, 64

Aswan Dam, 254, 279

Atlantic Charter, 41

atom bomb: China, 106, 269, 358, 392; U.S., 27, 76, 81–82, 103–105, 179; U.S.S.R., 77, 103, 106, 156, 168, 169, 214, 270. *See also* nuclear weapons

"atomic diplomacy," 94–95, 259

atomic energy, international control of, 103–107, 115. *See also* disarmament; nuclear test-ban treaty

Atomic Energy Commission, 283

Attlee, Clement, 184–85

Austria: peace treaty, 218, 219, 241

Badoglio, Pietro, 23

Baghdad Pact. *See* Central Treaty Organization

Balkan states, Stalin and, 48–49, 139

Baltic states, U.S.S.R. and, 12

Bandung Conference, 228, 304

Bao Dai, Emperor, 250, 344

Baruch Plan, 105–107, 229

Batista, Fulgencio, 314–15

Bavaria, 12

Bay of Pigs invasion, 319-20, 327

Belorussia, 9, 54

Ben Bella, Ahmed, 195, 318

Beneš, Eduard, 58, 136–37

Ben Gurion, David, 258

Beria, Lavrenti, 183, 196, 207, 239, 287; East Germany, 204, 206; firing of, 195, 197

Berlin, 73–74, 131, 204; Adenauer, 300–301; blockade, 133, 134, 148–51, 260; 1958 crisis, 294–95; 1962 crisis, 327–330; Cuban missile crisis, 332, 335, 378; U.S., 306, 389; U.S.S.R., 208, 299–300, 313–14

Berlin Wall, 322, 323

Bevan, Aneurin, 148

Bevin, Ernest, 118, 157

"body counts" in Vietnam war, 370
Bonn Republic. *See* West Germany
Bradley, Omar, 182
Brezhnev, Leonid, 340, 382; Vietnam, 359–62
brinkmanship: Dulles, 208, 212; in Berlin blockade, 149–50
British Commonwealth, 237, 271–72. *See also* Great Britain, colonial empire of
Browder, Earl, 24
Budapest, 41, 257. *See also* Hungary
Bulganin, Nicolai, 113, 222, 285n.; Geneva Conference, 234–35; and Khrushchev, 225–26, 267; 1956 "peace offensive," 240–43; Suez crisis, 257–58; Yugoslavia, 213–14
Bulgaria, 26, 42, 45, 48, 73, 117, 126, 139, 141, 169, 331
Byrnes, James, 54n., 71, 80n., 103, 117–118

Cambodia, U.S. incursion into (1970), 381, 382
Camp David: Eisenhower and Khrushchev at, 305, 384; "spirit of," 309, 376
Captive Nations Week, 302
Casablanca Conference (1943), 14, 79
Castro, Fidel, 156, 247; Algeria, 275; Bay of Pigs invasion, 320; Communism of, 314–16; Cuban missile crisis, 328; Khrushchev, 313
Castro, Raul, 328
Central Intelligence Agency (CIA), 208; Cuba, 316, 319; Guatemala, 203; Iran, 203; Laos, 345; Vietnam, 349
Central Treaty Organization (CENTO), 132
Chad, 272
Chamberlain, Neville, 13n., 95, 123n., 169, 355n.
Chambers, Whittaker, 143
Chiang Kai-shek, 80, 83; Chinese Communists, defeated by, 87–92, 351, 367; Hongkong, 83–84; Japan, surrender of, 76; MacArthur, 176–77; Matsu-Quemoy attacks, 211, 292–93; Stalin, 70; U.N., 17, 38; U.S., 98, 147, 158, 163–66, 170, 238, 354; Yalta agreements, 53
China. *See* Communist China; Nationalist China
China Lobby (U.S.), 237
China White Paper, 159, 164–65, 174
Chinese Communists, 53, 80; Hongkong, 84; Japan, 88–89, 91; Marshall's mediation with, 158; civil war with Nationalists, 45–91, 90–91, 100, 350; Stalin, 134; U.S., 143, 174, 212–13. *See also* Communist China; Mao Tsetung
Chou En-lai, 213; Albania, 323; Formosa, 228; Hungary, 268; nuclear-free zone, 302–303; Suez, 259–60

Churchill, Winston, 7, 12, 14, 15, 35, 50, 64, 66, 68–69, 71, 119, 203, 213, 214, 232, 252; on causes of Cold War, 96, 99; Germany, 46–47, 205; Greece, 49–50; "iron curtain" speech, 117–18; Japan, defeat of, 76, 82–83; Poland, 44–45, 49, 70, 75; at Potsdam Conference, 72–79; at Quebec conference, 45–46; Roosevelt, 13, 29–30, 63; Stalin, 15, 22–24, 33, 47; Truman, 63–64; U.N., 37–38, 88; U.S., 20–22, 32, 77
Clay, Lucius, 148, 322
Cold War: causes of, 92–101; "revisionist" historians on, 29, 82
collectivization: in U.S.S.R., 6, 10–11, 220, 326n.; in Yugoslavia, 213
colonialism (Western), 276–77
Cominform, 130–33, 138, 249, 269
Comintern, 24, 91, 131
Committee for the Marshall Plan, 134
communes (China), 287
Communism, 142, 394; in U.S. election of 1948, 144; Soviet ideology of, 109–112; U.S. attitudes toward, 191–92 (*see also* McCarthyism)
Communist China, 147, 151, 179, 306, 329; Berlin, 294; Bulganin, 242; Cuban missile crisis, 328–29, 332; Geneva Conference (1954), 215–16, (1955), 236; India, 304; industrialization of, 240 (*see also* Great Leap Forward); Khrushchev, 221, 307, 321, 340; de-Stalinization, 240, 247; Korean War, 173, 179–83; Stalin's successors, 199–200; U.S., 230, 238, 277, 286, 388; U.S. Formosa policy, 174–75, 228; U.S. Vietnam policy, 354–56, 358, 362, 374–75, 381; U.S.S.R. (*see* Sino-Soviet split)
Communist parties (Western), 168, 246–47. *See also under individual countries*
Communist Party of the Soviet Union: 19th Congress (1952), 196; 20th Congress (1956), 243, 245–48; 21st Congress (1959), 295–96, 299; 22nd Congress (1961), 323; 23rd Congress (1966), 364
Conant, James, 117n.
Congo crisis, 116n., 313, 338
consumer goods (U.S.S.R.), 11, 108, 209, 221, 224
containment policy (U.S.), 121, 124–25; Algeria, 276; Dulles-Eisenhower Administration, 200–201, 203; Eisenhower Doctrine, 278–81; Vietnam war, 373 (*see also* dominoes simile)
Council of Mutual Economic Assistance (Comecon), 136
Cuba, 310, 314–16, 273; Bay of Pigs invasion, 319–20, 327; missile crisis, 291, 325n., 328, 330–37, 346, 375, 384; U.S. policy toward, 389; U.S.S.R., 285, 364, 393

Cultural Revolution (China), 159, 364, 392–93*n*.; Vietnam war, 373–74

culture, Soviet regimentation of, 110–113

Curzon Line, 42–43, 55

Cyprus, 116*n*., 127, 251–52, 272, 338

Czechoslovakia, 58, 140, 169, 218, 239, 254; Communization of, 120, 133, 136–37, 149; Marshall Plan, 130; Munich conference, 355*n*.; Rapacki Plan, 290; U.S.S.R. invasion of (1968), 150, 264, 374, 378–81, 393, 394

Dairen, 53, 86, 167

Daladier, Edouard, 13*n*.

Dardanelles, 77–78

D'Argenlieu, Georges Thierry, 250–51*n*.

Darlan, Jean-François, 23

Davies, Joseph E., 67–69

Dean, Gordon, 282

Deane, Silas, 19

Declaration on Liberated Europe, 56–59

defection from U.S.S.R., 225*n*.

Defense of the Realm Regulations, 69

de Gaulle, Charles, 21, 23, 56, 76, 125, 244, 319, 340, 373; Algerian settlement, 275–76, 308; Eisenhower, summit postponement, 300, 302, 308–309

Democratic Party (U.S.), 146

de-Stalinization policy (Khrushchev's), 239–40, 245–48, 268, 324; in satellites, 203

détente, 156, 209

Dewey, Thomas E., 144, 147–48

Diem, Ngo Dinh, 156; elections under 1954 Geneva agreement, 343–44; fall of, 353–54; U.S. commitment to, 238, 250–51; 342, 348

Dien Bien Phu, 351

Dillon, C. Douglas, 311

disarmament proposals of U.S.S.R., 228–31, 235, 307

Djilas, Milovan, 140

Dobrynin, Anatol, 330

"Doctors' Plot," 196, 208

dominoes simile (Vietnam), 354–56

Dorticos Torrado, Osvaldo, 332–33

draft exemptions (U.S.), 368

Dubcek, Alexander, 378–81

Duclos, Jacques, 133

Dulles, John Foster, 130, 132, 206, 208, 213, 231, 275; effect of death on summit conference, 205, 300–301; massive retaliation doctrine of, 210–12, 224, 283; Nasser, 254–56; policies of, 147–48, 203, 214; U.S.S.R., 201, 243, 326–27, 385; Vietnam, 250, 342; Western Europe, 215, 237

Dumbarton Oaks Conference, 18, 36, 37, 39, 41

Dutch East Indies, 83, 168

Dzhugashvili, Yakov, 10*n*.

Eastern Europe, 65–66, 131, 236, 242, 250, 268, 324, 332, 340; Soviet conquest of, 26, 41, 57–58, 123, 141; Soviet policies toward, 100, 170, 277, 282, 379, 381–82*n*.; 386; U.S. relations with, 115, 277–78, 353, 388, *See also* satellite states

Eastern Front (World War II), 7, 52

East Germany, 75, 123, 131*n*.; Rapacki Plan, 290; refugees from, 322; riots in, 197, 203–206; U.S.S.R., 187; Warsaw Pact, 218

economic aid, foreign, of U.S. and U.S.S.R., 155–56, 274; Molotov's proposals, 97–98

Economic Cooperation Administration, 135

Economic Cooperation Agreement, 129*n*.

economic recovery: of Europe (*see* Marshall Plan); of U.S.S.R., 6–7, 108, 119, 226

Eden, Anthony, 49*n*., 271; Dulles, 203, 238, 256; Geneva Conferences, 232, 236; Molotov, 203; Suez crisis, 254, 258–60; Stalin's demands to, 11–12

Egypt: Great Britain, 188, 202, 248; Israel, 252–53; U.S.S.R., 254. *See also* Nasser; Suez crisis

Ehrenburg, Ilya, 111*n*.

Eisenhower, Dwight, 5, 94, 102, 113, 177, 275; Bulganin's "peace offensive," 240–43; Chiang Kai-shek, 199–200; Communist China, 213; foreign policy of, 233–34, 244–45 (*see also* Dulles); Geneva Conference (1955), 232; German question, 205; Khrushchev, 235, 302, 306; McCarthyism, 201; Matsu-Quemoy islands, 292–93; "open skies" proposal, 235–36; popularity, 148, 230–31; Suez crisis, 259–261; Sputnik, 271; travels, 228, 306, 309*n*., 318; U-2 flights, 311; Vietnam, 233, 342, 348; Western allies, 202–203

Eisenhower Doctrine, 278–81

elections (U.S.): Congressional, of 1948, 144; of 1962, 330;—Presidential, of 1940, 144; of 1944, 30, 144; of 1948, 124, 144–48; of 1952, 147; of 1956, 243, 256; of 1960, 312; of 1964, 358

Estonia, 119

European Defense Community (EDC), 187, 210; French rejection of, 215

European Recovery Program. *See* Marshall Plan

extraterritorial rights (China), 86

fall-out shelters (U.S.), 322–23

Far Eastern Republic of U.S.S.R., 307

fascism, 315, 395

Fierlinger, Zdenek, 58

Finland, 26, 45, 60, 137; Communists in, 120, 131*n*.; U.S.S.R., 100, 119–

120, 241, 379 (*see also* Russo-Finnish War)
For a Lasting Peace, For a People's Democracy, 132
forced labor camps (U.S.S.R.), 9, 11, 198
Formosa, 165, 170, 173, 236, 326n.; U.S. quarantine of, 172–74, 180, 199–200; U.S. policy confusion toward, 176–77. *See also* Chiang Kai-shek
France, 12, 16, 37, 39, 53, 127, 208, 215, 256; Algeria, 237, 252, 262, 272–276, 351; Communist Party in, 95, 131, 133, 168, 202, 247; Geneva Conference (1955), 215–16, 235; Indochina, 89, 167, 174, 188, 202, 236, 351; North Africa, 188, 202, 231–32, 236; Suez, 254; Vietnam war, 373
Franco, Francisco, 195, 309n.
Freudianism in U.S.S.R., 112
Fuchs, Klaus, 104

Galbraith, John Kenneth, 322
Gandhi, Mohandas, 167
Gauss, Clarence E., 89
"generation gap" and Vietnam, 372–73
Geneva agreement (1954), 215–16, 236, 343, 358, 360
Geneva Conference (1955), 216, 232–236, 243, 384; "spirit of Geneva," 235, 376
German Democratic Republic, 168. *See also* East Germany
German Federal Republic, 168. *See also* West Germany
Germany: Communists in, 25, 46, 91; peace treaty with as Cold War issue, 294–95, 301, 302, 321, 323–25, 327–331, 336–37; postwar settlements, 34, 53, 73–75, 117, 122–23, 133, 156, 168, 178, 185, 187, 209; rearmament of, 131, 145, 180, 215, 216; reparations, 53–54, 74–75, 122, 129; reunification, 204, 209–10, 231n., 236, 241; in World War II, 6, 8, 9, 11, 46, 60–61, 66. *See also* Berlin; East Germany; Nazi-Soviet Pact; West Germany
Gero, Erno, 264
Ghana, 195, 272
Giap, General Vo Nguyen, 350–51
Gilpatric, Roswell, 327
Glassboro meeting (Johnson-Kosygin), 376
Goebbels, Joseph, 31, 69
Goldwater, Barry, 358, 364
Gomulka, Wladyslaw, 133, 263–64, 338
Gottwald, Clement, 136–37
Great Britain, 11–12, 16, 74, 125, 127, 184, 214n., 244, 262, 340; colonial empire, 12, 167, 231, 250; Egypt, 188, 202, 248; Geneva Conference (1954), 215–16; Malaysia, 188, 363; Suez crisis, 252–54; U.N., 37–38; U.S. attitude toward (1945), 20–21

Great Leap Forward, 287–88, 293, 326
Great Purge, 27, 106
"Great Society," 368–70
Greece, 48, 103, 116, 139, 208, 213; civil war, 159, 347; Communists in, 23, 49–50, 131n.; Cyprus, 251–52; Truman Doctrine, 125–26; 278
Gromyko, Andrei, 27, 106, 234; U.S., 324–25, 329, 333
Guatemala, 203, 255, 316
guerrilla warfare, 350–53
Guevara, Ernesto "Che," 247, 328
Guinea, 321
Gulf of Aqaba blockade, 375
Gulf of Tonkin resolution, 358
Gusev, Fyodor, 27

Hainan, 170
Halifax, Lord, 83n.
Hammarskjöld, Dag, 313n.
Hanoi. *See* North Vietnam
Harriman, Averell, 19, 48, 59, 67, 97–98, 176
Herter, Christian, 301, 311
Hilsman, Roger, 346
Himmler, Heinrich, 65
Hiroshima, 79, 82, 84
Hiss, Alger, case of, 142–44
Hitler, Adolf, 5, 13n., 16, 25, 41, 81; treaty with U.S.S.R., 7, 12, 13 (*see also* Nazi-Soviet Pact)
Ho Chi Minh, 167, 354, 358; Geneva agreement (1954), 215–16, 343
Hoffman, Paul, 135
Hokkaido, 85
Hongkong, 83–84, 89, 326n.
Hoover, Herbert, 186
"hot line" (Kremlin-White House), 338
Hopkins, Harry, 38, 48, 67, 78n., 80; on U.S.-Chinese relations, 87–88
Hull, Cordell, 12n., 20, 21, 22, 24n., 56, 143; U.N., 17–19
Humphrey, Hubert, 288
"Hundred Flowers" speech, 240
Hungary, 41, 48, 61n., 117, 169, 262, 331, 338; revolt (1956), 150, 206, 238, 259, 262–66, 277, 351, 378, 380
Hurley, Patrick J., 88, 143–44
hydrogen bomb, 102–104; of U.S.S.R., 207, 214, 224, 270. *See also* nuclear weapons

Inchon landing, 176, 179, 181
India, 83, 265, 292; China, 304, 332, 363; Great Britain, 30, 167, 272; Korean War, 175, 179, 208; neutralism of, 227; Pakistan, 237, 363
Indochina: French war in, 167, 188, 202, 272, 351; Geneva agreements (1954), 215–16, 236, 256; U.S. policies toward, 174, 188, 233, 250–51, 354–56
Indonesia, 168, 227, 265; Communists in, 351, 363; U.S. policies toward, 355–56

industrialization: of Communist China, 287–88; of U.S.S.R., 11, 108–109, 206, 394
Inner Mongolia, 166
International Bank, 128
International Monetary Fund, 127
Iran, 137, 203; Britain, 188, 202; Soviet withdrawal from, 115–16, 118–19
Iraq, 257, 279–80
"Iron Curtain," 71, 119, 158
isolationism in U.S., 34–35, 92, 114, 124
Israel, 168; Arab nationalism, 251–54; Six-Day War (1967), 375–76; U.N. truce, 257; U.S., 237, 278; U.S.S.R., 208, 253–54
Italy, 17, 127; Communists in, 117, 131, 133, 168, 202, 247; NATO, 216, 223; in World War II, 5n., 13, 60–61

Japan, 16, 17, 76, 80, 84, 85, 88–89, 91, 158, 170–71; Communists in, 80, 86; defeat and surrender of, 6, 46, 77, 79–86, 92, 182; Soviet entry into war against, 32, 51, 52, 66, 69–70, 75–76, 79, 82–84; U.S. peace treaty with, 171, 184; U.S. postwar occupation, 34, 162–63, 176, 251
Jenner, Senator William E., 173
Jessup, Philip C., 151
Johnson, Louis, 157, 169, 172
Johnson, Lyndon: Berlin visit, 322; domestic reforms, 368–70; meeting with Kosygin (Glassboro), 376; retirement, 377; Truman compared to, 190; Vietnam war, 358–61, 364, 365–368, 373
Joint Chiefs of Staff (U.S.), 66, 283
Jordan, 280

Kadar, Janos, 265
Kaganovich, Lazar, 220, 264, 266, 267, 324
Kassim, Abdul Karim, 279–80
Kazakhstan, 222
Kennan, George, 19, 68, 121, 126, 128
Kennedy, John F., 275, 316, 327, 338, 339; Cuban missile crisis, 330, 333–337; foreign policy, 286, 316–18; Khrushchev, 312, 319–21; Vietnam, 342–43, 346–54
Kennedy, Joseph P., 186
Kennedy, Robert F., 330, 333, 334
Khan, Ayub, 309n.
Khrushchev, Nikita, 104, 115n., 197n., 213–14, 234–35, 264, 279, 300, 313, 320, 323; agriculture, 129–30, 222–223; Bulganin, 225–26, 243, 248; Castro, 314–16; Communist China, 287, 288, 312, 338–39; Cuban missile crisis, 328–30, 334, 337–38; Eastern Europe, 266, 379; Eisenhower, 235, 304–307, 311–12; foreign policy, 223–28, 243–244, 248–49, 273, 284–87; Germany, 288–90, 327–30; Kennedy, 312, 317, 319–21; Nasser, 279–80; Nixon, 301–

302; ouster, 245n., 266–68, 339–40, 360; Stalin, 8, 239–40 (*see also* de-Stalinization policy); succession struggle, 113–14, 195, 206, 320–22; Suez crisis, 257–60
Khrushchev, Nina, 305
Kim Il-Sung, 175
Kissinger, Henry A., 282–84
"kitchen debate" (Nixon-Khrushchev), 302
Knowland, William, 230
Kohler, Foy, 333
Konev, Ivan, 55, 322
Korean War, 156, 157, 164, 170–93, 208, 273, 342; armistice-truce in, 102, 182, 199–200; U.N., 116n., 184–185; U.S. involvement, 92, 119, 171, 189–90, 365
Kosygin, Alexei N., 340, 360–62, 376, 382; Vietnam war, 359–62
Kozlov, Frol, 301
Kuomintang, 87–92, 160. *See also* Nationalist China; Chiang Kai-shek
Kuril Islands, 53, 84–86
Kuznetsov, V. V., 183

Labour Party (British), 22, 78, 84, 99, 118, 128n., 175, 373
Laos, 326, 329, 345–46
Latin America, Soviet interest in, 275, 295, 313
Latvia, 119
League of Nations, 16, 36
Lebanon, U.S. Marines to, 280
Lend-Lease, 3–4, 47, 134–35
Lenin, V. I., 167, 220
Leningrad, 119
Lie, Trygve, 209
Lippmann, Walter, 126, 334
Lin Piao, 355
Litvinov, Ivy, 198
Litvinov, Maxim, 27, 113, 234
Liu Shao-chi, 326, 362
Lublin Committee. *See* Polish Provisional Government
Lysenko, T. D., 110

MacArthur, Douglas, 175, 205, 366; Chiang Kai-shek, 176–77; Japan, 82–86, 163, 176; Korean War, 176–77, 179–83, 244n.
McCarthy, Joseph, 141, 173, 191–92, 201
McCarthyism, 141–44, 173–74, 191–92, 201, 233, 237, 342
McCone, John, 331
Macmillan, Harold, 271–72, 300, 302, 313, 322, 332
McNamara, Robert, 333
Maisky, Ivan, 27, 113
Malawi, 272
Malaya, 167, 188
Malaysia, 250, 363
Malenkov, Georgi, 113, 132–33, 183, 196, 197, 206, 207, 219, 220; foreign

policy, 208–209; Khrushchev, 221–223, 266, 267, 287
Mali, 321
Malik, Yakov, 151
Malinovski, Rodion, 41, 325
Manchukuo, 53
Manchuria, 16, 80, 84, 86, 90, 91, 161–162, 166, 167, 170; U.S.S.R., 79, 117, 171, 221, 386
Manchurian Railway, 53, 86, 167
Mandate of Heaven, 160, 179
Manhattan Project, 52
Mao Tse-tung, 84, 91–92, 141, 156, 183, 310, 362; Cultural Revolution, 339, 364, 373–74, 392–93n.; de-Stalinization, 240, 246; guerrilla warfare, 350–351; Khrushchev, 221, 312; nuclear war, 293, 302–303; Stalin's successors, 199–200, 268–269; U.S., 98–99, 164–165; U.S.S.R., 170, 326, 338, 359, 393 (*see also* Sino-Soviet split)
Marshall, George, 61, 117, 122, 123, 130, 145, 146; China mission, 158, 162
Marshall Plan, 97, 102, 124, 126–32, 134–36, 145, 164, 173; "containment" policy, 121, 273; success, 187, 189; U.S.S.R., 169, 214n.
Marxism, 127n., 142. *See also* Communism
massive retaliation, doctrine of, 210–12, 214, 224, 283
Matsu-Quemoy islands, 211, 292–93
Mendès-France, Pierre, 238
Manshikov, Alexander, 301, 304n., 323
Michael, King of Rumania, 58
Middle East: Arab-Israeli conflict, 253–254; 1958 crisis, 292; Eisenhower Doctrine, 278–81; Suez crisis, 251–52
Mikhailovich, Draja, 26
Mikolajczyk, Stanislaw, 45, 49, 70
Mikoyan, Anastas, 220, 264, 301, 330
Mikoyan, Stepan, 198
"military-industrial complex," 94, 377
Mission to Moscow, 68
Mollet, Guy, 258–60
Molotov, Polina, 27n., 198
Molotov, Vyacheslav, 12, 26, 27, 56, 58–63, 63–64, 67, 72, 78, 90, 96–98, 113, 117n., 122, 145, 196, 197, 234, 264; Khrushchev, 220, 249, 266, 267, 287, 324
Mongolia, 53, 80
Monroe Doctrine, 386
moon landing (U.S.), 271
Morgenthau, Hans J., 116n.
Morgenthau, Henry, 74
Morgenthau Plan, 46
Morocco, 306, 309n.
Moscow conference (Churchill-Stalin), 47–49
Moscow Conference of Foreign Ministers, 122
Mossadegh, Mohammed, 203

multilateral nuclear force (MLF), 359–360
Munich conference, 123n.; "Munich analogy" (Vietnam), 355n.
Mussolini, Benito, 315
mutual security agreements, with Western Europe, 150–51

Nagasaki, 79, 82
Nagy, Imre, 264
Napoleon, 11, 180
Nasser, Gamal Abdel, 156, 227, 252–254, 278–80, 375
"national liberation, wars of," 169, 273, 274, 295, 350
National Liberation Front (NLF) of South Vietnam, 345, 361
National Security Council, 174
Nationalist China (to 1949; *see also* Formosa; Chiang Kai-shek): civil war, 86–92, 114, 117, 119, 158–66; U.N. Security Council seat, 17, 37, 39, 88; Yalta agreements, 53
Nazi-Soviet Pact, 14n., 55, 57, 108n., 109n., 242
Near East. *See* Middle East
Nehru, Jawaharlal, 179, 259–60
neutralism, 227, 249; of India, 309n.; Nasser, 252–53
New Frontier, 318
"New Left," 141–42, 315, 371–72
Nhu, Madame, 344n., 353
Nicolson, Harold, 123n.
Nimitz, Chester, 82–83
Nixon, Richard: Cambodia, 382; Khrushchev, 301–302; McCarthy, 201
Nkrumah, Kwame, 195
Normandy invasion, 3–5
North Africa: allied invasion (1942), 13; France, 188, 202, 232, 236
North Atlantic Treaty Organization (NATO), 119, 151, 156, 168, 185, 187, 214, 236, 373; effects of Geneva Conference, 232, 239; MLF proposal, 359–60; Suez crisis, 260–62; U.S.S.R., 169, 214n., 216, 224; Warsaw Pact, 217–18; West Germany, 168, 177, 215, 273, 288–89
North Korea, 79, 84, 86, 173, 362; *Pueblo* incident, 376; invasion of South Korea, 171–72. *See also* Korean War
North Vietnam: Communist China, 358; Geneva agreement (1954), 236; 1956 rebellion, 351; U.S. bombing, 356–57, 360–61, 364–65, 367, 370, 373; U.S.S.R., 360, 364, 378, 393. *See also* Ho Chi Minh; Vietnam war
Norway, 12, 103
Novotny, Antonin, 240
nuclear nonproliferation agreement, 328–29
nuclear test-ban treaty, 259, 310, 321, 325, 326, 329, 336, 338, 358

nuclear testing: Soviet suspension of, 292; Soviet resumption of, 322–23; suspension issue in U.S., 243

nuclear war: Communist China on, 269, 288; fear of, 148, 224–25, 282–84, 390–91

nuclear weapons: Communist China, 302, 303, 394; Formosa, Japan, and NATO, 289; Rapacki Plan, 290–91; U.S.S.R., 182, 224–25, 238, 295, 394; West Germany, 290, 325, 327. *See also* atom bomb; hydrogen bomb

Nuclear Weapons and Foreign Policy, 282–84

Nuri Es-Said, 279

Nye Committee, 141

Okinawa, 165

One Day in the Life of Ivan Denisovich, 9

"one-party democracy," 194–95

Open Door Policy, 86

"open skies" proposal, 235–36

Outer Mongolia, 90*n.*, 163, 221, 288

Pakistan, and India, 237, 272, 363

Palestine, 168

Panama Canal, 78, 255

"paper tiger" (Mao on U.S.), 165

Pasternak, Boris, 111

Paulus, Friedrich, 60

Peace Corps, 353*n.*

"peace offensives": Bulganin's (1956), 240–43; Johnson's (1965–66), 376*n.*

peaceful coexistence, 35–36, 109, 209, 295

Pearl Harbor, 81, 158, 354, 365

Peng Teh-huai, 303–304

Penkovsky, Oleg V., 327

percentage plan, Churchill's for Balkan states, 48–49

Perón, Juan, 64; Perónism, 315

Pervukhin, Mikhail G., 267

Petrograd, worker riots in, 205–206

Philippines, 81, 251, 347; Communists in, 95, 165–67; Truman's aid to, 174

Poland, 7, 13*n.*, 15, 41–45, 49, 58–60, 97, 122*n.*, 130*n.*, 218, 245, 268, 290, 331; Communization of, 12, 26, 38, 133, 149, 277; postwar division, 14*n.*, 64–65, 70; Potsdam-Teheran agreements, 75, 123; Truman, 63–64, 70; U.S., 261, 277–78; U.S.S.R., and 1956 revolt, 262–64, 351, 378–79; Yalta agreements, 50, 54–57

Polish Provisional Government, 43, 45, 50, 56, 58, 59, 64, 70

Pomerania, 42, 61*n.*

Port Arthur, 53, 85, 131, 167; U.S.S.R., 171, 183, 221

Portugal, 195

Potsdam Conference, 27, 67–69, 71–79, 81–82, 99, 123, 386

Powers, Francis Gary, 311

prisoners of war: German, 218–19; Korean, 190, 200; Russian, 9

Progressive Party (U.S.), 29, 192; 1948 election, 144, 146, 147

Pueblo incident, 376

Puerto Rico, 251

"Pumpkin Papers," 143

purge trials (U.S.S.R.), 141, 169

Quebec conference, 45–46

Quemoy, *see* Matsu-Quemoy islands

Rakosi, Matyas, 240, 264

Rapacki Plan, 290–91, 294

Republic of China, *see* Chiang Kai-shek; Formosa; Nationalist China

Republican Party (U.S.), 122, 144, 147; and Cuban missile crisis, 330–31

"revisionism" in Communist world, 268–69, 288, 393

"revisionist" historians, 82, 94–96

Rhee, Syngman, 172*n.*, 175, 350; Korean truce, 200; U.S., 224, 238

Rhineland, 12, 13, 16

Ribbentrop, Joachim von, 67

Rokossovsky, Konstantin, 264

Roosevelt, Elliott, 20, 122

Roosevelt, Franklin D., 12, 14, 19, 20, 23, 32–35, 68; China, 83, 158; death of, 62–63; German defeat, 46, 61–62; Hiss case, 142–43; historical reputation, 28–30; Japan's defeat, 82–83; Kennedy compared with, 318; Moscow conference (Churchill-Stalin), 47–48; Poland, 44, 59; Stalin, 15, 31–35, 59, 143; U.N., 18, 36–37, 40, 88; Yalta conference, 50–57

Rostow, Walt W., 169

Ruhr, 46, 75, 122

Rumania, 42, 45, 48, 58, 59, 117, 122*n.*; U.S.S.R., 12, 340, 379

Rusk, Dean, 317, 328–30; Vietnam, 346–47, 385–86

Russell, Bertrand, 104

Russian Revolution, 205–206

Russian S.S.R., 54*n.*

Russo-Finnish War (1939–40), 26, 31, 120

Saar, 46, 228

Saburov, M. Z., 267

Sakhalin Island, 53, 84, 86, 170

Sakharov, Andrei, 391

Salazar, Antonio, 195

San Francisco conference, 59, 64, 66

satellite states (of U.S.S.R.): de-Stalinization, 239–40, 246; relations with U.S.S.R., 262–66, 331, 349; Warsaw Pact, 217–18. *See also* Eastern Europe

Schlesinger, Arthur M., Jr., 124, 319, 321

second front (World War II), 12–15. *See also* Normandy invasion

Secretary of State (U.S.), role of, 317–318

Security Council of U.N.: Berlin blockade, 151; China's seat, 151; Churchill, 37; Czechoslovakia, 137; Iran, 118–119; Korean War, 175; Soviet boycott, 171, 178; Soviet use of veto, 115; voting procedures, 39–40; Yalta agreements, 50, 52, 54. *See also* United Nations

Senate Foreign Relations Committee (U.S.), 19; Vietnam hearings, 346–347, 385

Shepilov, Dmitri, 267

Sherwood, Robert, 32

Sholokhov, Mikhail, 305

Shtemenko, Sergei, 27

Sikorski, Wladyslaw, 45*n.*

Silesia, 42, 46, 55

Singapore, 30, 127, 274

Sinkiang, 80, 91, 166, 167, 170, 221

Sino-Soviet split, 138, 312–13, 325–26, 356, 392–93; Bulganin's peace offensive, 242; causes of, 206, 214*n.*, 221, 240, 282, 292, 307–308; Cuban missile crisis, 336–37; Khrushchev, 303, 323, 324, 338–39; Kosygin, 362; Matsu-Quemoy, 292–93; Vietnam war, 356–57, 359, 381

Sino-Soviet treaties, 79, 90, 167, 170, 171, 199

Six-Day War, 375–76

Smith, Walter Bedell, 116, 145, 147

"socialist realism," 110–13

Solzhenitsyn, Alexander, 9, 98, 391

Sorensen, Theodore, 330

South Korea, 163, 274, 347, 350, 373. *See also* Korean War; Rhee

South Vietnam, U.S. involvement in, 250, 342. *See also* Diem; Vietnam war

Southeast Asia Treaty Organization (SEATO), 132

space race, 225, 248, 270–71, 319

Spain, 195

Special Assistant to the President for National Security Affairs, 317

Spellman, Francis Cardinal, 251

spheres of influence (postwar Europe), 22, 35, 36, 45, 166

Sputnik, 270, 289

Stalin, Joseph: atom bomb, 76–77, 103; Balkan states, 48–49, 139; Berlin blockade, 149–51; Communist China, 84, 90, 133–34, 160–61, 167, 199–200; Dardanelles, 77–78; death of, 102, 132, 136, 183, 198, 209, 238; economic reconstruction of U.S.S.R., 108–109; Germany, 14, 25, 61–62, 74, 123; Great Britain, 11–12, 23–24, 118; Greece, 49–50; Iran, 118–19; Japan, 69–70, 76, 80, 84–85; Khrushchev, 245–48, 324, 339; Korean War, 171–72; Marshall Plan, 128–31; Potsdam Conference, 69–70; regime, 5, 9–10, 11, 14, 24, 27, 35, 60, 68, 76–77, 96–97, 111, 113–14, 195, 208,

220, 339, 391; re-Stalinization, 340, 374; second front, 4, 13; "socialist realism" of, 109–113; succession crisis following death of, 195–99, 206; Teheran conference, 14–15; Tito, 67, 126, 137–41; Truman (Potsdam Conference), 63–79, 146; U.N., 18, 26, 38–41, 88; U.S., 12, 24–25, 103, 122, 146–47, 156; Warsaw, 43; Western Europe, 260; World War II, 68, 27*n.*, 107; at Yalta conference, 50–57

Stalingrad, battle of, 5, 7, 8, 14, 60

Stassen, Harold, 122

Stevenson, Adlai, 147–48, 212, 243

Stimson, Henry, 94–95, 104, 134

Stockholm Peace Appeal, 169, 208, 228

Strategic Air Command (SAC), 259, 289

strategic arms limitation talks, 378

Sudeten Germans, 133

Suez crisis, 78, 203, 233–38, 251–52; Bulganin's peace offensive, 241; Great Britain, 271-72, 278; seizure of canal, 254–56; U.S., 252–53; U.S.S.R., 257–258

Sukarno, Achmed, 251, 318, 363

summit conference (Eisenhower-Khrushchev), 235, 299–301, 304–306, 308–309, 318

surface-to-air (SAM) missiles, 328, 331

Syria, 279

Taft, Robert A., 173, 186–87; influence in Republican Party, 147

Taiwan. *See* Formosa

"teach-ins" on Vietnam war, 370–71

Teheran conference, 14–15, 32, 42, 43, 46, 50, 55, 66, 75, 78, 143, 145

test-ban treaty. *See* nuclear test-ban treaty

TET offensive, 376

Thailand, 373

Thant, U, 358

38th Parallel (Korea), 86, 177, 178, 179, 181, 182

Thompson, Llewellyn, 319, 332

Tibet, 173, 304

Tito, 26, 58, 131*n.*, 134; Albania, 312; Catholic Church, persecution of, 140; Churchill, 64; Cominform, 132; de-Stalinization, 249–50; Greece and Turkey, 213; Korean War, 178; Stalin, 126, 137–40; Trieste, 67; U.S.S.R., 227, 228

Togliatti, Palmiro, 248

Trieste, 66, 67, 139, 213, 228

troika plan. *See* United Nations

Trotsky, Leon, 167, 197, 222

Truman, Harry, 29, 33–34, 83, 148; China, 92–93, 165; Churchill, 63–64; election of 1948, 144–46; foreign policy of, 186–87; Formosa, 172–74, 176–77, 199–200; Indochina, 174; Japan's defeat, 76, 79–86, 92; Korean War, 171; MacArthur controversy,

179–83; Marshall Plan, 127; Potsdam Conference, 67–69, 71–79; U.S.S.R., 63, 99, 146; U.N., 116, 175; Vietnam war, 342; Wallace, 118
Truman, Margaret, 64
Truman Doctrine, 102, 121, 124–61; 173; Eisenhower Doctrine compared to, 278; Vietnam war, 346–47
trusteeship plan (U.N.), 37
Tunisia, 309*n.*
Turkey, 116, 184, 213, 279, 348; Cyprus, 251–52; Truman Doctrine, 125–126, 278; U.S. missiles in, 335*n.*; U.S.S.R., 77–78, 208

U-2 flights (U.S.), 224, 235, 301, 335
"U-2 incident," 235, 316, 345; summit conference, 310–11
Ukraine, 9, 26, 39, 54
Ulbricht, Walter, 204–206, 309
Umansky, Konstantin, 57
"unconditional surrender": of Germany, 14, 25; of Japan, 69–70, 76, 79–84
United Nations, 133; Baruch Plan, 105–107; Churchill, 37–38; Congo-Cyprus, 116*n.*; failures of, 116, 121; Formosa, 177; Hungarian revolt, 265; Korea, 116*n.*, 177, 180, 184–85; Manchuria, 162; nuclear arms proposals, 229, 329; San Francisco conference, 64; Soviet leaders on, 38–41, 208, 241, 313; Soviet republics, representation, 17–18, 26; Suez, 257, 262; *troika* plan, 321; Truman Doctrine, 125; U.S. leaders on, 35–37, 116, 165, 385; U.S. views toward, 16–21, 31–32, 114–15, 186, 214; Yalta agreements, 54. *See also* Security Council
U.N. Atomic Energy Commission, 106
United Nations Relief and Rehabilitation Administration, 127
United States Information Service, 201

Vandenberg, Arthur H., 18, 19, 20, 114, 135, 150
V-E Day, 46, 65
Versailles conference, 73
Vienna meeting (Kennedy-Khrushchev), 319, 320–21, 324–25, 327
Vietcong, 352
Vietminh, 350–51
Vietnam war, 29, 35, 79, 81, 102, 141, 164, 187, 273, 341–89; debate on in U.S., 174, 186, 346, 365–68, 370–72, 376–77, 388; 1954 Geneva partition and, 215–16, 343–44; U.S.S.R., 167, 357–58, 374, 378
Vinson, Fred, 146
Vladivostok, 170
Voice of America, 157
Voroshilov, Kliment, 14, 196, 267
Voznesensky, Andrei, 393
Voznesensky, Nicolai, 247*n.*
Vyshinsky, Andrei, 98*n.*, 196

Wallace, Henry, 29, 92, 94, 115, 118, 120, 122, 124, 212; election of 1948, 144, 146–47
"war on poverty," 368–70
Warsaw Pact, 217–18, 236, 239, 250, 264, 379
Warsaw uprising, 41, 43–44
Wedemeyer, Albert C., 162
West Berlin, 274, 322. *See also* Berlin
West Germany, 74, 123, 145; creation of, 148–51, 187; East Germany compared to, 204; economic recovery of, 130–31, 202; NATO, 168, 177, 215, 273; nuclear weapons, 310–11, 329, 359–60; Rapacki Plan, 290; rearmament issue, 148–49, 185, 209, 244; U.S., 237; U.S.S.R., 129, 219, 288–90, 362, 393. *See also* Adenauer
Western alliance: Korean War, 187–189; Vietnam war, 373; *see also* NATO
Western Europe: economic recovery of, 216–17, 226, 271, 388 (*see also* Marshall Plan); Geneva Conference, 243; Khrushchev, 228, 260; U.S., 150–51, 237–38
White, Harry Dexter, 144*n.*
Willkie, Wendell, 13
Wolff, Karl, 60
World War II, causes of, 16, 20–21
Writers' Union (U.S.S.R.), 111*n.*

Yalta conference, 32, 50–57, 64, 78, 84, 143, 145; agreements reached at, 53, 74, 82, 386; China provisions of, 80, 90, 161; Eisenhower view of, 232; Stalin's conditions on Japan at, 70, 85
Yugoslavia, 213. *See also* Tito

Zhdanov, Andrei, 110–11, 113, 132
Zhukov, Georgi, 58, 113, 196, 222, 234; and Khrushchev, 195, 267, 287; memoirs of, 76–77
Zionism, 253–54
Zorin, Valerian, 136

Yalta
Russians into war with
Japan Port Arthur
Sold out Poland
German to be divided
  Mistake — Roosevelt mistook
Russians willingness to invoke
self in world peace. Should
have required sharp, specific
agreements
    Dumbarton Oaks —
UN — Veto for 5 powers

Possibility of Atomic
Diplomacy, Russia's weakness
allowed — Eastern Europe
Davies — Hopkins p. 69
US interested in Japan not Europe
Moralistic not pragmatic
Churchill's urge to reach capital
  political vs military objectives

Brit, France & US = "Western
German Republic —
Russian start blockade 1948
1949
NATO Formed